Men Who Are Making America

By
B. C. Forbes

Founder of FORBES Magazine

Vector Publishing Company
127 Charles Park Drive
P.O. Box 1822
Council Bluffs, Iowa 51502

Men Who Are Making America

By

B. C. Forbes

Editor "Forbes' Magazine"
Author "Finance, Business, and the Business of Life"

B. C. Forbes Publishing Co.
Equitable Building
New York

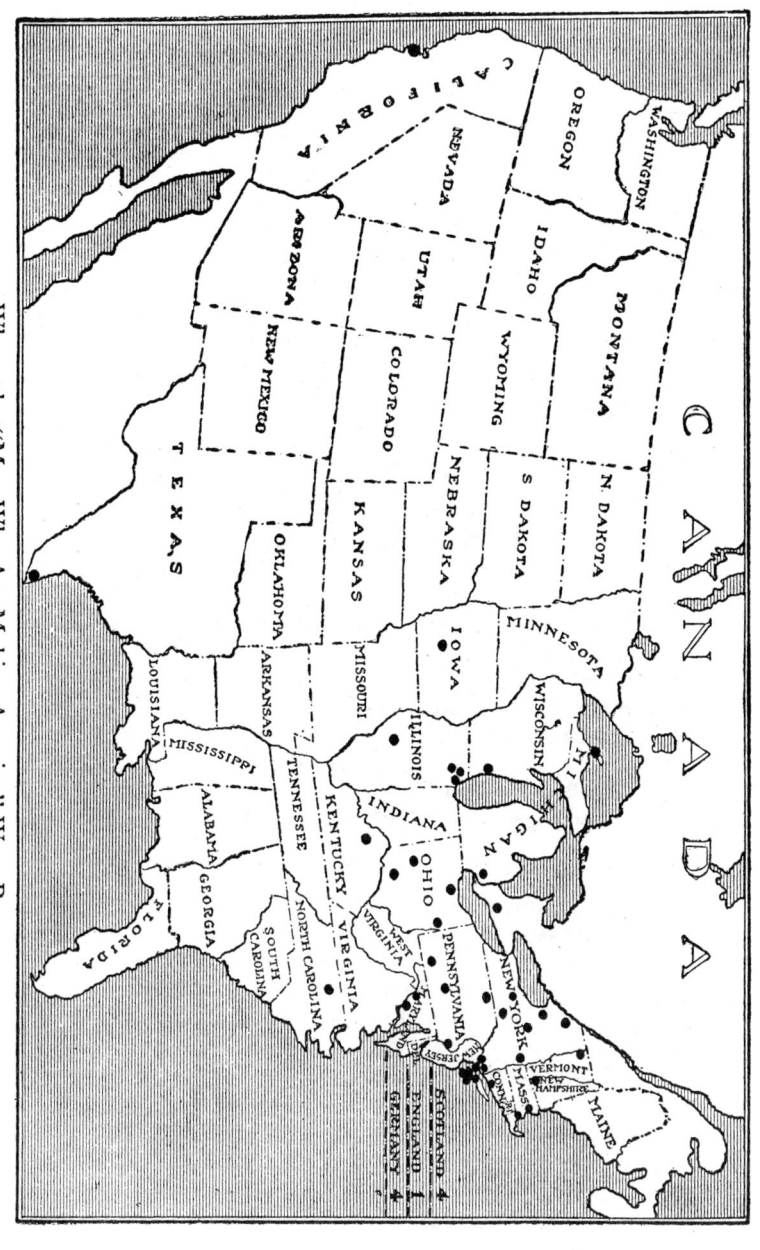

Where the "Men Who Are Making America" Were Born

INTRODUCTION

"How can I attain success?"

That is what every rational human being wants to know.

This book tells in an intimate way how fifty of America's foremost business and financial leaders of the present day have climbed the ladder of success.

The selection of the fifty is based on the replies received from business men all over the country to the question: "Who Are Our Fifty Foremost Business Men, Men Who Are Making America?" In all but a few instances, based on geographical or exceptional circumstances, the list represents those who were accorded the highest number of votes. Having been thus singled out as the most successful American business men now living they may be regarded as well qualified to speak illuminatingly and helpfully on the subject of achievement.

Who are the fifty men thus honoured by the business world?

In what fields have they made their mark?

Are they moderately young or are most of them elderly?

How many of them are native Americans and how many were born in other parts of the world?

Were their parents in a majority of instances poor, moderately circumstanced, or wealthy?

The table on pages vi-vii furnishes a succinct reply to these questions.

It will be seen that:

    24 were born poor.
    17 were born in moderate circumstances.
    9 were born rich.
    40 were born in the United States.
    4 were born in Scotland.
    4 were born in Germany.
    1 was born in England.
    1 was born in Canada.
    14 began as store clerks.
    5 as bank clerks.
    4 as grocery boys.

The compilation shatters the popular idea that most of the highest financial and business positions in the United States are held by

	WHERE BORN	CIRCUM-STANCES OF PARENTS	AGE 1917	BEGAN:	CHIEF SUCCESS WON IN:
Armour, J. Ogden	Milwaukee, Wis.	Rich	54	Packing Business	Meat Packing
Baker, George F.	Troy, N. Y.	Poor	77	Grocery Boy	Banking
Bedford, A. C.	Brooklyn, N. Y.	Moderate	53	Store Clerk	Oil
Bell, Alexander Graham	Edinburgh, Scot.	Poor	70	School Teacher	Telephone
Carnegie, Andrew	Dunfermline, Scot.	Poor	82	Bobbin Boy	Steel
Davison, H. P.	Troy, Pa.	Poor	50	Errand Boy	Banking
Dollar, Robert	Falkirk, Scot.	Poor	74	Cook's Boy	Lumber and Shipping
Douglas, W. L.	Plymouth, Mass.	Poor	72	Pegging Shoes	Shoes
Duke, James B.	Durham, N. C.	Poor	56	Peddling Tobacco	Tobacco
Du Pont, T. Coleman	Louisville, Ky.	Moderate	54	Coal Miner	Traction Cos. and Powder
Eastman, George	Waterville, N. Y.	Poor	63	Insurance Clerk	Cameras
Edison, Thomas A.	Milan, O.	Poor	70	Newsboy	Inventor
Farrell, James A.	New Haven, Conn.	Moderate	54	Labourer	Steel
Ford, Henry	Greenfield, Mich.	Poor	54	Machinist	Automobiles
Forgan, James B.	St. Andrews, Scot.	Moderate	65	Bank Clerk	Banking
Frick, Henry C.	West Overton, Pa.	Poor	67	Store Clerk	Coke and Steel
Gary, Elbert H.	Near Wheaton, Ill.	Moderate	69	Law Clerk	Steel
Gaston, William A.	Boston, Mass.	Moderate	58	Law Office	Banking
Goethals, Geo. W.	Brooklyn, N. Y.	Poor	59	Errand Boy	Engineer
Guggenheim, Daniel	Philadelphia, Pa.	Rich	61	Lace Business	Mining
Hammond, John Hays	San Francisco, Cal.	Moderate	62	Engineer	Mining
Heckscher, August	Hamburg, Ger.	Moderate	69	Coal Mining	Zinc and Real Estate
Hepburn, A. Barton	Colton, N. Y.	Moderate	71	Store Clerk	Banking
Insull, Samuel	London, Eng.	Poor	58	Clerk	Electricty
Kahn, Otto H.	Mannheim, Ger.	Rich	50	Bank Clerk	Banking

INTRODUCTION

	WHERE BORN	CIRCUM-STANCES OF PARENTS	AGE 1917	BEGAN:	CHIEF SUCCESS WON IN:
Keith, Minor C.	Brooklyn, N. Y.	Moderate	69	Store Clerk	Fruit, Central America
Kingsley, Darwin P.	Altburg, Vt.	Poor	60	Farm Hand	Insurance
McCormick, Cyrus H.	Washington, D. C.	Rich	58	Harvesting Business	Farm Machinery
Morgan, J. P.	New York	Rich	50	Bank Clerk	Banking
Nichols, William H.	Brooklyn, N. Y.	Moderate	65	Chemist	Chemicals and Copper
Patterson, John H.	Near Dayton, O.	Moderate	72	Toll Collector	Cash Registers
Perkins, George W.	Chicago, Ill.	Moderate	55	Office Boy	Banking
Reynolds, George M.	Panora, Ia.	Moderate	52	Store Clerk	Banking
Rockefeller, John D.	Richford, N. Y.	Moderate	78	Office Clerk	Oil
Rosenwald, Julius	Springfield, Ill.	Poor	55	Clothing Clerk	Mail Order
Ryan, John D.	Hancock, Mich.	Poor	53	Store Clerk	Copper
Schiff, Jacob H.	Frankfort, Ger.	Moderate	70	Bank Clerk	Banking
Schwab, Charles M.	Williamsburg, Pa.	Moderate	55	Grocery Boy	Steel
Shedd, John G.	Alstead, N. H.	Poor	67	Grocery Boy	Merchant
Simmons, E. C.	Frederick, Md.	Poor	78	Store Boy	Hardware
Speyer, James	New York, N. Y.	Rich	56	Bank Clerk	Banking
Stillman, James	Brownsville, Texas	Rich	67	Clerk	Banking
Vail, Theodore N.	Carroll Co., O.	Moderate	72	Telegraph Operator	Telephone
Vanderbilt, Cornelius	New York, N. Y.	Rich	44	Mechanical Engineer	Financier
Vanderlip, Frank A.	Aurora, Ill.	Poor	53	Machinist	Banking
Warburg, Paul M.	Hamburg, Ger.	Rich	49	Clerk	Banking
Willys, John N.	Canandaigua, N. Y.	Poor	44	Laundryman	Automobiles
Wilson, Thomas E.	London, Ont.	Poor	48	Railway Clerk	Meat Packing
Woolworth, F. W.	Rodman, N. Y.	Poor	65	Farm Boy	Merchant
Archbold, John D.	Leesburg, O.	Poor	69	Grocery Boy	Oil

Average Age 61

INTRODUCTION

young men. Only four in the list are under fifty years of age. And only a few of the others at fifty would have won entrance into any such list as this. Not only is the average age sixty-one, but no fewer than twelve are seventy or more.

There is encouragement in this fact for those earnest workers who have not yet reached places of conspicuous eminence. If the right kind of seed is being planted, the fruit may ripen by and by. Results are not always attained in a hurry.

Indeed, one great lesson the lives of these notable men convey is that patience, perseverance, stick-to-itiveness, and unflagging courage are essential qualities.

Another point revealed by this analysis of the personnel of America's ablest business leaders is that neither birth nor education, neither nationality nor religion, neither heredity nor environment are barriers—or passports—to success in this land of liberty and democracy. Worth alone counts. The only caste in America is merit.

The humble origin of the majority of these "Men Who Are Making America" would call for more comment were it not so typical of the nation's annals.

My study of the careers of these men has impressed me with this fact: Most of them had to pay the price of success. They worked harder and longer, they studied and planned more assiduously, they practised more self-denial and overcame more difficulties than those of us who have not risen so far.

How can one achieve big things?

What are the necessary qualifications?

What course must be followed?

For a full answer to these questions the reader must turn to the character sketches.

But I may remark, in a general way, that there would appear to be two sets, or classes, of qualities calculated to win success:

First—Qualities within the reach of all.

Second—Qualities attainable only by those favourably endowed by Nature.

The first list of qualities, if wisely cultivated and exercised, may be depended upon to earn at least a moderate measure of success.

But, as a rule, some of the qualities in the second category are requisite for the attainment of such exceptional success as has been achieved by many of the men whose records are outlined in this book.

Among the qualities all may weave into the fabric of their character may be enumerated: Integrity, self-denial, sincerity, industry, sobriety, self-culture, cheerfulness, self-reliance, good temper, courage, stick-to-itiveness, confidence, concentration, steadfastness, loyalty, ambition, optimism, politeness.

INTRODUCTION

The rarer and higher qualities, not within reach of every brain, include: Foresight, statesmanship, generalship—ability to select, to lead, and to inspire other men; great mental and physical stamina; superior judgment, abnormal memory, willingness to incur large-scale risks adjudged capable of being turned to profitable account, personal magnetism, dynamic force, imagination, commonsense.

Says Shakespeare:

> "'Tis not in mortals to command success;
> We will do more—deserve it."

My observation and investigation have convinced me that nine times in ten success is won by those who deserve to win it. Dame Fortune is not so capricious as superficial indications sometimes would suggest: fame, responsibility, and (uninherited) wealth usually seek shoulders broad enough to bear them worthily. The little man cannot continue to fill a big place creditably.

It is not always true that "What man has done, man can do." Not every man is so constituted that he could become a Rockefeller or an Edison.

But, on the other hand, the character sketches here presented abundantly prove that in this land of opportunity no normal person need fail because of early handicaps of birth or environment.

My main object in writing these brief biographies of notable doers is to inspire and assist the millions of ambitious, clean, forceful, diligent young men who are bending their energies, physical, mental, and moral, to make their way in the world, to become useful, constructive citizens, to leave behind them a worthy heritage.

Let me meet possible misdirected criticism by explaining in the clearest terms that these character sketches are confined to financial and business men and do *not* include any of America's innumerable men of national and international eminence in statesmanship, science, education, art, literature, medicine, etc. Nor are there any railroad giants in this list, as it is my purpose to devote a separate volume to them.

Objection may be raised that the dollar apparently has been used almost exclusively as the yardstick in measuring success.

In the nature of things, the man who creates or builds up a mighty financial, industrial, mining, or commercial organization usually makes money, often a great deal of it. In business, profit is the reward of successful achievement.

But the man who sets up money-making as his primary, his sole goal, who subverts everything to that end, seldom fulfils his narrow, Midas-like ambition.

It is not money but the joy of achievement, the joy of creating, of

INTRODUCTION

developing something, that spurs on most men who become factors of the first importance in the business world.

Providence would seem to have ordained that the man who *serves* most shall reap most.

Success is coming to be spelt Service.

The success that consists only of dollars is no longer accounted worth-while success.

Unless the men in this volume (with few exceptions) had a higher title to recognition than the size of their bank accounts, they would not have been honoured by their fellow business men throughout the country as the finest specimens of "Men Who Are Making America."

Most of them have been instrumental in providing employment on a large scale and at wages sufficient to enable the workers to become self-respecting citizens, able to marry and to raise families in rational comfort. Without men of this calibre, without stalwarts capable of organizing and successfully conducting business enterprises, no nation can long hold its place in the world. To become and remain prosperous and powerful a modern nation must have a thriving population and such foreign trade outlets as only brainy commercial and financial leaders of international vision can open up and conquer.

The United States owes much to its idealists, to its dreamers, to its cloistered intellectuals, to those calm, reasoning souls who point to higher things and refuse to be engulfed in the maelstrom of materialism. But other peoples have achieved more in these philosophic realms. It is not our achievements in abstract thought that have won us a unique place among the nations.

Our greatest distinction has been won by actions, not words, by deeds, not dreams, by concrete accomplishment, not airy theorizing. The world can match our statesmen and philosophers and poets and artists and composers and authors.

But no nation can match our galaxy of doers, our giants of industry, transportation, commerce, finance, and invention.

What other land could bracket names with such of our twentieth-century titans as Hill and Harriman; Morgan, Edison, Carnegie, Bell and Vail; Frick, Gary, Schwab and Farrell; Ford and Willys; Duke, Eastman, Rosenwald, Paterson, Keith and Woolworth; the McCormicks, the Armours and Wilson; Goethals, Guggenheim, Hammond, Ryan and Nichols; to say nothing of our leaders in international finance?

Old World heroes too often have been destructionists.

New World heroes are constructionists.

It is my hope that these sketches, brief, fragmentary, and light though they necessarily are, will do something to modify the too-general impression that "Oh, the rich guys were lucky; we weren't. That's the only difference." I have tried to give in specific detail some of the difficulties encountered by these men and to explain exactly how they overcame them, for by so doing I believe something will be done to promote understanding between the less successful and the successful.

So common throughout the volume is the story of early struggles sufficient to daunt and drive to despair the average human being that the sub-title might well be the motto of Kansas: "Ad astra per aspera"—Through difficulties to the stars.

The extent of the interest aroused by the serial publication of the articles in *Leslie's* has been deeply gratifying; indeed, that periodical stated editorially that no series ever printed by it in its long history had attracted so much attention and comment throughout the length and breadth of the country.

So numerous have been the requests to issue the sketches in permanent form that I offer no apology for bringing forward this volume. It contains quite a few biographies never before written from authentic, original material owing to the aversion of the subjects to talking for publication; only the conviction that the telling of their life-stories frankly and fully might serve to hearten others induced these men to narrate their experiences.

Were I not confident that the volume will have some inspirational value I would not have troubled to write it. The preparation of a series of real romances in financial and business, though of some current and perhaps historic interest, would not have justified the time, the labour, the patience, *and the diplomacy* which have been necessary to accomplish the task. It took from six months to a full year to induce more than one of the subjects to say one word about their careers. In a few cases, as will appear from the articles, there was no personal interview, so that the information in such instances—including, notably, Henry Ford and George F. Baker—must be accepted as second-hand.

Wherever possible I have let the subjects tell their own stories in their own words. I know of no volume which enables the ambitious young man to make the intimate acquaintance of so many of the nation's foremost men of affairs and to learn from their own lips the most useful wisdom their eventful experiences have taught them.

Please pardon this too-lengthy introduction to them.

MEN WHO ARE MAKING AMERICA

J. OGDEN ARMOUR

J. OGDEN ARMOUR is at heart as democratic as was his father and has larger vision. When Philip D. Armour died, sixteen years ago, Armour & Co. did a business of $100,000,000 a year; now they do $500,000,000. And the brains, the active directing, head, the planner and architect and developer of Armour & Co., is J. Ogden Armour. He is not an ornamental figurehead, merely the son of a rich father, but one of America's ablest, most forceful creative business men.

Since "J. O.," as his colleagues call him, took hold, auxiliary enterprises have been built up doing in the aggregate more business than the packing house—the Armour Grain Company handles more grain than any other concern on the face of the earth; Armour has the second largest leather business in the world; he ranks among the foremost manufacturers of fertilizers; he controls more refrigerator and other special cars than any railroad system in the country.

J. Odgen Armour is the largest merchant in Christendom or heathendom.

Also, he is the largest *individual* employer of workers—some 40,000 of them; Armour & Co. has no stockholders; it is purely a family concern.

Thanks to muckrakers, self-seeking government officials, and misled newspapers, I—doubtless in common with many others—had pictured Armour as an aristocrat too proud to mix with Chicago's Four Hundred, as an autocrat too overbearing to join other leading citizens in civic movements, as a mediocre business man but possessing sense enough to let brainier men run the organization bequeathed to him.

How false were such conceptions! How unfair such judgments!

I told Armour very frankly what my ideas about him had been—after I found out, by careful investigation, that they were all wrong. He laughed—and gave me straight-from-the-shoulder explanations.

"I have no social ambitions," he said. "My ambition is to run Armour & Co. successfully and to give a great many young men a chance to make their way in the world. My associates in the business are my closest friends, my chums. If it weren't for the fun there is in working with them and being with them, I wouldn't—I couldn't—stay in business. Without sentiment, the work would be too hard."

Years ago Mr. Armour was offered $130,000,000 for his company but unhesitatingly declined it.

"What could I do with $130,000,000?" he remarked when I asked him about this incident, now revealed for the first time.

The truth is that, instead of feeling too aristocratic to mingle with capital-S Society, Mr. Armour is too democratic.

He mentioned sentiment in business.

"Do you let sentiment enter into running your business?" I asked.

"Enter into running it?" he repeated. "Why, I run it on sentiment. If I didn't, it would not be successful—and it wouldn't be worth while running. What is it that makes an organization successful? Isn't it the loyalty and the enthusiasm of the many men engaged in it? And how can any man inspire these sentiments if he has no sentiment in his own make-up? No one man can run a big concern; he must depend upon others for the actual doing of almost everything.

"To get the right kind of men we begin early. We are more particular about the hiring of office-boys than about any other thing connected with Armour & Co., for the office-boys of to-day will become our department managers to-morrow. We select them with that in view. We practically never go outside for a high-priced man. Just as the fellow who starts with the Pennsylvania Railroad as a brakeman may one day become president, so young men who start with us at the bottom can hope to rise to the top."

Here let me digress. Mr. Armour happened to remark one day, in the hearing of a bright youth, that one of his greatest pleasures in life was developing young men.

"Mr. Armour," spoke up the youth, "you need not look any further. You can start right here," pointing to himself.

Mr. Armour did start right there. To-day the youth is vice-president of Armour & Co., Mr. Armour's right-hand man and most trusted associate, Robert J. Dunham, director in Chicago banking and business enterprises and having the income of a prince—all at 40!

I walked through every department at Armour's and I believe the average age of the executive heads is under rather than over 40. When men grow old enough to enjoy a life of leisure they retire on pension.

Mr. Armour is 53—past. I called him 54, as he was born in 1863, but he objected.

"Don't make me worse than I am," he protested, smiling. "I

never realized I was anything but a young fellow until one day I was late, for some reason or other, in reaching the stockyard. I used to get there by eight, but this morning it was half past. One office-boy, who didn't see me, looking up at the clock as I was passing, said to another: 'I wonder what's become of the old man this morning!' The '*old man!*' It stabbed me."

The world was accustomed to expect epigrams and all sorts of sage sayings from the original Armour. But nobody, so far as I know, has ever publicly attributed a like ability to the son.

Well, he has it. Read, for example, these sentences, dropped by him in course of our very informal, heart-to-heart talk:

"Business can no longer be done with a club but with a chemist—and a lawyer."

"The most valuable ability of all is the ability to select men of ability."

"The richer and bigger you are, the more considerate you have to be of other people's feelings if you are to succeed in taking the curse off being rich."

"The man who handles himself right is the man who puts himself on the level of the man he is with."

"The world is a worse place for a young man with a lot of money than for one without any."

"I have known a lot of men who were good men when they had no great amount of money but who let riches go to their head and make poor men of them."

"I don't worry. Worry kills more people than ever hard work killed."

"There *is* luck in the world. There may be luck in getting a good job—but there's no luck in keeping it."

Unlike some rich men's sons, J. Ogden Armour is a worker. For many years he was at the packing house by eight o'clock every business morning. He began at the bottom; pay, $8 a week. He learned the business in the stern school of experience—his intrepid father saw to that. And as "J. O." says in his well-written book, "The Packers and The People," the slaughtering, dressing, and packing of swine, cattle, and sheep is no parlour game.

Later, when he became the directing head, he used to receive at his home, by seven o'clock every morning, detailed reports of the livestock receipts at all the principal centres in the country and, after carefully analyzing the whole national and international situation, decide upon the general buying programme for the day.

Let me relate another incident, one that Mr. Armour will be surprised to read in this article, for he does not know I ferreted out the facts.

Britain's declaration of war had stampeded financial America. The New York Stock Exchange was afraid to open the flood-gates. Virtually every other exchange in the land was closed. The banks were clamouring for emergency currency, clearing-house certificates, and other panic appurtenances. Savings banks suspended cash payments.

The bottom had fallen out of everything.

No, not everything. The Chicago Board of Trade—the famous "Grain Pit"—remained open, was subjected to a terrific bombardment, but weathered the storm *without one grain-trade failure*.

The newspapers carried black headlines telling how George E. Marcy, president of the Armour Grain Company, had heroically saved the day, first by fighting against the closing of the board, and then, when pandemonium broke loose and grain prices began to soar, by selling first one million, then another million bushels of wheat at prices which prevented quotations from rising more than two to three cents a bushel—contrasted with opening skyrocketing to the extent of eight cents a bushel at Minneapolis. Marcy was proclaimed a hero.

"Yes," admitted Mr. Marcy when I quizzed him about the events of that exciting day, "I did go into the market and sell two or three million bushels of grain to keep the market from running away—but I advised with Mr. Armour over the telephone early that morning and I did nothing but carry out his instructions."

Mr. Marcy added this other bit of heretofore unwritten history:

"Mr. Armour also told me to step in and take care of anybody who might need help. I replied: 'You are assuming a great risk. Some may fail.' Mr. Armour repeated: 'Go ahead and help any you can. Go to the banks with people who are good and arrange to have them tided over.' I did—and not a single failure occurred in the grain trade. This was, of course, Mr. Armour's idea, not mine."

One writer, familiar with the facts rather than the fiction concerning the Armour family, has said: "J. Ogden Armour would be the last to acknowledge that he has outstripped his father as an originator, a creator, an economist, and a financier. But such is the fact."

A prominent Chicago business man told me: "'J. O.' has quadrupled the business that his father built up. 'P. D.' was not so optimistic, not so farseeing, not so ready to dare as his son. The son has gone beyond what his father would have approved in branching out. He has done it because of his extraordinary belief in the development of this country. 'J. O.' himself has said, 'The country has grown up to help me out of the hole when I seemed to have planned too far ahead.'"

The present Mr. Armour would subscribe to no such analysis, for few sons have so much reverence for a father.

Mr. Armour's modesty, indeed, is chiefly responsible for his having been misunderstood by a majority of the people. He shuns interviewers—"I had hoped to dodge you," he frankly told me when I waylaid him; "I told Dunham to steer you off."

You never read of Mr. Armour appearing in public and making a speech. "Because I happened to be born a rich man, I don't feel that that entitles me to foist my views on other people," he explained. "My father once said to me: 'You have to take the curse off being a rich man.' I have tried in my own way not to aggravate the offence of being a rich man or a rich man's son."

On civic and other committees formed to deal with important problems Mr. Armour often does much real work, but always outside the range of the limelight.

Society doesn't appeal to him. He divides his time between his business and his home, presided over by his wife, formerly Miss Lolita Sheldon. He is intensely fond of his only child, a daughter of about 21, who, it may be recalled, was a cripple until Mr. Armour brought over the famous Dr. Lorenz of Vienna, who operated upon her successfully and whose services were placed by Mr. Armour at the disposal of other children in the country similarly afflicted, an offer of which boys and girls from as far off as the Pacific Coast availed themselves.

The affection existing between Mr. Armour and his mother is beautiful. No matter how pressing business affairs may be, he never allows her to leave Chicago without him, and he insists also upon journeying to wherever she may be visiting to accompany her home. It was of this estimable lady that the late Philip D. Armour said, "My culture is mostly in my wife's name." From Belle Ogden—his mother's maiden name—J. Ogden has inherited his unassuming characteristics.

Mr. Armour has no false pride concerning the humble origin and early struggles of his father. He recounted to me how his father, when only 19, set off from his home in the village of Stockbridge, N. Y., in company with three other men, determined to walk all the way to California to make their fortunes in the then new gold fields— this was in 1851. One of the four died, two others turned back, but Philip Armour tramped on and reached the coast in six months! His first job was digging ditches at $5 a day and $10 a night—and oftener than once he worked day and night. By and by he took contracts to dig ditches and in five years had saved $8,000. With this fortune he returned with visions of marrying his village sweetheart and buying a farm, but, alas! she had married a worthy horse doctor.

On his way home, Milwaukee impressed him as an ideal centre for doing business, since it caught the streams of traffic and people crossing and recrossing the continent. There young Armour, in 1859, formed a produce and commission business partnership with Fred B. Miles. Each contributed as capital the humble sum of $500—the original partnership agreement now hangs in the son's office as one of his most cherished possessions. Smoked and pickled meats being in demand by travellers and others, young Armour later switched to that line, as junior partner of John Plankinton, the then largest packer in America. Then came the Civil War with its pressing calls for huge quantities of preserved meats and Plankinton & Armour prospered.

Chicago having outstripped Milwaukee as a growing commercial centre after the war, Armour, with characteristic foresight, moved to that city in 1870 and, with two brothers, formed Armour & Co., the firm which to-day, without a single stockholder outside of the family, is doing a business, with its allied enterprises, approximating that done by the billion-dollar Steel Corporation.

The founder died in 1901, after one of the most picturesque, inspiring, and successful careers in American history. His younger son, Philip D., Jr., died a year before his father. There were misgivings in certain quarters as to the ability of the elder son, J. Ogden, to fill his father's shoes. Indeed, Armour père at one time pictured no Napoleonic career for Ogden—and the latter shared his father's judgment! But long before he died the father had the satisfaction of seeing Ogden develop into a business man of the first calibre. As a matter of fact, "J. O." really ran the business quite some time before his father passed away, and he did it with a success that yielded the father the greatest happiness of his later years.

"I thought I was the most fortunate young man in the world when I inherited a huge business and a good name," said Mr. Armour to me reminiscently. "But it was not long before I changed my views, for I had nothing but trouble, especially when the United States Government brought all sorts of grave charges against me and other packers. I felt that I had tried to run Armour & Co. honestly and fairly—and certainly I did not need to do dishonest things to make money. The indictments, nevertheless, caused me terrible humiliation and unhappiness. I had been proud of my father's name and record, and had tried sincerely to maintain both unsullied. The courts gave us a clean bill of health, but not before the American packing industry had been so vilified that country after country shut its doors against American-made products."

Mr. Armour added: "The experience taught me that the rich man who chooses to enjoy his riches, without taking the responsibilities that ought to go along with them, is not much of a chap."

Armour & Co. has handsomely made up the ground lost by the Government's attack upon the packing business. The firm's sales are fivefold what they were sixteen years ago and innumerable side lines have been successfully established. Read these figures:

Armour & Co. to-day has 500 branches located in different countries.

It has spent $3,500,000 on one foreign plant alone—in Argentina. It has offices and permanent representatives in forty foreign cities and countries. Its foreign business alone last year approximated $100,000,000. It paid cash to American farmers to the amount of about $300,000,000 last year for live stock.

Armour & Co. to-day handles no fewer than 3,000 distinct products —a transformation from the days when Plankinton & Armour sold nothing but meats.

The Armour Grain Co., the largest in the world, has constructed in South Chicago an elevator holding 10,000,000 bushels, bringing the company's total elevator capacity up to 25,000,000 bushels.

The Armour Grain Company's lumber sales run into millions of dollars every year, thousands of farmers finding it convenient to take home prepared lumber when they bring their grain to depots.

During one recent month 14,000 visitors went through the Armour packing establishment in Chicago, where every single operation in the killing of live stock and the preparation of the products is wide open for inspection every day.

Armour's profits last year averaged less than three cents on the dollar on its total business.

Mr. Armour has served in every department both at the stockyards and in the office. Before he had finished his full course at Yale Sheffield Scientific School he was called home by his father to get into harness. With fewer vacations than the average clerk enjoys, Mr. Armour has been in harness ever since, working hours which would scandalize trade-union leaders!

In showing me over the Armour Grain Company he took me to a room in which was a miniature flour mill and bakery where an expert analytical chemist receives a sample of every load of grain bought by the company, ascertains the percentage of moisture it contains, then grinds the sample into flour, analyzes the food values of the flour, then bakes it into bread so that customers can be supplied with exactly the kind and colour of grain or flour they desire. This scientific process enables the company to sell first those shipments which contain the largest percentage of moisture, thus saving hundreds of thousands of dollars every year, for the evaporation in some cases would mean one to two cents a bushel loss if the grain were not promptly marketed. This is doing business, "not with a club but with a chemist."

I noticed that wherever we went Mr. Armour was continually

addressing the employees by their names, revealing a real interest in the men. I took occasion to speak to numbers of the workers when Mr. Armour was not with me and I found they regarded him more as a colleague than as a boss; they felt that they were all working together, that they were working *with* rather than *for* him. I could believe Mr. Armour, therefore, when he said to me: "The best thing about my work is the loyalty of our people. There are such wonderful fellows all round about me. If it weren't for that, I would not give two cents for holding on to Armour & Co. The boys who run the business with me make the work a pleasure."

One of the executives told me that he had never seen Mr. Armour so happy as when he visited a very wonderful farm—a scientifically conducted enterprise of great magnitude—owned by one of his employees. "Mr. Armour," he said, "was delighted to think there were people connected with the company earning and saving enough to own such an establishment."

No space is left to tell adequately of the Armour family's benefactions. The original Armour spent several millions on the famous Armour Institute of Technology, which annually turns out hundreds of graduates so skilfully trained that corporations and institutions clamour to engage them the moment they are ready to start work. Several years ago the present Mr. Armour and his mother gave the institute an endowment fund of $1,500,000, while not long ago Mr. Armour gave another $500,000. The running of the institution costs Mr. Armour several thousand dollars *every week.*

Incidentally, the institute came into being through a sermon preached in 1892 by the illustrious humanitarian, Dr. F. W. Gunsaulus, on "What I Would Do If I had $1,000,000." Dr. Gunsaulus, as president of the institute, has been doing it ever since, Mr. Armour having given him not one million but several.

At the stockyards nurses are kept to visit not only the homes of Armour employees who become sick but to unearth cases of need among other families, and these are given all necessary attention. "Within half an hour after we receive word in the winter time from one of our nurses that some family is without coal, a wagon is on the way to them," one of the employees at the stockyards told me with great pride. "That's the kind of a man Mr. Armour is."

When the United States entered the European war Mr. Armour promptly urged that all dealings in foodstuffs should be taken under control by the Government, an unselfish attitude which caused chronic critics of all capitalists to soften their views. Mr. Armour's action has convincingly demonstrated that it is possible to be both a packer and a patriot.

GEORGE F. BAKER

THE man with the hardest shell and the softest heart in America."

Thus did one of the country's leading bankers describe George F. Baker, the closest associate of the late J. P. Morgan and to-day the most powerful national banker in Wall Street, the dominating director of more corporations than any other man in the United States and perhaps the third richest living American.

I can personally testify to the hardness of Mr. Baker's shell. It is impenetrable. He affects absolute indifference to how he is regarded by his fellowmen.

"It is none of the public's business what I do," he told me, just as he had told the Pujo Money Trust Committee when summoned to the witness stand at Washington, an attitude which the investigators forced him to abandon.

Did every financier adopt the Baker attitude toward the public and toward public opinion there would be a revolution in this republic in twelve months.

The free citizens of a democracy some years ago taught capitalists a lesson. The younger generation have learned it. They realize that they cannot show contempt for the hundred million human beings, of as good flesh and blood as themselves, who make up this commonwealth. The idea that presidents of banks handling the public's money, that directors of corporations whose stock is held by thousands of public investors, that overlords of semi-public enterprises can snap their fingers at the public's will, has been pretty well drummed out of the heads of most men. George F. Baker, however, is the dean of the old school, the school of secrecy, the school that for a long time did not have to reckon with the power of public opinion.

Many of those who voted on the question: "Who Are Our Fifty Greatest Business Men, Men Who Are Making America?" accompanied their ballots with letters. One important publisher sent me this comment: "You will notice that I have not included in my list George F. Baker; I regard him as nothing but a money-making machine."

That is the general impression of Mr. Baker among those not in a position to peer under his mask, who know him only by his works, who never hear of him doing a single generous act, but see him only as the power behind many financial, industrial, and railroad thrones, rolling up a gigantic fortune and so conducting the First National Bank of New York that, by the aid of its stockholding adjunct, the First Security Company, it pours into the pockets of its stockholders dividends of from 50 to 70 per cent. or more a year.

"The profits of Mr. Baker's bank make the rest of us look like rank novices at banking," declared one prominent banker the other day.

Mr. Baker was the first New York banker to conceive the idea of doing things forbidden under the National Bank Act by means of a separate enterprise whose ownership in reality was and is identical with that of the bank itself, each share of the bank simply carrying with it a share in the "other" enterprise. One could not be sold without the other. The invention has proved highly profitable.

The career of no prominent American is more of a sealed book than that of George F. Baker. I tried repeatedly to learn something of his early career from both professional and social friends, but all in vain.

"I have met Mr. Baker many times socially, both at his dinner table and my own, but I could not tell you anything more about his history than a total stranger," one veteran remarked. "He never *made* any dinner party; I mean he never was the life of any little social function—but he was the next best thing: he was an excellent listener. He said little, but listened a lot."

When I sought to impress upon him that, for his descendants' sake, if not for his own, he should throw off his business shell and give to the public a heart-to-heart talk about his life's work, all he would say was: "Some day the public will understand the truth." I am recording these things because they give the only picture I can procure of him.

Yet those who know Mr. Baker intimately declare that he is the fairest of men, that the public are mistaken in thinking he is interested only in adding to a fortune of perhaps $150,000,000 to $200,000,000, that he has a charming personality beneath the taciturn exterior he shows to the masses, and that, though he had only one philanthropic deed recorded in his favour—a $50,000 gift to Cornell College—until he gave $1,000,000 to the Red Cross, he is given to doing little charitable acts.

Speaking of this $50,000 gift, I have been told a touching story. I record it because it is the only sidelight of the kind I have been able to obtain regarding Mr. Baker.

A friend made a remark to Mr. Baker about how gratifying it must be for him to note how well the newspapers had received his kindly act.

Mr. Baker shook his head sadly. "It comes too late," he remarked with a far-away look.

GEORGE F. BAKER

The friend realized that something was on the old gentleman's mind. So he waited. Mr. Baker then recalled an incident which his friend had witnessed several years before. Just after the 1907 panic had been brought under control, Mr. Baker arrived slightly late at a largely attended meeting at the Union League Club. In inner circles it was well known that Mr. Baker had rendered yeoman service during the storm, and his appearance was greeted with applause which swelled into resounding volume as he walked across the floor to his seat.

"I could not get home quick enough that night to tell *her* about it," remarked Mr. Baker very sadly.

His wife had died in the interval.

The part played by Mr. Baker during the 1907 upheaval was delved into by the Pujo counsel, Samuel Untermyer, in 1913, with this result:

Question.—Is not Mr. Morgan recognized as the great general in this financial army down in Wall Street?

Mr. Baker.—That is according to who is talking. When we talk about him, as his friends, we think he is.

Q.—Is he not generally so recognized?

Mr. Baker.—I think so.

Q.—And you and Mr. Stillman are recognized as his chief lieutenants?

Mr. Baker.—I do not think so; no, sir.

Q.—Who are his chief lieutenants?

Mr. Baker.—I do not know. The members of his firm.

Q.—Try to overcome your modesty, Mr. Baker.

Mr. Baker.—During the panic I think Mr. Stillman and I were.

Q.—You will confess that that is what happened during the panic—Mr. Morgan was the general and you and Mr. Stillman were his lieutenants?

Mr. Baker.—Yes.

Q.—In your judgment is Mr. Morgan the most dominant power in the financial world to-day, far above everything else?

Mr. Baker.—He would be if he were younger in years. I do not know his superior.

Q.—There is nobody as much so except yourself, is there?

Mr. Baker.—And yourself. Get us both in.

Q.—How is that, Mr. Baker, seriously?

Mr. Baker.—There is no particular dominant power.

Q.—When did there cease to be a dominant power?

Mr. Baker.—When activities ceased; during the panic it was so.

How George F. Baker rose to be so great a power, how he moved up the ladder step by step, cannot be told. His early career is more mysterious than the Sphinx—and Mr. Baker is as silent about it as the Sphinx. When I asked him for a few facts about his early career, he not only refused to furnish any information, but, when I suggested that I might obtain the necessary data from the person presumably in the best position to know, he replied: "He knows nothing about it." It was even so, for this man confessed to me that he had never dared ask any questions on the subject. I next approached a friend who has been intimate with Mr. Baker for a generation, but he held up his hands and exclaimed: "The Almighty could not draw a word out of Baker about his early days. I would gladly tell you if I could, but I don't know, and it is no use asking him."

When I turned to "Who's Who in America" in the hope of getting some enlightenment on the subject, this was what I discovered:

"Baker, George Fisher, banker; born, Troy, N. Y., Mar. 27, 1840. Chairman Board First National Bank of New York, Jan., 1909— (ex-pres.)."

That was as far back as this publication had been able to penetrate, to 1909. Just what he had done during the previous 69 years, "Who's Who" was unable to record.

There is a rumour, a legend, a story, call it what you will, that George F. Baker began life as a two-dollar-a-week grocery boy, that later he earned $5 a week as a night watchman, studied enough to qualify as a bank clerk and won promotion to the position of a bank examiner somewhere or other. The first authentic record available about his career is that he took a hand, along with John Thompson and the latter's two sons, in forming the first bank in New York under the National Bank Act, in 1863. Mr. Baker started as cashier, but in four years annexed the presidency.

A veteran tells me that young Baker plunged on United States war bonds, loading the bank up to the gunwales with them. His nerve won the admiration of Secretary Chase, who saw to it that the First National Bank received every possible Government favour. It grew. To-day it has about as large deposits as the total held by the whole fifty-four banks then operated in New York City.

A little folder sent to the bank's stockholders to commemorate the fortieth anniversary of the founding of the institution contains these sentences:

"From the beginning the First National Bank sought the business of banks and bankers and became the redemption agent and depository for a large number of out-of-town national banks. It took an active part in the negotiation of War Loans, thus employing a large part of its deposits during the first years of business, the results of which amply rewarded the management for their confidence in the credit of the Government. The bank from the start took a leading position among dealers in United States securities, for itself and as representative of the several refunding syndicates, in financing the various United States loans issued by successive administrations. During the year 1879 the bank handled $780,000,000 United States

Government bonds, completing their receipt and delivery without error or loss."

Mr. Baker was a member of the Liberty Loan Committee of the present year (1917) and his bank distinguished itself by subscribing for more bonds than any other institution in the country.

The First National's total original capital was $200,000. How small a matter a few hundred thousand dollars later became to Mr. Baker may be gathered from the fact that when asked by the Pujo probers if he held any interest in the Guaranty Trust Company, he said he did not think he had or, if he had any, it was so small he did not remember anything about it. His "small" holding, it was brought out, was worth between $700,000 and $800,000! Another item of his fortune amounting to almost $500,000 he forgot entirely, so small was it in his eyes.

Financiers declare that it has been Baker's brains that have made the First National Bank a veritable gold mine—indeed, something better than a gold mine, for gold mines wear out, whereas Baker's bank, still humbly furnished as in days of old, waxes more profitable with age, last year's (1916) dividends totalling 60 per cent., or $6,000,000, irrespective of the millions paid by its *alter ego*, the Security Company. The bank has paid between 2,500 and 3,000 per cent. altogether, including a dividend of 1,900 per cent. at one clip!

It was in 1901 that a special dividend of $9,500,000 was declared for the purpose of raising the capital to $10,000,000. Of the total 100,000 shares, Mr. Baker owns 20,000, his son 5,050 and, Morgan & Company 4,500.

In 1908 dividends of 126 per cent. were declared, 100 per cent. of this going to start the First Security Company, which took over securities which the Comptroller of the Currency had ruled the bank could not legally carry. Mr. Baker also turned into it some holdings he had acquired "in the interest of the bank." The stockholders of the Security Company have no voting rights whatsoever; the thing is run entirely by trustees who are officers of the bank. This organization can speculate all it wants, although Mr. Baker told the Pujo probers that its stock transactions did not average more than 100 shares a day.

Some of the securities which Mr. Baker put into this pot were 50,000 shares of the Chase National Bank, 5,400 of the National Bank of Commerce, 2,500 of the Bankers' Trust Company, 928 of the Liberty National Bank, 500 shares of the First National Bank of Minneapolis, and smaller amounts of the New York Trust Company, the Astor Trust Company, the Brooklyn Trust Company, etc.

Mr. Baker's sphere of influence extended not only to these institutions, but he became a power in the Guaranty Trust Company, in the

Mutual Life Insurance Company, with its hundreds of millions of assets, to say nothing of a long string of railroads, including the Lackawanna, Lehigh Valley, Central of New Jersey, Reading, Erie, Rock Island, Southern Railway, Great Northern, Northern Pacific, New York Central and New Haven. After his friend Morgan organized the United States Steel Corporation, Baker became a member of its Finance Committee. Few other industrial corporations worth bothering about were overlooked by him or, rather, few of them overlooked him, for he was sought as a director by most of them. One of his railroad co-directors tells me that Mr. Baker's knowledge and memory concerning the physical as well as financial condition of properties were astounding. He never missed inspection trips.

Quizzed about his mile-long list of directorships, and his voting trusteeships, Mr. Baker could supply very little enlightenment offhand. Next day, however, he reverted to the subject thus:

Mr. Baker.—You presented me before the public as such a great director man, more than I realized myself, that I would just like to interject here that I never have become a director or a voting trustee from solicitation of my own; it has all come to me.
Q.—Do you know how many you have?
Mr. Baker.—I know I have too many.
Q.—Do you know how many?
Mr. Baker.—No.
Q.—Have you got twenty-five?
Mr. Baker.—I guess so.
Q.—Have you got fifty?
Mr. Baker.—I do not know. I have never counted them up.

Mr. Baker was as ignorant, or indifferent, about his dividends as he was about his directorships, as this illuminating page from the record brings out:

Q.—Up to the time the Chase Bank's capital was increased to $5,000,000, which you say was about four years ago, what dividend did it pay?
Mr. Baker.—I do not remember.
Q.—What, with an ownership of 23,000 shares, you cannot tell us that?
Mr. Baker.—Oh, I could by looking back, but I do not happen to remember.

Morgan, it will be recalled, enunciated the famous dictum that in his eyes character was more important than collateral in granting a loan. Mr. Baker when examined on this point first corroborated Morgan's theory but then recanted, in this wise:

Q.—What is the test of a Stock Exchange loan?
Mr. Baker.—Oh, it is as much who the borrower is as anything. . . . Possibly the loans are made on the security more than the borrower.

Q.—As a matter of fact, does not the bank look to the security and not to the borrower?
Mr. Baker.—Generally. We would not accept applications for loans from some parties.
Q.—There are some people who could not get money from your bank even if they had any amount of collateral?
Mr. Baker.—Yes, sir.

It was natural that the Money Trust investigators should turn the searchlight upon the First Security Company. At one point the committee's lawyer asked Mr. Baker:
"Did you consider the organizing of the First Security Company a mere evasion of the Bank Act?"
Mr. Baker replied, "No."
This subsidiary immediately began to pay dividends ranging from 12 to 17 per cent. and in the first four years of its existence accumulated a surplus of 40 per cent. It has waxed richer since.
"There is no question that you control the First National Bank in its management and affairs?" asked Mr. Untermyer.
"I would not like to be so conceited as to say that."

Q.—Nobody has disputed your control?
Mr. Baker.—No, sir, and I haven't disputed anybody else's control.
Q.—Well, who else has undertaken to control the bank?
Mr. Baker.—Nobody, and nobody has undertaken to control it at all.
Q.—I understand; it controls itself?
Mr. Baker.—Practically. We are a very harmonious family, I am happy to say, and we can't get up any quarrels.
Q.—Well, on the basis of 226 per cent. in a few years, it ought to be.

It developed that Mr. Baker bought control of the Chase Bank with a view to amalgamating it with the First National, but it became strong enough to stand on its own legs, so the merger did not go through.
Since then Mr. Baker has resigned from several directorates, but is still on more than twoscore boards, representing a total capitalization running into the billions.
Although in his 78th year, he is as fleet-footed, as clear-eyed, as straight-backed, and as energetic as most men of 60. During his busy business life he found little time for sports of any kind, and it was not until he was 70 that he swung his first golf club. Then he got the golfing fever and has since spent many a day on the links. He would now give John D. Rockefeller a game tussle were these two gladiators to fight a match. At the same time as he began golf he smoked his first cigar, and has since revelled in that dissipation also.
Even the rankest Socialist would not quarrel with Mr. Baker's

mode of living. He has never indulged in offensive extravagances, never paraded unwonted luxuries, never flaunted his wealth in the face of people less wealthy than himself. His friends say that his domestic life was beautiful in its simplicity and harmony.

Certainly his only son, George F. Baker, Jr., who is following in his father's footsteps at the First National Bank, is universally regarded as a most worthy young man, a hard, intelligent worker, a clean-cut sportsman in the best sense of that term—he is Commodore of the New York Yacht Club—and rivalling his father in his unexceptionable domestic characteristics. In America's hour of need he stepped forth for national service, accepting, among other duties, the chairmanship of the Committee to Enroll Yachts for the U. S. Naval Reserve Forces. Later, with the rank of Lieutenant-Colonel, he headed a Red Cross Commission to Italy, braving all the dangers of the submarine-infested Atlantic.

George F. Baker's intimate friends talk admiringly, not to say lovingly, of him. They declare that he is not conscious of his tremendous financial influence, that he never attempts to lord it over other people, that he is actuated by the most patriotic motives in all his endeavours to develop America's financial, railroad, and industrial activities. They emphasize his simple habits and tastes, his aversion to all that smacks of ostentation, and his inordinate dislike of coming to the front in any way whatsoever.

The Baker his friends portray is the very antithesis of the stony-hearted, money-making machine the public pictures him. Certainly there has never been the slightest suggestion of any financial dealings even remotely crooked on his part.

ALFRED C. BEDFORD

WHEN Chester A. Arthur was serving his term as President of the United States, a young man walked down Broadway, New York, looking for a job.

Thirty-three years later he took his seat at the head of the directors' table in the most famous business building on Broadway, as president of the greatest business organization in the world's history.

"What was your first step toward success? What first elevated you above the rank and file? How did you get a foothold on the ladder of success?" I asked Alfred C. Bedford, recently elected president of the Standard Oil Company of New Jersey, the parent company of the whole Standard Oil organization.

"When I got a position as an office-boy I was always on the alert to make myself useful. I often volunteered, after my own work was done, to count the cash for the cashier, to draw off balances for the bookkeeper, make up vouchers, carry the books to the safe, and do every little job I could see needed doing," replied Mr. Bedford. "I was soon assigned to do the running for an expert accountant who came to reorganize the whole system of accounts and bookkeeping. Instead of merely getting out vouchers and other papers that he called for, I asked to be allowed to count up columns of figures, compare vouchers, and do the statistical drudgery. In appreciation, the accountant began to teach me not only ordinary bookkeeping but the principles underlying accountancy and the fundamentals of recording and analyzing business transactions.

"I applied myself diligently to this work, studying at home at night, and it was not long before I graduated from office-boy to a position of greater responsibility than that of a routine bookkeeper. This first promotion I attribute to my willingness to do more than was expected of me and to the insight I then obtained into business methods. This gave me a grasp and a vision such as the average clerk in an office too often fails to cultivate because of his machine-like performance of his allotted tasks."

The installation of A. C. Bedford as president of the Standard Oil Company marks the passing of the old and the advent of the new generation. John D. Rockefeller and his brother William Rockefeller are the only survivors of the original band of brainy stalwarts who conceived and created the organization which was to encompass the earth, bringing light into dark places, and now these veterans have no connection with the business. Gone are Rogers, Flagler, Payne, Pratt, McGee, Tilford, Worden, Brewster, and Archbold—all men of vision and force, enterprise and courage.

In their stead are rising up a new race, a younger group, of whom A. C. Bedford, W. C. Teagle, F. W. Weller, H. C. Folger, H. L. Pratt, Dr. W. M. Burton, and W. S. Rheem are among the most conspicuous. This second generation has not yet demonstrated beyond doubt its fitness to rule over the industrial realms to which it has fallen heir.

But it has made a promising start. New rulers have brought new rules. The old-time secrecy that beset 26 Broadway, engendering so much suspicion, irritation, and agitation, has been abolished.

"I mean to keep my door wide open to every person having a legitimate call upon my attention," was the revolutionary proclamation of Standard Oil's new president on taking office. Veteran newspaper men assigned to get particulars of Mr. Bedford's election, having in mind past experiences at No. 26, could scarce believe their eyes and senses when they were ushered into the presidential sanctum without more ado than if they were calling upon the executive of some corporation long converted to the principle of publicity.

They found in A. C. Bedford a rational human being, a man of heart as well as head; open, frank, congenial, ready to discuss labour or any other problem incidental to the conduct of corporate business. Barred doors and sealed lips henceforth are to have no place throughout 26 Broadway. President Bedford is an apostle of the doctrine of publicity.

Having himself travelled unaided every step of the way, from the valley of obscurity to the summit of success, I asked Mr. Bedford to tell some of the things he had learned during his journey, to give some suggestions or pointers for the guidance of other climbers.

"Well," he began, "my advice to every young man would be this:

"Do everything you are told—and do it with all your heart and strength—willingly, cheerfully, and enthusiastically—and then look around for more work to do.

"Don't measure your work by hours, but by what it is possible for you to accomplish from the time you enter in the morning—and be early rather than late—until the place closes in the evening; and don't quit the moment the place officially closes if there is work still to be done.

"Read and study and think along the lines of your business. Learn what it is all about, what service it contributes to making the world go round more comfortably and efficiently. Cultivate the habit of looking ahead, of acquiring as much foresight as possible. Have imagination and vision.

"Then try to plan out your life, to map out a course; consider and calculate the steps necessary to carry you toward your goal; go forward step by step—and don't get your sequences mixed. Do one thing at a time. If your job at the moment is to keep books, master bookkeeping thoroughly and study the fundamentals of accountancy —don't merely keep your books mechanically. From accountancy go on to study finance, and this will help to open other doors. Or, if you start in a manufacturing department, first master that department and then learn all there is to be learned about other departments. Thus will you become familiar with the whole process of manufacture.

"Your next step would be to learn the outlets and the uses for your manufacture—the market for your product. By studying what and how much your market will take or will not take you become a capable merchandise man. This double knowledge of manufacturing and merchandising qualifies you to fill an executive position and opens the way to rise to the very top, whereas the fellow who was content to jog along in a rut in one department will still be about where he began."

"You think, then, Mr. Bedford, that almost every fellow has a chance?" I asked.

"No, not *a* chance, not *one* chance, but *many chances*," he replied spiritedly. "Every fellow has chances coming his way constantly; it is not a question of having chances but of recognizing chances when they come. You sometimes hear a fellow say: 'I had a chance once but didn't take it.' Never mind the chance that is past; watch out for the next one and qualify to be able to seize it."

"You believe the young man of normal intelligence and abnormal diligence can usually make at least a moderate success of his life?" I queried.

"Yes—I have no patience with smart Alecks, with high-fliers, with brilliant young gentlemen who go up like sky-rockets, for they usually come down like sticks," he declared with emphasis. "Do the natural thing; do just what is reasonable whether you are dealing with an employer or a customer or a competitor or with labour. Avoid short cuts.

"Success that is worth while is, after all, very largely a matter of plain, every-day morality combined with tremendous industry and a deserved reputation for integrity and for fairness toward the other fellow."

Rather old-fashioned advice? Not much comfort in it, is there, for those who want to find some brand-new trick for lassoing success without working for it? Pretty much an endorsement of the eternal verities, of such matter-of-fact virtues as industry and honesty?

The more I dig into the lives of successful men the more convinced I become that all have had to travel the same sort of hilly road, sweating brow and brain, meeting and overcoming obstacles, but never losing sight of their lodestar no matter how great the provocation. The scale that weighs success and mediocrity, I verily believe, oftentimes is tipped by an extra ounce or two of energy, an additional hour or two of labour, an added yard or two of foresight.

From the day he began work Alfred C. Bedford did not neglect the needful extra effort. He was fortunate in his up-bringing. His father, of English parentage, was for years the European representative of an American watch company in London, England, though still retaining a home in Brooklyn. Alfred was educated first at Adelphi College, Brooklyn, and later at Lausanne, Switzerland, this place having been chosen because of the excellent linguistic and other advantages it offered. His mother, who is still alive at 84, a scholarly and intellectual woman, familiar with the best in art, music, literature, and history, spent much of her time supervising the studies of Alfred and a brother.

"To my mother I owe my love for art and literature and the finer things of life," was the son's simple tribute.

When nearing nineteen, Alfred, his European education finished, decided it was time he started work. He had no pronounced bent, no predilection for any special field. A friend offered him a place as stock boy in his department at the wholesale drygoods house of E. S. Jaffray and Company on Broadway. This was a chance to get on Broadway, so he took it.

Alas! within forty-eight hours he realized that he had made a mistake, that he had entered the wrong place. The whole environment repelled him. There were twenty other youths in the department, all being trained by its head, a high-grade, clean, large-hearted man who took a deep and active interest in helping youths to get on in life. But young Bedford could see no future here; everything seemed blocked ahead. Besides, ribbons did not appeal to his manliness.

But he did not quit. Preparation for the fall trade necessitated continuous work from seven or eight in the morning till ten or eleven at night. Bedford did his share, shirking nothing. From junior stock boy he was rapidly promoted to be a full-fledged stock clerk and later was allowed to do some selling.

"Distasteful and repugnant though handling ribbons was to me," remarked Mr. Bedford in recounting those early days, "I there learned the value of order and system, of inventory and proper keeping of stock and also of business discipline. The manager was a brilliant salesman, and we used to edge near to hear his talk when he was selling a bill of goods. His skill caused us open-mouthed wonder. We regarded him as a genius."

Then came a pause. I waited.

"I also learned another lesson there," Mr. Bedford resumed. "Our most important customer was coming and we made extraordinary preparations to fascinate him with our display of goods. Everything in the department, from the oldest, stalest stuff to the newest, was brought out and arranged with consummate artistry. Even the dead numbers seemed to glow with beauty, so cleverly were they interspersed with the choicest and freshest creations. Well, the buyer came—and succumbed. In two days he bought everything the manager suggested. News of the coup rang through the whole house. Congratulations showered upon our department head.

"Next season came—but not the buyer. He had found to his cost that in his purchases of the previous season there had been included a lot of old-fashioned, obsolete, unsalable stuff on which, of course, he lost money. It was whispered he would never buy another dollar's worth of merchandise from that department.

"This incident burned certain truths into my mind. It taught me that it is fatal to palm off on a customer something he doesn't want, that you have to be as zealous about the welfare of your customer as about your own, that you must inspire and deserve his confidence by advising him frankly and faithfully what you believe will best suit his purposes and enable him to make a satisfactory profit. Once you establish such relations with a customer, you rivet him to you 'with hooks of steel.' Your business, run on these lines, will grow."

When a chance came to better himself by going with a flour firm, Alfred wrote his father for advice. In reply he was told to see his father's friend, Charles Pratt. After investigation, Mr. Pratt counselled that the concern was too small to offer large opportunities. Shortly afterward (in 1882) young Bedford was asked to call at 46 Broadway, the offices of Charles Pratt and Company whose oil business was then in process of amalgamation with the Standard Oil Company. He secured a position. That was A. C. Bedford's initial connection with Standard Oil.

His first order was to draw off a balance sheet from the books of a small subsidiary company. He had never kept books, and, struggle as he might, he couldn't reach a balance. The bookkeeper finally noticed that the newcomer was in trouble and looked the figures over. "Try putting the cash in and see if it won't balance," he remarked dryly. And of course it did. Bedford realized that he had a lot to learn—but he was determined to learn it.

He needed determination to go on in this place, for the bookkeeper never tired of telling him what a terrible mistake he had made in coming to such an office, for he himself had been there for years and years but, though forty, was nothing more than a bookkeeper. "I would rather see any son of mine dead than starting in as you're doing," he told Bedford.

Bedford, however, was made of different stuff. He had clearer eyes, a more virile imagination, a stiffer backbone. In the readjustment of the Pratt business the pessimistic bookkeeper was dropped and an expert accountant was called in, as already related.

About this time Standard Oil was laying plans to extend its ramifications to the Far East. One of its representatives was sending from India long letters describing conditions and prospects there, and when the stenographer made copies for the use of the directors, he entrusted Bedford with the reading of the proofs. This opened up a new vista. The possibilities of this business with which he had become connected fired his imagination. Here was something big enough for any man to tackle—vastly different from ribbons!

The ability, the enthusiasm, the trustworthiness of his young friend won the fullest confidence of Mr. Pratt. Although at first nominally in the employ of the Bergen Point Chemical Company, Bedford gradually was given more and more responsible and confidential duties by Mr. Pratt, not only in business, but in the philanthropic work which latterly claimed so much of that noble, public-spirited citizen's life. When C. M. Pratt, a son of the firm's founder, took charge, Mr. Bedford became his assistant.

These were years of valuable training for the future president of Standard Oil. He became directly associated with the running of various important concerns outside of oil, as the Pratts had large interests in numerous enterprises. Thus it came about that Mr. Bedford became treasurer of the Long Island Railroad, secretary of the Ohio River Railroad, a directing force in an electric light property in Portland, Oregon, in coal properties in West Virginia, in water projects, in public utility enterprises and in railroad building. Every new activity, every additional experience, every fresh responsibility brought increased travelling, broader knowledge, and a constantly widening circle of friends in the world of affairs.

All this time Mr. Bedford retained his connection with Standard Oil through its subsidiary, the Bergen Point Chemical Co., of which he had become manager. He had a conviction that some day this association might prove extremely valuable. And it did.

One day in 1907, before the financial panic broke, H. H. Rogers came to Mr. Bedford and told him there would be an opportunity for him to join the Standard Oil directorate. The suggestion dumfounded him.

"I don't see what use I could be on the board, for I'm not essentially an oil man," protested Mr. Bedford.

"You have had a broad, practical, general business experience and that is what we want," Rogers explained in a tone of finality. "We think there is a place for a young man like you."

Next day the newspapers received a three-line announcement that "Alfred C. Bedford was to-day elected a director of the Standard Oil Company of New Jersey."

Mr. Bedford had broken all precedent. Never before had any but practical, dyed-in-the-wool oil experts been elected to the great Standard Oil board. Every man on it was a giant. Every name on that directorate was an epitome of important industrial history.

The news of Mr. Bedford's elevation caused widespread comment. It was so revolutionary. It was so different from anything the staid, heavyweight Rockefeller board had ever done before.

But Mr. Rogers and the Rockefellers and the others familiar with the facts knew what they were about. They knew they were making no mistake. Mr. Rogers had made it his special business to study the crop of new timber and he had had no difficulty in singling out Alfred Bedford as the most promising tree in the whole forest—Standard Oil then had some 60,000 employees.

"It was an invaluable experience for me to rub shoulders with these men daily at such an eventful time," Mr. Bedford recently remarked. "I drank in the business and financial wisdom they had accumulated during several decades of activity in the handling of gigantic affairs. It was an inestimable privilege for a comparatively young man."

Being the youngest director, whenever any important missions involving travel and fatigue had to be undertaken, Mr. Bedford was delegated to carry them out. England, Roumania, Italy, France, and Germany all claimed on-the-spot attention. He rapidly withdrew from outside interests and concentrated upon the producing, refining, transporting, and marketing of oil.

When the Government instituted dissolution proceedings against the company in 1908, Mr. Bedford was one of those selected to look after the preparation of the data necessary for the defence. If he had not known the Standard Oil business in all its kinks and phases before then, he assuredly had opportunity to gather all the facts during the succeeding year or two.

Dissolution was ordered in 1911, the decree of the Supreme Court of the United States resulting in the splitting of the organization into thirty-two companies. Although Mr. Bedford disclaims any credit for the masterful manner in which this was done without disturbance to a great industry affecting the well-being of hundreds of thousands of citizens and practically every railroad and manufacturing industry as well as a great foreign commerce, and attributes the achievement to the efficiency of the organization and its personnel, it is not illogical to surmise that his training and executive ability had not a little to do with the phenomenal care with which the vast, complicated task was carried out in conformity with the decree of the court.

All the veterans then retired from the board except John D. Archbold, who became president. Mr. Bedford, who had risen to the treasurership, was now promoted to the vice-presidency, and on the death of Mr. Archbold, he was elected to the presidency of the company, on December 26, 1916.

In newspaper interviews with Mr. Bedford, published on his election, these sentences occur:

"The stormy period of business recrimination and reconstruction is past. A clear road is open to extend America's domestic and foreign trade along lines of fairness and benefit to all."

"We shall have many difficulties to meet after the war that we did not experience before. Trade with other countries is a necessary means of expanding our commerce. Europe will be alive; so must we keep abreast of our opportunities."

"A friend from Europe recently told our company: 'We're going to get after you oil people in America and we'll control the oil business of the world because we can go ahead without unnecessary interference from government or people.' If we are to succeed in world competition after the war, the public, the government, and the press must adopt a fair and liberal attitude toward the men who are trying to do the business of the country."

"We have always treated labour well. We have not furnished workmen's houses and free baths and that sort of thing, because we believe that the cities should do these things. Most of the men live in cities where they should have opportunities for proper living and entertainment as a right and not as gifts from employers. Adequate wages and independence to my mind are best for the workingman—and in general he will agree with this."

I should add that the biggest thing Mr. Bedford has done in a business way has never been publicly commented upon, namely, his colossal development of natural gas resources, but that is another story.

Of Mr. Bedford's non-business activities I cannot here speak at length. I can only mention that he has been a moving spirit in erecting in Brooklyn a $1,500,000 Y. M. C. A. building where 500 men live permanently—in reality, a huge temperance hotel as well as a religious, educational, and recreation centre. Much of his spare time is devoted to helpful work among the young. Recently Mr. Bedford was appointed by the International Y. M. C. A. as one of its War

Work Committee. This body will organize a comprehensive plan for extending the work of the Y. M. C. A. in our Army and Navy during the present war.

The highest possible tribute to Mr. Bedford's ability as a master of the oil industry was recently paid him by his selection, by the Council of National Defense, as Chairman of the Committee on Petroleum. This committee is made up of the most prominent oil men in the United States, and will look after the vitally important matter of conserving and effectively utilizing our supply of oil.

Another high honour was paid Mr. Bedford recently by the United States Chamber of Commerce, in appointing him a member of the committee to which has been entrusted the very serious question of the regulation of the war pay rolls, that is, of wages to be paid during the continuance of the great struggle upon which we have entered. The necessity for wise action in this matter is so urgent that the United States Chamber of Commerce at Washington was called upon to make a canvass of the nation and to secure, from the most reliable sources of information, all the facts that would help to solve one of the grave problems of the war.

Mr. Bedford believes that sound health makes for success—and also for a better manhood. So he doesn't neglect exercise and recreation. He is a devotee of golf, rides a lot, has a country home at Glen Cove, Long Island, and enjoys outings with his family—he is married and has two sons.

A wholesome man, is he not, to have at the helm of one of America's most far-reaching industrial organizations?

ALEXANDER GRAHAM BELL

NEXT to the reaping machine, which drove famine from the world, America's greatest gift to modern civilization has been the telephone. The name of its inventor, Dr. Alexander Graham Bell, will live down the ages after all but two or three present-day Americans have been forgotten.

The world scoffed at the first telephone just as it scoffed at McCormick's first crude reaper, at Fulton's first steamship, at Field's first transatlantic cable-laying project, at Morse's first telegraph, at Goodyear's first rubber products, at Wright's first aeroplane, and at Edison's electric lighting experiments.

Unlike most famous inventors, Dr. Bell did not spring from obscurity and poverty. His father was a scholar and scientist of note, and young Bell received a ripe education. But he did not escape the common fate of inventors and pioneers. His struggles with poverty came in early manhood instead of in boyhood. And they were struggles as trying and as protracted as fall to the lot of few men. At one time, while fighting to establish his ridiculed "toy" as an article of genuine use, he was reduced to the extremity of borrowing occasional half dollars for a meal, sharing this lot with his dynamic colleague, Theodore N. Vail.

The world first learned of the telephone at the Centennial Exposition at Philadelphia in 1876. On January 20 of that year a young college professor of Salem, Mass., Alexander Graham Bell, had executed specifications and a claim for an invention embodying an improvement in telegraphy, which in reality was a telephone, and on February 14 his application for the American patent was filed at Washington.

The first telephone message of which there is record was this: "Mr Watson, come here, I want you." It was sent on March 10, 1876, by the inventor from the top floor of a Boston boarding-house to a colleague, Thomas A. Watson, in a room below. Watson heard every word and rushed to apprise Bell of the fact. Almost forty years later, on January 25, 1915, Dr. Bell sent the same message to Mr. Watson, only this time Bell was in New York and Watson in San Francisco.

I can give from Dr. Bell's own lips the story of the birth of the telephone, surely a narrative worthy of a place in history.

"As a young, unknown man," said Dr. Bell, "I had been experimenting with a multiple telegraph apparatus and I went to Washington to discuss with the venerable Professor Henry of Washington, a great authority on electricity, an idea I had conceived for transmitting speech by wires. He was so sympathetic and encouraging and expressed such deep interest that I talked to him quite freely. He told me he thought I had the germ of a great invention. I told him, however, that I had not the electrical knowledge necessary to bring it into existence. He replied, 'Get it.'

"I look back upon that as a crucial period in my life. I was encouraged instead of discouraged. I felt then that my difficulty was my lack of knowledge about electricity, but I now realize that I would never have brought forth the telephone if I *had* known anything about electricity, for no electrician would have tried what I tried.

"The advantage I had was that I had studied sound all my life and knew something of its nature, the shapes of the vibrations that pass through the air when you talk, and other facts about sound. I had to go to work, with the assistance of Mr. Watson, to learn about electricity by my own experiments. No electrician would have been foolish enough to attempt the ridiculous experiments we tried."

That was the very beginning of the telephone. Let Thomas A. Watson describe what preceded and what followed.

"In 1874 I was working in a crude little workshop in Boston where inventors came to have all sorts of apparatus made. A young man came in one day, and although I had found all inventors enthusiastic, I soon saw that not one of them had the boundless enthusiasm and confidence of my new client. He wanted apparatus made which would use the law of sympathetic vibration to send eight or ten messages simultaneously over a single wire. The scheme looked all right to me at first, but we couldn't get it to work. We kept on experimenting all winter—and it was a good thing we did not succeed at first, for if we had, the speaking telephone might never have emerged from Bell's brain. One evening Bell said to me: 'Watson, I want to tell you of another idea I have which will surprise you.' He then confided to me that he believed it would be possible to invent a simple contrivance to enable people to talk by telegraph. My nervous system never got a worse shock! On June 2, 1875, when we were hard at work on Bell's harmonic telegraph apparatus, I in one room trying to send messages and he in another receiving them, one of the transmitter springs stopped vibrating and Bell, hearing a strange sound, immediately yelled to me: 'What did you do there?'

"There and then he realized that the sound he had heard over the wire was the first real sound ever carried by electricity to the ear of man. The speaking telephone was born at that moment.

"Alexander Graham Bell grasped the momentous fact that the

mechanism could transmit other sounds, voices, to the human ear. Bell at once gave me instructions to construct the first speaking telephone the world has ever seen. Next day I made a small instrument, but I confess I did not then realize what a tremendously important piece of work I was doing. By means of the little instrument we then made I could hear his voice over a wire and could almost get a word now and then—that was all. It was plain, however, that Bell was on the right track. It took ten months to invent apparatus which could transmit a complete intelligible sentence.

"In October, 1876, the first long-distance telephone conversation was conducted, between Boston and Cambridge. We borrowed the use of the telegraph wire after work was finished for the day and attached our telephone instrument at either end. We could not get the thing to work at all. Finally, I discovered that another connection was interfering with us and when this was cut off I could hear Bell shouting: 'Ahoy, Watson, ahoy! what's the matter?' That marked the birth of long-distance telephony.

"Almost forty years later Bell and I, by means of that first telephone instrument, spoke over 4,000 miles, he in New York and I in San Francisco."

To-day the Bell system carries almost 30,000,000 messages every day, has 10,000,000 subscribers, connected by 20,000,000 miles of wires, a billion dollars' worth of property, and employs 200,000 workers. As an adjunct of military preparedness it has proved invaluable in these latter historic, strenuous days.

Alexander Graham Bell was the logical man to invent the telephone. The science of articulation and phonetics had no more illustrious exponent than his father, Alexander Melville Bell, lecturer on elocution in the University of Edinburgh, where the son was born on March 3, 1847. The elder Bell had devoted intense study to enable the deaf to speak by means of "visible speech" and was the author of a standard volume on this subject. Mr. Bell's grandfather, Alexander Bell, had also won national fame in the treatment of defective utterance. Then his mother contributed her share to the lad's talents; she taught him music, particularly piano playing, and this enlarged his knowledge of the science of sound.

The boy Bell had a healthy amount of mischief in him. His special chum was the son of a miller who, on catching the pair playing some prank one day, admonished them and ended by saying, "Now, boys, why don't you do something useful?" Bell meekly asked what, for example, they might do. The miller picked up a handful of wheat and replied: "If you could only take the husks off this wheat you would be of some help." Bell set his young brain to work and discovered that by diligently using a nail brush he could remove the husks. He next conceived the idea that the work might be done by putting the wheat into a rotating machine used in the mill and thrown around against brushes or something rough. The lad laid his scheme before the miller and it was adopted with complete success.

A little later the fertile-brained Bell founded "The Society for the Promotion of Fine Arts Among Boys," in which every member was at least a "professor." The founder was Professor of Anatomy, and, aided by his father, gathered a collection of skeletons of small animals cleaned by himself, birds' eggs, plants, etc. The Society was progressing famously, its "lectures," held in the Bell attic, being very well attended. A special treat was in store when Bell got hold of a dead sucking pig and, before a large and keenly interested audience, prepared to dissect the animal.

"Professor" Bell, with a proud flourish, stuck a knife into the carcass. Horrors! It emitted a groaning sound! A mad rush was made for the door, led by the terrified anatomist. After that the Society languished.

The noise had been caused by the sudden escape of some air which had remained in the animal.

The youthful experimenter was more successful and—much more entertaining—in trying to teach a very intelligent skye terrier how to talk. By a little aid in the manipulation of its lower jaw, the dog learned how to say "Ow ah oo, ga-ma-ma"—"How are you, grandmamma?"

After graduating, without any honours, from the Royal High School of Edinburgh, at fourteen, the boy lived for a year in London with his grandfather, who was his sole intimate associate and companion. Here he devoted himself to studying the science of sound, became serious-minded and "old for his age." On returning home he so resented the curtailment of the freedom his grandparent had allowed him that, in league with his brother, he determined to run away to sea!

"My clothes were packed and I had fixed the hour of my departure for Leith, where I expected to become a stowaway on a vessel," Mr. Bell relates.

It was well for the world that he changed his mind at the last moment. Still bent on gaining independence, the youth, now sixteen, applied for a position as teacher in an Academy, at Elgin, Scotland, and was allowed to go. His salary was £10 ($50) a year and board, with instruction in Latin and Greek to fit him for the University. The discovery that several of his pupils were older than himself did not frighten him!

Later he took a classical course in Edinburgh University and returned as resident master and teacher of elocution and music at

Elgin Academy. When the Bell family removed to London Alexander Graham resumed study, first at University College and then at London University.

Before he was twenty-one he had taught numbers of deaf-born children how to speak, and when his father left for a lecturing tour in America the son took up the parent's activities. He taught speech defectives, delivered lectures at schools and colleges, and generally looked after his father's practice. He was looked upon as a young man of extraordinary ability, as something more than the brilliant son of a brilliant father.

Fate took a hand at this juncture in giving the young man's life an entirely new twist. Two of his brothers died from tuberculosis, and as a precautionary measure the Bell family, in 1870, crossed the Atlantic and settled near Brantford, Ontario.

His fame as a teacher of the deaf won for him an appointment at Boston University as lecturer on vocal physiology, and Professor Bell removed to Boston in 1872 to devote his whole energy to his teaching and study of the science of speech in all its phases. It was while here that he became interested in multiple telegraphy and, as already related, in telephony.

A man of less enthusiasm, less faith, less patience, would have given up the task long before even partial success was attained. To analyze scientifically the exact character of the vibrations caused in the air by the human voice was in itself no easy undertaking. He became convinced that in order to talk by electricity he must produce a variation in the intensity of the electric current identical with that caused by an equivalent vocal sound. In more understandable language, Bell concluded that he must invent a continuous instead of an intermittent current. Finally, he evolved an instrument which he felt justified in patenting, as already told, early in 1876 when he was only thirty years old. In the following year he went to Europe and delivered a series of lectures on his epochal invention.

How completely Alexander Graham Bell then covered the ground with his invention may be gathered from the fact that not a single electric speaking telephone has been made from that day to this which is not based on the patent he then took out.

The world owes the telephone, in a sense, to the deaf. It was the painstaking, lifetime efforts of three generations of Bells on behalf of children and men and women afflicted with deficiencies of speech that enabled Graham Bell to solve the problem of electric telephony, since the professional duties of his ancestors and of his own early years had led him to study every phase of the science of sound.

Troubles, vexations, obstacles, opposition, disappointments came to Bell before honours and fame. His contrivance was ridiculed

ALEXANDER GRAHAM BELL

by the newspapers of Europe and America, and even technical journals at first refused to regard it seriously. Capital was equally skeptical.

One man who had faith in his revolutionary device was Gardiner G. Hubbard, the inventor's father-in-law, a man of means and of business talent. He threw himself into the project enthusiastically and fought valiantly to introduce the telephone into practical use. Not only were Bell and Hubbard confronted with all the initial troubles incidental to designing and manufacturing the necessary instruments and paraphernalia, but they were attacked and embarrassed at every turn by the all-powerful Western Union Telegraph Company, associated with which were some of the most powerful interests in the country. A young, unknown genius, Edison, was enlisted by this rival enterprise, and he invented a meritorious transmitter which enabled the Western Union to establish a competitive telephone service.

Europe began to ring with Bell's fame, but his fortune did not keep step. Materials were expensive, customers were hard to drum up, and one or two of the early long-distance lines would not at first work satisfactorily. It was at this stage that Theodore N. Vail, a young man of boundless energy and irrepressible enthusiasm, consented to join Bell and Hubbard. He had as much faith in the worth of the telephone as its inventor himself had. He also had extraordinary foresight and brilliant business ability.

Like most really great men, Alexander Graham Bell is modest, so modest that he never loses an opportunity to emphasize the part played by others in the development of the telephone.

"Great discoveries and improvements invariably involve the co-operation of many minds," he declares. "I may perhaps take credit for having blazed the trail for the others who have come after me, but when I look at the phenomenal developments of the telephone and at the great system that bears my name, I feel that the credit for these developments is due to others rather than to myself. Why, I do not even understand how it has been made possible to talk into a telephone at Washington and have a man on the Eiffel Tower in Paris hear what is said without wires having been employed, or how a man in Honolulu can overhear that conversation between this country and France.

"When I look back upon the past, to the very beginning of the telephone, I can remember men whose names are hardly ever heard of in connection with the telephone, yet who, by their advice and their sympathy and their financial support, laid the very foundations for what we have to-day."

The French Government awarded him the Volta prize of 50,000

francs for his historic achievement and it was characteristic of Mr. Bell that he applied this money, with a substantial addition out of his own pocket, to founding the Volta Bureau in Washington "for the increase and diffusion of knowledge relating to the deaf." Later he founded, at a cost of over $300,000, the American Association to Promote the Teaching of Speech to the Deaf, and became its active president. To this notable work of brightening the lot of persons unable to hear, he devoted himself wholeheartedly, even during periods when his labours might have been directed with greater pecuniary profit to business affairs. He became the author of "The Education of Deaf Children," "Memoirs on the Formation of a Deaf Variety of the Human Race," and "Lectures on the Mechanism of Speech."

Romance has blended with Dr. Bell's interest in the deaf. In 1877 he married Mabel Gardiner Hubbard, daughter of Gardiner Hubbard (a regent of the Smithsonian Institution), a young woman who had lost her hearing in infancy and had derived great benefit from Professor Bell's scientific research and teaching on this subject.

Had Alexander Graham Bell never brought forth the telephone his other achievements would have won him distinction. He is the father of a wonderful little device, the telephone probe, for revealing painlessly the presence and the location of bullets in the human body. He had an important hand in the invention of the graphophone, jointly with C. A. Bell and S. Taintor. Scientists rate highly, also, Bell's achievements in connection with the induction balance. A generation ago he told the American Academy of Sciences all about his discovery of the photophone. Even before then the Royal Society in London had been addressed by him on the action of light on selenium plates.

Twenty-seven years ago Dr. Bell established a modest fund to promote the then novel project of aviation. By evolving the tetrahedral kite he succeeded in lifting and sustaining in the air upward of 300 pounds, exclusive of the weight of the machine, a more substantial result than Benjamin Franklin's experiments with kites brought forth. Largely because of his undying international fame as inventor of the telephone, Bell's wonderful pioneer work in aviation and in other spheres of applied science has won him no universal recognition, although in scientific circles it is reckoned at its true value.

There is a Farmer Bell as well as an Inventor Bell. Although his chief residence is in Washington, he spends a large part of each year on his extensive estate in Nova Scotia. Here, also, the scientist in him crops up, for he has applied science to the breeding of sheep. He knows more about sheep than a Scottish shepherd and has written as illuminatingly on these humble animals as on abstract and applied sciences.

ALEXANDER GRAHAM BELL

The patriarchal figure of Dr. Bell is one of the best known in Washington, to whose intellectual life he has contributed immeasurably. His long white hair and ample beard, his striking forehead and his keen, kindly eyes at once attract attention, suggesting a man of distinction.

In his case it cannot be said that his attainments have not won him honour in his own country. He is a regent of the Smithsonian Institution, has been president of the National Geographic Society, president of the American Institute of Electrical Engineers, and an honorary or active member of a long list of various scientific and philosophic bodies. He is an officer of the Legion of Honour, while his contributions to the advancement and enhancement of civilization have also won him innumerable medals and degrees from scientific societies and universities in all parts of the world.

As Edwin Markham, the poet, so fitly expressed it on the occasion of the presentation to Dr. Bell of the New York Civic Forum "Medal of Honour for Distinguished Public Service" last March, the telephone, the child of Bell's brain—

> Dispels the distances, shrinks up the spaces,
> Brings back the voices and the vanished faces,
> Holds men together though the feet may roam,
> Makes of each land a little friendly home!
>
> The wires are everywhere,
> The tingling nerves of the air.
> Be-netting cities, speaking for all hearts,
> From floor to floor their whispered lightning darts.
> Looping the prairies, leaping hills and lakes,
> Over the world their whispered lightning shakes.
> They stitch the farms and link the battle-line:
> They tread the Alps and down the Congo twine;
> They throb among the Pyramids, and speak
> Where Fujiyama lifts her perfect peak.

America may proudly claim as her own the two most illustrious electrical geniuses the world has produced—no, not claim them as her own, for Edison and Bell belong to the whole human race, since the whole human family are their grateful debtors.

ANDREW CARNEGIE

ANDREW CARNEGIE probably will leave the smallest fortune of any modern American Croesus—perhaps nearly a billion dollars less than John D. Rockefeller, a hundred millions less than Frick, and less, too, than was left by Morgan, Hill, Harriman, the Harknesses, Russell Sage, Hetty Green, or John Jacob Astor.

Carnegie has given away $325,000,000 *and has, I am told, less than $30,000,000 left.*

Carnegie's original investment in steel-making was $250,000. In 27 years he sold out the Carnegie Steel Company to Morgan's Steel Corporation for $300,000,000 in bonds, nearly $100,000,000 in preferred stock and $90,000,000 common stock. Carnegie, canny Scot, took the bonds and left thes tock for his forty partners, who owned about 40 per cent. and Carnegie about 60 per cent. of the Carnegie Company.

In his "Gospel of Wealth" he formulated this cardinal article of his faith:

"The day is not far distant when the man who dies leaving behind him millions of available wealth, which were free for him to administer during life, will pass away 'unwept, unhonoured, and unsung,' no matter to what use he leaves the dross which he cannot take with him. Of such as these the public verdict will then be: 'The man who dies thus rich dies disgraced.'"

Elsewhere he has recorded: "I would as soon leave to my son a curse as the almighty dollar."

Carnegie has no son, only one daughter, born in 1897. She will not be one of the world's richest heiresses.

Carnegie, relatively speaking, will die poor. He is now 82 and feeble.

Modern history contains only one character comparable to Carnegie—John D. Rockefeller. Carnegie created "a new era," the era of stupendous philanthropy—no, not exactly a new era, for he had his prototype in the palmy days of Greece and of Rome, when rulers and wealthy nobles distributed largess with equally lavish hand.

No American has been more extolled—and few more execrated. He has been invested with all the virtues of a saint—and condemned as a bloodstained tyrant and slave-driver. To him some have ascribed wisdom, foresight, and ability not less than superhuman;

others have portrayed him as a popinjay, the incarnation of smug self-satisfaction, the fortunate creature of circumstances, whose only claim to distinction he himself set down in the epitaph he composed for his tombstone—"Here lies one who knew how to get around him men who were cleverer than himself."

He has been called both a capitalistic socialist and a czar who refused to countenance any man, even the brainiest, as his equal in the realm of business.

Because he has no fixed religious belief, the epithet "atheist" has been hurled at him all through his career, yet he has given donations for 7,000 church organs—"Listening to music, particularly that of the organ, is a form of religious expression to him," declares an intimate.

He has been accused of having quarrelled with and hoodwinked more of his associates than any other man in industrial history. "No man ever made so many men millionaires or shared his profits so lavishly" is the verdict of such men as Schwab and Corey who shared freely of his bounties and bonuses.

"The modern Patron Saint of Scotland" he has been called—yet the people of his native town, carried away by their indignation at his peace views in the early days of the war, splattered his statue with mud and filth.

In face of all this, what is the truth? Is he an enigma? Are there two Carnegies, saint and devil, Jekyll and Hyde?

Before I undertook a close study of Carnegie's life I had imbibed several unfavourable ideas from my elders in Carnegie's native country. They disliked his ostentatious "cantrips." Some resented the name "C A R N E G I E" being plastered over buildings he helped to erect —and then left the struggling tax-payers to support. Stories of his arrogance, his impatience of contradiction by even the greatest experts and specialists in any line, his overweening self-satisfaction, his atheistic preachments, his never-ceasing slurs upon the royal family— such stories were rife in Highland glens and hamlets and cities.

I want to say, however, that fuller knowledge has modified my preconceived views and removed many misconceptions. I am no hero-worshipper; but in my judgment Carnegie's admirable qualities far outweigh his foibles, many of which were inspired in the early days, not by vanity, but by business motives.

When as a young man he invited the Prince of Wales to ride on a Pennsylvania Railroad engine he had an eye solely to future business favours—and he got them. When he moved in prominent social places in New York, still higher political and diplomatic circles in Washington, and hobnobbed with European royalties, it was with no thought of shining in the society columns of newspapers; it was more for the sake of the "profit" columns in his ledgers.

Later, people of eminence and intellect sought the company of Carnegie less for the sake of his purse than for his personality. He travelled everywhere and saw everything with intelligent eyes. His scanty schooling was supplemented by subsequent study, guided and coached by a tutor. He became a man of genuine education and of wonderful knowledge. The volumes that appeared under his name were not written, as many supposed, by others. He could recite half of Shakespeare and all of Burns and was deeply read in many subjects.

Before his wealth became notable his close British friends included such intellectual giants as Gladstone, Rosebery, Morley, Herbert Spencer, Mathew Arnold, and James Bryce.

In such company Carnegie could hold his own. He was a fine story-teller; he was cheerful; he had unbounded faith in the future; he loved life and he loved the world and its inhabitants. He was not immersed completely in steel; the truth is, no steel man ever knew less about steel than Carnegie did—but no man ever knew how to capture bigger orders, how to secure better results from workmen, or how to pick from the ranks such able partners. After his youthful struggles he, like John D. Rockefeller, took life easier than any of his associates —and has outlived the majority of them.

Carnegie admittedly drove his partners, his superintendents and other aspiring hopefuls like slaves, both for their own financial advantage and his. But he treated the workmen "white" and was warmly regarded by them.

It is not difficult to analyze the causes of Carnegie's quarrels with other giants in the industry. His falling-out with Frick, for example, was inevitable in the nature of the men and the evolving economic conditions.

Carnegie ridiculed kings and monarchs, yet he set up a business monarchy and crowned himself king. His word was as autocratic as that of the ex-Czar of Russia or the Sultan of Turkey. His favourites became courtiers, but none must attempt to seek or force a place on the throne. Able men whom he raised from the ranks and made wealthy by his system of bonuses and profit-sharing, worshipped their maker. His arrogance, his slave-driving, his masterfulness they accepted as a matter of course. Since Carnegie paid the fiddler, it was fitting he should have complete right to call the tune. And they were content to dance to the Carnegie music.

These methods worked all right with subordinates, but equals would not stand his highhandedness.

Henry C. Frick was already a man of wealth and power when he joined Carnegie. He foresaw the coming evolution in the conduct of big business. He realized the interdependence of industrial, railroad and financial interests. He saw that the day of independent monarchs was passed; he believed in a more democratic form of business administration. Instead of a czar, there must be control by statesmen, by directors. Frick was at home among his equals in brains and power; Carnegie would admit of no equals and would share his sceptre with no one. Frick adapted himself to the new economic order; Carnegie was of the old school—where Carnegie sat that must be the head of the table.

It is not true, however, that Carnegie hoodwinked partner after partner into parting with his stock to him at cruelly low figures. The explanation in most cases was that, when storms of depression broke, his associates lost faith in steel, whereas Andrew Carnegie, from the first time he saw a Bessemer furnace in operation (in England), never once lost confidence in the metal. He could always peer beyond the darkest clouds and see in steel something of infinite importance to the progress of the world. Never for a moment did he doubt that molten streams of iron could be transformed into streams of gold.

It is no exaggeration to say that no employer ever shared his profits so generously with his co-workers as did Carnegie. But power he would not share.

If I were to attempt to describe Andrew Carnegie in one comprehensive sentence I would say that, as a boy and youth, he worked prodigiously and displayed extraordinary alertness in seizing opportunities; that he glorified his parents and treated his mother with the most beautiful reverence; that through intense study and very extensive travel he became a man of no mean culture; that he early manifested extraordinary skill in financiering and pulled off more clever deals than any man of his day; that he treated his workmen with consideration and inspired talent by his generous, adroit system of sharing profits with those who contributed to the attainment of successful results; that in temperament he was strong-willed to the point of arrogance, and distinctly vainglorious, though, at the same time, he had simple habits and democratic ways; finally, that, by his example of prodigal giving, mostly for worthy purposes, he has done much to take the curse from inordinate riches and to force other millionaires to spend large parts of their fortunes for the benefit of humanity, thus, by his own deeds and by his example, furthering incalculably the brotherhood of man.

And now let us rapidly trace the steps by which the immigrant son of a poor weaver rose to be emperor of the world of steel.

Born in Dunfermline in 1835, the son of a handloom weaver, Andrew Carnegie had little schooling and early sought to contribute to the family purse. When ten he saved enough to buy a box of oranges which he peddled profitably to retailers! The introduction of steam-driven looms forced the Carnegie family, consisting of the

parents and two sons, Andrew and Tom, to emigrate to America
when Andy was twelve. They took up their abode at Barefoot Square,
Slabtown, Allegheny, Pa., where relatives had settled. The father
got a job in a cotton mill and Andy was taken in as a bobbin boy
at $1.20 a week. His mother took in washing and sewed boots for
a next-door shoemaker named Phipps, with whose ten-year-old son,
Harry, the little immigrant became fast friends.

"The genuine satisfaction I had from that $1.20 outweighs any
subsequent pleasure in money-getting," Carnegie declared some
years ago.

He worked from darkness in the morning until darkness every
evening, with only forty minutes' respite at noon. The thought,
however, that he had been "admitted to the family partnership as
a contributing member" comforted and sustained him.

A friendly Scotsman next gave him work in his bobbin factory at
$1.80 a week, but here his duties included firing the boiler. "The
responsibility," he chronicles, "of keeping the water right and of
running the engine and the danger of my making a mistake and blowing the whole factory to pieces, caused too great a strain, and I woke
and found myself sitting up in bed through the night trying the steam
gauges. But I never told them at home that I was having a hard
tussle. No, no! Everything must be bright to them."

Next, a former resident of Dunfermline gave little Andy a job as a
telegraph messenger in Pittsburgh at $3 a week. Scared lest his ig-
norance of the city might cause him to lose his place, he drilled himself so industriously that he was soon able to close his eyes and rattle
off the name and address of every business house throughout the
business section of the city! He went to the office early and secretly
practised on the telegraph instruments.

One morning Philadelphia was clamouring to send a "death message," and Andy, in the absence of any operator, took the message
over the wire and promptly delivered it before the office opened for
business. Instead of being, as he feared, dismissed for his audacity,
he was soon promoted to be an operator, "and received the, to me,
enormous recompense of $25 per month, $300 a year." He did extra
work in copying press messages which brought him $1 additional
weekly and also brought him into contact every evening with the
morning newspaper reporters.

Thomas A. Scott, then the Pittsburgh superintendent of the Pennsylvania Railroad, who often visited the telegraph office to talk to
the General Superintendent at Altoona, noted the energetic young
operator, and when the railroad put up a wire of its own, Carnegie
was installed as clerk and operator at $35 per month.

An accident tied up the road one day when the Superintendent was not at hand and Carnegie, on his own initiative, made the wires sizzle with instructions signed "Thomas A. Scott." This was against all rules, but Carnegie had adopted as his motto one he has often quoted since—"Break orders to save owners." Scott made him his private secretary at $50 a month and started Carnegie on his way to fortune.

"Could you find $500 to invest?" Mr. Scott asked him one day. "Yes, sir, I think I can," he replied, although how or where he was to get so huge a sum he had not the faintest notion. Scott explained that an owner of ten shares of Adams Express Company stock had died and that it could be purchased for $50 a share. The Carnegie family savings had gone to purchase a small house in order to save rent. The resourceful mother, "The Oracle," as Andy termed her, solved the problem by taking a steamer next morning for Ohio and mortgaging the home to an uncle, "to give our boy a start."

His first dividend check, "a mysterious golden visitor," set Carnegie thinking. This way, he saw, lay fortune. Soon afterward Woodruff, the inventor, showed the private secretary the model of a sleeping car and he at once became enthusiastic. When offered a share in the venture, Carnegie accepted. Again he had not the necessary funds, but he boldly visited the local banker and asked for a loan.

"Oh, yes, Andy, you are all right," said the banker, and the name "Andrew Carnegie" was for the first time signed to a note—he was subsequently to be one of the world's most persistent borrowers.

Scott aided him at every turn in his financial operations, and when, during the Civil War, Scott was made vice-president of the Pennsylvania, Carnegie was chosen to fill Scott's place as superintendent at Pittsburgh. Both rendered yeoman service to their country in the transportation and telegraph fields during the war.

Carnegie was then 28 and something of a capitalist. The burning of a wooden bridge played havoc with railroad traffic and this set the keen-eyed Scotsman a-thinking.

"Why not go into the building of iron bridges?" he asked himself. Forthwith he organized the Keystone Bridge Company, and—wise man —secured J. Edgar Thompson, then president of the Pennsylvania, Colonel Scott, vice-president, and other influential railroad men as stockholders. With such influence behind it, the company booked huge orders at such prices that it paid a total of 100 per cent. in dividends in four years. He entered a successful oil venture and several metal enterprises, including the Kloman-Miller-Phipps-Carnegie Company, which owned the Union Iron Mills. Indeed, he became so much of a business man and capitalist that he gave up his railroad office.

Off he went for a nine months' tour in Great Britain, leaving his partners to run the iron mills. Then disaster came. Depression set in, iron prices fell and the Union Iron Mills faced disaster. Miller, the most wealthy of the partners, had to advance money for workmen's wages. In lieu of cash many workmen were given orders for groceries on a village store. Stocks of pig iron had to be pawned. Then, to cap the climax, the puddlers struck. Miller quit. He sold for $73,600 stock which thirty-four years later, when the steel trust was formed, brought millions of dollars.

Carnegie hustled for orders from his railroad friends, and although he knew next to nothing about steel, he booked more contracts than any other drummer of his day. By effective team-work among the young partners, they managed to pull through.

It is not generally known that Carnegie for a time was a bond broker. In 1872 he was given a commission to place in Europe $6,000,000 of bonds of a Pennsylvania branch road and cleared $150,000. Later he made a second trip and earned $75,000 commission.

When in England he saw the Bessemer process of making steel. The sight of iron being blown into steel captured his imagination. Henceforth steel was to be his life. Rushing across the Atlantic he organized Carnegie, McCandless & Company with a capital of $700,000 which built a new steel plant which he, wily Scot, named the Edgar Thompson Steel Works. Thus flattered, how could the president of the Pennsylvania refuse his namesake generous rebates?

The name "Carnegie" began to be sounded all over the United States and Europe, whither he made frequent and spectacular trips. This was just after the 1873 panic. Protected by a huge tariff on the one hand and aided by rebates on the other, profits were piled up thick and fast. In 1880 steel rails were run up to $85 a ton, the works were run twenty-four hours a day, and the year's profits exceeded $2,000,000.

The following year the company was reorganized as Carnegie Bros. & Co., with $5,000,000 capital, of which Carnegie owned more than half. From then until 1888 the profits averaged $2,000,000 a year, or 40 per cent. Carnegie had rolled up a fortune of $15,000,000.

As partners died or dropped out, Carnegie took over their interest in the concern. Finally, only Carnegie and Henry Phipps—with whom, later, he quarrelled—were left. Competitors, too, including the Homestead and Duquesne Companies, were astutely bought out until Carnegie became undisputed steel king.

Frick's enormous coke properties in the Connellsville district of Pennsylvania were acquired by Carnegie in 1882 and Henry C. Frick for years was Carnegie's most trusted associate. The combination lasted until 1899, when the two parted company.

ANDREW CARNEGIE

The Carnegie Steel Company was reorganized with Carnegie in undisputed control. How he surrounded himself with such brilliant practical steel men as Captain "Bill" Jones, Schwab, Corey, Dinkey, and Morrison, and paid them enormous bonuses for results achieved; how he threatened competitors by announcing that he would build new plants and even build a new railroad to bring the Pennsylvania to its senses; how he frightened the country's leading money kings, and how he finished up by selling out to the organizers of the steel trust, are too well known to call for recapitulation.

His benefactions have included $60,000,000 for over 2,500 library buildings; $125,000,000 for the Carnegie Corporation of New York; $17,000,000 for colleges; $6,000,000 for church organs; $22,000,000 for the Carnegie Institution of Washington; $16,000,000 for the Carnegie Foundation for the Advancement of Teaching; $13,000,000 for the Carnegie Institute at Pittsburgh; $10,000,000 for the Carnegie Institute of Technology; over $10,000,000 for Carnegie hero funds; $10,000,000 for the endowment of international peace; $4,000,000 for steel workers' pensions; $2,000,000 for the Church Peace Union, and $1,500,000 for the Hague peace palace.

It is as a giver, not as a maker, of millions that Carnegie will live in history.

HENRY P. DAVISON

"MR. MORGAN wants to see you in his library at three o'clock," was the message received one day by the vice-president of a New York bank.

He hadn't the slightest idea what the veteran financier could want with him. He had met Mr. Morgan, as most other financiers had, during the parlous days when the master mind of them all was trying to stem the 1907 panic, but had not seen anything of Mr. Morgan until the spring of the following year when, with Senator Aldrich and other members of the Monetary Commission, he had spent a Sunday at Mr. Morgan's London home. Between then and the receipt of the above message in the fall of 1908 he had seldom spoken to Mr. Morgan.

Promptly at three o'clock the young banker, wondering what the matter could be, rang the bell of the famous Morgan library. On being ushered in he almost collided with Mr. Morgan at the entrance to his private room.

Mr. Morgan shook hands and bade the puzzled visitor be seated.

"Do you realize it is pretty near the first of January?" he asked.

The young banker, very much at sea, agreed that it was—this was about the middle of November.

"Are you ready?" asked Mr. Morgan.

"Ready for what?" queried the astonished visitor.

"For what?" echoed Mr. Morgan. "You know I want you to come and join my firm on the first of January."

"You never said anything about it, Mr. Morgan."

"I thought you knew by my attitude what I thought of you," said Mr. Morgan.

A pause.

"Mr. Morgan, have you ever fallen from an 18-story building?"

It was Mr. Morgan's turn to be astonished.

"No," he replied, scrutinizing his visitor.

"Well, I never have before, and it will take me a minute or two to catch my breath."

Mr. Morgan laughed.

And that was how Henry P. Davison, then only 40, was notified of his selection as a partner in the greatest international banking firm in the United States.

The story of how this same young banker won his first foothold on the New York banking ladder reveals the stuff he is made of.

He had quickly risen from office-boy to receiving teller in a modest bank at Bridgeport, Conn., when he read in the newspapers that a new bank was being formed in New York. Young Davison wanted to go to New York. He wanted to go very badly. In fact, he made up his mind that he *must* get a position in this new bank.

Armed with a letter from one of his directors who knew the cashier, he took the afternoon train to New York and handed in the letter.

The cashier treated him most cordially—so cordially that the young man left smiling, although without any job.

His smiles wore off when he got into the train homeward bound and thought matters over.

But he was not to be so easily licked! Next afternoon, when the bank closed, he again boarded a New York train. The cashier, although somewhat surprised to see him back, again accorded him a very pleasant interview, but explained that it was out of the question to engage an out-of-town man as paying teller—that was the office Davison was after. They must have a man with New York experience and of wide acquaintance. The cashier was so frank and sympathetic, however, that for the second time it was a smiling youth who left his presence.

The homeward journey, however, again dissipated the smiles.

He would try again!

Next afternoon, for the third time, he started for New York more determined than ever to get the place he wanted.

"The cashier has gone for the day," was the chilling message he received.

"Where does he live?" asked young Davison, undaunted.

In half an hour he was inside the cashier's home. A servant explained that his employer was dressing to go out to attend a dinner. All right, the visitor would wait.

On entering the room the banker burst out laughing. So did Davison, but only for a moment. He at once got down to brass tacks.

He began with all the intense earnestness he felt: "I know I am the man you want for paying teller. I can help you. I feel embarrassed at having to say this myself, but there is no one to say it for me. Give me the position and I will try to see that you will never regret it."

The ardour, the sincerity, and the perseverance of the young man made such an impression upon the banker that he became convinced the choice would prove wise.

"How much salary would you want?" he asked.

"I would like $1,500 but I would take $600 or $700—anything you like, so long as I can live on it."

This time it was the paying teller of the Astor Place Bank, at $1,500, that said good-bye. To celebrate, he went to a theatre. The big news was overpowering.

"Say, do you know who I am?" he abruptly asked a stranger sitting next to him. The man looked at him and confessed he didn't.

"I am the paying teller of a New York bank!"

Alas, the news failed to make any tremendous impression—except, probably, that the man thought he had next to him a young lunatic!

Disappointment was in store, however. Hardly had Davison given up his position and returned home for a rest before entering upon his new duties when he received a letter from the cashier containing the news that the directors had not endorsed his action, and that it would save much trouble if Mr. Davison would forego the paying tellership and accept a lower position at a smaller salary. He added that if Mr. Davison insisted in standing upon his rights, of course the directors would have to agree.

"Perfectly satisfied to accept lower position and salary," Mr. Davison immediately telegraphed—he did not want his benefactor to be kept in any suspense during the time a letter would take to reach him.

That this telegram confirmed the cashier in his sizing up of the young man can readily be understood.

To save carfare, the ambitious bank clerk used to ride on a bicycle daily to and from the bank in Astor Place to 104th Street, a distance of more than ten miles.

Henry Pomeroy Davison had early learned the value of money—and, also, when he wanted to go to college, the terrible awkwardness of not having the wherewithal. His mother had died when he was seven years old—he was born on June 13, 1867—and the four children were scattered among uncles and aunts. He attended school in his little native town, Troy, Pa., until he was 15, and before he was 16 he was teaching. He then began to realize the value of education and applied himself diligently to study. His grandmother, with whom he was then living, remarked one day: "This boy may be worth doing something for." So she arranged to have him attend boarding school, the Greylock Institute at South Williamstown, Mass., where Charles H. Sabin, now president of the Guaranty Trust Company of New York, the largest in the country, was one of his classmates.

"Harry Davison," Mr. Sabin told me, "was at the top of every class he entered and was valedictorian—but he was not much at athletics. He was very popular because he used, every morning, to let a crowd look over his answers to problems and other stuff given at night. He was always willing to help a fellow out."

During vacations he worked on a farm. On graduating he returned to Troy, whose 1,200 people supported one bank run by his uncle. A place was made for Harry as errand boy in it. He immediately became intensely interested and for two years worked very hard. Troy, however, held out little of a future and he regretted deeply that he had not gone to college. He began tutoring with a view to entering college. But, when qualified, he realized that he did not have the necessary money! Then he made up his mind to strike out.

He went to New York, tramped the streets looking for a job, but failed to find one. He went to Bridgeport, Conn., where he had an old friend. There he was given choice of a job as a runner in the bank or a clerk in a grocery store. He chose the bank.

By starting early in the morning and doing as much as possible of his own work by noon, he found time to stand by the bookkeeper and learn from him how to keep books. In a few months he was doing most of the work for this bookkeeper, and when the latter was promoted the runner got the job. The new runner was at once taken in hand by Bookkeeper Davison and taught bookkeeping. Then the bookkeeper applied himself to learning all about the teller's work. When the next shift came Davison was able to step up to the tellership and the runner had been trained to become bookkeeper. He applied exactly the same method in his new position.

"Then and ever since I have found it a good system, not only to reach out and learn the work of the man ahead of you, but also to teach your job to the fellow below you," said Mr. Davison.

How the young Bridgeport teller broke into New York has already been told. Six months after starting as receiving teller in the new Astor Place Bank he was promoted to the position on which he had at first set his heart, that of paying teller.

Dame Fortune sometimes plays queer pranks to accomplish her ends. Davison was "shot" into his next place. One day a crank pointed a revolver at Teller Davison's head, presented a check for $1,000 drawn to the order of the Almighty and demanded the money. Davison coolly accepted the check, read it loud enough to attract notice and began to count out the money. Others grasped the situation, and while the gun was still cocked at Davison's head, the bank detective seized the madman.

The newspapers made much of the dramatic incident and of the teller's self-possession. The directors of the Liberty National Bank happened to have a meeting that day and the holdup was mentioned.

"I know that young fellow," said Dumont Clarke, a director of the bank. "He would be a good man to have in the bank."

Mr. Clarke had met Davison once or twice when the latter visited his fiancée (Miss Kate Trubee of Bridgeport) while she was spending a vacation with her friend, Mr. Clarke's daughter.

Forthwith Mr. Davison was installed as assistant cashier of the Liberty. Within a year he was made cashier, three years later he was elected vice-president, and in another year president. His rise was so rapid that it attracted general attention. New York financial annals had contained few if any instances of a man of 32 being chosen as president of an important national bank solely on merit and without influence of any kind whatsoever.

Ruts were and are avoided by Davison, for ruts are graves in the making. He was not long with the Liberty when he did something original. It is told that when he joined the bank he procured a full list of the stockholders, mostly business men, visited each and delivered this sort of exhortation:

"You own . . . shares of the Liberty National Bank. Of course you would like to see them become more valuable. Well, now, won't you try to induce some of your friends to do business with us? We will treat them right—and the increased business will mean increased dividends."

Laggard stockholders were re-visited until nearly all were inoculated with the Davison spirit of enthusiasm. It became something of a sporting contest, this competition among stockholders to bring in the largest possible amount of new business.

Such intelligent initiative impressed the bank's owners—and helped the institution to grow at a rate which excited comment. It soon outgrew its quarters in the Central of New Jersey building in West Street and more pretentious, as well as more central, offices were opened at 139 Broadway. The old lease had two years to run and Mr. Davison preferred to keep the place closed lest a new concern might open there and fall heir to much of the Liberty's custom. Empty offices, however, being detrimental to a building, the owners brought pressure to bear upon Mr. Davison to agree to the subletting of the space.

Mr. Davison felt strongly, however, about the danger of a new bank taking the customers before they had learned to find the way to 139 Broadway. What could be done about it?

One of the most brilliant ideas of his life flashed into his mind, an idea that was destined to raise Davison's prestige and influence extraordinarily, as well as to help out his bank account, which then was a long way from six figures.

"I'll organize a trust company. Our capital will be safe and we ought to earn at least 6 per cent. It will make a good tenant for the Liberty's old building and it will afford some of us pleasant associations," was the plan he mapped out.

The bankers and others to whom he outlined the plan became so enthusiastic that the capital of $1,000,000 was quoted at $200 per share before the doors were opened. It is known, however, that the originator of the enterprise refused all suggestions that he take a larger share than the other directors. Each was awarded exactly the same amount of stock, a procedure that enhanced Mr. Davison's reputation for scrupulous fairness. The name given Mr. Davison's financial child was the Bankers' Trust Company. To-day it owns and occupies the most notable financial skyscraper in Wall Street, has total deposits of approximately $300,000,000, making it the second largest trust company in America. Mr. Davison, naturally, was made chairman of the executive committee, which position he has held ever since. A tablet erected in the magnificent building contains this tribute to the founder:

> THE DIRECTORS OF THE BANKERS'
> TRUST COMPANY HERE RECORD THEIR
> APPRECIATION OF THE SERVICES OF
> HENRY POMEROY DAVISON
> IN THE ORGANIZATION AND UPBUILDING
> OF THE COMPANY AND THE ERECTION
> OF ITS PERMANENT HOME

Contrary to the impression sought to be conveyed by the Pujo Committee investigators, the Bankers' Trust was not built up by an oligarchy of New York's leading financiers. It was a young men's enterprise. Such enthusiasts as Albert H. Wiggin, Gates W. McGarrah, Benjamin Strong, Jr., and Davison, not veterans who had "arrived," were chosen for the executive committee and worked nights patiently, zealously, skilfully, unsparingly, to win the success which was rapidly achieved. The experience broadened all of them.

George F. Baker, the veteran head of the First National Bank and a financier ranking in power second only to his closest friend, the late J. P. Morgan, did not fail to note the calibre of this resourceful young banker, and in 1902 he induced Mr. Davison—then only 35 years of age—to become his right-hand man as vice-president of the First National.

It was Mr. Davison's work during the 1907 panic that first brought him prominently to the attention of Commander-in-chief Morgan. At Mr. Morgan's request he was on hand at all the important conferences held uptown and downtown during the dark days of October and November. In the following spring Senator Aldrich appointed him an adviser to the National Monetary Commission to investigate the financial systems of Europe.

"Homestaying youths have ever homely wits," said Shakespeare. Davison is not open to this charge. He has enjoyed unique international experiences. First, as an adviser to the National Monetary Commission, he visited Europe and there met the Finance Ministers and other leading banking powers in England, France, Germany, and other European countries, discussing with them the very foundations of finance, banking, and currency, a privilege of rare value to a banker under 40 years of age and quick to seize every opportunity to enhance his knowledge and his usefulness. Next, when the Six-Power Chinese Loan was bruited, Washington, then presided over by Taft and Knox, asked a group of American bankers to join it in order to strengthen America's position in the Orient, and more particularly to enable this country to have a potent voice in insisting upon the maintenance of Secretary Hay's famous "Open-Door" policy for China. It was Henry P. Davison, by this time a member of the Morgan firm, who was selected to proceed to Europe and conduct the negotiations on behalf of the American group, consisting of Morgan & Co., Kuhn, Loeb & Co., the National City Bank and the First National Bank. Not only that; it was Davison who was chosen by the British, French, German, Russian, and Japanese delegations to become chairman of the whole group.

The protracted negotiations entailed several visits to Europe and long stays there, affording the young American an insight into European finance that equipped him, as nothing else could, as a real international banker.

That the negotiations came to naught was largely due to the attitude assumed by the Wilson administration, which frowned on "Dollar Diplomacy." Since then the Administration has changed its attitude and is now anxious that our bankers should extend aid to China.

The wisdom of Mr. Morgan's choice of Mr. Davison as a partner needs no descriptive words; financial history bears record that the greatest banker America has ever known found in Henry P. Davison the greatest partner he ever had.

Not the least valuable of Mr. Davison's achievements has been his untrumpeted endeavours to bring about a spirit of greater friendliness and cooperation throughout the banking community. His own openness and frankness have encouraged others to adopt a like attitude in their daily dealings with one another and with the public. His organization of the Bankers' Trust Company contributed toward this end by bringing many bankers together in a friendly way. The improvement which has been brought about in the exchange of credit information is one fruit of this new and better live-and-let-live policy.

Davison, blessed with fine physique and an engaging countenance, is both likeable and liked, by employees as well as by other bankers. He does not know how to dissemble—not even when bombarded by awkward, not-to-be answered queries by prying reporters. He goes at everything directly. He has confidence not only in himself but in men that he picks—he has often helped institutions to find important officers and has not hesitated to accept entire responsibility for his judgment in making selections. He is a man of courage, unafraid to face difficult situations, since originality, resourcefulness, and diplomacy can overcome most obstacles.

"In climbing the ladder of success what have you learned that you could pass on to aid other struggling young men?" I asked Mr. Davison. "Did you conceive any shining goal and bend everything to reaching it?"

"No," he replied emphatically. "Whatever job I had was to me always the very best job in the world, and I tried to fill it. I made no elaborate plans for the future. If I had any system in my labour it was first to do my own work; second, to teach the fellow below me how to take my place; third, to learn how to fill the position ahead of me.

"Boys and young men should not imagine that their work is so unimportant that nobody takes note of how they do it. It does not take long to find out whether a boy is on his toes watching how he can best be of help in a situation or whether he merely sits down and waits to be told what to do. The simple virtues of willingness, readiness, alertness, and courtesy will carry a boy farther than mere smartness.

"Perhaps it will not be out of place for me to describe an incident which may carry a lesson for the young men you are anxious to help. One day when I was teller, a customer offered me a very fine gold pen. I went right into the office and asked if this man had any loan from the bank. I explained that he had asked me to accept the gift. The bank promptly acted and it was not long before the fellow was in bankruptcy. The simple course I took saved the bank a good deal of money.

"Following a plain, straightforward course avoids complications of all sorts. Life is really simple. If it becomes complicated it is because we ourselves make it complicated."

The American Government, through President Wilson, recently signified its regard for Mr. Davison's transcendent ability by appointing him Chairman of the Red Cross War Council, one of the most important and onerous positions in the whole country, for on the Red Cross devolves the vast, complicated task of relieving "the suffering and distress which must inevitably arise, out of this fight for humanity and democracy," to quote President Wilson's words. The hand of a master at the helm at once became manifest. The Society immediately undertook the reorganization and concentration of all Red Cross and similar efforts throughout the country, coördinated the activities of multitudinous smaller bodies, stirred up public interest and launched a brilliant campaign for the raising of $100,000,000, an unpredecented undertaking. Yet so ably was the movement conducted that the goal of $100,000,000 was passed handsomely.

F. Trubee Davison, one of Mr. Davison's sons, with a foresight worthy of his father, organized a flying corps of young college men to train as the First New York unit of the Aërial Coast Patrol and became an expert hydro-aeroplanist before he met with a lamentable accident, in July, 1917, while in active performance of his duties in the air. Harry P. Davison, Jr., began serving with the American Ambulance Corps in France before war was declared by the United States but he later returned and joined the more dangerous aviation service. Both became active members of the Naval Reserve Flying Corps. Mrs. Davison has set an example to other American mothers by the brave and patriotic attitude she has taken throughout the campaign. The expense of training the collegiate fliers was borne by her, and she has also maintained an active aviation camp at her summer home.

Although Mr. Davison was never a star at any games or sports, he contrives to get a good deal of exercise and pleasure. He plays a swift game of tennis, rides horseback, and is at home aboard his yacht, which in the summer takes him to business in the morning and back in the afternoon to his beautiful home on Long Island, where under normal conditions he spends much time. Since America entered the war, Mr. Davison has taken up residence in Washington, where he spends all his time.

For years Mr. Davison was president of the hospital at Englewood, N. J., where he used to live, and he has always done a lot of active Red Cross work. He has also done much, his friends declare, in helping young men to help themselves. He is entitled to write "Dr." in front of his name, having received the degree of LL.D. from the University of Pennsylvania. He is also a Knight of the Order of the Crown of Italy.

Recently he was given the military rank of Major-General in connection with his Red Cross governmental office.

Success has not spoiled General Davison. He is as democratic in spirit as in the days when he rode his wheel through ten miles of crowded streets to save ten cents car fare daily.

CAPTAIN ROBERT DOLLAR

THE cook-boy in a remote Canadian lumber camp was caught off guard.
"What are you up to?" demanded the boss.
The boy, startled, crumpled up a sheet of rough paper he had spread on top of a flour barrel.
"I've finished my work," he apologized.
"What were you doing?" asked the boss.
"When I have any spare time I like to learn," he explained timidly.
"Learn what?"
"To figure and write."
The camp manager picked up the rumpled paper. It was covered with figures and writing.
He said no more.
When Li Yuen-hung was chosen President of China one of the first things he did was to send this ex-cook-boy a cable expressing a desire for his friendship. Yuan Shi-kai, his predecessor, had decorated the former lumber camp lad. So had the last Emperor of China.
To-day the cook-boy is one of the most influential counsellors of the Chinese Government and almost an idol in the eyes of the Chinese people.
His name is Robert Dollar, the foremost producer and exporter of lumber in the United States; the owner of two fleets of steamers—one for coastal, the other for overseas trade; the greatest individual creator of commerce between the Pacific Coast and the Orient; a still greater creator and cementer of friendship between the Orient and the Occident, and this country's most potent worker for the establishment of a powerful American merchant marine. Also, a philanthropist.
It was Captain Dollar who led the unsuccessful fight against the enactment of the suicidal La Follette Seamen's bill which immediately swept the Stars and Stripes from the Pacific Ocean and gave the Japanese complete control of the commerce between the Orient and the United States before the American people had their eyes opened to the gravity of the situation.
"La Follette's name will go down to posterity as the man who drove the last nail into the merchant-marine coffin," the veteran captain declared when, despite all the protests of commercial and shipping authorities, the fatal measure was passed by Congress.

The law was found to be so impossible that Washington was obliged to announce that certain features of it would not—because they *could not*—be enforced.

Even so, the conditions brought about were so demoralizing, so subversive of all discipline, so productive of insubordination, that shipping casualties became so numerous on the Pacific Coast that insurance companies refused to accept risks.

An impressive tribute to the genius of American statesmanship!

Not content to legislate for American ships, then representing about one per cent. of the world's shipping tonnage, the Washington wiseacres actually attempted to make laws for the remaining 99 per cent.! Of course they had to crawl back into their shells. If they hadn't, America would have been left without ships to move her $7,000,000,000 of annual exports and imports. President Wilson sent for Captain Dollar, but, unfortunately, Congress did not promptly follow the sound advice given. America had not then had her eyes opened by participation in the world war.

"All we shipowners want," Captain Dollar repeatedly told the Government, "is to be put on an equal footing with other nations. Give us equal laws and we will give you a merchant marine rivalling that of a century ago, when the Stars and Stripes carried nine-tenths of the United States overseas commerce. To-day our naval vessels cannot go far from land without the support of foreign auxiliaries."

So ridiculous did our marine regulations become that American shipowners were compelled to fly the British flag and employ British Naval Reserve men on their vessels, thus helping to strengthen Britain's power at the expense of crippling our own.

"You may succeed in driving us out of the United States, but you can't drive us out of the business," Captain Dollar told Andrew Furuseth, the seamen's professional agitator, who really was the inspirer of the measure.

Patriotic American though Captain Dollar is, *he was compelled by our absurd laws to run his overseas fleet under an alien flag and from an alien port.* Whereas his ships used to sail from California, their headquarters is now Vancouver, British Columbia, which levies toll, of course, on every ton entering her harbours and gets the railroad haul of merchandise which ought to pass over none but American lines and be handled by none but American workmen.

By what steps and by what qualities did Robert Dollar climb from the cook's shanty to the ownership of steamship lines and a vast timber business, honoured by election to the presidency of both the Chamber of Commerce and the Merchants' Exchange of San Francisco, by selection as a director of the Foreign Trade Council, by appointment as a director of the $50,000,000 American International

Corporation, by decorations from Pekin and by receiving the Freedom of the Borough and the keys of his Scottish birthplace?

Not one of America's "Fifty Greatest Business Men" began more humbly. He was born in a little home above a lumber firm's office at Falkirk, Scotland, 73 years ago. When only 12 he was taken from school to earn a few shillings as office-boy with a shipping company. The family emigrated to Ottawa a year later and little Robert, when under fourteen, was dispatched 200 miles from civilization to a lumber camp. Even to-day lumber camps are not Sunday-school centres; 60 years ago they were—well, less so.

The most menial job of all was that of "cook's boy." When the food did not come up to the expectations of the hungry lumber jacks, the person who set it in front of them was lucky if he encountered nothing more damaging than a volley of oaths. Bob Dollar, however, manifestly was doing his best and most of the rough diamonds came to have rather a warm spot for him in their hearts—especially as he could be called in to read or write a love letter for those who could use axes very effectively but pens not at all.

When the camp manager, Hiram Robinson, caught the cook's boy struggling with addition and subtraction, multiplication and division, and caligraphy, he did not dismiss him for using the company's time for such a purpose, but quietly began providing the ambitious little fellow with books, and also saw to it that leisure was provided for study.

The lad did not confine his studies to books or to cookery. He learned how to fell trees, how to tell good lumber from bad, and, not least important, how to get along with the uncouth workmen. Before he had had his first shave he was playing the part, not of a boy, but of a man, able to hold his own when trouble broke out.

"Take a drive down the river Du Moine. Take fifty men with you," was the order he received one day from the camp manager. This was the first drive of saw logs undertaken from the Du Moine district over the Chaudière Falls, a route subsequently taken by many millions of Ottawa-bound logs. Dollar, though only twenty-one, managed the men and the venture successfully. As a reward he was made foreman over a big gang.

Two things all Scottish children are taught—the Bible and thrift. Lumber-jack Dollar had saved most of his hard-won wages, though the pay was only $10 a month at the start. Another trait is independence—the northern Scots claim that they are the only people the Romans failed to lick after trying. He had enough money when twenty-seven to buy a modest bit of timber land and, with high hopes and unbounded optimism, started operations.

Alas! "Wall Street" upset all his plans and plunged him into bankruptcy—not because he had speculated on a "sure-thing" tip; it was the panic of Black Friday which ruined him as it ruined many stronger business men.

He had learned, however, how to take knocks. Without difficulty he found a good job as manager of an important lumber establishment. He saved every penny that came within his reach and paid off all his debts in full within four years—he was and is an ardent believer in the Golden Rule and its Founder. His employer took him into partnership and this time things moved more satisfactorily. Their product consisted chiefly of hewn-board timber for export to England.

"Captain Dollar is from Missouri—from the heart of Missouri," one of his managers said to me. "He must always be shown; he wants to see things for himself—even if he has to travel one thousand or ten thousand miles to see them. He is one of the best-travelled men in the world. He always gets at the bottom of everything. He is intensely practical and has scant regard for untested theories. He keeps his eyes open all the time for new opportunities. He is the most resourceful man in America."

Perhaps this explains why he moved first to Michigan, where larger and better timber could be had, and later to the Pacific Coast. He began lumbering redwood in northern California but grudged the amount he was charged for transporting his output. He investigated. Discovering that if he could get a ship of his own he could cut the cost to half, he bought a little tub, the *Newsboy*, of some 300 tons. It paid for itself in less than a year.

This appealed to the Scotch in him! If one twopenny boat could earn so much, why not get hold of more boats? He did. And that was the birth of the now famous Robert Dollar Steamship Company with one fleet of vessels in the coastwise trade running all the way from Alaska to the Panama Canal, and another fleet plying between the Pacific Coast and the Orient, with branches in Shanghai, Hong Kong, Tientsin, Hankow, Kobe, Petrograd, Manila, Vancouver, Seattle, and New York.

The business did not grow of its own accord; it had to be built up from the foundation. It called for foresight, enterprise, energy, diplomacy, patience, perseverance, and the most scrupulous fair-dealing, for no race is more quick to resent questionable practices than the Chinese.

When Captain Dollar first began to ship lumber to the Orient the demand was solely for the very largest pieces. This left a by-product of small boards which could not be shipped. He knew that the Chinese did not use these enormous sizes but that nearly all of them were cut into small pieces by hand-saws. The resourceful Dollar began persuading his Chinese customers to take a sprinkling of these small sizes. He took a trip to the Celestial Empire and created a market for his by-product.

Return cargoes were then not to be had. As there was no profit in running empty steamers, trade must be developed. Off he went to find out what could be done about it. When he got to the Philippines he made arrangements to import mahogany and copra. Japan, he discovered, could supply oak, sulphur, coke, and coal. China yielded a grade of pig iron which Western mills would snap up as fast as it could be brought over.

The Dollar steamships were thus kept loaded both going and coming. Since the outbreak of war freight rates have been so high that lumber could not stand it. Outward shipments, consequently, have consisted very largely of general merchandise and munitions, the latter chiefly to Vladivostok. From that port the vessels proceed to China, Japan, and the Philippines for return cargoes.

While the Dollar Steamship Company trades with India, Japan, and the Philippines, its largest business is with China, where Captain Dollar has come to be revered to a degree not easily understood by the untravelled American.

"Never try to cheat a Chinaman," Captain Dollar impresses upon every one who would do business with the Chinese. Confucius taught them that "honesty is the best policy," and the Chinese live strictly up to this axiom. In addressing a meeting of the United States Chamber of Commerce he said: "In all our years of trading with the Chinese, involving many millions of dollars, we have never lost a single cent, never had one bad debt. I wish we could say the same of other countries, including our own."

Time and again Captain Dollar, on going aboard one of his ships on the Pacific to inspect the outgoing cargo, has ordered thousands upon thousands of boards dumped back on the pier because they were not in every particular exactly what the Chinese buyers had ordered. Sometimes the mills had sent better grades, but the Chinaman wanted just what he bargained for and would feel aggrieved were the contract not lived up to scrupulously.

"The Captain never bluffs and cannot be bluffed," one of his associates told me. "I remember once a customer sent in a large claim on the ground that the lumber delivered was of inferior quality. When we went to the yard the owner had two or three hundred boards lined up and told us they were a fair sample of the whole consignment and he wanted an adjustment on that basis. The rest of the boards had been stacked up in piles twenty-five or thirty feet high. 'It is all like this,' the customer declared, pointing to the inferior boards. 'Let's have a look at it,' said the Captain. 'Oh,' said the buyer, 'you can't climb up these piles.' There was no other way to get at the stuff, so the Captain, although nearly seventy, shinnied to the top almost as fast as a monkey. There was not a bad board in sight! He was from Missouri, as I told you before."

Great as have been the services of Captain Dollar in extending American commerce in the Orient and in creating a fleet of high-class steamers, both passenger and freight, as well as in striving heroically to have Congress adopt sensible shipping legislation, he has a much stronger title to the gratitude of the American people.

Robert Dollar has done more to prevent strife and promote peace between America and the Orient than any living statesman.

When war was threatened between this country and Japan over the San Francisco school question, Captain Dollar succeeded in getting up a party of commercial men from different chambers of commerce to visit Japan, where he is almost as well known and as highly regarded as in China. The Emperor himself received the delegation. The *entente cordiale* was reëstablished. After that the jingoes could make no headway with their militant propaganda.

Two years later Captain Dollar organized an influential commission to visit China. Their reception by the Emperor, by Governmental dignitaries, by cities and by commercial organizations eclipsed in ceremony and display anything before or since extended to foreign visitors. Captain Dollar's diary of this memorable trip (he has kept diaries without a break for sixty years) was later published for private circulation at the insistent request of friends; it gives a better insight into the nation which comprises one-third of the human race than any other publication I have ever read. It is sprinkled with wit and humour. The distinguished Chinese delegation, headed by Cheng Hsun-chang, which visited the United States and created nation-wide interest in 1915, was China's fitting way of returning the Dollar delegation's visit. This exchange of courtesies not only bore practical commercial fruits in the form of developing new business between the two countries, but proved infinitely more valuable in bringing the two nations into closer understanding.

Captain Dollar, as his photograph shows, is a patriarchal figure with his silver-white hair and gray beard. He works prodigiously, especially before most of America's 100,000,000 people are out of bed. He spends a goodly part of his time and his means in philanthropic and church work, being especially interested in furthering the Young Men's Christian Association movement throughout the world. His native town in Scotland has not been forgotten; his gifts to it include elaborate swimming baths.

I asked Captain Dollar what his vast experience had taught him were some of the qualities helpful to the attainment of success. I also asked him what ought to be done to enable the United States to attain a higher place among the commercial nations of the world.

The Grand Old Man of the Pacific thus replied to the first question:

"1.—Fear God and be just and honest to your fellow man.

"2.—Incessant hard work.

"3.—Frugality and saving your money.

"4.—Drink no intoxicating liquors; in these days of keen competition whisky and business won't mix—*you can't do both.*

"Foreign Trade is the answer to the second question. We are legislated to death. Stop legislating and leave our merchants alone and they will develop our foreign trade, and provide tonnage to carry our own products to market. Permit our shipowners to operate our ships exactly on the same terms and conditions as other nations are doing, and then our merchants will supply the cargoes and our shipowners will provide plenty of tonnage for our commerce in time of peace and auxiliaries to our navy in time of war, and, except for carrying our mails, it won't cost our country a cent."

A few months ago a septuagenarian visited octogenarian Hiram Robinson, at Ottawa.

"You don't remember me?" asked the visitor.

The old man peered at him a moment.

"Don't I?" he cried, holding out his hand. "You are Bob Dollar, my old cook-boy."

The millionaire ex-cook-boy left Hiram happy, for the aged lumberman was the boss who caught him learning to read and write and who made the ascent of the ladder of success a little easier.

WILLIAM L. DOUGLAS

FORTUNE rarely can be overtaken by following the beaten track. Most of the notable successes in business and finance have been won by those who either opened entirely new paths or greatly broadened and developed old ones.

John D. Rockefeller was the first to grasp and carry out on a large scale the idea of combining many small concerns into one powerful corporation. E. H. Gary did the same thing in steel in the early days. Henry Ford, John N. Willys, William C. Durant, and other forward-looking stalwarts jumped into the automobile arena and developed it from an infant industry to one of the most important in the country. Thomas A. Edison, Alexander Graham Bell, and Theodore N. Vail were all pioneers. Frank W. Woolworth made a fortune by seizing and holding on to a new method of merchandising. So did Julius Rosenwald.

Henry C. Frick took hold of the coke business when it was in its swaddling clothes and made of it a giant. George Eastman found photography the complicated plaything of a few and so simplified and cheapened it that he brought it within the reach of all. John H. Patterson did something similar with the cash register. William H. Nichols made up his mind to become a manufacturer of chemicals because he saw that the field could be tilled with greater scientific knowledge and to more profitable account than ever before. E. C. Simmons, of hardware fame, and James B. Duke, the tobacco king, took hold of existing industries but developed them along new and very much broader lines. Minor C. Keith penetrated Central America and achieved fame and fortune by his labours to transform it from a fever-stricken waste to a tropical fruit garden. Frank A. Vanderlip organized and developed a new phase of national banking and more recently conceived an improved method of conducting international financial and commercial operations.

W. L. Douglas, the subject of this sketch, has demonstrated that the track one follows is of less importance than the diligence and enterprise with which it is followed. Before his day no American had ever become a millionaire making shoes. Shoemakers were usually poor men, doing business on a puny scale.

Douglas, at the age of thirty-one, after having been bruised and buffeted on the stormy sea of experience, set out to become "The greatest shoemaker in the world."

It was a nervy ambition for a young man possessing nothing but his head and his hands, with liabilities in the form of a wife and three children. He was without capital, without influence, without commercial training.

But he did know how to make shoes and he had the will to succeed, come what might.

Let us first look at the young shoemaker's start and then at his present place in the world, a place so prominent that the mere pasting of his picture on an envelope in almost any country in the world will serve to carry the letter to him.

In 1876 a shoemaker rented one room in a building at Brockton, Massachusetts, and, by means of $875 of borrowed capital, installed some machinery and engaged five employees. Every day he trudged home from Boston with rolls of leather under his arms. This leather he personally had to select. He personally had to cut it up to be made into shoes which he personally had designed. He personally had to lay out the work at night for each employee and had to supervise its execution. The shoes made, he personally had to go out and find buyers.

All this seldom took him more than eighteen hours a day—if he worked twenty hours he felt he had put in a couple of hours overtime. His output was forty-eight pairs per day.

Although he soon outgrew his original factory and had to move into larger quarters three times—in 1879, again in 1880, and again in 1881, when he took a three-story factory and ran his output up to 1,800 pairs a day—he was still dissatisfied with his rate of progress. To reach the goal he had set himself, the proud position of the world's greatest shoemaker, he must travel faster or he might not win out.

He knew the shoes he was making were good shoes. He knew that more people would buy them if more people learned about them. He knew he could develop his manufacturing facilities to meet an increased demand. He knew also that to attain his ambition more people *must* be told about his shoes.

He did a revolutionary thing. In 1883 he began to advertise systematically, persistently, extensively. Advertising then, however, was not always taken seriously by the public. Much of it was downright fraudulent, more of it was grossly misleading, and little of it kept strictly within the truth. There was no association of advertising clubs to censor imaginative effusions of vendors of merchandise. Exaggeration was accepted as a matter of course. Indeed, the individual or firm who spent money freely on advertising was often regarded with skepticism. Surely if the goods were all right they could be sold without the expenditure of thousands of dollars on printers' ink!

W. L. Douglas had a product of which he was proud. To show how proud, he decided to stamp his own picture on the sole of every shoe that left his factory. Of course, he encountered a storm of ridicule. He was accused of unconscionable personal vanity. It was sarcastically remarked that he was apparently more anxious to distribute his photograph than his shoes.

The first results were discouraging. He paid out more money than the increase in returns justified. But W. L. Douglas was not one of that large army who expect strong, healthy plants to shoot up the moment seed is sown in the ground. He was not building for to-day but for to-morrow, for the time when his portrait and name on a pair of shoes would commend these shoes to men and women throughout the world. He could stand the scoffing of those ignorant of his ambition and barren of his vision. His confidence never weakened, his perseverance never wavered. He adhered to his well-considered course, spending $250,000 and more annually on advertising the shoes whose maker was not ashamed to stamp with his own portrait.

With what results?

The thirty-by-sixty feet one-room factory which was started on less than $1,000 capital, with five employees and an output of forty-eight pairs of shoes a day, has developed into one of the manufacturing and mercantile wonders of the present time. Its capital is not $1,000, but $3,500,000; it occupies not one room, but a group of spacious buildings covering 300,000 square feet; its output is not a few pairs a day, but over 5,000,000 a year (17,000 pairs per day) worth over $20,000,000. The force of five workers has multiplied into an army of 4,000 workers. The leather consumed is not transported under the arm of the owner, for it comprises the hides of 1,860,000 animals yearly. Nor does the proprietor personally sell the whole output, for it would fill every car of a train $6\frac{1}{2}$ miles in length. The "accessories" called for annually include over 1,000,000 yards of cloth and 15,000 miles of flax thread. A monument over 500 miles in height could be raised were a year's output of shoes stacked one on top of another.

W. L. Douglas has handsomely attained his ambition. His is the largest shoe factory in the world under one roof producing men's, women's, and boys' shoes. Nor is this all; but over a hundred W. L. Douglas shoe stores have been established here and abroad.

The portrait of W. L. Douglas has become one of the best-known trade-marks in the world and has earned for its owner greater fame and fortune than have fallen to the lot of his old-time scoffers.

The plucky young man who worked eighteen hours a day to gain a foothold on the ladder did not later permit himself to become a mere shoe-making or money-making machine. His vast business interests did not prevent him from discharging his full civic responsibilities. He became mayor of his town, a State Representative, a State Senator and, finally, Governor of the great Commonwealth of Massachusetts, an extraordinary tribute, for he was elected on a Democratic ticket in a State invariably controlled by Republicans. Among other honours that have come to him has been the honorary degree of LL.D. (from Tufts College).

No boy ever had a less auspicious start. He came into the world in a poor home in Plymouth, Mass., on August 22, 1845, and was only five when his father died. His mother was left in such straitened circumstances that she was obliged to give up little William Lewis when he was only seven years of age. At the time most boys are beginning school, this lad began work. He was bound for a term of years to an uncle who was less interested in what he could do for the boy than in what the boy could do for him, and the seven-year-old child was set to work pegging shoes in a dismal garret. So tiny was he that he had to stand on an empty box to reach the bench. His duties included also the gathering of enough wood to keep two fires going, a task that taxed the child's strength, and, combined with his general treatment, almost—but not quite—broke his spirit. When there were few shoes to peg, during dull seasons, the boy was permitted to tramp two miles to school and there spend a few hours.

For four years he stood being cuffed and scolded and ill-treated. Then one day he rebelled and set off home to his mother. Her circumstances had not greatly improved, and as the boy was too young (eleven) to be sent to work in the regular way, she re-engaged him to the uncle at $5 a month. Four more years he toiled and suffered amid the most heartbreaking environment. Nor did it brighten his lot to be denied the wages promised for his four years' servitude. All the uncle ever paid was $10.

His period of bondage over, the youth took a job in a cotton mill at Plymouth at thirty-three cents a day. A broken leg, however, incapacitated him for work. But nothing could daunt his spirit or weaken his determination to equip himself for the battle of life. The moment he could use crutches he hobbled off to school, a distance of two miles, and every day he covered the four miles in order to increase his scanty knowledge. Although reared amid such depressing conditions, where matters educational were lightly considered, the boy had enough commonsense to feel that ignorance was as a millstone hung on the neck. As soon as he could discard his crutches he went to work on a farm under an arrangement that permitted him to attend school as much as possible during the winter months.

All this William Lewis Douglas had passed through before he was sixteen years old. Before the average boy of his age had wrestled with anything more trying than school books, he had undergone the sufferings and encountered the difficulties of a lifetime. Only his unconquerable, irrepressible determination not to remain an ignorant drudge buoyed him up. At sixteen he had learned some things not always learned at school. He had learned self-reliance, he had grasped the value of knowledge, he had cultivated courage, he had imbibed ambition. Moreover, he had learned the rudiments of a trade. His clean habits, his frugal living, his apprenticeship in hard work had built up for him an iron constitution, a body that could withstand abnormal physical strain.

Winter on the farm over, he returned to his own calling. After a spell of making cheap brogans at Hopkinton, Mass., he decided to go to South Abington, Mass., and see if there was an opportunity to learn to make fine boots. On the train he heard the station called for South Braintree and, thinking it was his stop, got off. He canvassed the numerous small boot shops, but no one wanted an apprentice. It was getting dusk, and as he had not sufficient funds to obtain a lodging, he decided to walk to South Weymouth. He started off, thinking that perhaps he could get a job there. As darkness came on, however, he realized that when he reached South Weymouth he would not find anybody up. And he would have no home for the night. So he retraced his steps through the darkness to South Braintree.

Here he secured a job pegging boots, which was rough, coarse work. He had previously applied to Anson Thayer, a noted shoemaker, for work, and Thayer, on discovering him near by pegging boots, kept an eye on him a short time, and then agreed to take him in as an apprentice. Here for three years he learned to make fine calf boots—at $1.50 a week and his board.

The long hours which shoemakers, in common with most other workmen, then toiled did not prevent him from attending evening classes, so eager was he to make up for his early lack of schooling.

Out West there was a shoemaker, Zephaniah Meyers, whose shoes were known far and wide. Young Douglas sought him out, and under his distinguished tutelage he learned the art of designing and cutting shoes of superior style. Before long Douglas's skill began to be talked about. The pupil was becoming as famous in the trade as his master. A former resident of the Bay State, Alfred Studley, then in business at Golden City, Colorado, got into touch with Douglas and offered him a partnership. Douglas was quick to realize that this would afford him opportunity for experience in the selling of shoes, and thus before he was twenty-one years of age his name appeared on a shingle. Old-fashioned methods did not appeal to the progressive young man. Therefore, he induced his older partner to go in for advertising. The first Douglas shoe advertisement, the precursor of so many thousands on a more ambitious scale, appeared in a frontier news sheet in 1886.

It read:

> INDIANS!
> If you wish to run away from the Indians don't go barefoot, but buy a pair of
> BOOTS OR SHOES
> OF STUDLEY & DOUGLAS
> who keep constantly on hand a good assortment of Boots and Shoes, which they will sell cheap for cash. Particular attention paid to manufacturing and repairing. Store on Second Street, opposite the Boutwell House, Golden City, Colorado.

The making of shoes by machinery began to come into vogue in the late 60's, and the clear-visioned Douglas was quick to see that this opened up an infinitely wider field for large-scale operations. He knew every kink of the making of shoes by hand—how to select the best kinds of leather for specific purposes, how to design, cut, make, and fit shoes. Nor had he neglected to cultivate as best he could the art of pleasing customers. Douglas saw that the greatest possibilities lay in manufacturing in large quantities, and this was feasible only by machinery. Along that road fortune lay.

It was in 1870 that the man who was to make the town known all over the world arrived in Brockton, then North Bridgewater. He had no difficulty in receiving a responsible position with Porter & Southworth, who owned a factory where most of the work was done by machinery. Here his ability and industry won him promotion. By the end of five years he was superintendent of the plant.

Then he decided to strike out for himself, with results already briefly narrated.

In reply to my questions concerning his own career and the prospects for young men, Mr. Douglas said that, looking back, the most trying point in his career was that night when he was stranded on the outskirts of South Braintree in the dark, without a penny, without a haven for the night and without a job.

"Servants make the worst masters," is a common saying. It is sometimes, perhaps it is often, true that labourers or artisans who become foremen, superintendents, managers, or employers expect more and exact more from workers than do those who begin higher up the scale. Men who have climbed up by working abnormally hard themselves are apt to have little patience with those who do not show similar industry.

W. L. Douglas is not of this type. Indeed, he would be the first to admit that he could not have developed his colossal business had he not been able to inspire loyalty among his employees. He still regards himself as a worker and looks upon his employees simply as co-workers. The most satisfactory results can be obtained only when everybody is satisfied. He wants none of his workers to undergo such trials as he himself underwent when a youth.

It may not be generally known that Mr. Douglas is the father of arbitration in this country. It was largely through his labours that Massachusetts led the country in passing arbitration and conciliation legislation and established a State board to administer it. As early as 1886, while a State Senator, he introduced a bill "to provide for the settlement of difficulties between employers and their employees." He foresaw that only by such methods could peace be preserved between capital and labour. Too often in those days employers looked upon workmen merely as human material to be used exactly as other material was used—to the best advantage of the employer. What arbitration has done to maintain industrial peace and prevent grave disorder cannot be overestimated, and had Mr. Douglas rendered no other public service than this he would have deserved well of his fellowmen.

Among other reforms which he brought about was the passage of a law compelling employers to pay all their manual workers weekly, a stipulation that seems almost superfluous to-day, but one that was sorely needed a generation ago.

The Douglas employees are well taken care of. The services of a trained nurse and a physician are constantly at their command, gratis —the doctor may be called to the home of any employee at any time without charge. Mr. Douglas has donated a surgical department to the Brockton Hospital, has presented the City with a Day Nursery where working mothers may leave their children during the day, and is a liberal contributor to other worthy causes, although in his philanthropies he is as much opposed to advertising as he is in favour of it in business.

In addition to his services as local councilman and mayor, as State legislator and State governor (in 1905), valuable though these services were in raising the tone of politics, W. L. Douglas has done for business ethics something that should not be overlooked simply because his action was dictated by sound commercial considerations. I do not refer to his supplying the public with the kind of shoes that so many of them want to buy, but to his pioneer work in stamping on each shoe the price at which it must be sold. This clean-cut, straight-forward, one-price method of doing business is accepted almost universally now, but our fathers and mothers can well remember how difficult, not to say impossible, it was to make sure of fair, honest treatment at the hands of retailers. Buying then was a matter of bickering and bargaining, a gamble in which the customer usually was not the victor.

The Douglas system of selling direct from the factory through his own retail stores also marks a step forward in merchandising.

The boy who began pegging shoes at seven is still, at seventy-two, pegging away at shoemaking. Only, to-day his shoes are on sale at over 9,000 stores and are being worn by one member of every second family in America.

Verily, America is the land of romance in real life, the land where merit has opportunity to blossom.

JAMES B. DUKE

AMERICA has many merchant princes and captains of industry but only three industrial kings: John D. Rockefeller, the Oil King; Andrew Carnegie, the Steel King, and James B. Duke, the Tobacco King. The history of the first two is well known. The career of the third, with the whys and wherefores of it, is here printed for the first time.

Each of the three had the same rough road to travel, the same obstacles to cleave and clear. Each used the same methods and the same tools—intense application, ceaseless watchfulness for opportunity, unwavering courage and self-confidence, readiness to assume responsibility, rigid frugality during early years, with, above all, infinite love of work and achievement.

At fourteen—note the age—James B. Duke, after having experienced life in a log cabin and almost inhuman poverty, won the position of manager of the family's small tobacco factory—the factory which formed the nucleus of the greatest tobacco enterprise the world has ever known, an enterprise dominant not only in America but in virtually every country under the sun.

So frugal was Mr. Duke and so determined to conserve capital for the development of the business that, after he was earning $50,000 a year, he lived in a hall bedroom in New York, and ate his three meals daily in the cheapest lunch room in the Bowery! In his case, as in most others, phenomenal final success entailed phenomenal early sacrifices.

Young Duke deliberately set out to do in tobacco what John D. Rockefeller was doing in oil. And he succeeded in becoming the most powerful tobacco figure in history.

The reason? Here it is, in Mr. Duke's own modest words:

"I have succeeded in business, not because I have more natural ability than many people who have not succeeded, but because I have applied myself harder and stuck to it longer. I know plenty of people who have failed to succeed in anything who have more brains than I had, but they lacked application and determination.

"I had confidence in myself. I said to myself: 'If John D. Rockefeller can do what he is doing in oil, why should I not do it in tobacco?' I resolved from the time I was a mere lad to do a big business. I loved business better than anything else. I worked from early morning to late at night—I was sorry to have to leave off at night and glad when morning came so that I could get at it again. Any young man with common intelligence can succeed if he is willing to apply himself. Superior brains are not necessary."

Long before Schwab or Morgan had dreamed of a huge steel trust, James B. Duke conceived the idea of a gigantic tobacco organization having such a volume of business as to be able to sell superior goods at lowered prices. Volume, he saw, was the key to industrial economy, efficiency, and success. As long ago as 1888 he began to lay foundations for what became, in 1890, the American Tobacco Company, which succeeded so well that it supplied 80 per cent. of America's cigarette, pipe, and chewing tobacco and snuff before the Government "dissolved" the so-called tobacco trust, in 1911.

Mr. Duke, moreover, had meanwhile crossed the Atlantic, waged a terrifically fierce but successful war in England and, through the British-American Tobacco Company, had gained for Americans control of a similarly powerful organization in Europe, an organization which set up factories in Germany, England, Holland, Denmark, Finland, Belgium, Australia, China, India, South Africa, Canada, Jamaica, Egypt, etc.

The United States Government's action, however, caused the practical control to fall into English hands.

"If any British manufacturers had accomplished half as much for British trade as was accomplished in America, they would have been knighted; here you are indicted and they want to put you in jail," declared Mr. Duke with a tinge of bitterness. "It discredits a man to succeed in a large way in this country nowadays.

"Why, in North Carolina, in the part where we made cigarettes, the largest tobacco crop the farmers ever had up to 1890 did not amount to more than from $4,000,000 to $6,000,000. The crop now yields the farmers of North Carolina from $50,000,000 to $60,000,000 a year. I did my own share in making this development possible and I refuse to feel ashamed of it."

Mr. Duke's share was, I might add, at least ten times that of any other individual. He was the dynamo that energized the whole machinery.

The evolution of the obscure Duke tobacco business into the American Tobacco Company contains all the elements dear to the writer of fiction—war and ruination, log cabins, dire poverty, struggles born of necessity, pluck and perseverance, progress, and ultimate triumph.

James Buchanan Duke—so named after President Buchanan, last of the ante-bellum Democrats to hold that office—was a four-year-old motherless toddler on a farm three miles from Durham, N. C., when the war broke out, in 1861. After the struggle had been in progress a year or more his father joined the Confederate Army, selling out everything he had for Confederate money with the exception of a number of things which were to be paid for in tobacco, settlement to be made at the end of the war. The children were sent to their grandfather's, thirty miles from Durham. When the elder Duke returned in the spring of 1865, the purchaser of the farm was unable to make payment, but he was in possession, running the farm and occupying the dwelling house. There was nothing for Duke to do but to become temporarily a farm labourer for the other man, getting, in return, a portion of the crop.

Little James B., with his father and two brothers—his mother was dead—lived throughout the winter in a log cabin on the farm. All four slept on a straw tick in a corner of the cabin. Their sister was given a bed at the farmhouse.

The hardships suffered by the Duke family were almost heartbreaking. First Wheeler's Cavalry, of the Confederate Army, and, later, part of the Northern Army, had been stationed in that neighbourhood—the surrender of Johnston to Sherman took place near Durham. The soldiers had cleaned up everything eatable for miles around. Parched corn was the staple food of the people in those days. Washington Duke, the father, regained his farm in the spring and eked out a livelihood for the family by buying small quantities of tobacco and other goods in one district and bartering it in the eastern part of the State for meat and flour, which he brought back and peddled.

Farmers had begun to grow tobacco, and those who owed Duke money before the war paid him in that commodity. He began to peddle it along with what he was able to grow himself. As the sons became old enough they helped both on the farm and at peddling. Having made a little headway, the Dukes bought the tobacco crops of other farmers and made arrangements to ship it to South Carolina, Alabama, and other points. By 1871 the business had grown to from 40,000 to 50,000 pounds a year.

James B. had contrived to attend a free school during the fall of each year when work on the farm was slack; but although he was smart enough at his lessons, business appealed to him far more than booklearning. By the time he was fourteen he had shown extraordinary aptitude in handling and peddling tobacco. He was full of ambition. He was keen to build up a big trade. And so it came about that he was installed as superintendent of the little log factory of the Dukes. Here at 14, he was bossing about a score of workers and continually challenging the best of them to race with him at the work—there was, of course, no machinery then.

JAMES B. DUKE

By the time James was eighteen his father was worth $10,000 or $15,000 and was anxious to send the bright youth to college.

James astonished him by replying: "I don't want to go to college. I want a partnership in this business. I want to work and make money."

Thinking to test the mettle of the ambitious youth, the father said he would give him $1,000 and let him go off on his own account for a while.

The lad promptly prepared to launch out and paddle his own canoe.

In a day or two, however, the father agreed to give James and another brother each a one-sixth interest in the business. The partnership boomed. The log factory no longer sufficed. A factory was built in Durham. "Duke of Durham" tobacco was finding an ever-widening market.

Then, in 1878, there was a consolidation. The Dukes took into partnership George W. Watts of Baltimore and also the oldest Duke brother, Brodie L., who had established quite an extensive tobacco business of his own at Durham. The five partners were W. Duke (the father), B. L. Duke, Mr. Watts, James B. Duke, and B. N. Duke.

The capitalization of W. Duke, Sons & Company was $70,000. James B. had saved $3,000 and his father lent him $11,000 to make up the $14,000 which each partner contributed.

The growing of tobacco was given up and all energies were centred upon the manufacturing and selling of leaf bought from other farmers. Again the growth was rapid. But as the only field covered was granulated smoking tobacco, the younger partners, full of ambition, were anxious to break into new ground.

The cigarette business was then in its infancy, the total sale in the United States being well under 200,000,000 cigarettes a year. In 1883 the Dukes took what was to prove an epochal step: they decided to enter the cigarette field. To insure success, James B., although the youngest partner in the business, being only twenty-seven, was put in full charge. He had such driving power, such boundless energy, such physical stamina, such ambition and vision that the others unanimously voted to serve under his lead.

From the start the new move proved successful beyond their dreams, more business being offered than they had capital to handle. Advertising was used most effectively; indeed, the Dukes became the largest advertisers of that day in the United States, their annual bill reaching as high as $800,000.

Within a year a very large brick factory had to be built in Durham, whither the business had moved in 1875. It was decided, also, to invade New York with a factory for the manufacture of both cigarettes and pipe tobacco.

James B. Duke came to the metropolis to build up the business. They could secure more orders than the firm had capital to handle. It was at this stage that Mr. Duke lived in his hall bedroom, ate regularly in a Bowery lunch room near the factory, and plowed back into the business $49,500 of the $50,000 a year he was making. Not that; but he insisted, against much opposition, that no other partner, married or single, be allowed to withdraw more than $1,000 a year salary. He was after big and ever bigger business. To facilitate credit and other operations, the firm incorporated in 1885. The output of cigarettes quickly mounted to a billion a year, equal to 40 per cent. of the total cigarette business in the country, notwithstanding that others had had a long start of them.

The Alexandrian head of W. Duke, Sons & Company, Inc., however, was still not satisfied. He had not yet reached in tobacco the stage Rockefeller had reached in oil. There were still other lands to conquer.

Why not take over the principal tobacco concerns in the country, form one huge company, float stock and obtain capital to cover the whole land—and, incidentally, pave the way for the invasion of Europe?

With Duke, dreams never long remained dreams; they were made to take concrete form. This one was so revolutionary that he spent nearly two years in bringing it to fruition. At last, in 1890, he formed the American Tobacco Company, which included four of the principal tobacco concerns in the country in addition to the Duke business.

"What was your main idea in bringing about such a gigantic merger?" I asked.

"I wanted volume and organization," he replied. "A business in order to succeed must serve the public better and cheaper than the other fellow, and to do that you must have volume. Our aim was to serve the people better and cheaper than anyone else, and to do that we had to have volume. We were not especially after competitors; we wanted to develop tobacco consumption and provide a good article cheaply. We thought that if we did this—and we knew we could do it— the majority of the public would find it advantageous to buy our product.

"That was just what happened. The American Tobacco Company went ahead so fast that before the disintegration, in 1911, we were doing a business of about $325,000,000 a year. This was 80 per cent. of the entire tobacco business. The goods of other concerns were offered by retailers all over the country, but our product was better and cheaper and the public naturally preferred it.

"Another reason was that, while our firm had a very strong position in the cigarette end, I wanted to play a much larger part in the to-

JAMES B. DUKE

bacco end. In those early days the total cigarette business in the country was only about $8,000,000—2,000,000,000 cigarettes—whereas over $100,000,000 was spent for other tobacco."

For the business which started in the little log factory on the Duke farm $7,500,000 was received in 1890!

But that $7,500,000 secured for the American Tobacco Company something even more important—the services and the brains of James B. Duke. These services and these brains were needed. It was not all smooth sailing for the "trust." English manufacturers invaded territory supplied by America and were playing havoc with the export division of the business.

Mr. Duke packed a trunk, stepped on board a steamer, in 1901, and landed in London. His mission was merely to lick the English manufacturers to a frazzle in their own country!

He had never been abroad before in his life. He knew nothing of England or of England's prejudices and practices. But did the prospect of having to fight the most plutocratic tobacco interests of Britain intrenched for many, many years, daunt him? Not at all. He was confident he could "do the trick."

In ten days he had secured weapons to do it and had $5,000,000 transferred by cable to clinch matters!

"However did you manage to do it so quickly?" I asked.

"I had nothing else to do," Mr. Duke replied, as if that explained his achievement fully and satisfactorily.

"Just how did you go about your famous fight?" I persisted. I happened to have spent some time in England at that period and had vivid recollections of the nation-wide excitement that raged there, with the English newspapers lashing themselves into a fury over the Yankee tobacco invasion.

"I went to our London office," replied Mr. Duke after indicating that there was nothing remarkable in what he did. "I looked over the product of the chief English manufacturers, learned all about their position, their size, and so forth. In two days I decided that I wanted control either of Player's or Ogden's.

"I first went to Player's, at Nottingham, told them exactly what I was after and asked their terms. They named what I thought was too much. So I next went to Ogden's, at Liverpool. The managers were willing to accept the offer I made them, and within a few days the directors approved the deal, subject, however, to the sanction of the stockholders.

"By this time the English manufacturers were thoroughly alarmed. They had hastily laid their heads together and formed a combination under the name of the Imperial Tobacco Company to fight us. They showed up at Ogden's the day the stockholders met and tried to queer my deal by offering to pay a higher price. The Ogden directors stood by their agreement, however, and we bought the business."

Then the real fight began. Every manufacturer in Britain turned his artillery upon the Yankee-controlled Ogden's. Wholesalers and retailers alike joined to boycott Ogden's goods. The newspapers thundered against the "treason" of Ogden's in selling out to Americans and urged every loyal Briton to down the audacious Yankee.

James B. Duke, however, stood by his guns. Even when sales of Ogden's goods dropped 50 per cent. and the Englishmen were hurrahing over their success, he never for a moment flinched. He tried first one selling wrinkle and then another. It was during this historic tobacco war that "souvenirs" were distributed lavishly in even the smallest packages of cigarettes. Some of the things cost almost as much as the tobacco. Prices, of course, were cut ruinously. And hundreds of thousands of dollars were spent in advertising.

Every day the war lasted cost $3,000!

But Duke won before a year had passed.

While he agreed to sell out all his company's English interests to the Imperial, the English combine, at millions of profit, in due course he formed the British-American Tobacco Company and secured control of the export business of the Englishmen's combine, the Imperial Tobacco Company, so that he became and still is the dominant force in the foreign tobacco business!

When, however, the United States Government ordered the disintegration of the American Tobacco Company, the splitting-up process resulted in a great many shares of the British-American Tobacco Company being thrown on the market, and these were grabbed up by English buyers to such an extent that it is now to all intents and purposes an English instead of an American concern, with the stock usually selling several dollars a share higher in London than in New York. When British-American was dominated from New York the company naturally favoured American goods in its conquering of foreign markets, but now Chinese, Turkish, Indian and other tobacco is pushed. The bulk of the profits, also, now go to English pockets instead of to American. Its sales of cigarettes alone approximate 100,000,000 a day.

Mr. Duke remains at the head of the British-American Company but has severed all official connection with American tobacco companies, although he remains a large stockholder in numbers of them.

Although before the war he found it necessary to spend about half his time abroad, Mr. Duke's heart is still in his native land, and particularly in the South. He conceived a gigantic project for the industrial development of his native State and its sister, South Carolina. He organized the Southern Power Company to supply electric power

JAMES B. DUKE

for cotton mills and other plants, including street railways, lighting plants and other activities demanding electric current. This company is already serving 75 towns and over 200 cotton mills operating more than 3,500,000 spindles, while it also runs an electric railroad of 125 miles. Thanks partly to this furnishing of electric power at reasonable cost, the Southern cotton mills have passed those of New England in annual output.

Though he scraped and saved every penny possible during the long struggle to provide sufficient capital for the development of his business, and urges all ambitious young men to do likewise, Mr. Duke feels that he is now entitled to enjoy the comforts of the best home money can procure. His estate at Somerville, N. J., has 1,000 acres of lawns and is one of the show places in the State.

Although rich, Mr. Duke does not believe in giving away money promiscuously. He declares that it requires even more study and investigation to distribute money wisely than to make it. His ideal in this direction is John D. Rockefeller, whose benefactions, he believes, will carry Mr. Rockefeller's name down through the ages as the greatest man and the greatest benefactor to humanity the world has yet produced.

T. COLEMAN DU PONT

"HOW did you come to think of putting up the largest building in the world?" I asked T. Coleman du Pont, owner of the $30,000,000 Equitable Building of New York, the business home of 15,000 people, with 2,300 offices, 1,225,000 square feet of rentable space, 487 building employees and 59 elevators serving its 40 floors, which rise to a total height of 548 feet, and on which New York reaps taxes of $9,000 every week, or almost $500,000 a year.

"Why, someone had, I imagine, learned that anything constructive appealed to me," replied General du Pont, "whether it's erecting the greatest skyscraper in the world or only a dog kennel, whether building a road or a street car line, developing a coal mine or a steel plant, building up a powder company or creating a real farm out of barren land.

"The Equitable people wanted a building on this site. I found they had the largest single plot in the financial heart of New York—the very best site in the world. The idea of erecting the largest office building in the world appealed to me. When I found I could get a long-term mortgage at a fair rate of interest and that the fundamental conditions were logical and the time for building economically right, I undertook the work. The finished undertaking speaks for itself.

"Now that the building has been completed and its organization working smoothly, it does not call for my attention. I like conceiving, planning, organizing, systematizing, and getting a project established successfully. Then I want to start something else. Just now I am out of a job."

Out of a job, although in addition to being interested in the running of the world's largest building he controls the Equitable Life Assurance Society with its $600,000,000 assets; controls, also, important coal mines in Kentucky; runs an enormous farm in Delaware and Maryland; is spending $2,000,000 out of his own pocket in building a model highway from one end of Delaware to the other; is actively interested in several large hotels; said to be the political leader of the Republican party in Delaware (this he denies), member of the Republican National Committee from Delaware, and I do not know what else!

"Why did you buy control of the Equitable Life from J. P. Morgan & Co.?" was my next question.

"It was after the building was completed. The Equitable Society was the largest tenant. They had been very fair in dealing with me, so I thought it would not be a bad idea to buy the Equitable Life stock and mutualize the Society. I am a thorough believer in the mutualization of the company. It should have been mutualized years ago. I am ready and anxious to coöperate to the full in carrying out any plan of mutualization that is fair to the policy-holders and desired by the directors."

The American public regards the name "Du Pont" as spelling powder and riches. Coleman du Pont had nothing to do with powder until after he had made a fortune—*and he made his own fortune*. At thirty-eight he had given up active business to enjoy a life of leisure.

"It would be very interesting to tell just how you became associated with the Du Pont Powder Company," I suggested.

"Certainly I'll tell you," he replied with his characteristic directness and brevity. "Eugene du Pont, head of the company, had died and no other member of the family cared to take his place. One day I received a message from my cousin, Alfred I. du Pont, asking me to consider going into the business. After talking with Alfred, the matter was taken up with the other members of the family in the old firm. None of them was willing to take on the active duties of management. I then got in touch with Pierre S. du Pont, who was living at Lorain, Ohio, and he came east. We told him of the plan. The result of the conference, between the members of the family in the old firm and Pierre S. du Pont, Alfred I. du Pont, and myself, was that we three younger cousins took over the concern.

"When we took hold of it there were seven clerks in the main office of the company we went into. This company, however, had important interests in other explosive companies."

"How many clerks are there now?" I asked.

"I think between 1,600 and 1,700 in the main office when I left and I believe there are now between 2,500 and 3,000 employees in the main office."

The effectiveness of a good organization was demonstrated, when the unfortunate war broke out in Europe, by the way the Du Pont Company responded to a call for an increase of output multiplied by 100. They have anticipated many of their deliveries although it did take 40,000 men on construction work at one time to do it! There have been no strikes.

"How was it done?" I asked.

"The first thing we did was to amalgamate all of the many different companies and the scores of sub-companies controlled by the Du Ponts into one corporation. This meant efficiency and economy in every department. The consolidated concerns were systematized and standardized and the best methods put into practice, departments created and the managers given responsibility and offered premiums for results.

"I knew nothing of the manufacturing of powder except the general chemistry which I had learned at school. My cousins had this knowledge and experience. I was familiar, however, with the use of it commercially and had had successful experience in organizing and systematizing several industries.

"We engaged the best men we could find. We paid six men very large salaries—and they were the cheapest labour we had, for their brains could make thousands for the company annually."

For four or five years Coleman du Pont worked from early every morning till late every night. He thought powder, talked powder, ate powder, dreamed powder. In three years success was assured—and the company has continued to grow by enormous strides ever since.

The skilful utilization of by-products was also taken up by the aggressive new management. To-day the Du Ponts are not only the largest makers of explosives, but are the world's largest manufacturers of leather substitutes—60 per cent. of the 1,500,000 automobiles manufactured within the last twelve months have been upholstered in Fabrikoid, one of its products, thus tending to keep down the price you and I have to pay for shoes. Its output of ivory and shell substitutes is enormous. Moving picture films are largely composed of Du Pont basic materials. The wonderful anesthetic, ether, which enables surgeons to work painless miracles, is produced in larger quantities in the Du Pont plants than anywhere else in America. [I have in front of me a list of commodities made and sold by the concern; the total is 251.]

It was characteristic of Coleman du Pont, however, when the company's success was absolutely assured, that he should get out. He had done the job he undertook; the business was running perfectly; everything had been systematized and standardized, so it possessed no more attraction for him!

It will astonish the public to learn that in normal times less than 2 per cent. of the Du Pont Powder Company's output went for military purposes. The company supplies the United States Government with the larger part of its powder requirements every year, but this did not mean more than about one per cent. of its entire output. Some 99 per cent. of the output made was sold for mining purposes, railroad building, road construction, quarry work, farming operations, sport, leather substitutes, and miscellaneous uses.

Coleman has in him some of the stuff that makes heroes. His friends are sanguine he may one day become a great national figure, somewhat of the Roosevelt type. Physically, he is a giant—when nineteen he stood six feet four inches and weighed 210 pounds. He went in for every form of athletics—he was stroke of the crew, captain of the football team, captain of the baseball nine, ran 100 yards in 10 seconds, could break in broncos with the skill of a cowboy, was and is a good shot, can swim like a Trojan, was a star man in tug-of-war competitions, and held his own in the boxing and wrestling ring.

"If I had been as good at my studies as I was at athletics I would, no doubt, have been a professor," he laughed, referring to his college days. So thoroughly has he kept in trim that his weight has not increased five pounds from the day he left school. His shoulders look as broad as Jess Willard's and his muscles are of veritable whipcord.

He is democracy personified. His democracy is not assumed; it is not make-believe, artificial, or calculated. He acquired it when driving mules and swinging a pick down in Kentucky coal mines, and the inflow of millions of dollars has not swept it out of him. No multi-millionaire in America is easier to approach. The people who have worked for him worship him. He mingles with them like one of themselves—and is more ready to give them a helping hand than to trounce them.

He is the kind of man—he did this very thing—who can collect fares on a trolley car for several blocks to relieve the conductor, help off elderly ladies with a child in each arm, and do it with the same interest as if a vital twenty dollars were coming to him for it at the end of the week.

Also, Coleman du Pont is a man who has done things—and Americans like doers rather than talkers. Starting at the bottom, he rose to be head of a Kentucky coal property and upbuilt Central City, making it a place working people wanted to live in. He became head of other coal companies and is still largely interested in them. He succeeded as a steel man and then as a street-railroad builder and operator. Next he took the lead in making the Du Pont Powder Company one of the most efficient and prosperous enterprises in the United States. The $2,000,000 highway across the State of Delaware is already far advanced and when it is finished he will present it to the State. He is an enthusiastic trustee of the Massachusetts Institute of Technology (his Alma Mater), has contributed about $1,000,000 to its expansion, and names his pleasure boats "Tech"—"Tech Jr. II" broke all records for speed in 1915. He farms, and farms successfully, on a gigantic scale, breeding the finest draft horses, and owns herds of registered cows, pigs, and sheep.

While at Wilmington he threw himself into the work of creating an efficient National Guard, his belief being that the nation's citizens should fit themselves to defend their homes rather than saddle the country with a huge standing army. He was made Brigadier-General on the staff of three successive governors of Delaware.

He was not a politician, but in order to rid Delaware of "Gas" Addicks, who for twelve years had prevented the state from being represented in the United States Senate, he jumped into the arena and drove Addicks out bag and baggage. He became State Chairman but declined the offer of a Senatorship then and also later. As a member of the Republican National Committee in 1908 he supported Taft and for a time was in charge of the speakers' bureau in that campaign. In 1916 his Delaware friends insisted upon bringing his name forward for presidential honours, but the General told them he did not admire their judgment!

Coleman du Pont's father, Antoine Bidermann du Pont, was not in the powder company. Early in life the father, with a brother, went West to seek his fortune. They finally settled in Louisville, Ky., where Coleman du Pont was born, on December 11, 1863. The two brothers acquired an interest in a paper mill, street railroads, coal mines in western Kentucky, and had their average share of ups and downs. Coleman du Pont early contracted a fondness for constructing things and was sent to the famous Massachusetts Institute of Technology, where he received the customary thorough training as a mining engineer.

From the "Tech" he went to Central City, Ky., and learned coal mining from underground up. He shouldered a pick and dug coal, drove mules, looked after the horses, served in the blacksmith's shop, shod mules and horses, did carpenter work, filled a fireman's job, ran an engine and tackled engineering problems. He lived the life of a miner, mixed with miners, attended their weddings and funerals and other functions, and became the most popular man on the property. He was elected a member of the Knights of Labour, the miners' union of that day.

He rose to be superintendent and was largely instrumental in developing the Central Coal and Iron Company into an extensive enterprise. From a village with but one general store and less than ten straggling dwellings when he started there, Central City grew to be a prosperous industrial town of 7,500 inhabitants with row after row of model dwellings for the working people. Superintendent du Pont, as the principal figure in the community, took the lead in remodelling Central City. He got the people to work with him enthusiastically in improving their living conditions and environment. His popularity and democracy enabled him to become an effective leader in this movement.

This he accomplished before he was thirty! At that age he left Kentucky for Johnstown, Pa.

"Why did you pull up stakes and leave your native territory?" I asked.

"The best man in western Kentucky coal fields, the president of the biggest coal company there, was getting $4,000 a year," he replied. "I felt I wanted to try and see if I could not do better than that. I made up my mind to break into the biggest industry in the country.

"Arthur J. Moxham, the steel man of Johnstown, Pa., and Tom L. Johnson, afterward Mayor of Cleveland, had started to work for my father at fifty cents a day, so I got a job as general manager with their concern in Johnstown, Pa." What was then the Johnson Company afterward became the Lorain Steel Company, now a subsidiary of the United States Steel Corporation.

After five or six years, he became interested in street railways, and went into this on a large scale—for example, he bought the car line in Johnstown, and built in New Jersey, New York, and Alabama.

"I never liked work," he remarked.

"What?" I exclaimed. "For a man who never liked work you seem to have done a fair share of it."

"I mean it. I would rather play than work any day. I worked and worked hard while I was at it—only because I had to. I could not get along any other way to do things worth doing. I don't give a snap for money except that you cannot get on without it—and you cannot do little things for your friends, to say nothing of big constructive jobs, without capital."

It was at this stage of his career that the Du Ponts of Wilmington called him in to take the helm and try to steer the business into prosperous channels. How he succeeded is a matter of history.

Coleman du Pont has his own theory about roads and their upkeep. No man has done more to arouse the American nation to the necessity for good roads, both as a peace and a war measure.

"I believe that more money will be spent in the next twenty-five years in building roads than has been spent in the last twenty-five years in building railroads," he declared. "I have been building good roads since I was nineteen. At that age I found it was cheaper, and a little easier on my temper, to fill up the holes in the road than to be continually lifting wagons out of these holes.

"Provision must be made for maintenance; to keep a road good it must be maintained. This costs money—a lot of it. My plan to provide for this at first and to keep down road tax (one of the banes of modern life), is to have the State, the county, the city, or whoever builds a road, set apart a width of, say, 250 feet, permanently reserving, say, 50 feet in the centre for road purposes, pipe line, railways, telephone, etc. The building of a good road always advances the value of the adjacent land. Let the State, county or city, lease the remaining 200 feet, 100 feet on each side of the roadway, and in a very short time the income will far more than maintain the road.

"As an example: About 1791, I have been told, a law was passed in New York State, appropriating $30,000 to build a stone road from Canal Street, New York City, north as far as the money would go. Suppose the State or city had acquired 100 feet on either side of Broadway from Canal Street to, say, Tarrytown, the income would probably amount now to $100,000,000 annually.

"This is the system I am following in building the road through Delaware. I am going to give the road to the State and put the adjoining property in trust, the income from which will be forever available for roads or for other purposes."

Coleman du Pont married a second cousin, Miss Alice du Pont, of Wilmington, in the days when he was working at the coal mines in Kentucky. He has three daughters, two of them married, and two sons, the elder a student at the Massachusetts Institute of Technology, the younger at Hill school.

GEORGE EASTMAN

THE story of the birth and cradling of the Kodak has never before been told.

It is a story containing all the elements of poverty and pluck, of plodding and perseverance, of hope and despair. Also these other fitting elements: a widowed mother, broken in health, suddenly plunged into financial misfortunes and a young son determined to overcome the necessity for her keeping a boarding-house. The picture gives a glimpse of the youth working all day as a clerk and then working and experimenting in a little improvised workshop all night, snatching an hour's sleep now and again while his chemicals were cooking, for several nights on end his bed knowing him not.

Then came sufficient success to warrant giving up the clerical position and providing a modest home. Fame, even, came to the young inventor. His photographic plates were recognized as the best the world had ever produced. He branched out as a manufacturer.

Then black, inexplicable, unfathomable failure. His formula, the sensation of the photographic world, refused to work. Sleepless investigation and experimentation were of no avail. Disaster—mysterious, incurable—had befallen. Ruin faced him and his little band of workers.

How defeat did not daunt the young man, how his resourcefulness triumphed, crowns the story, the story of George Eastman, the man who made us all photographers, the man whose ingenuity has made America the fountain-head of photographic supplies for every nation on earth.

Nor is the story lacking in respect of how the poor boy, on becoming rich, used his millions. To his titles of inventor, chemist, scientist, manufacturer, merchant, and financier can be added very truthfully that of public benefactor, for George Eastman in his later years has devoted almost as much time to the intelligent giving of money as to amassing it.

Also, the story can be rounded out with the statement that its hero is the embodiment of modesty. When he goes camping for weeks in the woods or exploring among mountains he does his own cooking, and when he visits the large model farm he established in North Carolina for the teaching of scientific agricultural methods to Negroes he is not above taking tools or implements in his own hands and showing them how a job ought to be done.

Now let us tell the story in detail.

Six years after he was born, on July 12, 1854, at Waterville, N. Y., George Eastman's family moved to Rochester, N. Y., where his father died within a year. The father was the originator of the business college idea, and the successful establishment he founded was managed for a time after his death by a brother. But it did not survive its founder many years.

George, the only son—there were two sisters—was taken from school when fourteen years old, and set to work in an insurance office at $3 a week. The mother, though a semi-invalid, was a woman of unusual ability and resource and played well her part in supporting the little family.

"I then conceived a terror of poverty," Mr. Eastman told me reminiscently. "It haunted me by day and by night. I was so careful of my pennies that, although I clothed myself and helped in a small way at home, I managed to save $37.50 the first year and put it in the bank."

Young as he was, he realized that hard work was the only road leading from the slough of poverty to the hilltop of success. He was soon drawing a salary of $600 a year, the maximum the insurance office could pay; but his employer, realizing young Eastman's worth, recommended him for the position of bookkeeper in a savings bank which paid $1,000 a year.

An abnormally active brain, deft fingers, and a love for tools had induced him to become an amateur mechanic after office hours. Soon he had quite a little workshop where most of his spare time was spent in making things, especially little contrivances of original design. He longed to travel, to see some of the wonderful things the world had invented and constructed. He had an unquenchable thirst for knowledge. His thoughts of travel gave birth to another thought: he must equip himself to take pictures of the sights he would see.

To a Rochester photographer he paid $5 for detailed instruction in photography, then conducted by the wet-plate process. This impressed him as an awkward, clumsy, unsatisfactory way of doing things. His first achievement in the field of photography was the construction of a handy, portable outfit. Experiments to improve on the wet-plate process were temporarily interrupted by promotion at the bank, entailing the learning and execution of more important and more onerous duties.

Then came news from England of the discovery of the gelatine dry-plate process. Eastman immediately became interested, and though without any information, outside of scraps to be picked up in photographic journals, he resumed his experiments. After repeated failures he began to get results—and, almost of equal importance, he grasped the idea that this could be made a manufacturing business, that dry plates could be produced and sold, whereas under the old wet process only materials to make them could be marketed, the buyer having personally to take the raw materials (nitrate of silver, colodion, and a piece of glass), hide himself in a dark tent, smear the glass with the colodion, and dip it in a bath of nitrate of silver. Few amateurs cared to undertake such a job for the sake of trying to take a picture which oftener than not would turn out a failure. Dry plates, on the other hand, could be manufactured in large quantities and sold.

George Eastman discerned vast possibilities. Opportunity was holding out her arms to him. He would become a manufacturer of dry plates.

But what of his domestic responsibilities? He was now (1879) drawing $1,400 a year at the bank and was the sole support of his mother. The new venture at best was speculative. Lots of other people abroad and at home had taken up the making of dry plates and there was no certainty that he could earn a living at it. The spectre of poverty awed him.

Both intuition and ambition, however, urged him on, and his alert mind, his keen perception, his sound commonsense, quickly solved the problem. He hired a room as a workshop for a few dollars a month, engaged a young man to look after the routine work during the day, and he himself did all the delicate chemical operations at night, after finishing at the bank. Usually his office hours were short, but during interest and balancing periods, overtime was necessary, and on such occasions it was not uncommon for young Eastman to toil all night in his little factory without a chance to undress or to go to bed, his sleep consisting only of very brief naps while chemicals were working. When Saturday night came he went home to bed and usually slept straight through until Monday morning, aroused only to eat a meal or two on Sunday.

Eastman plates, however, were rapidly becoming famous. There was a demand for more than he and his youthful assistant could make.

"What was the secret of the superiority of your plates?" I asked Mr. Eastman.

"I just happened to hit upon a good formula; it was more or less luck," he replied modestly. "Even to-day, after thirty years, the making of the proper emulsion is somewhat empirical, and only a few men can do it satisfactorily. The actions and reactions connected with the producing of sensitiveness are still only imperfectly understood by chemists. For example, the difference between a solution which makes a picture in 1,000th part of a second and a solution that takes seconds to print by gaslight has not been thoroughly and scientifically defined. The securing of great sensitiveness is a matter of experiment, and has been worked out by only about a dozen people in the world to-day. I chanced to strike a combination that was very good at that time."

The local photographer who had taught Eastman how to use wet plates readily bought the greatly improved product of his former pupil. While this photographer was taking pictures at the Thousand Islands, the head of a leading firm of importers and jobbers of photographic supplies noticed him taking pictures without using any dark tent and asked him what he was doing. Told that gelatine dry plates, made by a young fellow in Rochester, were being used with excellent results, he induced Eastman to bring to New York samples of his product. Convinced they were superior to anything else on the market, the firm arranged to purchase quantities at wholesale prices, Eastman retaining the right to sell to retailers at a higher figure.

Eastman advertised his plates and from that day on was oversold. At the end of a year he gave up his bank job, as the wholesalers, dissatisfied because the shipments they received would not half fill their orders, made a deal to take all the plates he could make. The attractive feature of the arrangement for Eastman was that they agreed to take a minimum amount each month, including the dull months of winter, and pay promptly.

"Capital was not overabundant with me then," Mr. Eastman recalled. "I regarded the arrangement as a fine one, but subsequently it nearly ruined me."

The Eastman factory branched out. Henry A. Strong, a former boarder with Eastman's mother (and now vice-president of the Eastman Kodak Company), was taken in as a partner on January 1, 1881. The force, originally consisting of one, had multiplied. The output rose to about $4,000 worth of plates a month, all of which were shipped to the wholesalers, who allowed the unsold ones to accumulate during the winter.

When spring came complaints began to pour in about the poor quality of the Eastman plates. Every day brought more "kicks." The firm communicated with Eastman. He could not believe any fault could be found with them. However, conditions became so bad that he hurried to New York and on testing samples from the stock discovered that they had lost a great part of their sensitiveness. Puzzled, Eastman put on his thinking cap. Finally he noted that the older the plates the poorer the results—the plates had simply been piled on one another as received, the newer ones consequently being sold first. He at once realized, what till then was unknown, that age dulled the sensitiveness of the solution.

Eastman unhesitatingly agreed to take back every unsold plate. The misfortune almost ruined his infant industry, but he was determined that nothing faulty should go out under his name. By increasing their activities, Eastman and his co-workers quickly replaced the supply on the market and the sun of prosperity again shone on him.

Then the bottom fell out of everything!

Eastman could not produce a single good plate. Try as he might, he could not get the right sensitiveness.

Day after day and night after night Eastman studied and worked and worried, desperately seeking to fathom the trouble. He had not changed his formula one iota; yet it would no longer work. He tried everything he could think of, but all in vain. He had lost his key to success.

His factory must come to a standstill. There was no use manufacturing plates which would not meet requirements. What could he do? Must he close up and seek another office job?

"Compared with what I then went through all the subsequent troubles of my life have been as nothing," Mr. Eastman recounted the other day. But adversity could not master him. It but served to draw out his resourcefulness, his courage, his determination and stick-to-itiveness.

Suddenly Eastman disappeared. One week, two weeks, three weeks, four weeks passed. Not a wheel was turning in the factory.

Then one day Eastman returned. He carried in his head and in his pocket a new formula. He had been to England. He had gone to Mawson & Swann, of Newcastle, whose plates were the best made in England. He had bought their formula and had worked two weeks in their factory to make sure that he understood every phase and kink of the operation.

Without loss of an hour the Eastman plant began to hum, and although the plates were not so good as formerly, they were better than anything else manufactured in America, and as good as the best obtainable abroad. The stoppage of the factory had but served to increase the clamour for Eastman goods, and everything was quickly driving along as satisfactorily as before—except that Eastman's hair had turned gray over the inexplicable loss of his art.

The explanation? Eastman, who would not rest satisfied until he unearthed the cause, found that he had been using from the very start one particular batch of gelatine for one delicate process in the making of his emulsion and that it had given out. No other gelatine he could obtain would give the same results—just why or how he could not analyze. Every other consignment he tried was of no use; it would not work with his formula.

From the one room of 1879-80, the Eastman factory developed. They had moved into a small building of their own after the partnership with Strong was formed in 1881, and in 1882 it had to be doubled. The making of dry plates was recognized as a very profitable business, but so many concerns were attracted to the field that prices fell and the market became oversupplied. By 1884 the outlook had become cloudy.

Instead of brooding, Eastman pondered how to improve matters. From the start he had had a mania for improving everything handled. This time he set himself the problem of finding a substitute for glass. With characteristic foresight, he realized that the greatest future in the photographic business was to be in the amateur field. If he could only make the taking of photographs simple enough there would be no bounds to the potential demands.

Securing the services of William H. Walker, who had given up the dry-plate business because of its apparently poor future, Mr. Eastman began experimenting with film photography. The problem involved not only the creation of a satisfactory film, but a portable contrivance to hold it. Their joint efforts to coat flexible material with sensitive emulsion proved successful, as also did their construction of a holder for the roll of film. Innumerable technical and chemical difficulties had to be overcome, but sufficient progress was made to justify the incorporation, in October, 1884, of the Eastman Dry Plate and Film Company, which later bought the European patents from Strong, Eastman, and Walker.

It was in April, 1885, that the first roll holders with paper film were put out and Mr. Walker was despatched to England to open a branch there. Their roll holder with negative paper was a real commercial article, the only workable thing of its kind, although the idea of a roll holder had been patented the year Mr. Eastman was born.

This forward step, however, did not satisfy Eastman. Why not, instead of merely selling the roll holder and film to be inserted in existing cameras, invent a camera that could be sold loaded so that the novice could snap pictures? This was the origination of the famous Eastman slogan; *"You press the button, we do the rest."*

This camera was called the Kodak. It was born in June, 1888.

"Why did you choose the name Kodak?" I asked Mr. Eastman. "What does it mean?"

"It does not mean anything," he replied. "We wanted a good strong word, one that could not be misspelt or mispronounced and, most important of all, one that could be registered as a trade-mark that would stand all attacks—we had had serious trouble before then through infringements and imitations of our product and the names we used."

GEORGE EASTMAN

The first Kodaks were sold with a roll of 100 sealed exposures and cost $25. When the whole 100 had been used, the camera could be returned to Rochester or taken to a dealer who forwarded it to headquarters. The film had to be taken out in a dark room. The Kodak threw photography open to the whole world.

Of course, the Kodak of 1888 was not the Kodak of to-day. One hundred pictures had to be taken and developed before the results could be seen. The paper films used had to be handled by experts, and in other respects they were not quite satisfactory.

Mr. Eastman spent much brain-sweat in trying to discover a substitute. He described minutely his ideas to a clever young chemist who, after much experimenting, evolved a honey-like substance, a solution of guncotton and wood alcohol. This was not what they were after, but Mr. Eastman at once saw that this substance might be worked into a substitute for paper and into a transparent film, a long-cherished object. Experimentation revealed that the best way to make transparent films of uniform thickness was to spread a thick solution evenly along glass tables, and apparatus was at once constructed for making films on tables 100 feet long. The film strips could then be cut to any desired length.

From Edison's laboratories came an inquiry as to whether it was true that the Eastman Company had invented a transparent film; if so, Mr. Edison wanted some immediately.

This film made the motion picture possible. Indeed, when Mr. Edison tried to sustain one of his early "movie" machine patents the judge declared that the principal part of the invention lay in the film. Mr. Edison since has acknowledged the part played by Eastman in the birth of moving pictures.

The Eastman Company was immediately swamped with photographic orders. A great many amateurs had dark rooms and could thus do their own developing. Different sizes of Kodaks were manufactured to hold rolls of a dozen films. Hundreds of additional workers had to be employed, and Kodak Park, since become famous throughout the world, was opened.

How to overcome the necessity of having a dark room to re-load the camera and for development purposes was the next hurdle. Mr. Eastman got up a special line of cameras which employed a film having black paper attached to the roll at each end. This permitted of daylight re-loading, but another inventor, Samuel N. Turner, devised the now-familiar method calling for a window on the back of the camera and black paper running the whole length of the film with a number for each picture. He was paid $40,000 for his little contrivance, a big sum in those days—1894.

The next milestone in the path of progress was the invention of the developing machine, in 1902. This was the work of a young man, Arthur W. McCurdy, then private secretary to Alexander Graham Bell. He had almost given up in despair, after many months of unfruitful toil, when he brought his contraption to Mr. Eastman and was shown how it was unpractical. The idea was all right, but there was a fatal flaw in adopting it for practical purposes. Mr. Eastman explained matters to him, advised him to continue his efforts and return when he had succeeded. McCurdy went straight to the Kodak experimental room and within twenty-four hours again submitted his achievement to Eastman. From that day to this he has not needed to do another stroke of work; he has drawn a handsome royalty from the Kodak people ever since and is now in retirement in Vancouver, B. C.

A non-curling film was perfected in 1904, and this seemed to mark the final development in photographic appliances.

Nothing further of importance was discovered until 1914, when the Autographic Kodak was announced. When its inventor, Henry J. Gaisman, first approached Mr. Eastman, his ideas were not practicable, but, on having the defects pointed out, he went at it again; turned down once more, he returned time after time, always exuberantly enthusiastic, and finally went off with a check for $300,000, refusing to have anything to do with any royalty arrangement.

The growth of the Eastman Kodak business has been one of the commercial wonders of the world. From one assistant, Eastman's force has expanded to 13,000, not including over 10,000 dealers deriving the whole or part of their livelihood from handling Eastman products. Kodak Park Works at Rochester comprise ninety buildings, with fifty-five acres of floor space, including one building 740 feet long. The other four factories also are located in Rochester, the whole employing 8,500 workers. These workers represent 22 distinct industries and 229 different occupations, as classified by the United States Census!

Before George Eastman began to sleep in his clothes at night in his one-room shop, America imported all its photographic materials. Within the last forty years—and particularly within the last twenty —the Eastman Kodak has brought a stream of gold from every part of the world to this country, filling the pay envelopes of many thousands of workers and enriching investors in Eastman securities. The Kodak rules the whole camera world, a tribute to American inventive, scientific, and mechanical genius, but more particularly a tribute to George Eastman.

The innate modesty of Eastman has kept his achievements from being more generally recognized. Lord Kelvin, the greatest scientist of the last generation, regarded Eastman as a chemist and scientific inventor of unique standing, and for years coöperated with him as one of the Eastman Company directors. Eastman's rise over innumerable difficulties, the ever-increasing demands for his products, and the world-wide reputation of everything bearing the Eastman stamp have been due to a rare combination of brains, industry, and ambition to provide nothing but the best, no matter what the cost. Millions of dollars have been spent not only in continuous experiments to improve quality, but in providing experts to test rigidly every cent's worth of material leaving the plant. "Excelsior" has been the motto throughout.

Like most other notably successful American enterprises, it became a target for the puny-brained politicians who were swept off their feet by the "trust-busting" madness. To be big was a crime. For Americans to turn out a product better than anything else in the world and to build up an organization of world-wide ramifications was accounted a criminal offence. When Washington announced that the Eastman Kodak was to be attacked, the company offered to change any of its methods not satisfactory to the Department of Justice, but a voluntary adjustment would not have afforded sufficient political fireworks. These proceedings are still dragging along, although events abroad and at home have thoroughly chastened the "trust-busting" spirit and have demonstrated the necessity for large business units.

Of course, the Eastman people strove with all their might to become the undisputed leaders in their industry. Like John D. Rockefeller in oil, James B. Duke in tobacco, Theodore N. Vail in telephony and other giants, Eastman fought competitors tooth and nail and doubtless employed methods not in harmony with the resurrected Sherman Law; but these methods were common and accepted as perfectly legitimate at the time, even by successive Attorney Generals.

George Eastman has little love for money except as an instrument for accomplishing worthy aims. He has always lived unostentatiously. Having no children of his own—he is a bachelor—he has become a sort of father of his city. His gifts to Rochester have included large sums to the University of Rochester and to the General Hospital, while other benefactions have been made to the Hahnemann Hospital, the Homeopathic Hospital, the Friendly Home, the Children's Hospital, the Y. M. C. A., the Y. W. C. A., and the City Park. He is providing a dental dispensary for children which will be perhaps the finest in the country. He has spent both time and money in securing good civic government, one of his steps toward that end having been the establishment of the Bureau of Municipal Research. He is erecting a building for the Chamber of Commerce. He also took a leading part in the organization of the Rochester Art Commission and has personally striven to adorn the city and its public buildings and parks. His love of art is equalled only by his fondness for good music, in the cultivation of which he has been active, his efforts to give Rochester a superior orchestra having been only one of his activities in this direction.

He has also distributed money freely outside of Rochester, but usually anonymously. He was one of the late Booker T. Washington's ardent supporters, and his farm in North Carolina is supplementing the practical training of Negroes carried on at Tuskegee.

His own employees have been Mr. Eastman's special care. Kodak Park Works is an example of how attractive a large plant and its environment can be made. Moreover, he has enabled hundreds of the older employees to amass a competency through ownership of Kodak stock, while his annual distributions to all classes of employees have been notable—the latest wage dividend approximated $900,000.

Although I spent hours with Mr. Eastman I could not draw from him one fact about his benefactions. All he would admit was:

"I have believed in trying to do some little things as I have gone along. I don't believe in men waiting until they are ready to die before using any of their money for helpful purposes."

Incidentally, Mr. Eastman was one of the largest individual subscribers to the Liberty Loan.

George Eastman is an excellent specimen of the type of "Men Who Are Making America."

THOMAS A. EDISON

YOU and I think of inventors as geniuses who suddenly are hit by a brilliant idea from out the air and forthwith patent it in workable form. We picture them as eccentric fellows who for the most part sit around waiting for a stroke of inspiration.

Edison is not of that type. He angrily resents being called a genius or a wizard or a magician. "Genius is one per cent. inspiration and 99 per cent. perspiration," he declares. "The three great essentials to achieve anything worth while are, first, hard work; second, stick-to-itiveness; third, common sense."

Edison is acclaimed as the world's greatest inventor. After he had achieved success as an inventor and manufacturer, he deliberately dropped everything else and adopted invention for his profession and life work, in 1876. After that he simply *had* to make good or become a laughing-stock. Edison made good.

He is also the world's greatest experimenter. He tries thousands and thousands of ways—sometimes fifty thousand—to do a thing, and never quits, even should it take ten years, until he has either found a way or proved conclusively that it cannot be done.

Edison has worked harder and slept less than any other great man in history—he once worked continuously, without a moment's sleep, for five days and nights, while perfecting the phonograph. He has conducted more experiments than any other human being. He has taken out upward of 100 patents in one year and has secured a grand total of over 1,000 patents, a record unapproached by any other individual in this country or abroad.

He has tasted the bitterest defeats and lost all his money time and again. He spent five solid years and over $2,000,000 creating a plan and a plant to extract ores by magnets from powdered rock, only to find that the discovery of unlimited quantities of rich Mesaba ore rendered his whole process profitless and it had to be abandoned, leaving him grievously in debt, but unbroken in spirit. Again, after years of toil on his electric storage battery, he began its manufacture on a large scale, but flaws were discovered in a small percentage of the output, and although buyers clamoured for more shipments, he refused to market a single additional battery until he had sweated and studied and experimented with it for five more years, when, this time, he achieved his desired goal.

Difficulties which would drive normal mortals to despair only light up Edison's enthusiasm and stimulate his determination to triumph. If a thing won't work one way, he tries it another way—5,000 other ways, 10,000 other ways, 20,000 other ways, if necessary. He has sent botanists, mineralogists, chemists, geologists, and others into the most remote, uncivilized nooks of the earth in search of some fibre or other elusive material which the indefatigable experimenter calculated might prove the missing link in a chain of experiments—one expert circumscribed the globe in search of a species of bamboo which Edison figured might supply just the right filament for his in-the-making incandescent lamp, while other explorers combed the fastnesses of South America for a fibre which might still better serve the purpose.

With Edison, inventing is the result of successful experimenting on definite lines. His greatest achievements have not been in originating ideas for new achievements, but in carrying to fruition what others have dreamed of accomplishing but failed to attain. Edison is a doer rather than a dreamer. He, too, of course, has dreamed, but his fame rests less upon his dreams than upon what he has done.

He did not originate the telegraph or the telephone; he was not the inventor of electric lighting; the electric railway was not first thought of by him; others had made moving pictures—of a kind; the recording of the human voice for reproduction was not an idea born in his brain; nor was he the first to think of storing electric energy in a battery.

But without Edison the world would not be enjoying these adjuncts of progress as it is to-day. His has been the master mind, his the master hand, in bringing them to flower and fruition. Where others failed, he has succeeded. Where others brought forth only ideas, he has created actualities. While all predecessors and contemporaries were working along the wrong track, Edison, by his ceaseless industry, his matchless insight and tuition, his unequalled knowledge—gathered in part from complete familiarity with the past but far more from his infinite investigations, experiments, and experience—discovered the right track and pursued it relentlessly, undaunted, year after year, if need be toiling twenty hours a day, seven days a week, and sacrificing in the cause every penny of his fortune. For Edison time has no meaning when he is striving toward a goal; if the end takes ten days or ten months or ten years, what's the difference? The end is the thing.

He has a philosophy of failure which all of us might well adopt. If after thousands of attempts, the expenditure of hundreds of thousands of dollars, and the apparent waste of precious years, he has only failure for his reward, he does not complain, he does not feel downcast. When his assistants commiserate with him and themselves on the futility of all their pains, Edison will cheerfully reprimand them thus: "Our work has not been in vain; our experiments have taught us a lot. We have added something to the total of human knowledge. We have demonstrated that it cannot be done. Isn't that something? Now let's take up the next thing."

That is Edison. Don't waste time and vitality bemoaning the past when the present and the future are calling so loudly to have great and small things accomplished. Look forward, not backward.

Not long since a minister asked a number of successful men: "What are the greatest safeguards against temptation?" Edison replied: "I have never had any experience in such matters. I have never had time, not even five minutes, to be tempted to do anything against the moral law, civil law, or any law whatever. If I were to hazard a guess as to what young people should do to avoid temptation it would be to get a job and work at it so hard that temptation would not exist for them."

Edison literally works day and night. At crucial points in his career, when the invention, the manufacture, or the installation of some contrivance has demanded every ounce of his energy and every moment of his time, he has not touched a bed for weeks and weeks, contenting himself with lying down for a brief spell on a floor with a book for a pillow, or curled up on a roll-top desk, or stretched on a pile of metal pipes. Remonstrated with once for not relaxing his labours and devoting some part of his life to recreation and amusement, Edison replied, not so very long ago:

"I already have a schedule worked out. From now until I am seventy-five years of age, I expect to keep more or less busy with my regular work, not, however, working as many hours or as hard as I have in the past. At seventy-five I expect to wear loud waistcoats with fancy buttons, also gaiter tops; at eighty I expect to learn how to play bridge whist and talk foolishly to the ladies. At eighty-five I expect to wear a full-dress suit every evening at dinner, and at ninety—well, I never plan more than thirty years ahead."

Inventors proverbially are eccentric. Edison is not an exception. He has not been inside a tailor's shop or had a tailor's tape applied to him in a quarter of a century! Some time before the close of the nineteenth century he was inveigled into allowing a tailor to measure him for a suit of clothes and every subsequent suit has been made from what he calls "that jig pattern!"

He is likely to appear at his laboratory in a light summer suit in the middle of winter. But he does not freeze to death, as Mrs. Edison has ingeniously contrived to supply him with three or four layers of underwear! Edison is reported to have received a foreign dignitary, delegated to cross the Atlantic and present Edison with a signal honour, almost stripped to the waist, his hands and face smeared with grime and grease—and it had taken supreme diplomacy and pressure on the part of his colleagues to persuade him to receive the visitor at all, so immersed was Edison in a vital experiment.

Last year when a university conferred upon him the honorary degree of LL.D., it had to be done by telephone—he was too busy to go to accept the honour. One of the greatest universities in England announced that it would honour Edison, but he would not give up his work long enough to cross the ocean for the ceremony, and the proffered degree was withdrawn. Once he received a greatly prized gold medal in New York and mislaid it on the ferry-boat on his way back to his Jersey home. "I have a couple of quarts more of them at home," he commented.

When France, at the Paris Centennial Exposition in 1889, made him a member of the Legion of Honour, at a memorable ceremony, Edison balked when it came to placing the sash upon him and positively refused to have anything to do with it. He did consent to wear the coveted little button in the apel of his coat, but whenever he was to meet Americans he turned down the lapel so that they couldn't see the button—"I didn't want to have my fellow-countrymen think I was trying to show off," was his explanation.

Edison often begrudges the time he is impressed into wasting in receiving visits from foreign potentates and other celebrities. He is of the common people and his heart is with the common people. Perhaps the most pleasing tribute he ever received was during the great Preparedness Parade in New York in May, 1916, when the route of the procession resounded with shouts of "Edison! Edison! Edison!" as the veteran inventor marched at the head of his colleagues on the United States Naval Consulting Board. He was to have dropped from the ranks at a certain point, but, though the heat was intense, he refused to fall out. "I like it and they seem to be liking me," was his ultimatum to those who sought to persuade him to stop and rest. The acclaim of his fellow-citizens, this spontaneous, enthusiastic reception mile after mile, went straight to his heart. The sincere applause of the multitude, of the rank and file of his own people, were more gratifying to Edison than all the diplomas and parchments and medals in the world.

Edison, like his friend Henry Ford, has always sought to produce things that would benefit the masses. Has any other living being added so much to the comfort, enjoyment, enrichment of the lives of his fellow mortals?

Edison has stretched out his hand, seized hold of the evanescent sounds of the human voice, and made them imperishable.

Every phase of the panorama of human life, formerly gone from sight with its own passing, can now be preserved and reproduced for posterity as well as for the day-by-day edification or amusement of the people by means of Edison's invention of moving pictures.

That the human voice can span continents and bridge oceans is in no small measure due to Edison's early achievements in telephony.

The flooding of the world with light second only to that of the sun itself is another of Edison's gifts to humanity.

Edison has been and is the benefactor of the common people. Not only has he given them, for a nickel, entertainments previously beyond their reach; not only has he brought music into their homes, but one of his consuming ambitions to-day is to lighten the burden and the drudgery of every housewife in the land through the invention of simple, inexpensive devices for performing many domestic tasks which now bear heavily upon overworked mothers and other harassed domestic workers. If he lives long enough—and he is come of an extraordinarily long-lived race—he promises to achieve as much in this field as he has in others.

Milan, Ohio, has the distinction of being the birthplace of Edison. The book of life opened for him on February 11, 1847. His paternal ancestors were Dutch, but the family had lived in America for several generations. The members were noted for their longevity. The family, of modest circumstances, moved to Gratiot, Michigan, when Thomas Alva was seven. There the elder Edison dabbled in farming, the lumber business, and the grain trade. The boy had such an extraordinarily shaped head that the doctor predicted brain trouble! The teacher at school pronounced little Thomas, who was always at the foot of the class, "addled," and at the end of three months he was given up as too stupid to receive instruction. That was all the regular schooling Edison ever received, his instruction thereafter being attended to by his gifted mother.

He did some queer things. When six he was missing for a while and was found sitting on goose eggs trying to hatch them. He built a fire in a barn, watched it go up in flames and was publicly whipped in the village square as a warning to other boys. He had part of a finger chopped off, was nearly drowned, and, becoming interested in chemistry, when about ten gorged another boy with seidlitz powders, confident that the gas generated would cause the boy to fly! That was, apart from his egg-hatching, his very first experiment. Before he was eleven he had gathered together a fearful and wonderful chemical "laboratory" in the basement of his home, and, to make sure that nobody would interfere with his materials, he marked every one of his 200 bottles " POISON."

Then, with another boy, he started cultivating ten acres of his father's farm and sold as much as $600 worth of produce in one year.

He became newsboy on the train running between Port Huron and Detroit, started two small stores in Port Huron in charge of other youths, met with no great success, and turned to extending his news vending by installing newsboys on other trains. His ambition was equalled only by his industry, as is shown in Dyer and Martin's excellent "Life of Thomas A. Edison," from which these early facts are drawn.

He started a laboratory on his train, using part of the unventilated smoking car which was never used by passengers. Next he installed a printing press in the car and actually collected, wrote, set up and printed all the news for his *Weekly Herald* and sold as many as 400 copies weekly, a feat which the London *Times* described as notable in that this was the first newspaper ever printed on a train in motion. His ingenuity manifested itself in diverse ways. During the War between the States he bribed railway telegraph operators to send bulletins to each station announcing the most sensational events of the day with the result that when "Newsy" Edison came along with his papers there were crowds waiting at every station to buy them. On special occasions he charged exorbitant prices. His laboratory was growing steadily, until one day the train lurched badly, a stick of phosphorus fell on the floor and the car caught fire. The enraged conductor pitched Edison and all his belongings off at the next stop, boxing Edison's ears hard enough to cause the acute deafness from which he has ever since suffered.

A printer's devil persuaded Edison to join him in changing his publication's name to *Paul Pry*, which contained so pointed personal gossip that one victim threw the youthful editor into the river and *Paul Pry* died shortly after. Edison's literary abilities had been greatly aided by his extremely zealous reading in the Detroit Library during the long period he spent in that city between the early arrival and the late departure of his train. His method was to tackle the books shelf by shelf and read everything indiscriminately.

His chemical experiments led him to take up telegraphy and he and a chum erected a wire between their homes and enjoyed talking over it nightly until a stray cow pulled the wire down. Edison having bravely saved the life of the local station agent's child by snatching it from an approaching train—at the expense of numerous cuts—the grateful father offered to teach young Edison telegraphy. For six months Edison worked eighteen hours daily. He became proficient enough to build a line a mile long from the station to the village and was appointed telegraph operator at Port Huron. As he used to leave messages unsent and undelivered while he conducted experiments, his services were dispensed with.

Edison's next move, in 1863, was eventful. He found a job as railroad telegraph operator at the Grand Trunk Station of Stratford Junction, Canada. Here also his experiments landed him in trouble. Night operators had to tap the word "six" every hour to the superintendent to make sure they had not gone to sleep. Edison promptly invented a contrivance which clicked off the required signal every hour so that he could enjoy snoozes in comfort! One night a train was allowed to pass, and as another train was coming from the opposite direction on the same track, Edison, having frantically but vainly tried to send the engine driver a warning, promptly bolted for the border. For the following five years he was a roaming telegraph operator.

Sometimes he almost starved. His inventive talent, however, found vent every now and again. One office was terribly overrun with rats and Edison fitted up a little device which electrocuted them by the score. A similar invention for electrocuting cockroaches at another office was written up in the newspapers and Edison was immediately dismissed. A more ambitious invention during this period enabled the dots and dashes to be recorded on strips of paper at lower speed than sent, a contrivance which, years later, led Edison to invent the phonograph.

He drifted in time to Boston where he bought Faraday's complete works and applied himself with intense diligence to experimentation. His first patent was taken out on June 1, 1869; it was designed to enable Congress to record and count votes instantaneously, through each member pressing a button at his desk. The proud inventor proceeded to Washington expecting to be received with open arms, but left bitterly disappointed, having been peremptorily told that the inordinate time consumed in taking a vote was one of the accepted methods of delaying progress and harassing opponents. This initial experience determined Edison to confine his efforts ever after to things for which there would be a keen and wide demand.

While in Boston Edison made a stock ticker, established a small stock quotation business, and also introduced a method of telegraphing between business concerns, a method so simple that anyone could understand and work it.

How great a contrast was there between Edison's entry into New York in 1869 and his reception in 1916, when he was the hero of the Preparedness Parade!

So hard up was he on leaving Boston that he had to let his books, instruments, etc., remain as security for debts. Arriving by boat in New York he had not a cent to buy food, for which he was starving. Seeing a tea-taster at work, Edison begged him for some tea and this formed his first breakfast in New York.

Three days later Edison was sitting in the offices of the Gold &

Stock Telegraph Company watching the gold ticker at work—speculation in gold was then at fever pitch. Suddenly scores of boys rushed into the place excitedly explaining that the ticker in their employers' offices had stopped working. Dr. Laws, head of the concern, also arrived breathless. The apparatus had broken down. Edison calmly told Laws that he thought he could fix it and proceeded to do so. The grateful and astonished doctor asked the stranger his name, and next day, after a searching quizzing-bee, put him in charge of the whole business at a salary of $300 a month. When the hungry, penniless, out-of-work operator heard the amount he was to receive he nearly fainted.

In his new surroundings Edison found vent for his genius in improving the ticker and bringing out many allied patents. He also at the same time formed the firm of "Pope, Edison & Company, Electrical Engineers and General Telegraphic Agency," and began to do important work for the Western Union Telegraph Company. When the head of the Western Union asked Edison how much he would consider reasonable for a certain patent, Edison tried to summon up enough courage to ask $5,000, but the sum was so much that he could not bring himself to name it.

"How would $40,000 strike you?" he was asked.

Edison, being very hard of hearing, could not believe his ears. He received a check for $40,000 but didn't know what to do with it. Finally, he went to the bank it was drawn on, laid it down unendorsed, and waited to see what would happen. He suspected that the Western Union executive was playing a trick on him and that the $40,000 offered was a joke. Of course, the teller would not cash the check because he did not know Edison, but by going to the Western Union office he got a clerk to return to the bank with him and identify him. The teller meanwhile had been tipped off and he paid over the $40,000 in small bills, the whole forming a big parcel. Edison trundled home with it, nervous as to what might happen, for he had no safe. Next day, however, they took compassion on him and showed him how to open a bank account.

With this capital he started a plant of his own in Newark, declaring he did not like the idea of "keeping money in solitary confinement." He was soon employing fifty men making stock tickers and other instruments. Business prospered to such an extent that two shifts were employed. Edison acted as foreman of both, working night and day with only occasional half-hours for sleep in out-of-the-way corners of the shop. Here he began in earnest his life of invention. Among the earliest of his patents was an automatic telegraph which could send and receive 3,000 words a minute and record them in Roman type. He also took hold of a typewriting machine and developed it into the practical Remington now of universal use. In 1873 he went to England to introduce his automatic telegraph and also his quadruplex telegraph instrument, which had cost him prolonged study and experiment. The mimeograph was another important achievement of the early 70's. At one time forty-five different inventions were being worked on in Edison's plants—by this time he had five shops going.

His early "system" of bookkeeping was at least original, but it did not do credit to his inventive powers. All bills were slapped on one spike and not one of them was paid until legal proceedings had been taken; then, when the order for payment came along, Edison paid the bill plus the legal costs and transferred the bill to another spike. Tax assessments were treated the same way, but on one occasion it was impressed upon him that if he did not pay a certain tax by a specified date 12 per cent. additional would be levied, involving quite a sum. On the very last day of grace Edison took up his station at the end of the long queue, but when he finally got to the tax receiver his mind was so full of other matters that he forgot his own name and, being absolutely unable to recall it, was summarily turned back to the end of the line, with the result that, as closing time came before Edison could again reach the desk, he had to pay the extra levy.

For his famous carbon telephone transmitter Edison was offered a lump sum of $100,000 from the Western Union, then in a death-grapple with the Bell people. Edison, knowing his weakness for making money go, stipulated that the sum be paid him at the rate of $6,000 annually for seventeen years, an arrangement which the W. U. jumped at, for this was virtually only interest on the money. He repeated this extraordinarily poor business arrangement some time later when the Western Union offered him $100,000 for his electromotograph. The Western Union did not lose anything by these deals with Edison, for the company sold out to the Bell interests for a big figure, including a substantial royalty on the use of certain of its patents. English interests cabled Edison an offer of "30,000" for certain of his apparatus and Edison promptly accepted, well pleased with the sum. When the money arrived he received not the $30,000 he had expected, but £30,000—$150,000.

One of his most notable inventions worked at the very first experiment. This was the phonograph, originated in 1877, and the machine to-day is one of the precious exhibits in the South Kensington Museum, London. When Edison's workmen heard the little hand-turned cylinder reproducing the human voice they were positively incredulous; they were quite sure that Edison, always fond of a joke, was playing a trick upon them, that ventriloquism was the explanation. It was not until they had examined the little machine microscopically and made sure that there were no wires connecting it with any other contrivance and that no ventriloquist was near by that they finally accepted the entrancing truth that their chief had scored a historic bull's-eye at the very first shot.

It was characteristic of Edison, however, that he spent ten years improving it before he exploited it commercially, among his final sessions on it being one of five days and nights without a moment's sleep.

The hardest and perhaps the greatest of all Edison's achievements was begun in the late 70's, and now his labours in this field are yielding employment to hundreds of thousands of wage earners and many hundreds of millions of capital. I refer, of course, to his system of generating, regulating, measuring, and distributing electricity for light, heat, and power. In evolving his incandescent lamp Edison ransacked the earth for suitable materials. He tested 6,000 vegetable growths, brought from all parts of the globe in his search for an ideal substance for use as a filament inside the glass bulb. At first a piece of carbonized cotton thread was used, later a certain kind of bamboo yielded a better fibre, but finally all carbon filaments were discarded in favour of metallic ones.

The immensity of Edison's task in inventing and establishing the first electric lighting plant in New York, at Pearl Street, in September, 1882, involving not only the construction of absolutely new forms of machinery and apparatus, but in laying the necessary wires, in originating methods and apparatus for regulating and sub-dividing the current, in inducing people to agree to the installment of the little-tested invention, and in solving a thousand problems never solved before—the immensity of this burden, I say, cannot be grasped at this day when a generation of experience and familiarity with electric lighting has led us to accept everything pertaining to it as a matter of course. At the end of 1882 only 225 buildings in New York had been wired, including the offices of J. P. Morgan, who became one of Edison's admirers and supporters. For three months the current was supplied free to those brave enough to allow their places to be threaded with the mysterious wires which, it was feared, might start fires or cause explosions at any moment.

The story of the multiple-arc system, of the revolutionary three-wire system which saved 60 per cent. of the copper formerly used, the introduction of central stations against all opposition and ignorance, the invention of a meter for measuring consumption of the current—this story of the birth of a new era in human progress is too full of incident to permit its being even outlined here. Suffice it to say that Thomas A. Edison's accomplishments in this field stamped him the greatest inventive figure of the age.

Electric railway experiments next arrested Edison's chief attention, and by using the track for a circuit, he achieved wonderful results. He built an electric line at Menlo Park, N. J., in 1880 and 1882, then his headquarters, and it attracted railroad builders and engineers from all parts of the world; but somehow they were not so quick as Edison to grasp the possibilities of the field thus opened up.

The worst financial blow Edison received was the abandonment of his extensive plant at Edison, N. J., for magnetic ore milling. This was "the most colossal experiment Edison ever made," his associates record. When it was given up, chiefly because of the discovery of unlimited quantities of rich ore in the Mesaba Range, Edison's whole fortune had gone and he was heavily in debt. Some of his associates were broken hearted. But Edison was undaunted. "As far as I am personally concerned," he declared philosophically, "I can at any time get a job at $75 per month as a telegraph operator and that will amply take care of all my personal requirements"—a touching testimony of the simplicity of his mode of life.

There followed Edison's epochal inventions for the manufacture of cement—half the Portland cement produced in America was later made in Edison kilns. In one day, of almost twenty-four hours, Edison personally prepared detailed plans for his first cement plant covering a length of half a mile, a feat regarded by experts as the most stupendous ever performed by a human brain in one day. From the manufacture of cement to the "pouring of cement houses" was a logical step—and, incidentally, Edison believes this method of construction is only in its infancy.

Of late years the electric storage battery, wireless apparatus, the Edison-Sims torpedo and other submarine problems, improvements in the phonograph, the dictating machine, the inventing of "speaking motion pictures," and household labour-saving devices have claimed most of the master inventor's time and talent. Naval problems have been his chief concern for the last two years, and just at present "I am working day and night for my Uncle Sammy" is the typical Edisonian message sent me.

President Wilson, in paying tribute to Edison on his seventieth birthday, wrote: "He seems always to have been in the special confidence of Nature herself." If he is, it is because he has worked harder and more intelligently than any other living man to wring her secrets from her. His success has been paid for.

Notwithstanding that he has given to the world more than any man of his generation, Edison has not received a corresponding financial reward. He is not a multi-millionaire. Nor has he any desire to be one. He eats as little as he sleeps—just enough, he says, to keep him at the same weight (about 175 pounds) year after year.

His attire is simple and unstudied and he both smokes and chews tobacco, but this is his only form of dissipation. Until latterly he indulged in no recreation or amusements except parchesi, but he has now taken to automobiling, often in company with Mrs. Edison or one of his children.

"Edison is not a Christian but an atheist," is a remark sometimes heard. Let Edison speak for himself on this subject: "After years of watching the progress of Nature I can no more doubt the existence of an Intelligence that is running things than I do of the existence of myself."

Although now past the allotted span of three score years and ten, Edison's brain has not lost its brilliancy nor his right hand its cunning. It is not yet time to write "Finis" to his career.

"Don't you feel a sense of regret in being obliged to leave so many things uncompleted?" he was asked.

"What's the use?" he replied. "One lifetime is too short and I am busy every day improving essential parts of my established industries."

These industries give employment and sustenance to an appreciable percentage of his fellowmen, and comfort, convenience, recreation, education to every civilized race, enriching the lives of all of us.

JAMES A. FARRELL

THE president of the largest corporation the world has ever known began life as a common labourer.

To-day he is one of the greatest practical industrial executives in America.

I know no man possessing more knowledge of his business—practical, theoretical, detailed and general—than James A. Farrell, president of the United States Steel Corporation. He carries in his head more steel facts than any other human being.

Not only does he know how to make steel, not only has he had practical training in every phase of manufacturing steel products, but he has done more than any other person, past or present, to send American merchandise into every corner of the earth. Before others began even to talk about the vital importance of outlets for American products, James A. Farrell, working literally day and night and journeying hither and thither across the seven seas, was blazing the trail for American goods and actually creating markets now yielding millions of dollars a year to American workmen and American business enterprises. He is known as "the father of the export steel trade."

Mr. Farrell holds the record for securing foreign orders for American goods. He is the greatest international salesman America has ever produced.

So modest is he, so averse is he to talking about himself or his achievements, that he was unknown to the American public until his name was proclaimed to the world as the new president of the Steel Corporation seven years ago. "Who is Farrell?" the people and the papers asked. Newspaper "morgues" were ransacked in vain for data about him. So were "Who's Who" and other publications chronicling the careers of notables.

Even now James A. Farrell is imperfectly known to all but those in the steel industry. Here are a few facts—and they are facts—about him:

When a boy he began training his memory and he has disciplined it so thoroughly throughout his life that he admittedly has the finest memory of any business man in the country.

Though working twelve hours a day as a labourer in a wire mill, he studied systematically every evening, and in fourteen months became a mechanic, rising to be foreman in charge of the 300 men in the works before he was of age.

Having made several voyages with his seafaring father when a schoolboy, he became interested in foreign lands and now he is as familiar with every foreign country as he is with Pittsburgh or New York. He has been called "a walking gazetteer of the world."

His knowledge of shipping, of steamship lines and lanes, of how best to transport merchandise from any one point of the globe to any other point is so far beyond that of any other human being that he has won the nickname "the American Lloyd's Register." In peace times he could tell the location any day of hundreds of vessels plying all over the seven seas.

Twenty years before the average American realized the importance of foreign outlets for domestic products, Mr. Farrell, in face of obstacles which would have driven others to despair, inaugurated, singlehanded, a campaign for the conquest of overseas markets for American steel products and built up an export business before the war of almost $100,000,000 a year, a record not approached by any other individual. Since then the annual total has been far more than doubled.

As the first president of the Foreign Trade Council, he rendered invaluable service to American manufacturers in aiding them to overcome obstacles in entering foreign markets.

In nine days' examination during the Government's suit against the Steel Corporation, Mr. Farrell astounded everybody by answering thousands upon thousands of questions of every conceivable variety without having to refer to a single scrap of paper. The replies in many cases called for the recital of average, maximum, minimum, and percentage figures involving decimal points, yet the witness recited them from memory as easily as if he had records in front of his eyes.

He can enter the mills and mines of the company and greet hundreds of co-workers by their first names even though, as occasionally happens, he runs across a workman he may not have met since the days when they sat together as common labourers or artisans on the cinder pile.

His associates declare that he has the uncanny faculty of being able to do two things at once; for example, he can listen to and digest everything said to him by a caller and at the same time read and absorb everything in a letter or report submitted to him for consideration and decision.

He has read every important book published on the iron industry and every worth-while volume on the history and conditions of other countries, his library on these subjects being second to that of no other individual. When electricity promised to become a factor in manufacturing and transportation he paid $1,500 for a complete library of books on electricity.

With all his amazing knowledge, his unique standing in his field and his power as president of an organization employing 280,000 men, James A. Farrell is still "Jim" Farrell, as democratic as when he first answered the whistle of the wire mill, and as hard a worker.

A scene incongruous in these supposedly hard, materialistic days of rushing business, unceasing pressure, and lack of sentiment, was witnessed in a busy skyscraper in downtown New York six years ago.

Several hundred men and women waylaid one of their number to present him with a loving cup. He had received signal promotion, and they pressed around him to offer congratulations and bid him God-speed. They were quite happy until the presentation speech was made, when it dawned upon them that they were saying farewell and that they were to lose their colleague.

A sob was heard—from a stenographer or a telephone girl. In two minutes there was hardly a dry eye in the whole house. Enough tears were shed to fill the loving cup.

The employees were those of the United States Steel Products Company and the man was their chief, James A. Farrell, who had been promoted from the presidency of that subsidiary to the presidency of the billion-dollar parent company.

When Mr. Farrell was sitting day after day on the witness stand during the Government's investigation of the company, newspaper writers described him as a machine rather than a man, as carrying on his shoulders, not a human head, but a Pandora's box filled with every conceivable variety of figures and knowledge, as wearing an expression as immobile as the Sphinx, and as talking without apparently moving his lips—a statue rather than a mortal. They portrayed him as all head.

The truth is that James A. Farrell's heart is larger than his head. But he doesn't wear it on his sleeve. He hasn't the conquering smile of Charles M. Schwab, one of his predecessors. He is not given to making an ostentatious fuss when meeting or welcoming anyone. He affects none of society's artificial "gush."

An intimate analysis reveals James A. Farrell as a man of intense sympathy—he is what his Spanish friends call "simpatico" in an unusual degree. He understands human nature as well as he understands iron. Interested as he has been beyond almost any other man in developing America's steel industry, he has been still more interested in the human beings who sweat and toil to produce the steel. His ceaseless efforts to find foreign markets have not prevented him from striving incessantly to improve the conditions of American workmen —indeed, the revolution which has taken place in conditions at steel plants since Mr. Farrell first entered the wire mill as a boy has been due in no slight measure to his efforts.

Perhaps, too, an inherited sense of Irish humour has had something to do with enabling him successfully to meet difficulties and men at home and abroad. Even the responsibilities that press upon the president of a concern doing a billion dollars' worth of business a year have not crushed the love of fun—nor the boyishness of heart —from "Jim" Farrell. When off duty—particularly when, clad in oilskins and high boots, he skippers his sailboat—he enjoys playing pranks with his family or friends.

But let us go back and trace Mr. Farrell's career from the beginning.

At school in New Haven, Conn., where he was born on February 16, 1863, James A. Farrell developed a keen interest in geography. He learned to draw maps from memory and to fill in correctly the principal cities, seaports, rivers, etc. He took pains to remember what he learned and his naturally good memory developed. The Farrells had been seafaring people for several generations, and when James was a mere lad his father took him on several voyages. Foreign sights still further stimulated the lad's interest in geography.

One day the elder Farrell's ship, of which he was both owner and captain, sailed away from New York and was heard of no more.

With the vanishing of the vessel vanished the son's dreams of a college education. Instead of entering a university he entered a wire mill as a labourer. Although only fifteen and a half, his sturdy physique and excellent health, which have never failed him, enabled him to perform the duties of a man. Twelve hours' manual toil every day did not dampen his ardour for study. Returning from the works after a full round of the clock he applied himself diligently to his books. As a little boy he had a fondness for swapping things and for other juvenile business transactions and he now had ambition to become a salesman.

While performing the tasks of a common labourer he had kept his eyes open and had used his scanty opportunities to such purpose that in fourteen months he was promoted to the position of a mechanic. In this capacity he learned how to draw all kinds of wire, from the thickness of a human hair to a hawser strong enough to pull a ship. Before he was twenty he left the New Haven Wire Mill and went to the Pittsburgh Oliver Wire Company as an expert wire drawer. By the time he cast his first vote he was foreman over all the 300 men in the mill.

All this time, however, he was daily and nightly striving to fit himself to become a salesman. In addition to having learned every trick of the wire-drawing trade he had assiduously sought to learn other branches of the iron and steel industry and had also improved his general education by systematic study. When twenty-three he attained his object: his company appointed him salesman with the whole of the United States as his territory.

Of course he succeeded—succeeded so well that the important Pittsburgh Wire Company of Braddock, Pa., made him its sales manager three years later. His office headquarters were in New York and this enabled him to rub shoulders with many influential steel men and also served to broaden his training and his outlook.

Here again he made his mark, and when only thirty he was promoted to be general manager of the whole organization.

"The explanation of Farrell's success as a salesman," one of his intimates impressed upon me, "is that he knew the business so thoroughly from the ore up that he could not only talk intelligently about his wares, but often he could give buyers sound advice as to the kind of material that would best suit their purpose. He did not build up his business by the methods then too often in vogue. He did not take buyers to saloons or clubs and sign contracts over booze. He is a teetotaler. He was not even a 'good mixer.' It was not glib talk that won him customers, but something more solid. He was a delightful companion—his Irish wit was always on tap—and serious-minded people found him an excellent conversationalist because he was so well read. Farrell was really a salesman plus; he knew more about goods than nine-tenths of the men he did business with. And he had a reputation for being straight. You could depend upon 'Jim' Farrell's word."

Unlike many Americans, Mr. Farrell's vision was not confined to the country's geographical boundaries. As a schoolboy and as a barefoot lad scampering about the decks of his father's ship he had learned that a large part of the world lay beyond the Atlantic and the Pacific coasts and south of the Rio Grande. His selection as general manager of the Pittsburgh Wire Company came in 1893, the panic year. The steel business was prostrated. Farrell's first year as manager threatened to prove a bad one. Nobody would buy substantial amounts of anything. What was to be done? Most business men resigned themselves to conditions on the theory, "We must wait until the storm passes and things come our way again."

Farrell didn't wait for orders to come his way. He went after them. And here the knowledge he had absorbed came to his aid. He had studied foreign countries exhaustively and knew a great deal about their internal conditions, principal industries, steel requirements, and tariffs.

Forthwith he invaded the foreign field with might and main. By December 31st he had sold one-half of the plant's product abroad! This feat became the talk of the steel trade.

For three years Mr. Farrell lived within a stone's throw of the mill at Braddock. Many a time he was called out of bed at night to straighten out some unexpected tangle. He nursed the mill with the fidelity of a mother to her child. Naturally it grew. Although no additional capital was put into it, its value trebled during Farrell's six years' managership.

Control having been purchased, in 1899, by John W. Gates and others who formed the American Steel & Wire Company of New Jersey, the position of foreign sales agent of the merger was offered Mr. Farrell. When, in 1901, the United States Steel Corporation was organized, with the American Steel & Wire Company as one of its principal subsidiaries, Mr. Farrell was unanimously chosen as the best man to develop the foreign end of the giant's operations. The choice of Mr. Farrell for this difficult position was inevitable, so completely had he outdistanced all others as a master of foreign business.

In order to coördinate the overseas activities of all the subsidiaries, the United States Steel Products Company was incorporated in 1903, and Mr. Farrell became its president. His work here formed a notable page in the history of our foreign trade.

In the first year, 1904, sales of the Steel Corporation and of its subsidiaries to foreign countries totalled $31,000,000; by 1912 the figure had exceeded $90,000,000, while the 1916 aggregate exceeded $200,000,000. The cost of doing this foreign business when Mr. Farrell took hold ranged from 7 to 11 per cent.; it is now well under one per cent. and he hopes to cut it down to one-half of one per cent. The whole world has been dotted with agencies, some 260 having been established in more than 60 countries. Finding steamship service inadequate, Mr. Farrell induced the corporation to acquire a fleet of its own and to charter additional vessels; now it owns or has under long-term charter 30 to 40 ships. Its exports of over 2,500,000 tons a year usually load about three steamers every two days. Steel Corporation steamers penetrate far-off places not touched by other vessels and carry goods of other shippers, including competitors, to such places.

The products handled include everything in iron and steel from special nails for China to bridges for Iceland, wire for the Holy Land and skyscrapers for South America.

Only those who have tried to penetrate new markets can understand the labour, the skill, the patience, that the creation of such an organization demanded. Without his phenomenal knowledge of international transportation, Mr. Farrell never could have opened up so many new trade lanes—the active head of the Cunard Line once described Mr. Farrell as "A good shipowner spoiled by being in another industry." Nor could he have attained such results had he not trained for just such a position during previous years, for his comprehensive study, combined with his amazing memory, enabled him to compute such intricate matters as foreign customs duties, the rail and water transportation, facilities of other countries, and the degree of competition to be encountered, all without having constantly to consult printed records or continually to cable abroad for information.

"Mr. Farrell did the work of four men," declared E. P. Thomas, then one of Mr. Farrell's co-workers and later his successor as president of the Steel Products Company. "He seemed to know everything and could remember everything. He had a tremendous capacity for work; after putting in a full day here at the office he would take home bundles of business papers, and 'clean up,' as he called it, at night. He often worked fourteen hours a day. We received several hundreds of cables and letters every day and the way he contrived to digest all important matters in this mass of material and answer personally a great part of it was astounding.

"Of course, we all pitched in and helped all we could, for there never was a man of greater personal magnetism. Every employee regarded him as a sort of father and counsellor, who could be depended upon for guidance and sympathy in domestic or other trouble."

When the presidency of the Steel Corporation became vacant there was little difference of opinion as to the ideal man for the job. James A. Farrell towered above any other figure. He knew every detail of the mining, transportation, and transmuting of ore into iron and steel, of manufacturing all classes of products, of how to sell at home and, not least in importance, of how to cover the whole earth with American steel manufactures—for that, of course, is the goal of the greatest industrial organization ever created by the human brain.

"Jim" Farrell had one other qualification. He knew how to inspire workmen and win their loyalty. For example, he was inspecting a mine when the superintendent cautioned him not to enter a certain heading because it was dangerous owing to falling slate. "Aren't there men working in there?" asked Mr. Farrell. "Yes," he was told. "Very well," replied Mr. Farrell, "if it is right for the men to be there it is all right for me to go in." And in he went. The incident spread all over the mine and a reporter wrote a "story" about it. When it was widely reprinted and commented upon, Mr. Farrell was astonished, for he did not consider his action as having been anything out of the ordinary. But among miners, steel workers, and other employees it stamped him as unspoiled by success. They felt that he still regarded himself as simply one of them.

Just after his election to the Steel Corporation presidency a friend invited Mr. Farrell to join a theatre party. When they arrived Mr.

Farrell absolutely refused to sit in a prominent position in the box. His picture had been appearing in publications throughout the country and he feared he might be recognized by some of the audience and perhaps stared at, not to say talked about, as pushing himself into the limelight!

When not working, which is not often, his favourite recreation is handling his boat, with members of his family and perhaps a few friends on board. His charities, of which nothing is ever heard, run chiefly to children's homes and hospitals.

When I asked Mr. Farrell what his life's experience had taught him, what he could pass on to the myriads of young men ambitious to succeed, he cited these as some of the essentials—in addition, of course, to honesty, integrity, and other to-be-taken-for-granted qualities:

"*Application.* If a task is to be done, do it no matter how unimportant it may seem.

"*Concentration* and *Specialization* on definite lines of work.

"Cultivation of a *good memory* and a practical imagination, with ability to analyze conditions and evolve new plans and methods—that is, *originality*."

Pressed to explain how to develop a strong memory, Mr. Farrell, in an interview with him published in the *American Magazine*, replied, in part:

"To cultivate a good memory at first requires effort—great effort. In time it becomes easy and natural to remember things. To retain things in your mind becomes a habit.

"Conan Doyle, in his writings, propounded the right idea. You must concentrate. You must not carry any useless mental baggage. You must concentrate on the things in which you are interested and expunge from your memory everything you are not interested in. There must be not only a spring cleaning but a daily cleaning of your memory, so to speak, in order to make room for fresh stores of helpful information.

"James J. Hill, who had perhaps one of the most remarkable memories of any man in the country, used to say that it is easy to remember things in which one is interested. Any one wishing to acquire comprehensive knowledge of his business, or of any specific subject, must not try to store his mind with endless details about other things. For example, I have tried to learn all I could about the steel business in its mining, manufacturing, selling and transportation branches; but, to enable me to carry business information in my head, I have not attempted to retain in my mind minute detailed data about politics or baseball.

"Absorb what to you is essential—that is, everything pertaining to your field of endeavour. Abolish from your mind non-essential,

JAMES A. FARRELL

extraneous subjects. No human brain has cells enough to store up all the facts about all subjects under the sun. Don't clog your brain cells with impedimenta. Feed them only with vital material, with things that will enhance your usefulness in your sphere of activity by increasing and improving your stock of needful information."

"How can a young man start in to improve his memory?" I asked.

"The best foundation on which to build a strong memory is to cultivate a capacity for work. Good habits also contribute to a good memory; careless habits tend to distract and spoil the memory. A clear head is necessary to a keen memory.

"It is essentially true of the mind that it grows on what it feeds. Youth is the time when the mind and memory are most sensitive, most retentive, and most plastic. It is especially important, therefore, to begin the proper training of the mind at an early age. It is as difficult to dislodge cumbersome, useless things from the mind as it is to acquire new and better supplies of knowledge. What was done badly has to be undone—often at considerable cost. As with most worth-while things in this world, a good memory calls for the paying of a price. Any youth or man who desires to train his memory must be prepared to pay the cost. He must be prepared to forego an endless round of even harmless pleasures. He must not hope to shine continually and conspicuously in social or society circles during his formative years. He must study while others play. His reading must be limited very largely to books and magazines and papers which will help him to acquire facts and a better understanding of whatever business or subject he is determined to master. He must utilize most of his spare time and not idle it away."

When a witness at the hearing of the Government's suit against the Steel Corporation he was asked: "Can you remember what percentage of the business of each of the subsidiaries of the Steel Corporation was foreign in 1910 and in 1912?"

Here is his reply, given without consulting a single note or figure: "Yes; the Carnegie Steel Company, 21 per cent. in 1910; 24 per cent. in 1912. The National Tube Company, 10 per cent. in 1910; 12 per cent. in 1912. The American Sheet & Tin Plate Company, 11 per cent. in 1910; 20 per cent. in 1912. The American Steel & Wire Company, 17 per cent. in 1910; 20 per cent. in 1912. The Lorain Steel Company, 30 per cent. in both periods. The American Bridge Company, 6 per cent. in 1910; 8.5 per cent. in 1912. The Illinois Steel Company, 1.2 per cent. in 1910; 2.4 per cent. in 1912."

"That man's mind is a self-working cash register and adding machine combined," remarked one of the attorneys.

The brain-work, the detailed knowledge, the intricate practical calculations necessary to solve export trade problems can be gathered from the way Farrell solved the difficulty of shipping goods from New York to Vancouver, British Columbia, at a cost that would enable our manufacturers to meet European ocean-borne competition. Europe could send material for $6 to $7 a ton, whereas the rate from Pittsburgh was $18 a ton. Mr. Farrell started a line of steamers which left New York, went through the Straits of Magellan, called at various ports on the west coast of South America, Mexico, and up to Vancouver.

"How were these steamers brought back to New York?" queried the attorney.

Mr. Farrell replied in these words:

"We go into the merchandise business to work the ships around the world economically to enable them to load out to British Columbia with steel. The steamers are chartered for lumber or coal from Puget Sound to the Gulf of California—that is, to Guaymas or Mazatlan. They then go across to a place called Santa Rosalia and load full cargoes of copper matte from the Boleo Mining Company, owned by the Rothschilds; from there to Dunkirk, France, or Swansea, England, to discharge this copper. They are then chartered again to bring them across the Atlantic in order to get them back here to go on a triangular run again. They generally come over with chalk; occasionally with other commodities. Just now we are bringing over a cargo of tin plates in one of our steamers from Swansea."

QUESTION: How long does that trip take—the round trip?

MR. FARRELL: From seven and a half to eight months.

In view of the international commercial conditions that will arise after the war it is comforting to know that there is such a man as James A. Farrell as president of America's largest industrial organization. He is a national asset.

HENRY FORD

HENRY FORD has sprung into greater international fame or notoriety than almost any other civilian, American or European, within the last five years. More epithets and encomiums have been showered upon him than upon any other man in private life.

He has been called the most foolish, and the sagest of men.
He has been called idealist, and scheming, self-seeking egotist.
He has been called humanitarian and slave-driver.

His historic "Ford Peace Ship" to Europe to "get the boys out of the trenches by Christmas" has been lauded as the noblest incident of the European war, and condemned as the most childish, farcical idea ever born in the brain of a notoriety-seeker.

His $5-a-day-for-every-worker plan has been hailed as marking the birth of a new and better era in industrialism, and it has been ridiculed as injurious to many of the participants and contrary to all concepts of economics.

His gigantic factory has been described as a model, and characterized as the most ingenious invention ever conceived for turning men into machines, each being compelled to toil at tremendous pressure with clock-work precision, speed, and monotony.

Some have seen in his spectacular exploits nothing but adroit strokes of self-advertising; others see them wholly and solely as the earnest efforts of an altruist.

"He has affected to despise money, yet has rolled up more millions for himself in the last few years than perhaps any other man, save Rockefeller," declare one set of critics, while admirers aver that Ford has shown more contempt for money and greater anxiety to get rid of it usefully than any other modern multi-millionaire.

Many look upon Ford as the plainest and simplest and most lovable of men, while others declare he has completely lost his head and is obsessed with the idea that he is the greatest figure in America, if not in the world, and able to do the impossible.

"With all his money Henry Ford lives as plainly and modestly as when he was a working mechanic," claim some of his friends, but others counter that he now delights to hobnob in the limelight with the President of the United States, with Edison, and with other national figures and that, not content with spending money lavishly on a million-dollar palace and 5,000-acre estate in Michigan, he must needs have a pretentious house in the most fashionable resort of the idle rich in the sunny South.

Ford is a seer, a superman, able to read human nature and human conditions better than any other business man in America contends one faction; intimates have declared that he brags about never having read a page of history in his life and is in love with his colossal ignorance, boasting he needs no guidance from the past to enable *him* to solve all the world's problems of the present and of the future.

"The most loyal and lovable of friends" and "Impossible for any self-respecting man to get along with him," are two diametrically opposite comments.

The Ford car has been the butt of more jokes than any other thing or any person in modern times—and bought by more people than any other car evolved by the brains of man!

What is the truth about Henry Ford? Is he knave or saint, fool or sage, egotist or altruist? Is he one of the world's really great men, or is he merely a commonplace mechanic who hit upon a good idea and was fortunate in finding friends able and willing to enable him to develop it and exploit it?

Henry Ford, as I analyze him, was a hard-working, ambitious mechanic who overcame innumerable difficulties and discouragements in his pursuit of an idea which did credit to both his head and his heart. He was fortunate in being befriended by two or three able business men who helped to steer the infantile Ford industry along right channels. Ford was, or became, as much interested in producing the right type of men as in manufacturing the right kind of machine, but his intoxicating success went to his head, and he became obsessed with the notion that there was nothing, human or superhuman, that he and his money could not accomplish.

His motives, however, have always been unimpeachable; no ulterior, selfish thought of self-advertising or self-glorification was for a moment in his mind. He is a humanitarian through and through, an idealist, an evangelist of the doctrine of industrial reform for the benefit of the labouring classes. His boasted ignorance of past human experience and history, his innocence of economics, and his latter-day arrogance are directing him into activities for which he is unfitted. His hands and his intentions are worthy of admiration, but his experience has not fitted him to fill the rôle of Sir Oracle to which he aspires.

Before he permitted his fairy-like prosperity to warp his judgment and his perspective, Henry Ford was the most modest and lovable of men, simple in his tastes, humane in all his ideas, determined to better the lot of the working people. He is still sincere. He is still prompted by humanitarian motives. He is still unenamoured of money-making for money-making's sake, and his spectacular dashes into the limelight are not prompted by any thirst for notoriety or other selfish purpose. Unfortunately, however, he is not bearing the strain of suddenly won international fame with quite the same degree of success that he bore the strain of earlier adversity.

But were he without faults he would not be human. He has done so much good, he has shown such a humanitarian example to other big business men, his achievements have been so praiseworthy, and his motives have been so irreproachable that it seems ungracious to indulge in even impartial criticism.

The early career of Henry Ford is inspiring to the youth of America. The boy Ford was no different from other boys in the neighbourhood of his father's 300-acre farm at Greenfield, near Detroit, Michigan, where Henry was born on July 30, 1863, except that he more often played with mechanical tools than with other youngsters. It is recorded that, when a mere lad, he played truant from church one Sunday to demonstrate to a young companion who had a new watch that he could take every wheel and screw apart and reassemble them. When still a schoolboy, he built an engine, it is said, out of odds and ends. He was proud of his invention but was chagrined at the lack of enthusiasm over it.

One day, before he was sixteen, instead of going to school according to programme, he jumped on a train for Detroit, walked boldly into the works of James Flower & Company, manufacturers of steam engines, and booked a job at $2.50 a week. He succeeded in finding an old lady willing to board him for $3.50. To balance his accounts, he set out to find night work and prevailed upon a jeweller to pay him $2 a week for four hours' work every night. He worked from seven in the morning to six in the evening and then from seven to eleven o'clock at night—a 15-hour day, leaving him about six hours for sleep.

Young Ford proved a capable mechanic, so capable, indeed, that he began to find fault with the inefficient, labour-wasting methods employed. He was quite sure he could run the thing much better himself. At the end of nine months his pay was increased to $3, but a fortnight later he quit and entered the Dry Dock Engine Works, where he could learn something new—about the manufacturing of marine machinery. The chance to enlarge his knowledge and experience, he calculated, was worth incurring a reduction of fifty cents a week in pay—his new wage was only $2.50. But it didn't stay at that figure long; in a short time it was doubled.

This enabled him to give up his night work, as he didn't need the extra money —"I really had no use for spare money; I never have known what to do with surplus money for I cannot squander it on myself without hurting myself. Money is the most useless thing in the world," was and is the Ford dictum.

For a period at this stage of his life it would appear—from Rose Wilder Lane's biography of Ford, from which many of these early facts are derived—that he became "one of the boys," joining the other youths of the Dry Dock plant in their skylarking. However, he soon became recognized as a sort of leader of some of the youths, whom he inspired with towering ambitions.

Ford planned that they should organize a watch factory which, he demonstrated to their satisfaction, could turn out 2,000 watches a day at a cost of 37 cents each, to be sold for 50 cents. They would buy their raw materials in great quantities, start it going at one end of his dream factory and have the complete watches tossed out with lightning rapidity at the other end—exactly what Ford is doing now, except that it is automobiles he thus tosses out, the daily total is not 2,000 but 3,000, and the selling price of the finished article is not 50 cents but several hundred dollars.

"What about capital?" asked one prospective partner, an inhabitant of this glorious castle in the air.

Before Ford could solve that little problem he was called home to look after the farm on account of his father having been injured and his older brother having fallen ill. Alas, this cheated the young band of their promised millions and deprived the world of 50-cent Ford watches.

After two or three years on the farm he married a neighbouring farmer's daughter, Clara J. Bryant, in 1888, and they settled comfortably on forty acres of the Ford farm, having built a snug house of their own.

Henry now had leisure of an evening for the study of things mechanical, and while reading a technical magazine he came upon an article describing a novel horseless carriage which a Frenchman had invented. The idea set his imagination on fire and off he went to Detroit one day for materials to start the building of an engine which would outdo the Frenchman's. Detroit had recently acquired a fire engine driven by steam and, as good luck would have it, it went roaring down the street at the rate of fifteen miles an hour while Ford was returning to the station. The engine carried a tremendous water boiler—a ponderous, heavy, awkward load whose weight consumed a serious part of the propulsion power. Ford was immediately struck with the waste entailed by this undue weight and bulk and set his mind in motion to think up something that could do away with it.

After much thought, he started to utilize gasoline as the motive power. A full knowledge of electricity, however, would be necessary before attempting to put his theories into practice. And he had only a book acquaintance with this mysterious current.

To the amazement of the neighbourhood, to the grief of his family, and against the entreaties of his wife, he announced that he was going to Detroit to get a job. The good folk of Greenfield thought poor "Hen" was crazy.

The moment he and his wife had found a boarding-house in Detroit, Ford made for the Edison Electric Light & Power Company. Fortune favoured him. An engine in a sub-station had rebelled and the engineer in charge could not manage it. Did Ford think he could tame the balky engine? He guessed he would like to have a try at it. Almost in a twinkling he had that engine running smoothly and musically. He was there and then engaged as night engineer of the station at $45 per month. In six months he was brought to headquarters as manager of the mechanical department at $150 per month.

Ford found that much of the trouble the plant had been experiencing was due to the indifferent service rendered by the men, who had to work twelve hours a day. It was characteristic that he introduced an 8-hour day for all the men—except himself; he continued to work twelve, at least.

His new wealth emboldened him to seek a home of his own. By working every night, often by the aid of a lantern held by Mrs. Ford, the mechanic built a modest home and a capacious shed for a workshop. Then he settled down to construct his gasoline-driven carriage.

In that shed the unknown mechanic was making history. He suffered the fate common to inventors and pioneers. As he toiled there far into every night, renouncing all social diversions, his mind intent upon the one consuming idea of evolving an engine that would revolutionize transportation, the neighbours, seeing the light straggling through the cracks in the dilapidated building at all hours of the night, began to regard him as a crank. When he passed on his way home from work, neighbours would look at one another significantly and tap their foreheads. An inoffensive creature, too bad he had gone crazy.

Months passed. Then one night, long after midnight, amid a downpour of rain, Henry Ford chug-chugged out of the shed and down Edison Avenue, Mrs. Ford pacing him on the sidewalk. He crawled along for several blocks until he suddenly realized he did not know how he could turn his machine homeward. He stopped, got out, pulled and tugged until he had turned it around and then drove triumphantly back to the shed. The Ford car was a thing of reality—even though it was only a wheezy one-cylinder engine mounted on a buggy frame and four bicycle wheels refitted with strong tires.

The local newspapers mentioned the mechanic's wonderful invention, but the little stir it caused soon died down. The thing was crude, extremely crude. Ford well realized he must spend much time in devising improvements before he could think of giving up his position and devoting himself to making horseless carriages. Mrs. Ford having returned for a temporary stay with her mother, Henry was obliged to do his own housekeeping, and often of a night, after working on his engine for hours, he would jump on board and ride down to have a sandwich and a cup of coffee from "Coffee Jim," who kept an all-night lunch wagon in the city. The two became close friends.

For eight more years—yes, *eight* long years—Henry Ford kept working twelve hours a day to earn his living and the living of his wife and little son, and regularly spent half the night evolving improvements on his car. By this time automobiles were beginning to come into vogue. They were expensive, luxurious things, appealing only to the rich. Ford's idea was to make a car that the man of ordinary income could buy and use. Finally he devised a two-cylinder engine which worked splendidly, built a real car, rode it about the streets of Detroit to advertise it, and then tried to raise capital to become an automobile builder. But no capitalist would risk backing the venture.

Ford did not lose courage. Even then he had adopted as a motto, "Anything founded on the idea of the greatest good for the greatest number will win in the end." He knew he would win.

"Coffee Jim" came to his rescue. He financed Ford, enabling him to give up his job at the Edison plant and to build a car to compete at the automobile races at Grosse Point. Ford had his little two-cylinder racer ready on time, but the crowds laughed when he pulled out to compete with the redoubtable, unbeaten Alexander Winton. Ford, the unknown, was the only man who dared to enter against the famous champion in the all-comers' race.

But the jeers soon turned to cheers as the little car shot around and around the track—and won.

At one bound Ford had become the most famous automobile racer in America. Everybody crowded around wanting to know who had built this wonder-working car. Ford modestly admitted he was its maker.

The limelight was immediately turned on Ford and his car and his little workshop. Capital was now offered, but only on condition that the capitalists were given control. They wanted to build motor palaces costing thousands of dollars. Ford's dream was to establish an automobile factory exactly along the lines of the watch factory of his boyhood day-dreams. So no Ford automobile factory sprang into being just then.

HENRY FORD

However, several men of modest means became interested in Ford and his plans, and enough capital was furnished to build a car to startle the world at the next race. Ford constructed a four-cylinder monster that developed eighty horsepower, Barney Oldfield was induced to drive it, and in a three-mile race he defeated his nearest competitor by half a mile! This feat, which rang around the world, brought the necessary capital to form a company. Ford became vice-president, general manager, and everything else, at a salary of $150 a month. At last Ford had visions of making his dream a reality. But again, for similar reasons, he was doomed to disappointment. His new backers wished to turn out regal chariots to sell at a profit of two or three hundred per cent. Ford would not deviate from his plan to make cars within reach of persons of small earnings. The clash left Ford, then over thirty years old, with a wife and child to support, and with neither capital nor job.

James Couzens and one or two others stuck to Ford, and enough money was scraped together to rent a large shed, hire a couple of workmen, and buy enough material to start making a few low-priced cars. The company was nominally capitalized at $100,000, but only $15,000 was actually paid in. Ford worked literally day and night. His two mechanics also cheerfully worked overtime. Customers came to the shed unsolicited and planked down deposits on cars not yet made. Before long Ford was employing forty men and was ordering material by the car load. He got long enough credit to enable him to turn the material into finished cars and collect his money. Every cent he could save was put into the business and no fancy salaries were paid, yet it was often a case of nip and tuck to meet bills. His sales soon were at the rate of 1,000 cars a year. The price was $900.

Winter was coming on with threatened dearth of orders. Then Ford conceived the idea of breaking the world's speed record with a new four-cylinder car. On the frozen Lake Sinclair Ford himself drove his new car a mile in 39 1-5 seconds, lowering the world's record by the astonishing margin of seven seconds. That would bring orders aplenty for the coming year.

Alas, when Ford returned to the shop after his amazing performance he was informed, the story runs, that there wasn't a dollar in the till to pay the men's wages! And, to make matters worse, it was just on the eve of Christmas. When his workmen trooped into the office for their pay, Ford made a clean breast of conditions. If they would stand by him everything would be all right, but if they deserted, the jig was up. To a man the workers pledged their loyal support, and the way cars were turned out during the following days was eye-opening.

This proved the turning point in Henry Ford's career. Success came fast.

In January, 1914, the world was startled by Henry Ford's announcement that he would pay all his unskilled workmen a minimum of $5 a day and reduce their working hours from ten to eight. The news caused such an invasion of Detroit that the police were powerless to handle the thousands of clamourers for employment, and finally the fire department had to turn out in force and charge the mob with volleys of water from their most powerful hose, a species of disorganization and excitement not repeatable, as no man is now engaged who has not lived for six months in Detroit.

Recipients of the $5 a day—and that included the most illiterate men of the fifty-five nationalities employed in the works—had to comply with certain conditions calculated to induce, or compel them to lead a mode of life approved by Ford. This mild form of coercion incited resentment among numbers of the workmen and it was soon found necessary to modify the conditions. By establishing schools for teaching English, by instituting an extensive welfare department, by providing hospitals, gymnasiums and the like, and encouraging the labourers to use their new-found wealth wisely, astounding results were obtained, for both Ford and the men.

Thus in February, 1914, under the new plan, less than 16,000 men, working only eight hours a day, made 26,000 cars against only 16,000 cars made by fully 16,000 men in the previous February working ten hours a day, an increase of 10,000 cars. The plan paid with a vengeance!

Five months after the profit-sharing scheme, as it was called, went into effect, the average bank account of the beneficiaries had increased almost threefold, the value of homes owned by them increased almost 90 per cent., the value of lots bought on contract increased 135 per cent., life insurance among the men increased nearly 90 per cent. and the number of employees living under unsatisfactory conditions was reduced from 23 per cent. to only $1\frac{1}{2}$ per cent. The profit-sharers now include several hundred ex-convicts, a class in which Ford takes intense interest. "The way to mend a bad world," says Ford, "is to create a better world. The way to create a right one is to give people enough to live on so that they are not discouraged and want to go into destruction"—meaning war, revolution, and the like.

Having satisfied his workers, Ford next announced that he would distribute $10,000,000 or more of his year's profits among his customers, provided that a certain output was reached. And, of course, it was reached; the actual amount distributed was approximately $15,000,000.

One Ford motto is: "To make money, make quantity." Here

are figures from the report of the Ford Motor Company for the fiscal year ended July 31, 1916:

Profit for the year	$59,994,118
Gross business done	206,867,347
Number of cars made	508,000
Total employees, all plants	49,870
Employees getting $5 a day or more	36,870
Cash on hand	52,550,771

Ford's own share of the 1916 profits was computed at $35,000,000. No wonder Ford says: "I don't have to worry about the banks, they have to worry about me. They have to sit up nights scraping together enough to pay me my interest."

His output of cars is now approaching the 1,000,000-a-year mark, or over 3,000 every week day—the plant is closed on Sundays.

The Ford plant at Detroit with its 35,000 men and its Aladdin-like machinery is now regarded as one of the greatest industrial wonders of modern times and is visited by as many as 5,000 sightseers a day.

Ford now has large branch factories in Canada and England, is building one in Ireland, and is planning the erection of huge factories at Chicago, Kansas City, and in New Jersey.

He is arranging to bring his own ore from his own mines, smelt it in his own furnaces, mould it in his own plants, forge it in his own works and, in short, become as far as possible self-sufficient.

His greatest unrealized business ambition is to supply the farmers of the world with very low-priced tractors. This Thor's task will devolve mainly upon Ford's only child, Edsel Ford, who is following worthily in his father's footsteps.

"I would like," Ford declares, "to put the farmers in possession of the land, to destroy monopoly and leave the producers free to develop. I would like to liberate the farmer from his debt. And we can do it, too. In the past a man couldn't get enough variety of experience on the farm; but now with the telephone, the phonograph, the moving pictures, the automobile—so that he can get away to the big cities when he wants to—the farmer can live in the country and have all the experience in the world. The high cost of clothing and implements and transportation hampers the farmer, and the Trusts cheat him, and the banks soak him an awful price for his money. I want to do away with all those things."

Not long ago Mr. Ford—although he declares "I don't believe in boundaries; I think nations are silly and flags are silly too"—told President Wilson that he could arrange to turn out 1,000 one-man submarines a day, the tiny craft to sneak up to the enemy ship, stick what he called a "pill" into its vitals and submerge before the pill exploded, causing the ship to sink, a job, however, less to his liking than housing and nurturing thousands of birds on his novel farm. The one-man submarine has not yet taken possession of the ocean.

Here are two of Ford's recent notable utterances:

"Money doesn't do me any good. I can't spend it on myself. Money has no value, anyway. It is merely a transmitter, like electricity. I try to keep it moving as fast as I can, for the best interests of everybody concerned. A man can't afford to look out for himself at the expense of any one else, because anything that hurts the other man is bound to hurt you in the end, the same way."

"I am going to keep the American flag flying on my plant until the war is over and then I am going to pull it down for good; I am going to hoist in its place the Flag of All Nations which is being designed in my office right now."

It is not yet time to attempt to fix Henry Ford's place in history.

JAMES B. FORGAN

"I WISH my career were beginning instead of drawing to a close."

A sigh of regret accompanied these words, by James B. Forgan, the great national banker of Chicago.

I had asked Mr. Forgan whether the opportunities for young men were as great to-day in the banking field as when he won his spurs.

"There are certainly at present," he declared, "greater opportunities than ever before and more of them for young men entering the banking business. Banking in this country is now in an evolutionary stage. The deplorable European war has created the opportunities, and the Federal Reserve system—not yet fully understood or appreciated—affords us the means of taking advantage of them.

"We are just at the beginning of an era of banking development in this country through which our banking system will take its place among and rank with the great banking systems of Europe in national and international trade and finance. The prestige and power of these older systems for years to come will be seriously weakened and 'their extremity will be our opportunity.' There are untold opportunities ahead for competent bankers ready to take advantage of them."

Fearlessness and a superlative sense of honour are outstanding characteristics of James B. Forgan. Let me recite an illustrative incident.

A friend was in Mr. Forgan's office one day when a visitor came in and engaged him in conversation at the far side of the office.

The two talked together quietly for some time, but the banker then began to exhibit symptoms of annoyance. Presently Mr. Forgan jumped up and angrily ordered him out of the office.

"Excuse me for having acted this way," said Mr. Forgan, returning to his friend, "but what do you think that fellow put up to me? He tried to bribe me to make him a loan with the bank's money."

Very early James B. (the "B." is for Berwick) Forgan learned the value of keeping his eye on the ball whether playing the game of life or of golf. His father was a golf-ball and golf-club maker at St. Andrews, that ancient seat of learning and of "the royal game" and one of Auld Scotia's most historic, picturesque, and revered towns, once the see of Scotland's patron saint, where stood for centuries a cathedral "of which the very ruins are stupendous." He learned how to swing a club before he aspired to become a cashier.

Unlike the majority of men who have made an impress upon American history, young Forgan started without the handicap of poverty or a poor education. So expert was his father that he built up a business which employed quite a number of men and yielded him a very considerable fortune, the Forgan product having been in demand the world over. They were godly people, Mr. Forgan's parents, and had the satisfaction of seeing two of their sons become ministers, while the only daughter married a member of the cloth. James B. and David R. became bankers, while the other son succeeded to the father's business. Incidentally, the business has been shot through and through by the war, the head of it, Mr. Forgan's nephew, having gone to the front as an officer soon after hostilities began, while some thirty of the workmen also entered the service, leaving only old or infirm workers.

From Madras College, St. Andrews, James B. went to Forres Academy, where his uncle was rector for half a century and head of the boys' private boarding school connected with it. On graduating he was given the choice of entering the famous St. Andrews University or going into business. A local lawyer had discerned the makings of a legal luminary in the youth and induced him to enter his office. It was young Forgan's intention to attend the necessary classes in the university and study law at the same time, but his employer died and another lawyer, who was local agent of the Royal Bank of Scotland, got hold of him. So James B. Forgan became a banker's apprentice.

The ambition of most Scottish youths is to go farther afield and see the wider world. On finishing his three years' training, Forgan got a job with the Bank of British North America, in London, as a stepping-stone to service across the Atlantic, the goal of so many ambitious Scotsmen. In 1872, when twenty years of age—he was born in 1852—he was sent to Montreal, then to New York, and next to Halifax.

The Bank of Nova Scotia spotted the clean-cut young giant, noted his ability, and engaged him as paying teller. He worked conscientiously, studied banking from every angle, and won the confidence of his superiors.

Then he had what he calls "a stroke of luck."

The manager of the branch at Yarmouth had diphtheria in his family and was quarantined. Someone had to be sent to take charge without delay. Teller Forgan was the bank's choice.

"When can you go?" asked the general manager, Thomas Fyshe.

"Right now," Forgan replied.

"I didn't—and don't—believe in procrastinating when Opportunity

JAMES B. FORGAN

knocks at the door," Mr. Forgan has since said; "I hurriedly packed my bag and caught the first train out.

"I believe there is some mysterious influence outside of ourselves which gives us opportunity. If I had not proved efficient, the opportunity would not have come to me—it would have passed to someone ready to grab it. So I believe in the destiny that shapes our ends—and in keeping your powder dry!"

When at Yarmouth he was asked to make a thorough inspection of the bank. He did, and his report was as exhaustive and lucid as research and care could make it. The finished document stamped him as a master banker in the eyes of the directors. They had him inspect other branches.

His Scottish thoroughness, plus brains, won him that coveted prize in the life of every aspiring bank clerk, appointment to an official position. He was made manager of the bank's Liverpool, Nova Scotia, branch. Other promotion followed. When expansion necessitated the election of a regular Inspector of Branches, young Forgan —he was then only thirty—was the man chosen for this responsible work. The compilation of that first report was still bearing fruit.

The United States was virgin territory, the Bank of Nova Scotia never having ventured to invade it. But the directors were progressive. They were anxious to conquer new fields. Why not enter the heart of the States?

Hadn't they a level-headed, forceful young officer who had proved himself equal to any task? Let him blazon the trail.

At thirty-three James B. Forgan set out to establish a branch at Minneapolis. He knew business and how to handle business men. He had given special study to credits, having learned in the school of experience that one of the easiest ways not to make money is to make losses. His early steeping in the theory of banking had been supplemented by practice in many places and under various conditions. Already his name and fame were not unknown in financial circles.

His work in Minneapolis quickly told. Beginning modestly, the business grew. And James B. Forgan was recognized as bigger than his position. Within three years the important Northwestern National Bank of Minneapolis offered him its cashiership. Here also he applied himself to building up his institution. His previous experience enabled him to multiply the bank's connections and ramifications. The Northwestern became one of the strongest institutions in its section and Forgan had carved for himself a niche among America's leading bank executives.

Lyman J. Gage took note of the young banker's progress and in 1892 took Mr. Forgan into the First National of Chicago as first vice-president. A spell of ill-health delayed his acceptance of the presidency when Mr. Gage became Secretary of the Treasury, but on his recovery (in 1900) he stepped into the highest banking position in Chicago.

And this is what happened in fifteen years.

BANK'S GROWTH UNDER JAMES B. FORGAN'S PRESIDENCY

ASSETS	JANUARY 9, 1900	JANUARY 31, 1915*
Loans and Discounts	$27,781,462	$134,762,853
United States Bonds	879,160	3,824,000
Other Bonds and Securities	3,391,913	38,728,312
Bank Building	500,000	1,250,000
Cash and Due from Banks	16,827,327	79,847,616
	$49,379,862	$258,412,781

LIABILITIES		
Capital Stock Paid in	$ 3,000,000	$ 10,000,000
Surplus Fund	2,000,000	20,000,000
Other Undivided Profits	531,951	2,713,680
Special Deposit of United States Bonds	....	3,340,000
Circulating Notes	450,000	924,000
Dividends Unpaid	....	550,000
Reserved for Taxes	50,319	575,264
Foreign Bills Rediscounted	83,214	393,798
Deposits	43,264,378	219,916,039
	$49,379,862	$258,412,781

On January 1, 1916, Mr. Forgan was made chairman of the board, but he is still active in the business.

Those impressive figures, though almost unmatched in American banking annals, do not tell the whole story of Mr. Forgan's achievements.

Mr. Forgan early realized the value of inspiring and stirring to enthusiasm those working with him, and, to this end, he established in 1903 a generous pension fund for employees. He is as solicitous for the welfare and advancement of the youngest office-boy who comes under his wing as for the officers. Told that he used to have a long, fatherly talk with every new boy entering the Minneapolis bank, impressing upon him that the shaping of his career would begin from that moment, and advising him how to comport himself to win promotion, I asked Mr. Forgan about this.

"Yes," he replied. "I took a great deal of pride in the selection of

---

*Includes First Trust and Savings Bank, organized by Mr. Forgan in 1903 and owned by the stockholders of The First National Bank of Chicago.

young men entering the bank. I became friendly with the principal of the high school, and asked him to suggest likely young men. In this way we built up an exceptionally fine force, the result of which is that the young men then engaged are now at the head of the institution.

"I used to take the boys into my office and impress upon them that their ambition should be to become bankers, not mere machines or bookkeepers; that they should keep their eyes open to everything that was going on, and endeavour to understand what the figures they made on the books actually represented. I also pointed out to them that they should be observers of men, and that they could form opinions of the business methods of the bank's customers and of the other business men on whom they had drafts to collect on their rounds as messengers. By exercising intelligence they could see things and gather information and impressions which might be of value to the bank's officers."

Both Chicago and the nation's bankers have honoured James B. Forgan. He has been chairman of the Chicago Clearing House Committee since 1901; was elected not only a director of the Federal Reserve Bank of Chicago, but president of the Federal Advisory Council, a signal national tribute by fellow bankers to his outstanding ability. He is chairman of the Security Bank and the Second Security Bank, a director in various local enterprises and of the Equitable Life Assurance Society.

Oftener than once Mr. Forgan has been called to New York to aid in cracking banking nuts, particularly in times of crisis and when the reorganization of our currency system was under way. "The best practical banker in America," he has been called by more than one high authority.

I recall that at the last annual conference of the American Bankers' Association I attended, no other man's hand was quite so continuously being shaken by delegates during the intervals between the formal proceedings. His was a commanding, distinguished figure, dignified, yet not forbidding, his face often wreathed in smiles as he received a constant stream of friends from all parts of the country.

He is a man of broad sympathy. Chicago recognizes in him one of her foremost citizens, a great moral force, a leader and director of charitable movements, a (Presbyterian) hospital trustee, a patron of many philanthropies.

His advice to young men—he has three sons of his own—is to equip themselves for higher and higher positions—and save money! Being a Scot, he absorbed the spirit of thrift with his porridge and his Shorter Catechism.

"Extravagance," he declares, "is America's national sin. Most young people make no effort to save; few even of older years save systematically. My method was to start the new year by fixing the sum I would save during the year. If I decided to buy a $1,000 bond I would pay perhaps $100 in cash, borrow the balance from the bank, and repay $75 every month. That $75 was the first thing I paid on receiving my salary. The remainder had to last the whole month. December found me sole owner of the bond. I never speculated—I can't read the Stock Exchange tape intelligently even now."

If the United States is to seize the financial and commercial opportunities now offering, the example of James B. Forgan must be followed widely, for bankers cannot create capital. You and I and our fellow-citizens have to attend to that.

HENRY C. FRICK

ONE day a young man walked into the office of Prof. O. S. Fowler, prominent as a phrenologist, in Pittsburgh. The bumps discovered by the Professor caused him to rub his eyes. His "reading," dictated to his stenographer, contained such sentences as these:

"Your brain is large. You have more force, energy, vim, and get-out-of-my-way drive, push, courage, pluck, than one man out of thousands. Grapple with difficulties with both hands and dash through hard and easy. Actually enjoy life's struggles. Love antagonism as you love food. Do best when pushed most. Are actuated by the highest sense of character. Become terribly enraged if your character is aspersed. Love of making money is strong."

That was written on April 10, 1879.

To-day the man, no longer young, lives in one of the most costly and most artistic palaces on Fifth Avenue, New York, amid one of the world's finest private collections of paintings, panels, statuary, pottery, etc. He is the largest owner of land and buildings in Pittsburgh, including an open space of some 250 acres.

But neither the Fifth Avenue palace with its priceless treasures of art nor the great open park in Pittsburgh has been acquired to indulge any luxurious personal taste. Both are to be left to the public with endowments of millions, the one as an art gallery, the other as a public park and children's playground.

The bumps did not lie. Their possessor, starting without enough money to keep himself decently clad, was employing thousands of men and was worth millions of dollars in his early thirties and later became, not only the foremost business leader in Pittsburgh, but one of the very ablest industrial giants America has ever produced. Very abundantly, too, did he justify the phrenological indications of courage, combativeness, and stick-to-itiveness. The world was later to resound with an exhibition of his fearlessness, his bravery, his relentlessness.

The young man of the extraordinary bumps was Henry Clay Frick.

Mr. Frick's rightful place in the steel history of the United States is imperfectly understood, largely because he had neither faculty nor inclination for the bringing of himself and his achievements to public notice. He preferred to work and to let his one-time partner, Andrew

Carnegie, do the talking. Mr. Frick is popularly known merely as "The Coke King." Yet his achievements in the coke field were exceeded by what he accomplished in the steel industry. Practical steel men declare that Frick did more to make the Carnegie Steel Company than Carnegie himself did; he found it an unorganized, unsystematized, haphazard affair earning less than $2,000,000 a year, and in twelve years he evolved a huge, self-contained, integrated, coherent, symmetrical organization earning $40,000,000. Nor is it any secret in the iron trade that H. C. Frick was urgently called in by the Morgan-Rockefeller interests to save the United States Steel Corporation from the rocks to which it once seemed headed—indeed, Carnegie at one time was quite sure the whole billion-dollar Steel Trust would fall into his hands through default in the payment of the interest on the Steel bonds he held.

And here let me relate a little bit of unrecorded history.

Although Mr. Frick had been named one of the Steel Corporation directors on its formation, he had not attended one of its meetings. Along with the Mellon and Donner interests of Pittsburgh, he had formed the Union Steel Company, a wire enterprise, as a counterstroke to John W. Gates's action in invading the coke field. For the purpose of inducing Mr. Frick to become active in the direction of the Steel Corporation, the latter purchased the Union Steel Works, and Mr. Frick at once threw himself enthusiastically into the task of aiding in steering the great organization through its troubles.

The first thing he did was to insist upon the stopping of the dividend then being paid on the common stock. Even this, however, threatened to be insufficient to avert financial disaster.

Mr. Frick, bent upon reducing the preferred dividend, went to Mr. Morgan to convince him of the absolute necessity of this drastic step. The discussion was nearing a climax on board Mr. Morgan's yacht, the *Corsair*, as she steamed toward lower New York.

Rising from the breakfast table and going on deck with Mr. Frick, Mr. Morgan, with tears in his eyes, pointed to the financial district, and with a sweep of his hand, murmured brokenly: "If you reduce the dividends on that preferred stock I could not face going downtown to-morrow."

Mr. Frick, realizing how keenly Mr. Morgan felt, assured him that not another word should be said on the subject. And as it happened, Mr. Morgan was right and Mr. Frick wrong, for good times set in almost immediately and the billion-dollar steel craft sailed safely away from the rocks.

From that day to this, Henry C. Frick has been one of the most active and influential directors of the Steel Corporation, Judge Gary finding in him one of his ablest of associates and counsellors. Mr.

Frick was one of the first to recognize the calibre of James A. Farrell, who has made so successful a record as president of the Steel Corporation during the last seven years.

To the masses Mr. Frick is known chiefly as the man who refused to compromise the bloody Homestead strike even after he had been grievously shot and stabbed by an anarchist bent on assassinating him. The only other occasion when Mr. Frick figured prominently in the newspapers was when he brought suit against Andrew Carnegie to prevent him from seizing Frick's interest in the Carnegie Steel Company on terms which Mr. Frick contended were confiscatory and unfair in the last degree, a contention which led to a readjustment of the deal very much more in favour of Mr. Frick. The career of Mr. Frick, however, is worth recording, for it is typically American. It illustrates with unusual clarity what an admixture of hard work and brains can accomplish without financial or family favours. It drives home the old, old lesson that there is nothing mysterious, nothing occult, nothing inexplicable about the attainment of success, for, though the road to the summit is steep, rough, and barrier-strewn, yet incessant effort, unflinching courage, concentration of purpose and intelligent foresight can climb the steepest hills and overcome the greatest of obstacles.

Mr. Frick expressed it very simply, not to say humbly, when I asked him to explain how and why he had succeeded.

"The secret of my success?" he repeated. "There is no secret about success. Success simply calls for hard work, devotion to your business at all times, day and night. I was very poor and my education was limited, but I worked very hard and always sought opportunities.

"To win in the battle of life a man needs, in addition to whatever ability he possesses, courage, tenacity, and deliberation. He must learn never to lose his head.

"But, above all, hard work is the thing. For six years—from 1889 to 1895—when I first took hold of the Carnegie Steel business, I did not have a day's vacation. I reached the office every morning between seven and eight and did not leave until six. My example had an influence upon the others. Carnegie often remarked to me! 'You *do* get work out of these fellows:' They worked because they saw that I, then the chairman of the company, worked."

This habit of working hard was contracted very early by Henry Clay Frick—at first under the sharp-pointed spur of necessity. His mother had incurred the ire of her father, Abraham Overholt, the richest man in western Pennsylvania, for marrying an impecunious young farmer of Swiss descent, John W. Frick, when a money-match could doubtless have been arranged. It was at West Overton, Pa., that Henry Clay Frick was born, on December 19, 1849. On his parents' small farm, near by, the children had to help to the limit of their strength. Before he was eight, little Henry had learned how to drop corn, help in the harvest field, tend cattle, and perform a hundred varieties of chores. So badly were his services needed in the earning of the family living that he was allowed to go to school only in the winter months.

"I recall that, by running barefooted most of the year, I was able to make a pair of boots last two winters," Mr. Frick was not too proud to relate in discussing his boyhood days. When fourteen he left school, where he had not particularly distinguished himself except by the ease with which he could prepare his lessons and his rapidity in solving problems in arithmetic.

His first job was in a general country store in Mt. Pleasant, partly owned by an uncle, with whom Henry took up his abode. The experience he gathered in weighing sugar, measuring calico, handling butter and eggs, in getting up early to sweep out the store and to remove the tobacco and other traces left by the coterie of village worthies who used to sit around the stove smoking, chewing, and yarning until eight or nine o'clock every night—this experience Mr. Frick later came to regard as "an excellent education."

Even thus early his visions went beyond the narrow sphere of a village grocery. His eyes and his dreams turned toward Pittsburgh, and before he was seventeen he boldly cut the Gordian knot and set off to the big city, some fifty miles distant. After considerable tramping of streets he found an opening in an Allegheny store which sold trimmings and other folderols for women. His pay was six dollars a week, barely enough to keep body and soul together. From a relative he procured a loan of $50 and with part of this money he bought his first suit of clothes fit for church-going.

He went to the Third Presbyterian Church, built by William Thaw and Asa P. Childs, who was later to become Mr. Frick's father-in-law. Many years afterward the trimming-store clerk bought this church property and supplied several million dollars to erect on the site the William Penn Hotel, equal to anything New York can boast.

From selling lace, under the direction of a woman head of the department, young Frick gladly accepted an offer from a Pittsburgh store, at eight dollars a week. Here he contracted intermittent fever and had to go home—not, however, before he had greatly impressed the storekeeper, who begged him to return, at a substantial increase in pay.

Very wisely, as it turned out, the young man seized an opportunity to become bookkeeper and man-of-all-work in Grandfather Overholt's flour mill and distillery at Broad Ford, Pa., in the very heart of the

Connellsville coal region—it had not then become a coke centre. He not only kept the accounts, but weighed grain, sold flour, measured lumber, and made himself generally useful. What his salary was to be he did not know; when, two or three months later, he was informed he would receive $1,000 a year he could scarcely believe his ears.

From this establishment, built on the river bank, could be seen Connellsville coal outcropping. The $1,000 a year did not long satisfy young Frick's ambitions. When there arrived from the West, with money in his pockets, a man who had been born on a farm within sight of the Overholt office window, and who suggested that money might be made by buying land and starting the infant industry of cokemaking, Frick was ready to respond—more ready in mind than in pocket. However, Joseph Rist, the newcomer, took a fancy to the young bookkeeper, who was able to borrow enough to pay his share of the first instalment on the land bought. Rist contributed three-fifths and Frick and his cousin, Abraham O. Tintsman, who was managing the flour mill and distillery, one-fifth each. Upon Frick's shoulders, however, devolved the whole responsibility for the management of the enterprise and it was accordingly named Frick & Company.

One of his first duties was to journey to Pittsburgh and persuade Judge Mellon, the city's greatest banker, to lend them $10,000 for six months. Frick got the money—paying interest at the rate of 10 per cent. per annum. A beginning was made with 50 coke ovens. Thus humbly was inaugurated the career of the man who was to become the owner of virtually the whole Connellsville coke region and to supply coke every year to load a train long enough to circle the globe. But the climb from the bottom to the top, from 50 ovens to 12,000 was not achieved at one or two bounds, nor without difficulties grave enough to discourage a less resolute, less resourceful, less dauntless aspirant.

From 50 ovens Frick & Company expanded to 100 ovens, a second loan of $10,000 having been successfully negotiated by the bookkeeper financier—yes, he still continued keeping books, handling flour, and measuring timber. A second farm was purchased and the erection of an additional 100 ovens was begun.

Then, like a thunderbolt, came the 1873 panic. The whole country was littered with financial wrecks. Both Frick's partners, Rist and Tintsman, went under with the rest. But Frick, young and inexperienced though he was, and with less capital than debts, resolved that he would stand up against the hurricane and battle it out. He staggered Pittsburgh's principal banker by the amount he wanted to borrow!

And here let me relate an incident conveying a moral to every ambitious young man who reads this.

Judge Mellon sent a man (an uncle of W. E. Corey) to Broad Ford to investigate the character and calibre of this daring financial Napoleon. Instead of finding H. C. Frick to be one of the leading citizens of the place, living in sumptuous style and owning a wealth of property, the investigator discovered him to be merely a youth of twenty-four, employed as a bookkeeper and living, not in a mansion, but in two small rooms over a drug store. Inquiry elicited that the young man was held in the highest regard, that his industry and ability were the common talk of the place; and that his handling of the new coke concern had proved both able and successful. Judge Mellon, instead of feeling disappointed over the humble circumstances of the would-be borrower, decided that a young man of such enterprise and talent and courage, with horse-sense enough to live on a few dollars a week in order to increase his capital, deserved to be helped. So the loan was granted.

Not only did Frick buy out his two partners, but he gathered in other properties at bankruptcy figures. Frick's readiness to buy or lease other coal lands and coke properties—the whole coke industry amounted to only a few hundred ovens—caused the townspeople to look upon him as a lunatic. Wasn't coke bringing only 90 cents a ton, which was less than the cost of production? What profit could there be in such a business? To wade in deeper was sheer madness.

Frick said little but worked a lot. "It was an awful time," to use his own words. He borrowed and borrowed, but, though often kept awake at nights wondering how he could pull through, never once did a note bearing the signature "H. C. Frick" go to protest.

One deal which he brought off during this period helped him greatly. With others he had built a 10-mile railroad through the coke regions, from Broad Ford to Mt. Pleasant, and had leased it to the Baltimore & Ohio. Like almost everything else, it was in trouble. Frick hurried and scurried around securing options from other stockholders and succeeded in selling the little line to the Baltimore & Ohio at a figure which yielded the young negotiator nearly $50,000 profit—his first big killing.

The return of financial calm found Frick the sole owner of Frick & Company. Output rose above 50 tons a day and the price went from ninety cents to above two dollars; later (1879-80), when the boom set in, coke soared to above five dollars a ton, and every day the sun rose Frick sold over $30,000 worth of the fuel and pocketed a net profit of over $20,000.

Meanwhile Mr. Frick had, of course, given up his bookkeeper's job. At first he sold his coke through dealers, but during the dark days of the early seventies he opened a little office in Pittsburgh and attended to the selling end himself. He got out of bed every morning by six o'clock, set things in motion at Broad Ford, visited the coke ovens and, most mornings, took a train for Pittsburgh at seven, arrived about ten, worked until three, returned home about six and cleaned up whatever needed his attention.

As business grew he was obliged to employ managers for the coke plants and to go to Pittsburgh to live, the better to attend to the selling of the coke and the financing of the business. Every evening, after dinner, he went to the post office for his mail, proceeded to his office, and never left until he had attended to every communication. He worked more than a round of the clock daily.

Before he was thirty, Mr. Frick was a millionaire. In 1880, when thirty-one, he had his affairs so organized that he felt able to enjoy a long tour in Europe, in company with three other young Americans. Happening to be at Killarney Castle on the Fourth of July, they hoisted on its flagpole the Stars and Stripes, almost sending the distracted caretaker out of her wits—until a substantial tip mollified her. Mr. Frick had contrived somehow to find time to study and to read fairly extensively and was able to "do" Europe intelligently. The art galleries of Paris especially impressed him and sowed in him seed which was to bear rich fruit for the American people. Shortly after returning home he met Miss Adelaide Howard Childs, of Pittsburgh, became engaged in the summer, and married her in December of the same year, 1881. Notwithstanding that he was then wealthy, Mr. Frick, with the cordial approval of his bride, did not set up an ostentatious style of living. For eighteen months they lived in one room at the Monongahela House and the $25,000 home which at the end of that time they purchased in the East End, Pittsburgh, has remained, with some additions, their Pittsburgh home ever since.

Andrew Carnegie and his partners were beginning to branch out in the steel industry at this time and needed coke badly. In 1882 Frick sold them a half interest in his company. It then owned over 1,000 ovens and more than 3,000 acres of coal land.

It was reorganized with $2,000,000 capital and in the following year the amount was increased to $3,000,000 to cope with the rapidly expanding organization which Frick was developing. By then everybody recognized what Frick had known for years, namely, that the coke manufactured from Connellsville coal was superior to anything else in the country.

Six years later (1889) the H. C. Frick Coke Company owned and controlled 35,000 acres of coal land, almost two-thirds of the 15,000 ovens in the Connellsville region, three water plants with a pumping capacity of 5,000,000 gallons daily, several short railroads, and 1,200 coke cars. The number of men then in the employ of the "H. C. F. Co." was 11,000. The monthly output was steadily approaching 1,000,000 tons, a figure actually exceeded a few years later.

The silent, plodding, far-seeing Frick was a more important, though less advertised, factor in the industrial world than Carnegie. The steel-maker made several unsuccessful attempts to induce the young genius to become a partner in the Carnegie steel enterprise. One afternoon, in 1889, however, when sitting in his private office, Mr. Frick was told that Mr. Carnegie and all his partners were in the outer office anxious to see him. They offered the Coke King a substantial interest in Carnegie Brothers & Company, Ltd., if he would accept the chairmanship. Mr. Frick agreed. He also became a director in Carnegie, Phipps & Company and resumed the presidency of the H. C. Frick Coke Company which he had resigned some time previously owing to differences with Carnegie.

Frick was astounded to find, on assuming the management, how utterly unorganized and chaotic the Carnegie affairs were. He immediately rolled up his sleeves, addressed himself to the task of evolving system out of disorder, and for six years did not take a single day's rest. Astounded to learn that there were no regular meetings of directors or executives, Frick instituted weekly board meetings at which, to save time, lunch was served. Managers were brought to these meetings to submit statements and answer questions, and presently similar meetings were held by the executives at each plant. The discouragement which reigned before Frick was called in to reinvigorate the concern was quickly transformed into enthusiasm. Everybody entered into the spirit of the thing, stimulated by the example of the chairman, who worked hardest of all. He added immensely to his reputation by acquiring, in 1890, the famous Duquesne Mill, a thorn in the Carnegie flesh, without the expenditure of a single dollar—$1,000,000 of bonds were issued and were eventually paid for several times over from the millions of profits.

But tragic days lay ahead. Mr. Carnegie had, in 1885, made his first public address, and from then on he had talked and written copiously about the rights of labour. His "Triumphant Democracy" became the labour agitators' Bible. Carnegie had laid down the dictum "Thou shalt not take thy neighbour's job," a sentiment that won plaudits wherever labour men forgathered at home or abroad. The effect upon labour leaders, foreseen by others, became more and more manifest until, in 1891, a strike occurred and considerable intimidation and disorder ensued. There had been labour troubles before then, but in each case Carnegie had capitulated.

The burden of the 1891 ructions fell upon Mr. Frick. During the disturbances, when Mr. Frick scarcely had time to spend an hour

HENRY C. FRICK

or two with his family, his youngest child, a beautiful six-year-old girl, fell ill and died. She had been his favourite, and her death was felt all the more keenly because Mr. Frick blamed himself for not having been able to attend her more constantly during her fatal illness.

The climax of the labour discontent came, as all the world knows, at the Homestead Works the following year, 1892. Carnegie by then had learned by bitter experience that he could not put his idealistic preachments into practice. He laid plans with Frick and others to put the mill on a non-union basis—and then skipped off to the most secluded spot he could find in Scotland until the fight should be over. Only one or two of his partners knew the address of his hiding place. Frick was left to face the music alone.

What occurred during the bloodiest labour battle in the annals of America is too well known to call for recapitulation here. The creation of a semi-military organization by the strikers, their drumming of the sheriff's representatives out of the town, their defiance of all local authority, the mortal combat between several hundred Pinkerton strikebreakers, brought to the works on barges, and thousands of blood-thirsty strikers on either bank of the river; the reign of terror until the military took control, the attempted assassination of Mr. Frick, his uncompromising refusal to accept anything short of unconditional surrender by the men, and the conduct of Carnegie—all are matters of history.

Even those who condemned what they called Frick's stubbornness could not deny his heroism. After the Russian anarchist had entered his office and shot him through the ear and neck, had fired two other shots, and then with a barbarous stiletto had ripped open Frick's hip and leg, wounding him so grievously that the doctors despaired of his life—after this frightful experience, when the mob burst in and were about to shoot the anarchist, Frick commanded: "Don't kill him."

This clemency of Mr. Frick, reminiscent of that final scene on Calvary when the prayer went up: "Father, forgive them, for they know not what they do," prompted me to ask him what his surging thoughts were at that terrible moment.

"I was as cool at that moment as I am now," Mr. Frick replied very simply. "I had no desire to see him killed or even ill-treated."

When I questioned Mr. Frick more closely about his experience he confided that the only remarkable feature of it was that, when the anarchist pointed at his head and fired, he saw his little girl, who had died the previous year, standing beside him as clearly and as real as if she had been physically present—indeed, for an instant her presence was so real and corporeal that he felt like stretching out his arms to her.

Such was Mr. Frick's physique that he amazed the doctors by his rapid recovery. When they probed for the bullet that had lodged in his neck he gave directions for the guidance of the instrument. His chief worry was for his wife, who was then ill. To add to the tragedy, he buried a child born during the stress of the excitement. Tremendous pressure was brought to bear on Mr. Frick to reach a compromise with the strikers but, lying on his back wounded painfully, he declared that if President Harrison and all his cabinet and Carnegie to boot were to come to him on bended knee and implore him to capitulate, he would not recede one inch. Some of his partners wailed that no men would be left to work the plant when a settlement finally came.

"The morning after the labour leaders admitted defeat and called off the strike, you could not get near the place for men crowding around to get work," Mr. Frick told me. "The vital importance of winning that strike was not generally realized. We had reached the point where the men had become dictators of how our business should be run. We could not promote a man without their permission. We installed expensive machinery but they would not permit it to be fully worked. They restricted output arbitrarily and unreasonably. We had a mill that could produce 500 tons a day but they would not let it make over 250 tons.

"The defeat of the labour leaders under such circumstances was the best thing, not only for the steel industry, but for the men themselves. Their fears that the introduction of more machinery would cause wholesale unemployment were, of course, unfounded. We put in one contrivance that saved over 400 men, but the reduction of costs enabled us to employ more workers than ever before. Machinery, too, subsequently did some of the most trying work formerly performed by hand.

"Nobody could have more sympathy than I have for the poor. Poverty had been my own lot, and knowing from experience the kind of life led by the poor, I felt, when I first entered the coke business, that by treating workmen properly I never would have any labour troubles. By the time the Homestead strike came I had learned that the more a certain type of workmen got, the more arrogant and unreasonable they became. In the end they wanted to run our business, to be dictators. Of course, there could be only one boss."

A happy thought placed Charles M. Schwab in charge of the reopened works, and his inimitable good humour, infectious enthusiasm, and unaffected democracy quickly inspired loyalty and contentment among the men.

How guiltless of the spirit of vindictiveness was Mr. Frick, came to light long afterward. It was discovered by some one that he had

HENRY C. FRICK

quietly provided for the families of several labour agitators imprisoned for their lawlessness.

Frick resumed his task of planning and creating the most self-contained industrial enterprise in the land—with perhaps the exception of the Standard Oil Company. He believed in doing business on a big scale. He believed in unification, standardization, and other policies now general but then rare. The various Carnegie interests, except coke, were merged into one symmetrical whole. By building the Union Railway, to join the scattered works with one another, he regained possession of the yards and placed them on a better transportation footing than any competitor.

One link was still missing in the Carnegie chain of profits: ore had to be purchased from outsiders. By a masterly stroke, conceived and carried out against the outspoken opposition of Andrew Carnegie, Frick acquired a dominating interest in the Oliver Mining Company and thereby obtained an ample supply of high-grade Bessemer ore for a mere song. This proved one of Frick's most profitable stratagems. But it cost him the illwill of Carnegie, who prophesied—very erroneously—that the deal would prove disastrous.

Frick, industrially, was an Alexander the Great. For him it was not enough to own all the coal and coke, all the ore, all the plant, and all the local railway facilities necessary for the production and handling of steel products. Why not enter the railroad field? Why pay millions of dollars for the transportation of mountains of ore from the Lake Erie district? Why not build a railroad of their own and pocket all the profits? The Pittsburgh, Bessemer & Lake Erie Railroad was the result. Its financing was done by means of a bond issue, the interest of which was from the start earned several times over.

Not satisfied even then, Frick looked farther afield. Why pay huge sums every year to steamships for bringing ore across the Great Lakes to the shipping point? Why not acquire ships of their own? Forthwith a fleet of six steamers was bought.

Frick, by the sweat of his brain, had fulfilled his dream. From the moment the crude ore was dug from the earth until its transformation into thousands of finished products, not a profit or royalty was paid into any treasury other than that of the Carnegie Steel Company.

From earnings of less than $2,000,000 when he took hold in 1882, the company's earning power rose to $40,000,000 by 1899.

Frick had become too big to suit Mr. Carnegie, whose genius for picking and handling brilliant young subordinates was in distinct contrast with his inability to get along with his equals. Carnegie was dictatorial; Frick was stubborn, never afraid of a fight. In his early days Frick had played the game according to the rules then in vogue; it was not a Sunday-school picnic game, nor were the rules those of the Sermon on the Mount. But though the game had often been rough, and weaklings had gone to the wall, Frick, though he may not have been suffused with sentiment, had never been accused of dishonesty, doubledealing, or cowardly underhandedness.

When the inevitable clash came, in 1899, over the price the Carnegie Company should pay for Frick coke, Carnegie attempted to drum Frick out of the company on terms which Frick successfully contested in court and received for his holdings many millions more than Carnegie had decreed.

Into the pros and cons of this epic quarrel I cannot and need not enter; the whole case occupied columns and columns of the newspapers at the time.

For years Carnegie was anxious to get out of business. He had enunciated his famous creed about dying disgraced if dying rich. He wanted to cash in, to get millions which he could use as his fancy suggested. Negotiations with English investors in 1889 fell through, and so did a project hatched by what was known as the Moore Syndicate in 1899. Henry Phipps and Frick had been induced to put up $85,000 each to add to the $1,000,000 the Moore Syndicate paid for its option to purchase, as Carnegie wanted to have his partners associated with the transaction. But the memorable Flower panic burst, and this quashed the deal. Mr. Carnegie's retention of his partners' option money, which they alleged he had agreed in advance to return, made bad blood between these two and Carnegie.

When, finally, negotiations were opened in 1901 for the formation of the United States Steel Corporation, it was found necessary to call Frick in to negotiate with the Rockefeller interests for the purchase of their vastly important ore properties and Great Lake steamers, one of the most profitable acquisitions of the trust.

Mr. Frick's only comment upon the Carnegie Steel Corporation deal was: "I never could have sold the property for such a sum."

"What of the future?" I asked Mr. Frick. "Are we to see other huge combinations, or has the trust movement passed its zenith?"

"Without great, powerful organizations, America cannot hope to compete successfully with the world," replied Mr. Frick. "Without strong organizations how could we meet Germany's combinations, supported and coöperated with by the government? To capture foreign markets we need heavy artillery. Organization, combination, and coöperation—these are the essentials to safeguard our future.

"The tariff? If we had a couple of crop failures with men thrown out of employment on all sides, it is hard to tell what the result might be if we had no adequate means of insuring tariff protection.

"As for the farther future, I don't think we should have serious

HENRY C. FRICK

trouble in my time or even in yours, because we have such a wonderful country to develop. There is room for everybody."

I cannot close this very inadequate sketch of Henry Clay Frick's career without recalling an incident, very small in itself, yet throwing a suggestive light on his real character. Two or three Christmases ago a bank in Pittsburgh failed just before thousands of children and others were ready to withdraw the Christmas Club money they had saved and deposited throughout the year. Weeping and wailing immediately arose. The whole country was touched. Then came the joyful tidings that a benefactor had agreed to pay every dollar of this money. This benefactor turned out to be Mr. Frick. He could not resist the appeal of the little ones. His heart goes out to children. All that he does for them no one save himself knows. Every check used for such purposes bears a picture of the little daughter he lost.

Mr. Frick's large fortune is not to be disposed of after the Vanderbilt and Astor plan. "I do not believe in leaving children a great many millions of dollars," Mr. Frick told me. "Of course, I shall provide very amply for my son and also for my daughter—but she will receive no notoriety as one of America's 'richest heiresses.' The American people are fond—and properly so—of going to Europe, chiefly to see the famous paintings and other works of art there. I have tried to bring some of them here, and will leave the whole collection, along with my home and the additions I am building to it, for the benefit of the people."

Mr. Frick's chief reason for explaining this to me was to apologize for living amid what he called "such apparent luxury." He is one of the most unostentatious of men. Incidentally, the memorable French mission, headed by ex-Premier Viviani and Marshal Joffre, which visited the United States in the spring of 1917, was graciously permitted to use Mr. Frick's residence as its headquarters while staying in New York.

I would rank H. C. Frick as one of the six greatest business men in the country.

ELBERT H. GARY

NEXT to the presidency of the United States, the biggest job in America is the chairmanship of the United States Steel Corporation.

Elbert Henry Gary is the head of a corporate empire greater in income, resources, and area than the average European nation.

Its gross receipts in 1916 reached $1,230,000,000, exceeding the normal revenue of the United States Government.

It has an industrial army of 275,000 men, or more than the American army and navy combined, more than the entire regular and volunteer force engaged in the Spanish-American War, enough to plant one man every mile between the earth and the moon and leave enough to girdle the earth with human milestones. Standing side by side, the solid line would stretch a hundred miles.

The corporation's payroll this year will total some $320,000,000. Since its organization, in 1901, it has paid $2,500,000,000 in wages.

It has a fleet of over 100 steamers, which, drawn up, would form an unbroken line ten miles in length, a greater array than the navy of any second-rate Power.

Its own railroad system, straightened out, would stretch from San Francisco to New York and project several hundreds of miles into the Atlantic. Yet it pays in freight charges to other railroads $3,000,000 every week of the year. Its freight bill in sixteen years has aggregated $1,800,000,000.

It mines as much coal as the greatest of America's coal companies and makes over a million barrels of cement every month.

It has 122,000 stockholders, who in 1917 will receive perhaps $70,000,000 in dividends. Since organization $433,700,000 has been paid on the preferred stock, while common stockholders have received fully $305,000,000, or more than half the amount of stock outstanding.

Employees have been given the privilege of subscribing for 357,000 preferred and 268,000 common shares on which special bonuses are paid.

The corporation's original total capital of $1,400,000,000 was equal to two-thirds of all the money then in circulation in the United States. If it had been all paid in gold the weight would have been 2,330 tons;

in dollar bills it would have circled the earth six times with enough left to stretch from northernmost Alaska to Cape Horn.

Its assets exceed $2,000,000,000.

Not less than $7,000,000 is spent annually on welfare work to make employees healthier, happier, safer, and, therefore, more efficient.

Allowing five to a family, the Corporation supports 1,400,000 persons, twice the population of Boston.

It has industrial ambassadors or consuls in sixty countries.

It has some sixty subsidiaries, and twenty corporation presidents serve as the aides of the chief executive.

Yet the man who presides over this unparalleled enterprise is never flustered, never excited, never confused. He is master of his job; indeed, his associates agree that there is no job in America better filled and that no job will be harder to fill when he retires.

There is nothing of the autocrat in Judge Gary's make-up. He is human—humane. He often smiles—his smile is famous; he seldom frowns. There are no hard lines in his face and his blue eyes are kindly.

His office, on the seventeenth floor of 71 Broadway, is hung with autographed photographs of men who have played foremost parts in making America. These breathe a friendly atmosphere.

Let me relate an illuminating incident.

J. P. Morgan was in Europe.

Times were bad—it was in 1909. Prices were falling, orders were dwindling, wages were being reduced all over the country. The Steel Corporation directors concluded that they must follow the general trend by cutting wages. Action was proposed at a meeting of the Finance Committee. Many favoured the step. Judge Gary was uncompromisingly opposed.

"I move," interposed Judge Gary, when he saw how the discussion was going, "that we postpone action for a week," and this was agreed to.

Mr. Morgan, before sailing, had said to Judge Gary: "If you want me to do anything while I am away, cable me."

Judge Gary hated to bother Mr. Morgan, but the welfare of the workmen lay near the Judge's heart. He cabled Mr. Morgan a request to see two prominent members of the committee travelling in Europe and then cable a recommendation on the part of the three that wages be maintained.

Mr. Morgan acted with his customary promptitude and effectiveness. He summoned the directors then vacationing in Europe and, with his characteristically persuasive powers, which few men could withstand, secured their vote.

Back came the cable the Judge wanted, and when the proposal next came up it was defeated. The day was won for the workmen, and the courageous stand taken by the Steel Corporation had such an inspiriting effect upon sentiment that general industry soon revived.

This little incident, heretofore unpublished, gives a better insight than anything else I know of into Judge Gary, the man, the true friend of the workingman, the humanitarian.

Judge Gary did more than any other "Big Business" captain to bring about the renaissance in the attitude of corporations toward the public. Ten years ago, condemning the high-handed, secretive on-goings of financial and industrial leaders, he said publicly: "All this must be stopped by the rich themselves or the mob will stop it. There would have been neither growth nor spread of antagonism to capital unless there had been something to justify it."

Judge Gary could afford to speak out.

He was the most powerful pioneer for corporation publicity America had known. He inaugurated the publication of monthly statements years before the agitation for publicity became a force. His annual reports were models of lucidity and detail—so much so that they were adopted by German colleges as standard.

His fairness toward labour from the very start was revolutionary. In this he encountered tremendous opposition from his own directors.

"The only way to deal with labour is, whenever it shows its head, hit it," declared one very influential director at an early board meeting.

"Then you will have to engage someone else to do the hitting," was the ultimatum Judge Gary flung back.

The principles he laid down for treating competitors were also scoffed at by old-school capitalists as Utopian.

Because Judge Gary refused to squeeze buyers when a boom brought a steel famine, these same old-school financiers were convinced that they had picked an idealist instead of a practical man, and some of them sighed over the millions his new fanatical notions were costing the corporation.

Elbert H. Gary, however, stuck heroically to his guns. "This corporation is so big that, unless you deal fairly with the public, with competitors, and with customers, you are bound to encounter trouble sooner or later," he told the directors once and again.

And what has been the result?

When the United States Government brought suit to dissolve the corporation as a "bad trust" it scoured the whole country for witnesses to testify against it. Yet not one rival, not one customer, not one employee, not one member of the public came forward with one word against it! The only complaints made were by lawyers and others in the pay of the Government.

Mr. Schwab, testifying in the Government's suit against the Steel Corporation, made this explicit statement when questioned about steel pools:

"To the best of my knowledge Judge Gary did not have anything to do with these pools. He was opposed to them. When I was president of the Steel Corporation, one of the things that I had to contend with was Judge Gary's opposition to these things that I had been so long accustomed to."

All opposition to Judge Gary's above-board methods of conducting the corporation long since ceased. The idealist had proved the worth of his Utopian policies!

Judge Gary has always insisted that the success of the corporation has been due to the splendid ability of the Finance Committee and the Board of Directors, but his associates, with more truth, declare that the policies and labours of the chairman have been the main factor.

No stock ticker encumbers Judge Gary's office. He frowns upon speculation and never indulges in it himself. In the early days the steel directors' meetings were held at noon and some of the men who were then on the Board used to plunge heavily, using their inside information to hoodwink the public. However, that is a thing of the past.

The meetings of the Finance Committee are now held at two o'clock and then for the first time the quarterly statements, showing earnings, are produced. Soon after they are given to the Board of Directors and then to the public, so that no director has any advantage over any other stockholder.

"Looking back, what gives you the greatest satisfaction in your whole life's work?" I asked Judge Gary.

He sat silent for a moment, apparently letting his mind run back through the years.

"If I were to point to just one thing," he replied very deliberately, "I would say it has been securing the friendship and confidence of the large majority of our great family of employees. Yes," nodded the Judge, more to himself than to me, "that has been most worth while achieving. That yields more real satisfaction than anything else in my life."

"And what would you name next?" I asked.

"Assisting to bring about a friendly and coöperative spirit amongst the iron and steel fraternity, for this has resulted in eliminating the old methods of unreasonable and destructive competition which not only did so much to demoralize the steel business in times of depression and to drive into bankruptcy many connected with it, but periodically had a disastrous effect upon the general business of the country, to say nothing of the hardships and idleness it brought upon the workmen."

Henry C. Emory, former Professor of Political Science of Yale and Chairman of the United States Tariff Board under President Taft, in course of an analysis of Judge Gary's services to America says:

"What I have chiefly in mind in this regard is the treatment of stockholders. I spoke of him as the author of the 'open door' policy. Few people realize what a dramatic thing was the first publication of the quarterly statement of the affairs of that corporation. Powerful men protested that the public had no right to know. Gary insisted that 100,000 stockholders had a right to know about their own property and that he proposed to tell them. Some thought it a bluff; that when the lean quarters came the Judge would not dare to print the facts. They didn't know the man or his indifference to the men who hang around the ticker. Fat years or lean, whether the common stock sold for $10 or $100, the facts as to the condition of the company have been revealed every three months. The adoption of such a policy of 'pitiless publicity' was as much a landmark in our industrial history as the organization of the great merger itself—more so, in fact. We have heard much recently of the necessity of doing away with 'secret diplomacy' after this war is over. By this action toward his stockholders and the public Judge Gary dealt a historic blow to the policy of secret diplomacy in corporation finance."

A witty chronicler once said: "Elbert H. Gary was born a barefoot boy." That was both true and untrue. On his father's farm where he came into the world, in 1848, in Du Page County, twenty-five miles west of Chicago, the boy Gary did sometimes run about without shoes or stockings, but from choice, not necessity. His father, an upright, rigid New Englander, by hard work, carefulness, and frugality earned more than enough to clothe his family. He was a sternly practical man. His growing children were given the choice between study and work. Elbert preferred school to chores, with which he had extensive first-hand acquaintance.

Curiously, the holding of blackboard races in arithmetic by his teacher shaped young Gary's career. One day an uncle, H. F. Vallette, a lawyer of local note, visited the Garys, and the father, proud of his boy's mathematical ability, arranged a competition between the two. Elbert won. And the uncle, as a reward, offered him a place in his office at Naperville to read law. The father's verdict was: "Some day Elbert may have a little property and a knowledge of the law may help him to keep it."

He attended Wheaton College, taught school in the country during two winters, then entered his uncle's law office for eighteen months, went to Chicago as a student and, at twenty, graduated from the law department of Chicago University. He got a job at $12 per week with the Clerk of the Courts in Cook County, having been recommended by the head of the law school as the most promising graduate of the year. He proved himself capable, and by and by rose to the highest position in the office. His uncle then took him into his Chicago office.

The day after the great Chicago fire young Gary hired a room in a wooden building and hung up a lawyer's sign.

He made $2,800 in the first year.

His ambition was to become a judge. By way of gaining standing and influence he became the first Mayor of Wheaton. He did not have long to wait to realize his ambition: he was duly elected a County Judge.

Some time after this he became interested in iron and steel, as he foresaw the world was entering the steel age. On leaving the bench he became attorney for several corporations, though retaining his general practice. Even in those early days (1891) he contracted the combination habit. Through his instrumentality, several plants were rolled into the Consolidated Steel & Wire Company of Illinois, a $4,000,000 concern, then regarded as a veritable leviathan. More mills were secured seven years later and the enlarged enterprise was incorporated as the American Steel & Wire Company, with $12,000,000 capital.

Gary realized very clearly that combination meant strength. He evolved the theory that if he could combine all the units of iron and steel manufacture and transportation into a single management, enormous economies could be effected, unprecedented efficiency could be attained, and, as a corollary, handsome dividends earned.

He had already become a factor in the Illinois Steel Company and was on its board. He advocated the formation of a huge consolidation which would comprise the Illinois Steel Company; the Minnesota Iron Company, which owned the mines; the Lorain Steel Company, which had works on Lake Erie in Ohio; the Minnesota Steamship Company, which would supply the water transportation; the Duluth and Iron Range Railroad, which would carry the ore to the lake; the Elgin, Joliet and Eastern Railway and the Mt. Pleasant Coal and Coke Company of Pennsylvania.

Along with Robert Bacon, then a member of J. P. Morgan & Co., Judge Gary created the famous Federal Steel Company, the $200,000,000 corporation which caused both America and Europe to rub eyes. Mr. Morgan was fond of declaring that this was a bigger industrial and financial feat than the subsequent organization of the United States Steel Corporation.

Mr. Morgan sent for Judge Gary and told him that, of course, there was only one man fitted to take charge of the combination.

The Judge replied that he didn't care for the job.

"Why?" demanded Mr. Morgan.

The Judge explained that he was making more than $75,000 a year from his law business in Chicago, that his income was steadily growing, and that he was not anxious to leave Chicago.

"We expect to pay you for coming here," bluntly replied the banker. "You can name your own salary—anything you want—and for any number of years you want."

Finally Judge Gary agreed to go for three years, at $100,000 a year, until then the highest salary on record.

"I expected to return to Chicago at the end of the three years," said the Judge not long ago, "but here I am."

How the Steel Corporation came to be formed is this:

One day Charles M. Schwab, the brightest of all Carnegie's protégés, approached Mr. Bacon and intimated that Carnegie might be persuaded to sell out. Mr. Bacon promptly went to Judge Gary, the central figure in the great Federal Steel merger.

The first time Judge Gary broached the matter to Mr. Morgan, the latter was unresponsive. A dinner was given shortly afterward by the late J. Edward Simmons, president of the Fourth National Bank, in honour of Mr. Schwab, and it was on that historic occasion that Schwab, with irresistible eloquence and optimism, painted steel rainbows. Mr. Morgan, who was present, was impressed.

Next morning Mr. Morgan sent for Judge Gary. He was interested but said he would do nothing until he first received an assurance that Carnegie would sell. However, he spent several hours with the Judge going over the possibilities of the proposition. The desired assurance from Carnegie was in time forthcoming, and the machinery for forming the greatest business organization the world has ever known was set in motion.

Much has been said and written about the "Gary dinners." It was the panic of 1907 that started them. The first was held in the dark days of November of that year when the financial heavens were falling and industry was prostrate.

Instead of cut-throat competition, unbridled demoralization and wholesale discharge of employees, it was there and then resolved to act unitedly in an effort to stay the panic. Committees were appointed covering every branch of the iron and steel industry, and, to make a long story short, prices were steadied, bankruptcy-breeding tactics were checked, and order evolved out of chaos and threatened ruin.

Whether this was technically legal or illegal, I do not pretend to

ELBERT H. GARY

judge. But I do know that the results for business, for labour, and for the country as a whole were invaluable. As soon as the Administration intimated opposition to these gatherings (in 1911), they were discontinued.

E. N. Hurley, then vice-president of the Federal Trade Commission, in making an eloquent appeal for coöperation at the 1916 dinner of the Iron and Steel Institute, proudly proclaimed that the commission had recommended the passage of a bill removing all legal restraint of coöperation and combination among manufacturers to build up foreign trade. His peroration was a rousing appeal for such coöperation.

When the deafening applause had subsided Judge Gary, who was presiding, rose and said: "'Do I sleep, do I dream, or are visions about?' I could close my eyes and imagine I was attending one of the old-fashioned Gary dinners. If coöperation is wise in respect to export business, why is it not a good principle with reference to domestic business?"

Was there ever neater retort?

The esteem in which Judge Gary is held by the steel trade was demonstrated by a notable tribute paid him by competitors and customers at a complimentary dinner given in his honour in 1909 by the independent iron and steel manufacturers of the United States and Canada.

It was not the presentation to him of an enormous solid gold loving cup that made the occasion memorable in steel annals. It was the character of the gathering and the tenor of the addresses delivered. Here were chiefs of rival concerns paying a unique tribute to the head of the most powerful rival of them all. And they spoke of him, not as a foe, not even merely as a friend, but as a father, the far-seeing, beneficent father and counsellor of them all. It was on this occasion that Mr. Schwab, the first president of the corporation, magnanimously admitted that in his differences with Judge Gary the latter had always been right and he (Schwab) wrong.

"I am thankful for this opportunity of saying one thing, Judge," said Mr. Schwab. "You and I have been associated in business, or we were, for some years; we have had many differences, and I am glad of this opportunity to say publicly that with my bounding enthusiasm and optimism I was wrong in most instances—indeed, in all instances—and you were right. The broad principles that you brought into this business were new to all of us who had been trained in a somewhat different school. . . . This, sir, is the first time in the history of the industry when the great heads of all the big concerns in the United States and Canada have gathered to do honour to a man who has introduced a new and successful principle in our great industry. Judge Gary, you should be a very happy man to-night."

It was on this occasion, too, that Mr. Morgan made one of the extremely few speeches of his lifetime.

He was so overcome by emotion and nervousness that, to hold himself up, he grasped the back of his chair with one hand and leaned upon the shoulder of another diner. Before he sat down, tears were trickling down his cheeks and he whispered to his friend that, had he not leaned upon him, he never would have been able to remain on his feet. Mr. Morgan's speech contained one touching sentence. The speech is perhaps worth giving in full:

"I wish it were in my power to say all that I would like to say on this occasion. What I might say at another time would be pretty poor, but to-night I am very much overcome by all that I have heard said, for Judge Gary and I have been working together now for ten years in a way perhaps none of you appreciate, or how much it has meant to me. *I feel as though we were all just together.* It is impossible for me to say more, and I must ask you to accept my appreciation of how deeply I feel for the kind evidence of your sentiments toward me to-night. Gentlemen, let me ask you to excuse me from saying more."

Judge Gary has come to be recognized as one of the most effective public speakers in the country. Indeed, the addresses of no private citizen attract more universal attention. He does not indulge in flights of high-falutin' oratory; it is the worth, the weight, the wisdom of what he says that commands the respect of all classes, rich and poor, capitalists and workmen.

During a visit to the Orient in 1916 Mr. and Mrs. Gary received a reception such as is usually reserved for royalty. How much he then accomplished in fostering goodwill between the Orient and the United States cannot easily be gauged. His friendly attitude, his frank utterances, his full understanding of these often-misjudged peoples did much to dispel misconception and to pave the way for warmer international relations in the future. He followed up his "unofficial diplomatic visit," so to speak, with a series of magazine articles which further contributed to drawing together the Oriental nations and the United States in bonds of friendship and respect.

Judge Gary is married but has no son to fill his shoes.

The Judge can seldom be persuaded to talk of his part in the upbuilding of the greatest industrial enterprise mankind has ever known, hence most of the facts here set forth have had to be collected from the published records, from his intimates, and from personal knowledge covering almost the entire life of the corporation.

WILLIAM A. GASTON

A GROUP of notable Americans, all self-made but one, were patting themselves on the back. Each was telling how poor he was at the start, how hard he worked—and, well, here he was to-day, something very big that had grown from nothing.

The one man of wealthy parentage listened politely to the recital. Then he blurted out: "You fellows worked because you had to. It was a case with you of work or starve. I didn't need to do a stroke of work unless I wanted to. As you know, my family had money. But I have worked just as hard as any of you, not from necessity, but from choice. You had no alternative. I had."

William A. Gaston, head of the largest financial institution east of New York, was not the man who said this. But he might have been. Instead of selecting the primrose path of ease, he chose to enter the lists and win his own spurs. Instead of contenting himself with being an onlooker, he decided to become a doer.

He has succeeded. Colonel Gaston has won recognition and high place, not in one line of endeavour, but in three—and the end is not yet. He first distinguished himself as a lawyer; then as a business man and corporation executive; later as a banker and financier. He has also rendered useful service in civic and political life, and his intimates prophesy that he is destined to make his mark as a statesman.

There is none of the proverbial Bostonian haughtiness about "Billy" Gaston. He is democratic not only in politics, but in person. John L. Sullivan is just as real a friend as Theodore Roosevelt, his second at Harvard when young Gaston, in a memorable fight, won the middleweight boxing championship of his university in days when boxing meant hard fighting.

Nearly all successful business men possess fighting qualities. Commodore Vanderbilt was a fighter. Harriman, Hill, and Morgan were fighters. Men who aspire to do big things must have daring, must have courage, must have self-confidence. They must be prepared to accept risks. They must exhibit boldness when others show timidity.

Gaston's valour did not forsake him when he left college. He carried it with him into his business life. And New England once had reason to be grateful that he did. During the 1907 panic, when industrial foundations became as quicksand and the strongest of enterprises became shaky, William A. Gaston stepped to the front and fought to check the débâcle. It will be recalled that hundreds of banks throughout the country began to scramble for gold, while business men were harshly ordered to pay off loans, and influential city financial institutions acted panicky, hoarding their specie like misers and dunning borrowers to pay up instantly at any cost.

Gaston had not been many months in the banking business when this occurred. But the courage he showed in his college days and later at the bar and in business again distinguished his conduct. Instead of following the stampede, he adopted the historic policy pursued by the Bank of England in times of grave crises and used his resources freely, encouraging others to meet the panic with confidence.

Many New England institutions looked to the National Shawmut Bank, the largest in the New England field, for a cue as to what course should be followed. Some of the bank's directors urged that self-preservation was the first law of finance as of life and that the institution should look out for number one. President Gaston had larger and less cowardly ideas of banking and of his responsibilities. On November 15, when the demoralization was at its height, he sent out the following letter to every bank in the country having relations with the Shawmut, counselling calmness, courage, and financial boldness:

"Dear Sir:—In the period of such stringency of the money market as we are now experiencing, it is of the utmost importance that the banks shall renew, so far as it lies in their power, the notes which may be maturing of merchants and manufacturers and others who are worthy of credit.

"In many cases it is utterly impossible for perfectly solvent business houses either to borrow new money or to collect their receivables, which ordinarily are paid, or to sell their merchandise, and if they are forced unnecessarily by the banks to pay their notes, bankruptcy or receivership is sure to follow.

"In order to restore business affairs to a normal state, a general liquidation of business must take place. This, we believe, every merchant is attempting to do to the extent of his ability, but the banks and trust companies must, in our opinion, do their share by extending maturing notes in whole or in part. The fewer the number of solvent merchants who are forced to pay their debts where it means hardship, the fewer the failures, and, consequently, the sooner a restoration of confidence and a normal condition of the money market will ensue.

"We therefore urge you, as far as is in your power, to help the serious mercantile situation in this way."

I emphasize this incident because such conduct was rare rather than common in those dark days. I mention it because this action is characteristic of Gaston. I dwell upon it because the service he then rendered industrial and financial New England cannot be measured in dollars. In these current days we are learning to appreciate personal valour.

Blood will tell, they say. If so, Gaston's moral and physical strength and courage are entirely logical. He comes of good blood on both sides. From his mother he inherited the blood and spirit of the Beechers, a family that for a hundred years has given to the republic a succession of men and women devoted to religion, high principle, and humanity. Colonel Gaston's mother was a cousin of the famous preacher, Henry Ward Beecher. On his father's side, he is directly descended from a Huguenot family who left France because of religious troubles; went to Scotland, thence to Ireland, where was born his great-great-grandfather who emigrated and settled in this country in Killingly, Connecticut, where Mr. Gaston's father first saw the light of day. Gaston's home influence was the very best. His father was Mayor of Roxbury, Mayor of Boston during the Great Fire in 1872, State Representative, Senator, and finally Governor of Massachusetts in 1875, being the first democratic Governor after the Civil War. Until his death in 1894, Governor Gaston continued to have a great influence in Massachusetts affairs. His utter lack of race or religious bigotry, his friendship for the newer peoples that came to this country and his assistance and counsel to them; his record as a statesman and lawyer, made him one of the great characters in Massachusetts during the last generation.

This story of Colonel Gaston's ancestors is told merely to show what lies back of him, and to explain the principles of tradition and honourable living, square dealing and public service which he was taught as a child. Born in Roxbury on May 1, 1859, he was educated in the Roxbury public schools, in the Roxbury Latin School, and finally at Harvard University, from which he graduated in 1880 with the degree of A.B. He was never a prize scholar but had a record as a normal, wholesome lad more interested in athletics than academic honours. His Harvard class has since become famous; it included such men as Theodore Roosevelt; Robert Bacon, later to become a partner in J. P. Morgan & Company and ambassador to France; Robert Winsor, head of the great banking house of Kidder, Peabody & Company; Josiah Quincy, and Richard L. Saltonstall, later to become one of Mr. Gaston's partners. These were close companions and have remained so to this day.

Gaston entered the Harvard Law School and was admitted to the bar when twenty-four. His education was rounded out by a long tour through Europe. On his return he took up legal work in his father's office. He earned $400 in the first year—and lived on it.

He first began to show his worth in arguments before juries; but his grasp of business problems developed so markedly that important corporation cases were turned over to him. The acute depression of 1893 brought many business troubles, and the courts for several years had their hands full. Young Gaston distinguished himself by his business sense, his aptitude for straightening out financial tangles, his ability in aiding the reconstruction and rehabilitation of weakened enterprises. J. Ogden Armour recently remarked to me that business must nowadays be done with a lawyer and a chemist; in those days a lawyer was a very necessary adjunct to most corporations.

In the late nineties, when street transportation interests of Boston were getting into a very bad way, the West End Street Railway was a series of separate companies, and consolidation into one central corporation was decided upon as the only feasible course to avert bankruptcy. This proposition met with legislative opposition, and everything became hopelessly muddled. One night Col. William A. Gaston was called out of bed by a committee of West End stockholders who appealed to him as a public-spirited citizen to sacrifice his lucrative law practice, at least temporarily, and straighten out the situation before the threatened total wreck occurred.

He at first demurred, but it was probably the sporting side of the proposition which appealed to him; at all events, he assumed the duties of active manager and reorganizer of the local traction companies and organized them into one large company, now known as the Boston Elevated Road. He continued to manage this organization for about five years, during which time he built up the road, improved the service, giving Bostonians a longer ride for a nickel than any other community in the United States had gotten up to that time, and in the meanwhile by sound business methods strengthened the company's position financially until it was an attractive investment. Wages of the employees were raised to the maximum level then current in the United States. Workmen's compensation methods were introduced ten years before this legislation was passed by the legislature. Benefit societies were put on a sound business booking; an insurance system was instituted, and satisfactory arrangements were made for the handling of promotions on a civil service basis.

The era of trusts set in shortly after President McKinley's election in 1896 and was in flood tide during the years Mr. Gaston rehabilitated Boston's street and elevated railway systems. The task involved the spending of many millions of dollars, the letting of numerous contracts, the purchase of great quantities of material, etc. Under the code prevalent in the late nineties and the early years of the new century, it was considered entirely permissible for corporation directors and heads to form little companies or firms which were allowed to earn enormous profits from dealings with the larger enterprises dominated by those owning these side lines.

Gaston refused point-blank to countenance any such flimflamming. All contracts were advertised and awarded in the open. Not only did he scorn to participate in profits illegitimately filched from the Boston Elevated, but he saw to it that no one else took advantage of the company. There would be nothing creditable about taking such a stand at this time of day. But his insistence on such methods more than fifteen years ago called for a good deal of independence and self-assertion. Having spent nearly five crowded years in this work (from 1897 to 1901) he handed over the management of the property to others.

It has been said by one of our great American publicists that if all railroad executives during the last twenty years had viewed their responsibilities like "Billy" Gaston we would have been saved the railroad troubles of the last fifteen years.

Mr. Gaston since boyhood entertained a natural desire to succeed his father as governor of Massachusetts. In 1901 the Democratic Party had reached a very low point in regard to votes and influence. He accepted its nomination for governor, and put the same business abilities and methods which had built up the elevated road and made his other lines of enterprises active and successful into party reorganization, and the campaigns of 1902 and 1903 gave the Republican organization much to worry about. The time, however, was not politically propitious. Although as a result of this reorganization the Democratic Party in the state was put on an effective fighting basis and has since succeeded in electing three democratic governors, Mr. Gaston, though he doubled the party vote and could have remained in the field without contest, and undoubtedly elected, refused to be a candidate after his second campaign.

He has been honoured many times by his party—as Colonel on Governor Russell's staff, which gives him the title by which he is best known; as a delegate-at-large to the National Democratic Convention; as Democratic National Committeeman; and as president of the Massachusetts Electoral College which chose President Woodrow Wilson—the first body since 1820 in Massachusetts to vote for a Democratic president.

It may be recollected that in the spring of 1907 there were ominous financial rumblings. Security values declined silently but alarmingly. Far-sighted financiers accepted the warning and pulled in sail. There had been enormous industrial and commercial growth, involving a corresponding expansion in bank credit. The situation contained ugly elements. Colonel Gaston had returned to the practice of law in 1904 and his firm had become one of the foremost in New England. But again he was called upon to undertake a highly responsible task. The directors of the Shawmut National Bank were not blind to the unnerving financial undercurrents, and they were anxious to have at the head of their institution a man of the very first calibre.

In May Colonel Gaston was installed as president. Almost before he had time to find his bearings the storm broke. Hundreds of banks and trust companies throughout the country, among which many in New England were included, began struggling to hoard gold. Mr. Gaston realized that a critical time had come. If business men were harshly ordered by their banks to pay off their loans, and the influential financial institutions were to lead in the cry of panic and in hoarding their cash like misers, while dunning borrowers to pay up instantly, the end would be a national panic with general suffering which would equal the panic of 1893. Mr. Gaston thereupon adopted a characteristic attitude. He called a meeting of his Board of Directors, showed them concrete instance after instance where banks and trust companies had been hoarding gold instead of helping business men, and as a result solvent concerns were being forced to the wall. The letter already reproduced was the result. It was later admitted that this act more than anything else mitigated in New England the severity of the crisis. Its bravery and altruism even had an effect all over the United States, where its example was followed.

Another example of Mr. Gaston's far-sightedness was shown shortly after he became president of the bank, when he helped to finance a journey to South America of graduates of the Boston High School of Commerce, primarily to acquaint them with the possibilities of South America, but more especially in order to bring home to New Englanders the fact that its future business was bound up in that direction. As president of the National Shawmut, he has been working quietly but persistently with the idea of extending our trade in the South American countries. The Shawmut Bank is to-day being represented by, and is in turn the American agent of, powerful financial South American institutions.

Mr. Gaston headed the Finance Committee which collected funds for the Wilson campaign in 1912. When certain financial interests were incensed over the appointment of William G. McAdoo as Secretary of the Treasury, and opposed from the beginning the passage of the new Currency Bill, the attitude of many Boston bankers was that the worse the Democratic measure could be made the better, since it would defeat itself. Mr. Gaston took the contrary view.

During the discussion of this financial legislation, which resulted in the enactment of the Federal Reserve Law, he made a score of trips to Washington to consult with the members of the committee on behalf of the House and the Senate and with such leaders as Representative Glass and Senator Owen, and, of course, the Secretary of the Treasury. Perhaps more than any other man in New England, his opinion was sought in the passage of this bill, which in the opinion of the practical financial interests of the United States has been a great success.

While this was going on, the Clearing House Committee, appointed by the Clearing House Association, to which belong most of the national banks of Boston, held a preliminary meeting, and proposed to call a general meeting of clearing house banks to pass resolutions condemning the pending legislation in Congress. Mr. Gaston took the position in this matter that if such a meeting were called, he would attend and dissent from the vote and would do everything he could to influence similar action by other financial institutions. The proposed meeting was abandoned.

About this time the American Bankers' Association held their annual meeting in Boston, and an attempt was made to organize a movement to discredit the Currency Act then before Congress. Determined action on the part of Mr. Gaston and his associates prevented the contest in this convention which would have followed the introduction of the proposed condemnatory resolutions.

This assistance to the administration was wholly impersonal and patriotic.

Again, when a critical situation was created by the urgent need for gold after the European war began and it became necessary to form a gold pool, powerful opposition was exerted on the ground that the gold was needed here more than in England. The National Shawmut Bank in New England contributed very heavily to the Gold Pool, which was the means of producing a proper exchange basis between the two countries. To-day financial men then opposing this measure see and admit the courage and wisdom of Gaston's attitude.

Another instance where Mr. Gaston was wise enough and brave enough to oppose those immediately around him who thought he was temporarily acting against their interests, was in relation to the Cotton Pool, formed after the opening of the great war. England's attitude on cotton exportation had made imminent the danger of a collapse in the price of cotton, and threatened southern cotton producers, cotton buyers, and dealers with bankruptcy and ruin. In this crisis the government asked northern and eastern banking interests to put up money in order that the Federal Reserve Board could buy cotton and keep its price within reasonable bounds. The Clearing

House Committee of the Boston Banks was asked to meet the representatives of the cotton manufacturers of New England, who took the position that inasmuch as they had paid excessively high prices for cotton for years, the profits on their manufactured cotton goods being reduced or wiped out because of former high prices of cotton, now that cotton was down to a low price, Boston banks had no right to help to keep the price up artificially by such a means as the proposed pool, especially as the money contributed for this pool would come from institutions largely interested in low-price cotton. At this time there were six or eight cotton mill treasurers on the Board of Directors of the Shawmut Bank and many other directors interested in cotton manufacturing. Under Mr. Gaston's leadership the Shawmut Bank voted, with a few dissenters on the Board of Directors, to authorize the President to contribute to the Cotton Pool, which, however, was not called for.

While a number of Boston banks refused to go into this Cotton Pool, those most strenuous in their opposition now realize that it was the broad, patriotic thing to do, and they like Mr. Gaston all the better for his insistence. They are never in doubt as to what his position is, and experience has taught them that his judgment is unbiased by selfish considerations.

Colonel Gaston's reputation for ability to pull a desperate cause out of the hole is constantly bringing him to the front—often against his innate desire to remain out of the limelight. When the Young Men's Christian Association wanted a new $500,000 building, Colonel Gaston was coaxed into leadership of the campaign—and succeeded.

Next he organized the $300,000 campaign to get a Young Men's Christian Association building in Charlestown, Mass., for the enlisted men of the navy.

When John L. Mott, general secretary of the Y. M. C. A., wanted somebody to get money contributions in New England to the fund for maintaining the prison camps in the war countries, it was Colonel Gaston to whom he came.

When the Liberty Loan Committee was threatened with a desperate situation, it called on Colonel Gaston, who got together at an hour's notice two hundred of New England's leading capitalists in the Exchange Club and from that moment there was no more doubt of the success of New England's efforts.

As a member of the Executive Committee of the Red Cross to raise the $100,000,000 fund he did more than his share. And so on in every work for patriotic purposes he is to be found quietly inspiring others to work while carrying the major burden himself.

Mr. Gaston's capacity for leadership is demonstrated even in his country life. About ten years ago he bought a farm in Barre,

Mass., to which he devotes a great deal of attention. As a lover of animals he uses this as a breeding place for all kinds of fancy stock, and has interested himself in the affairs of the local community, being elected president of one of the oldest agricultural societies in the country, the Barre Agricultural Society.

His Alma Mater conferred upon him the coveted honour of election as a member of its Board of Trustees when he was only forty-six years of age.

With his wife and four children he is very happy in his home life. His eldest son, who inherits the family name of William and with it its qualities, is now training as an aviator and by the time this appears will probably be in active service in France.

New England needs such men as William A. Gaston. For almost 100 years after the American Revolution, New England held undisputed primacy in the nation's industrial and commercial leadership. After the Civil War, New York clinched the financial control in which it has been growing stronger every year, carrying with it far-reaching consequences to New England—consequences all the more serious because up to a few years ago the conservatives in control of New England business and finance refused to face or accept the facts.

It was New England capital that had built up and developed Western farms, mines, and railroads. The returns from these investments were so satisfactory, and the sense of power inherent in this ownership so tickling to New England sectional pride, that the fact that financial control of the money market had passed to New York, which not only secured control of the Western, but also of the New England railroads, and with this the right to restrict and even to deny to New England the needed transportation improvements, was, if considered at all, not discussed or openly admitted.

The fact that New England had each succeeding year turned out more shoes, cotton, and woolen products than the year previously was accepted as sufficient proof of progress.

Only within the last ten years has New England begun to awaken to the knowledge that relatively it is slipping behind. While its absolute primacy in the manufactures of its standard staples continues, the relative progress of Missouri in shoe manufacture and of the Carolinas in the production of cotton fabrics, make those states press Massachusetts hard for first place.

In addition to the false security engendered by the belief that without contest New England was destined permanently to retain the industrial leadership of the United States, there has come to be accepted in Massachusetts without much protest and even with some complacency, the belief that the state, which has always prided itself on leading all the commonwealths in regulating hours of work and protecting the child and woman labour, is the natural laboratory to try out all kinds of half-baked, socialistic theories. Railroad and banking laws, copied by Western states twenty-five years after being enacted in Massachusetts, were used to justify the claim of these frontier states to leadership in radicalism, the fact being that most of these laws have been so long in force successfully in Massachusetts that their origins are forgotten.

The result of transportation isolation and socialistic domination in legislation is that manufacturers are not encouraged to build factories in a state in which taxes are disproportionately high and the laws under which business is done more stringent than competing states in which every inducement is offered to new enterprises and a premium placed upon their coming. Massachusetts has skilled labour and competent employers, but this is not enough.

Massachusetts bankers who have been satisfied with the volume of bank clearings, because they were larger each year than the year before, have also only recently awakened to the fact that the percentage of this increase is but half that of the nation as a whole. Only recently are Massachusetts manufacturers waking up to the knowledge that their transportation system is intolerable, not only making it difficult for domestic competition in local products, but operating to retard the growth of the chief asset of New England—its water front—because of the impossibility of ships to get outcargoes for export from New England ports.

Only within the last few years also have New England manufacturers and the people generally awakened to the fact that the American market for New England goods is no longer sufficient to keep their factories going full time. New England competitors in manufacturing, in other parts of the country, with nearness to hydro-electric facilities, fuel, raw material, and better transportation facilities, have an unquestioned advantage in the home market. The only hope for constant employment of American wage earners after the war is a share of the world's foreign trade, and there again the transportation handicap against New England becomes important.

What New England needs to-day is Men, and fortunately for the section, it is meeting the demand. Foremost in this company of captains whose opportunity and privilege it is to lead New England in this struggle for its future, is William A. Gaston.

GEORGE W. GOETHALS

WHEN the news came that an army engineer would be chosen to build the canal, we all immediately thought of Goethals," declared General Mackenzie, then chief of the United States Corps of Engineers.

Why did General Mackenzie and other eminent army engineers at once know that a mere major was the ideal man for the job? Why did Theodore Roosevelt appoint him? Why did Secretary of War Taft decide that this little-advertised officer was the best man in the land for the biggest job confronting the nation?

Because Goethals was born under a lucky star? No. It was because he had fitted himself to meet the opportunity and to measure up to it. It was not because of good fortune, but because of his record. It was not because of any influence, but because of his demonstrated ability. It was not because of chance, but because of his character. It was not because of "pull," but because of his personality.

When the Goddess of Opportunity sought a man she went straight to Goethals's door. When she knocked he was ready, ready to go forth and link the Atlantic and the Pacific, to break the backbone of two continents, to overcome obstacles that had defied others, to perform the greatest engineering and constructive feat of all time.

His antecedents, his record up to that date?

A Brooklyn lad of Dutch descent, born June 29, 1858, he went to work as an errand boy in New York when only eleven. At fourteen he began keeping books for a produce market man after school and on Saturdays. His pay was gradually increased from $5 a week to $15, and he contrived to put himself through the College of the City of New York. He matriculated at Columbia with a view to becoming a doctor, the favourite family profession, but the day-and-night work and study having affected his health, he decided to gain admission to West Point. President Grant ignored a letter on the subject, but young Goethals, undaunted, prevailed upon "Sunset" Cox, then a notable political figure in New York, to recommend him after he had given an assurance that he would make good—which several young blades sponsored by Cox had not done.

Entering West Point on April 21, 1876, the slender, light-haired, blue-eyed youth exhibited the same grit which had enabled him to earn a college education and developed the qualities which were to win him international fame. Thus: He graduated second in scholarship in a class of fifty-four and was one of the only two graduates considered worthy of selection for the coveted Engineers' Corps. He was chosen one of the four captains of the Cadet Corps. He was elected president of his class. He had, therefore, won the highest distinction in scholarship, in military skill, and as a leader of his associates, a rare trinity.

His first commanding officer, knowing the tendency of young army engineers to indulge in strutting, set Goethals to work carrying a rod. He did not object; he merely told his superior, "I am here to learn." And learn he did. In two years he was promoted from second lieutenant to first lieutenant, and gained his captaincy nine years later, in 1891.

It was not his rank, however, that distinguished him from other army engineers, but his abilities and his achievements. "Whatever I gave him to do I immediately dismissed from my mind because I knew it would be done right," said one of his superiors. While still in the twenties, he was chosen instructor in civil and military engineering at the United States Military Academy; later he was placed in charge of the Mussel Shoals Canal construction on the Tennessee River; was signally honoured by being called to Washington as a member of the General Staff, and was made a member of the Board of Fortifications (for coast and harbour defence).

No matter what his station, no matter what the nature of his duties, no matter with whom he had to deal, Goethals displayed not merely technical skill of high order, but the rarer quality of statesmanship in handling men. Wherever he went, among whomever he worked, he inspired a loyalty and enthusiasm that produced 100 per cent. results.

"To accomplish successfully any task," Colonel Goethals told a graduating class at West Point, "it is necessary not only that you should give it the best that is in you, but that you should obtain for it the best there is in those who are under your guidance. To do this you must have confidence in the undertaking and confidence in your ability to accomplish it, in order to inspire the same feeling in them. You must have not only accurate knowledge of their capabilities, but a just appreciation and a full recognition of their needs and rights as fellowmen. In other words, be considerate, just, and fair with them in all dealings, treating them as fellow-members of the great Brotherhood of Humanity."

Goethals did not dig the Panama Canal with steam shovels. He dug it with men. Since everything must be done through men, Goethals's rule is to give first attention to men. By picking the right kind of men and then by treating them with absolute fairness, anything within the power of man can be accomplished. To join two oceans had been the dream of great men for centuries; but while others only dreamed or failed, Goethals went ahead and achieved triumphant results.

"As a soldier," he says, "I have always considered 'Do' an essential element of duty. In analyzing men for detail duty on the canal, I found that the man with military training had an advantage in knowing how to obey. Service is nothing more than obedience in a broad sense. If you escape duty you avoid action. Stern duties do not require harsh commands. Knowledge of our duties is the most essential part of the philosophy of life."

And again: "How many business men ever make an inventory of their employees? Do they give as much attention to the human equation as they do to machinery?"

Goethals is the Kitchener of America. Both were trained as military engineers. Both developed remarkable executive force. Both had the faculty of enthusing and inspiring men. Both became leaders of the same type—extremely insistent upon obedience, intolerant of excuses for failure, implacable of delay, autocratic in certain respects, yet just and considerate. Kitchener's eyes were not unlike those of Goethals'—keen, searching, piercing. Goethals has studied Kitchener's career and it is safe to assume that Kitchener studied the achievements of Goethals.

Goethals once remarked: "The world demands results. It is recorded that Lord Kitchener, when a subordinate during the South African war began to explain a failure to obey orders, said, 'Your reasons for not doing it are the best I ever heard; now go and do it!' That is what the world demands to-day."

Both Kitchener and Goethals have been called despots. Certainly no man not wearing a crown ever wielded such autocratic authority as was invested in Goethals during the building of the Panama Canal. He ruled with all the old-time freedom of the Sultan of Zanzibar or the Russian Czar. But his rule was founded on exact justice. Goethals accepted and acted upon the principle that there is a Brotherhood of Humanity. His fearlessness was never divorced from fairness. Power, he recognized, is only opportunity to do what is right.

When he held informal "court" every Sunday morning at his office and heard every comer, white, black, or in-between, he had wider authority than the United States Supreme Court; yet he played the rôle of fatherly adviser rather than a cold legal functionary. Wives of all colours came to him to reclaim erring husbands; labourers with a grievance against their foremen received respectful attention; men dismissed could lay their cases fully before him. These Sunday morning sessions made the administration of the Canal Zone possible.

They were a unique combination of theoretical autocracy and applied democracy. They were Panama's safety valve. Wrongdoers knew that "The Colonel" could deport them from the Isthmus with a stroke of his pen—but they also knew that if they did the right thing he would see to it that they got a square deal.

What the public wants to know is how Goethals achieved the apparently impossible; how he found time not only to meet and solve engineering problems, not only how to succeed in building the canal, but also how he, an army officer, was able to become so successful an administrator; how he managed to keep a formerly lawless land peaceful and law-abiding—how, in short, he achieved such signal results in dealing both with machinery and with human beings.

The situation that confronted Goethals when he was dispatched to Panama was appalling. The great De Lesseps, builder of the Suez Canal, when he tackled the problem of sundering the American continents had declared confidently: "The canal will be built." But after spending $260,000,000 and losing many thousands of lives the French had to acknowledge defeat after ten years' labours. President McKinley had appointed a commission to investigate Central American canal routes in 1899, but it remained for President Roosevelt to get action. In his own words: "I took Panama and left Congress to debate it later," paralleling the late E. H. Harriman's reputed method of ordering boards of directors to vote first and talk afterward. By paying French interests $40,000,000 and Panama $10,000,000 in cash and agreeing to an annual payment of $250,000 in perpetuity, the United States on May 4, 1904, took over the ten-mile Canal Zone stretching from Colon on the Atlantic to Panama on the Pacific. Colombia had tried to prevent the secession and was disgruntled.

Of machinery for the administration of the new territory there was virtually none. There had been over fifty revolutions in that region in about as many years. Crime, violence, vice, disease, had held revel there for decades.

Congress appointed a "seven-headed" commission to administer the affairs of the Zone and to dig the canal. The job proved too big, too complicated, too difficult, too discouraging for the septette. The canal was being dug from Washington. Before a roll of mosquito netting could be procured it had to be wound with red tape. Requests for machinery were similarly treated. John F. Wallace, chief engineer, threw up the sponge at the end of twelve months after having fought valiantly against disheartening odds.

John F. Stevens stepped into the breach and wrestled with red tape, fever epidemics, discontented labour, and construction setbacks. Moreover, the chief engineer's acts were open to disapproval by the chairman of the Commission, who usually reposed comfortably in Washington, D. C., instead of Culebra, C. Z. Stevens, too, gave up.

President Roosevelt was angry. He had set his heart upon having the Panama Canal built but had encountered nothing but disappointment after disappointment, delay after delay, and resignation after resignation. This time he determined to appoint a Chief Engineer who could not quit, one accustomed to doing things, one who could straighten out tangles and "send the dirt flying." He turned to the army and there found his man.

At first merely chief engineer, Goethals within six weeks was appointed chairman of the Canal Commission and given practically unlimited control. Colonel Goethals proceeded to do things without holding perpetual pow-wows with members of boards. His definition of boards, committees, and commissions is now historic: "All boards are long, narrow, and wooden."

At last President Roosevelt had found a man after his own heart. Hardly had the soldier-administrator reached the Isthmus, early in 1907, before he abolished all the municipalities, wiped out offices galore, divided the Zone into administrative districts, and set up an entirely new order. Without specific legal authority, President Roosevelt gave Goethals virtually carte blanche. New laws were promulgated without bothering with red tape; the whole administrative machinery was reorganized; new methods of dealing with labour were enforced. All this went under the description of "benevolent despotism." Colonel Goethals later described his course thus:

"While there was probably truth in the assertion made at that time that the chairman had exceeded his authority and usurped the prerogatives of the Commission, the end not only justified the means, but could have been accomplished in no other way."

The soldier-become-statesman had been sent to Panama to build the canal and he meant to build it. Everything else was subsidiary. If the susceptibilities of certain ornamental gentlemen at Washington were hurt—unfortunate but inevitable. If things had to be done without preliminary cabling and corresponding—the things were done. If the health and well-being and recreation of the workers called for undiluted paternalism—the necessary steps were taken. Whether the President of the United States had a legal right to act without specific sanction of Congress was none of the engineer's business. He was there to obey Presidential orders and to have his own orders obeyed in turn.

Asked the chairman of the House Committee on Appropriations during the inevitable Congressional "investigation":

"Did you ever inquire into the right of the Panama Railroad Company, under the laws of the State of New York, to go into the hotel business, Colonel Goethals?"

"No, sir; I got an order from the President of the United States to build that hotel and I built it"—referring to the Washington Hotel at Colon.

At first the Panamanians, like a good many others, scoffed at the appointment of an army engineer to rule over the Isthmus and carry out the greatest constructive job ever attempted on Mother Earth. The workmen opined that they had better learn how to salute just-so or run dire risk of instant dismissal. They pictured a ha-ha! Colonel, gaily decked in a richly trimmed uniform, his chest adorned with half-a-dozen medals, his hands carefully protected by gloves, with a numerous, obsequious staff of high-born young officers dancing attendance wherever he travelled by auto or carriage. They expected a martinet of martinets.

Goethals arrived unheralded and was received with no pomp or ceremony. He was mild-mannered. This led to a little misunderstanding which Goethals settled very characteristically. Union leaders waited upon him and told him that if he did not do a certain thing they would all resign that evening and stop the whole works. Goethals listened politely and shook hands with them as they left—without committing himself one way or the other. When evening came without any decision they telephoned Goethals. "I thought you had all resigned," was his reply. "But you surely don't want to tie up the work?" they queried. "I shall not be tying it up; you'll be tying it up. You forget this is not a private enterprise but a Government job." Puzzled, they next asked, "Well, what are you going to do?"

"Any man not at work to-morrow morning will be permanently dismissed. Good-night." Next morning the full force was promptly on the job and that virtually ended Goethals's troubles with canal employees.

They soon learned that he regarded them as friendly co-workers on a great task for the Government, that he was prepared to work harder than any of them, that he went everywhere and saw everything with his own eyes, that he would allow no official, high or low, to browbeat a single labourer or treat him unjustly, that his door stood wide open every Sunday morning to hear complaints and have justice meted out with even hand. They also came to realize that the Colonel was master of the job, that he was able to swing it—and that commanded respect. Moreover, he was even more careful of the employees' health than of his own; instead of living in state at Panama or Colon, his office headquarters were on Cucaracha Hill, overlooking defiant, rebellious Culebra.

Doctor Gorgas, to whom mankind is debtor, found in Goethals an ardent supporter of his brilliant campaign to rout the malarial mosquito and banish fever from the Zone, without which efforts the story of canal building under the Americans might have more closely and tragically resembled the attempts of the French.

Napoleon, when an obscure subaltern, used to pore over manuals of government as painstakingly as over manuals on manœuvres. Goethals acted as if there were no problem of civil administration which he had not pondered for years in anticipation of just such duties as now were laid upon his shoulders. He handled the volatile Panamanians with consummate skill. He handled 50,000 employees, comprising over seventy nationalities, as if his sole study and sphere in life had been that of a great industrial executive, arousing in them the competitive spirit to the highest pitch through dividing the canal into three sections, Atlantic, Central, Pacific, and pitting them against one another in their digging. These were the qualities—it was not merely technical engineering knowledge—that built the canal. Colonel Goethals modestly says there were no new engineering problems to be solved, but that there were endless novel problems in government.

His attitude toward human beings under his charge is well illustrated by the following passage from another of the inescapable Congressional quizzes, the point at issue being an item of $52,000 for a club-house:

Chairman: "A $52,000 club-house?"

Colonel Goethals: "Yes, sir. We need a good club-house, because we should give the men some amusement, and keep them out of Panama. I believe in the club-house principle."

Chairman: "That is all right, but you must contemplate a very elaborate house?"

Colonel Goethals: "Yes, sir. I want to make a town there that will be a credit to the United States Government."

The Panamanians were finding Goethals not a martinet but very much a man, a human being who understood human beings and wanted to treat them as human beings. Everything he did was done openly and above board. There were no cabals, no star-chamber intriguing, no political wire-pulling, Indeed, Colonel Goethals was a practitioner of the gospel of publicity in all his relations with his force —just as, at college, he had aligned himself with the anti-secret society order, Delta Upsilon. Every man knew his job was safe as long as he filled it. His own conception of duty Goethals has defined in these words:

"We are inclined to accept praise or reward for doing nothing more than our duty, when as a matter of fact we are entitled to neither, since we have done only what is required of us. The plaudits of our fellows may be flattering to our vanity, but they are not lasting; by the next turn of the wheel they may be changed into abuse and condemnation."

The world intently watched Colonel Goethals cleave the continent in twain. They saw him not merely directing the engineering, constructive and other physical phases of the epochal task, but discharging the multifarious duties of civil administration. And the world pictured him as among the most heavily burdened men on the planet.

"Load?" repeated Colonel Goethals to a recent interviewer. "There never was a load on me. It was my business to load!"

He did load, and saw to it that each man properly carried his load. By way of example: A rather pompous official with a grievance against the Colonel for having sent him certain instructions, entered the office one morning and began:

"I got that letter of yours, Colonel."

"I beg your pardon, but you must be mistaken; I have written you no letter," replied the Colonel.

"Oh, yes, Colonel—about that work down at Miraflores."

"Oh, I see," replied the Colonel imperturbably. "You spoke a little inaccurately. You mean you received my orders, not a letter. You have the orders, so that matter is settled. Was there anything else you wished to talk about?" That ended the interview.

Colonel Goethals was and is a great stickler for having orders obeyed to the letter and also to the minute. "My first text-book was the calendar," he remarked in reviewing his work at Panama. "Few realize the importance of definite dates. It is amazing what men can accomplish when given definite task, specific order, and time limit. A good many things an executive complains about in his men are due to his own lack of preparation and definite instructions. A task is either done or not done to-day. The first things I studied in building the canal were the time-books."

When chief of staff in South Africa, Lord Kitchener once sent for a railroad manager and asked him what was the shortest time in which a train could be run from Johannesburg, then Kitchener's headquarters, to a certain town farther south. The official did some figuring, then replied: "Thirty-six hours."

"Have a train ready for me at six o'clock to-morrow morning and have me there by six o'clock the following morning," commanded Kitchener, and the member of the staff who told me of the incident shortly after it occurred added: "We were there by six o'clock, you bet." Goethals is like that. He knows what it is physically possible to do within a certain time—and then orders that it be done without a tick of delay.

GEORGE W. GOETHALS

Not many erring mortals could have been granted the regal powers of a Czar, entrusted with the performance of a colossal, many-sided task, obliged to deal with some four-score nationalities and emerge from the ordeal successfully, without having engendered revolutionary sentiments, without having incurred a breath of scandal, without any warping of character. A man of smaller calibre would have abused his powers, would have misused his prerogatives, would have developed into an insufferable and intolerable autocrat. Goethals has carried immortal honours as lightly as he carried his canal-building "load." He has become as little puffed up by the military and civil recognition showered upon him as he became depressed when great slices of Culebra Hill insisted on sliding into the laboriously hewn canal, filling the passageway.

The view he takes is that he was ordered to do a certain piece of work and that he did it. Divided control and scattered responsibility having proved unsatisfactory to the Government, it was deemed necessary to concentrate authority. "And in principle," he says, "there is no difference in delegating legislative authority to fifty or one hundred men or to one man; the proposition is the same."

Curiously, the United States Government a second time called upon General Goethals to undertake a task in which the public interest was second only to that which centred in the building of the Panama Canal. That job involved the devising and constructing of much new machinery, new tools and new equipment for use both on land and water. Enough soil was excavated to fill a train long enough to encircle the earth many times, and entailed, also, enough dynamite-hole boring to have bored straight through the earth from New York to the roots of some tea garden in China. The new task assigned Colonel Goethals was also one of building, not, however, a passageway for ships, but ships themselves.

Colonel Goethals soon discovered that conditions at Washington were not wholly unlike those he first found at Panama. A Governmental board, inspired more by faith than fact, had proclaimed to a world unnerved by submarines that one thousand wooden ships of 3,000 tons or more would be turned out within eighteen months. When the time came to turn promises into performances the canal builder was called in. To his utter astonishment he discovered that "birds were still nesting in the trees from which the great wooden fleet was to be made" and immediately saw "how hopeless the task appeared." Nor had the bonds set aside to raise the necessary money been sold.

"As I regard all boards as long, narrow, and wooden, and being a believer in authority, I wanted both money and authority," Colonel Goethals told a great gathering of steel manufacturers in New York. Realizing that the construction of a thousand wooden ships from trees still in the leaf was an impossibility, the Colonel turned to the possibilities of steel shipbuilding. And he adroitly asked the nation's iron and steel men if they would rally behind him in an effort to launch 3,000,000 tons of steel ships within a year and a half, a question that was instantly put to the manufacturers by Chairman Gary of the United States Steel Corporation and answered in the affirmative with unanimous acclaim.

As I sat listening to the Colonel address my first impression was that his criticisms of conditions at Washington were undiplomatic; but when he led up to his straight-from-the-shoulder appeal to the body of men who alone could make his plans feasible, everyone realized the efficacy of his action. Having secured thus a pledge of loyal support, Colonel Goethals was in an advantageous position to deal with these men when it came to making hard-and-fast contracts.

No one realized better than Colonel Goethals the magnitude of his new assignment. However, he has a motto: "Begin a work and in its accomplishment problems will often solve themselves."

"Colonel Goethals has been so long accustomed to deal with subordinates and having his will enforced as law that trouble may rise when he comes to deal with his equals, men not accustomed to being bossed or to render military obedience," someone suggested when Goethals was named to build ships. That, however, was not the full explanation of his failure to carry out his programme. When he found, after protracted, to-be-deplored delays, that he could not have sufficient freedom to do effective work, he simply let the President know that he was ready to step aside. To get results was more important than retention or resignation. He went without a murmur.

In 1884 General Goethals married Miss Rodman, member of a venerable Quaker family, and there is another Goethals working his way to the front as an army engineer as well as a young Doctor Goethals, the latter in accordance with family trait and tradition.

I should add that Colonel Goethals was accorded a very high place in the vote taken for this series on "Who Are Our Fifty Greatest Business Men, Men Who Are Making America?" showing how he is esteemed by men of affairs throughout the country.

DANIEL GUGGENHEIM

MEYER GUGGENHEIM one day opened his heart and his purse to aid a friend who was wrestling heroically with a little mining property in Colorado which was threatening to ruin him.

That act of kindness over forty years ago was the basis of the extraordinary achievements of the Guggenheims in the smelting and mining business.

From control of one tiny smelter in far-off Pueblo, Colorado, the famous Guggenheim family, by industry, tenacity, and sacrifice, have built up the greatest mining and metallurgical enterprise the world has ever known.

To-day the Guggenheims handle and control 1,000,000,000 pounds —500,000 tons—of copper annually, or almost half the entire production of the world (2,250,000,000 pounds). They and their associates control the three largest copper mines in the world, the Chile Copper, the Utah Copper, and the Kennecott Copper properties.

Two of the Guggenheim companies alone, the American Smelting and Refining Company and the American Smelters Securities Company, do a business of over $300,000,000 a year—this exclusive of their mining activities. The Guggenheims, too, are the most powerful factors in the silver industry in the world, and are very large factors in gold, lead, zinc, and a variety of by-products.

As employers of labour they rank among the very largest in the world. They were the first employers, so far as known, to pay several employees, in salary and percentage of results, compensation running into hundreds of thousands a year—rumour said one man drew upward of a million a year.

The man mainly responsible for the phenomenal success of the Guggenheim organization is Daniel Guggenheim, whose judgment, whose faith in the future, whose ability to inspire men, whose capacity for hard work, first under the most trying physical conditions in remote, uncivilized mining camps, and, later, in the financial arena, have won for him a high place among the developers of America.

Many sides of Daniel Guggenheim are more or less familiar to the public—his philanthropies, his long record of welfare work among employees, his practical encouragement of American painters, his furtherance of musical culture, his love of literature, his interest in thoroughbred horses, his fondness for flowers, and his extraordinary knowledge of different races and countries, begotten of travel in almost every part of the globe.

But to this list I can make one addition: Mr. Guggenheim is no mean philosopher.

It took all my ingenuity, born of a fairly extensive experience in the art of interviewing, to draw Mr. Guggenheim into revealing this phase of his character. He did not "open up" until I had suggested that a great many people had the idea that men like himself had not really won their spurs and their wealth by any unusual effort but had simply been "lucky."

"Yes," said Mr. Guggenheim, "men—not always young men, either—sometimes come in here and, looking around my office, say: 'I envy you your luxurious office and your opportunities to enjoy the best in life.' I tell them: 'It has taken me forty years to earn my luxurious office with its beautiful pictures, fresh flowers, and leather-cushioned furniture. Year after year I put up with tremendous hardships, travelling in Mexico, in other foreign countries, and in remote parts of the United States.

"'You prefer the luxuries and refinements of the city, with its automobiles, its splendidly appointed homes. You do not care to make the sacrifices necessary to attain the success which can make the luxuries possible.'"

"What are some of the things necessary to achieve success?" I asked.

"Sacrifice, sacrifice, sacrifice!" Mr. Guggenheim repeated with impressive earnestness and ardour, his mind dwelling upon what he himself has undergone.

"Then, above all, you must have *tenacity*," he went on. "That is the greatest quality. Without it, no man can possibly succeed. Whether in college, in a profession, or in business, unless a man is tenacious, unless he sticks to a thing until he has mastered it, he has little chance of succeeding.

"One failure, you know, leads to another failure—and one success leads to another success. Win out in one thing before giving it up and trying another.

"Give me the choice between a man of tremendous brains and ability but without tenacity, and one of ordinary brains but with a great deal of tenacity and I will select the tenacious one every time.

"Then, tact is very important. I would rather employ a person of no extraordinary ability but who had great tact, than one of conspicuous learning and intelligence without tact.

"Judgment, initiative, energy, all these are most desirable and valuable qualities. But, above all and beyond all, you must have *tenacity* and *tact*."

"How did you manage to get this interview with me?" Mr. Guggenheim suddenly asked. "You didn't get it the first time you tried, nor the second. But you showed both tenacity and tact. You kept at it until you discovered a channel of approach that you knew would probably succeed. Your tenacity got you in here, and your tact has induced me to talk to you in a way I am not in the habit of talking for publication."

One of Mr. Guggenheim's favourite aphorisms is, "What is everybody's business is nobody's business." He therefore sees to it that all details in connection with the business are carefully and efficiently looked after.

I asked one of Mr. Guggenheim's closest colleagues what were his most notable qualities, how he had gained leadership in the smelting and mining business, why he had outdistanced all competitors. The reply, after careful deliberation, was:

"First, because of his phenomenal judgment, his ability to size up a situation correctly. Second, because of his unfailing optimism, his faith in the future, his confidence that the country and the metal industry and science would progress and develop. Third, because of his extraordinary faculty for handling other men, for influencing them to see things in the large way in which he sees them himself; his knack of inspiring courage and determination in those associated with him. Fourth, because of his policy of treating his people thoughtfully and generously—I mean his work-people as well as his executives and engineers and others high up; recently, as an instance, American Smelting insured the lives of all its salaried and daily-wage employees without a penny of cost to them. Fifth, because he has not been afraid to take chances, to spend one million dollars in the chance of making ten millions or fifty millions—as in Chile, for example, where a huge sum was spent in a most inaccessible part of the world before there was any possibility of immediate return."

A tiny craft which left the shore of Europe in 1847 and was storm-tossed on the Atlantic for four long, painful months bore to this land Simon Guggenheim, the first of the Guggenheims to come from Switzerland to this country. With him came his son, a young lad, Meyer Guggenheim, founder of the Guggenheim fortune and father of Daniel, the present head of the family. Meyer gradually built up a manufacturing business of considerable size and variety. He married a Swiss lass, Barbara Myers, and to them was born the "Seven Guggenheims." The elder boys entered the Swiss lace business and developed it wonderfully. This field, however, was limited—too limited for the combined energies of the maturing sons.

Having, through kindness, aided a friend to handle a mining property, Meyer Guggenheim's attention was directed to that sphere, and, he concluded, was a field broad enough for the activities of all his sons.

He summoned them all to the family home in Philadelphia, where all the children had been born. He related to them Æsop's fable about the seven sticks which could be broken easily when separated but which, when bound together, could not be broken. He told them that if they would all join and work together loyally and industriously, they could achieve what none of them could hope to do singlehanded. "In union there is strength" he impressed upon them.

Then he portrayed to them the potentialities of the smelting and mining industry, offered to help them to get a modest foothold in it, and asked their views of the project.

No sons ever had greater respect for a father—and few fathers have more richly deserved it, for Meyer Guggenheim was a man among men. They realized the wisdom of his proposal and immediately prepared to act on it.

He impressed upon them that, while he would aid them, both financially and with advice, to get a start, "you must kick for yourselves; you must build up your own enterprise."

As already told, their first venture was a smelter in Colorado. But they shortly acquired other interests. There were seven of them, all active, ambitious, optimistic, ready to rough it and ready to go anywhere, do anything, and suffer anything to contribute to the success of their new enterprise. No mountaineer, no prospector knew more hardships than the Guggenheim brothers voluntarily went through to reach a desired goal. Mountain fastnesses, untamed valleys, arid wastes, possessed no terrors that the daring young Guggenheims shrunk from facing.

The Creator, they soon discovered, had invariably deposited mineral wealth far from settled centres of civilization and had surrounded it with obstacles which only the pioneer and the brave elected to encounter. A price had to be paid to Nature for the giving up of her treasures.

Daniel Guggenheim, with the other brothers, uncomplainingly paid the prescribed price. Distance had no meaning for him or for them; wherever there was a chance to achieve something, he went, no matter what the cost in physical discomfort. He slept in tents or wagons amid wild surroundings as often as under a roof. The food he not infrequently ate would have been scorned by a Negro slave. His business demanded that he proceed to the firing line of advancing civilization, and he did not flinch from the ordeal.

But the readiness of Daniel Guggenheim and the other brothers to undergo personal hardships was not the only reason they forged

ahead. They had courage and wisdom enough to engage the best
and most expensive engineering and mining brains procurable. Not
only did they pay perhaps the largest salaries then known, but they
shared results with those who made results possible. From the time
he first became an employer Daniel Guggenheim adopted this now-
popular but then-revolutionary system. In this way the Guggenheims could get their pick of the world's mining, engineering, and metallurgical talent.

Nor is this all; but pains were taken to surround the workmen with
as comfortable conditions as circumstances would permit. Perhaps
no family has built more schools, hospitals, churches, and recreation
halls for employees. In inaccessible regions where itinerant enter-
tainers never venture, the Guggenheims' own welfare-workers get up
entertainments and other diversions.

The smelting industry was revolutionized by the Guggenheims.
Before their advent smelting contracts invariably were made for only
one year, smelting interests being afraid to take the risk of advancing
wages and rising costs over a series of years. Daniel Guggenheim
began taking five-year, ten-year, and even twenty-five year smelting
contracts at prices which sometimes appeared suicidal at the time.
But he was enough of a student of history, of science, of engineering,
of chemistry, of transportation, and of economic evolution to have
faith amounting to conviction that improved processes would be
devised to reduce smelting and mining costs sufficiently to yield a
profit in the future.

"If we can't discover scientific methods to lower our costs long
before this contract expires, we deserve to lose our business," was how
he expressed himself to one associate who questioned the advisability
of a certain proposed contract.

When the Guggenheims embarked in the Utah Copper Company,
in 1905, few people believed that the property could be made to pay,
the ore was of such low grade. Yet Daniel Guggenheim championed
the building of a $6,000,000 smelter and a $2,000,000 copper refining
plant to handle material which previously had never been handled
at a profit. It contained only twenty to thirty pounds of copper to
pay all the expenses of mining, smelting, refining, transportation,
selling, etc. His daring expenditure of this $8,000,000 has proved
one of the most profitable things the Guggenheims ever did, as the
mine is now ranked as the second largest in the world and pays handsome dividends.

Then look at what the Guggenheims are doing in Chile. The Chile
Copper property is ensconced in a remote, barren, mountainous desert
9,500 feet above sea level, in a region where rain has not fallen within
the memory of man, where vegetation is unknown, where water has

to be carried a distance of forty miles to the mine, where power has to be transmitted a distance of eighty-five miles from the power house to the mine, where roads are non-existent—where, in short, there is nothing to attract and everything to repel human beings. Into that forbidding region went the Guggenheims, decided to spend many millions in making it habitable, at once set the necessary complex machinery in motion—and now the Chile Copper Company has the largest developed body of copper ore in the world.

Daniel Guggenheim, I have learned from his associates, was the man who, in face of universal skepticism and discouragement, insisted upon the investment of many millions of dollars in Alaska. The Bonanza mine, now belonging to the Kennecott Copper Company, was simply a large body of copper which had been melted by nature, then corroded by glaciers and left perched on a hill. Although it contained from 65 to 85 per cent. copper, not a pound was won from it between its discovery (in 1901) and 1911 because it was beyond reach of transportation. Daniel Guggenheim set about the purchase of a half interest in the mine and agreed to build transportation within two years to get the copper out.

When questioned, Mr. Guggenheim said: "If we think it is good business we will go anywhere in the world whether it is Alaska, Chile, Mexico, or South America, Africa, or the Orient. If a lot of metal were found in the Arctic we would go after it. We know no distance and no barriers in our business." Before he was 40 Mr. Guggenheim had crossed the Atlantic Ocean seventy times.

"Roasted pigeons don't fly into one's mouth," Mr. Guggenheim went on to explain. "You have to discover a pigeon, you have to be able to shoot him, then you must clean him and roast him before you can eat him. So it is with business.

"The Almighty has put ores far away from where human beings are. That is why the mining business appeals to so few people. The average New Yorker wants to stay in New York, surrounded with luxuries. He is not willing to go to foreign countries or to uncouth regions, putting up with all sorts of inconveniences, to find properties and develop them. He shrinks from spending twenty or thirty or forty years meeting tremendous hardships.

"You cannot find copper, lead, silver, or gold mines in New York City. You must go to inaccessible and sometimes uninhabited places, where everything is crude and rough and uncomfortable and unsatisfactory. About the only enjoyment you get is the enjoyment of developing your business. You can get very little music and you have no cushioned chairs or rugs or fine pictures. You have to work all day like a slave and then perhaps read a little at night by the light of an oil lamp.

"The opportunities are as plentiful to-day as they ever were, if a man is willing to make the necessary sacrifices. No man, no matter what his vocation, can attain genuine success without making sacrifices. Nothing worth while can be got anywhere for nothing. Things we get for nothing we do not enjoy. The enjoyment comes from the hard work, the severe effort, and the sacrifice entailed in getting the thing—and the greater the sacrifice the greater the pleasure. Work and labour and study and sacrifice are all necessary to winning the kind of success that brings satisfaction with it.

"When we started in the metal business my father, I well remember, said to us: 'You boys have got to do the trick yourselves by hard work and by not being afraid to make sacrifices. But let me tell you, no sacrifice is too great to accomplish what you go after. You will be fully repaid if you will use your brains and make sacrifices until you reach your object.'

"When you ask me, therefore, for some advice for young men I would repeat that given us by my father—and, I may add, what I have already said: 'Roasted pigeons do not fly into one's mouth.'"

For twenty years or more the "Seven Guggenheim Brothers," Isaac, Daniel, Murry, Solomon, Simon, Benjamin, and William, worked hand in hand enthusiastically and unsparingly. Their ramifications in their field had already eclipsed all rivals when, under the leadership of Daniel, they merged their interests and took over the American Smelting & Refining Company. The truth of the words of their father, "In union there is strength," has been abundantly demonstrated by the record of his sons.

When the United States Government first wanted to obtain a large quantity of copper for war purposes Daniel Guggenheim took a lead in seeing that it was provided promptly and at a figure only half that prevailing in the open market.

Although Daniel Guggenheim is still head of the American Smelting & Refining Co. and the American Smelters Securities Co., he does not work quite so hard as of yore, because he has other interests which now appeal to him more than money-making. Also, many of his mining burdens are now being capably carried by his son, Harry F. Guggenheim, who, after distinguishing himself both as a scholar and an athlete at Cambridge University, England, carried out the traditions of his family for industry and sacrifice by spending a number of years "at the bottom of the ladder" in mines and metallurgical plants in Mexico, before taking his place at the council table of the great mining firm.

Although an ardent believer in hard work, Mr. Guggenheim is a strong advocate of vacations. "I believe," he told me, "that a man who works twelve months in the year does not work more than six months. It is the man who works ten to eleven months and does something else for one to two months who works twelve months. I insist upon every man and boy in our employ taking an annual vacation.

"Another rule we have is that boys must be treated with just as much consideration as any one else in the whole organization. If a boy comes with a message from others, or on any other duty, he must not be kept waiting, for his time is just as valuable to him as mine is to me."

Next to the Rockefellers, the Guggenheim family is probably the wealthiest in the country. Both Mr. and Mrs. Guggenheim are noted philanthropists. In dispensing their benefactions they make no difference in the matters of race, creed, or religion. In their early days Mrs. Guggenheim did not hesitate to share her husband's hardships on the firing line.

Having sowed wisely in the morning and forenoon of his life, he is now, in the afternoon, reaping a full harvest.

JOHN HAYS HAMMOND

AMERICA can claim the man who more than any other human being has coaxed Mother Earth to give up her hidden precious metals. No other figure in history ever added so much to mankind's supplies of gold and silver. Through his efforts mines in the United States, Africa, Mexico, South America, Central America, and Russia have added hundreds of millions of dollars to the world's wealth.

Latterly his activities in discovering riches in the bowels of the earth have been supplemented by operations on a colossal scale to irrigate and fructify the earth's surface for the sustenance of mankind. He has been a pioneer in the building of electric tramways in South Africa and Mexico, and hydro-electric power plants in different parts of the world.

These achievements have entailed adventures, dangers, and hardships such as have befallen few men. Besieged and shot at by semi-savages, perilous journeys among cannibals, stranded and starved for three days in a fastness far from civilization, imprisoned and sentenced to death, with the gallows oiled and manned ready to do its work—these are some of the experiences the shuttle has woven into the life of John Hays Hammond, recognized as the world's greatest mining engineer.

"How did it feel to be sentenced to death?" I asked Mr. Hammond. [I had lived in South Africa and was familiar with the circumstances of the memorable Jameson Raid which led up to his arrest and trial by Paul Kruger, then president of the Transvaal Republic.]

"I was angry, not afraid," Mr. Hammond replied with some fire, for we had been recalling those historical days. "As you know, we had arranged to plead guilty under one code of laws which punished treason by imprisonment, but were tricked and trapped by the Boer prosecutor into being sentenced under another code carrying the death penalty. I felt mad, indignant, outraged.

"I have had experiences more exciting and dangerous than those I went through in South Africa, only they were not so spectacular," Mr. Hammond added, when I questioned him. Almost from the time he could toddle, John Hays Hammond wanted to get at the inside of things, to explore, to make discoveries. His father, a graduate of West Point and an ex-officer of artillery in the Mexican War,

encouraged this inquisitive spirit, while his mother, a sister of John
Coffee Hays, the famous Texas ranger and later the first sheriff of
San Francisco, sympathized with his love for outdoor activities. He
early learned to ride, shoot, swim, penetrate forests, camp out, hunt,
and the like. From the public schools in San Francisco, where he
was born on March 31, 1855, he went to grammar school in New
Haven to prepare for the Sheffield Scientific School of Yale University.
He was bent upon being an engineer, a mining engineer for preference,
since he could then burrow into the ground and find out hidden things,
including perhaps gold, of which he had seen a great deal, having
lived in the mining districts of California during summer vacations.
His father was old-fashioned and erudite enough to prescribe a full
classical course in addition to the regular scientific curriculum, for he
wanted the boy to understand Greek and Latin as well as ore and
chemicals. Graduation from Yale, in 1876, with a Ph.B. degree, was
followed by a post-graduate course at the Royal School of Mines
at Freiberg, Saxony, until 1879.

The young man wanted to see something of the lands that lay
beyond the curve of the Atlantic. The Hammond boys—John Hays
was the oldest of four—had early earned a reputation as travellers
and explorers in California. Indeed, they used to hold competitions
regarding the number of counties each would visit.

Once, while under the temporary guardianship of an aunt, John
Hays, then fifteen, and a younger brother started to explore the tracks
of the Yosemite Valley and became so fascinated with their exploit
that they went on and on, staying a night or two at a mine, another
at some prospector's shanty, another sleeping out in the open, riding
sometimes fifty miles a day until they turned up nearly 500 miles
away, in Nevada, after the countryside had been searching for them
for two or three weeks!

"That trip," said Mr. Hammond reminiscently, "taught us self-
reliance, for we had to learn how to take care of our horses, how to
handle ourselves, how to meet all sorts of people, and how to get
accustomed to having the starry heavens as our bed-chamber ceil-
ing."

An attractive railroad position was refused by young Hammond
on his return from Freiberg. Senator Hearst, father of William Ran-
dolph Hearst, was then a foremost mine owner in the West, and Hammond tackled him for a job. The Senator was a hard-headed, practical man, and had had reason for being little enamoured of collar-and-
cuff, theoretical mining engineers.

"The only objection I have to you is that you have been in Freiberg
and have had your head filled with a lot of fool theories. I don't
want any kid-glove engineers," the brusque Senator told him.

"If you promise not to tell my father, I will tell you something," Hammond countered.

The Senator promised.

"I didn't learn a single thing in Germany!"

"Come around and start work to-morrow," clinched the Senator.

Young Hammond started next morning at seven o'clock and kept on the job daily for at least twelve hours. Senator Hearst was then negotiating for a number of properties and Hammond conducted ore tests on the results of which his employer invested millions of dollars.

A year later a wider door opened; Hammond joined the United States Geological Service as an examiner of gold mines. He kept his eyes open, noted the different formations at different mines, studied geology enthusiastically, and gradually cultivated a nose for mines. In the following year, 1881, he took practical training as a miner, as a foreman, and as a handy man in the mills. He contrived, also, to pay return visits to mines he had previously examined, and in this way was able to note the unfolding of their development. His knowledge enabled him to diagnose, analyze, and appraise ore bodies beyond the miner's pick. The whole thing fascinated him. It was not merely a thrilling way to earn a living and spend a life, but it added to the world's wealth, it brought new resources into existence, and it afforded profitable employment to thousands of workers. He enjoyed—and still enjoys—visiting a mine more than visiting the opera house or theatre.

Hammond's first professional trip to alien soil proved perilous. He was commissioned in 1882 to penetrate into Mexico some 250 miles from Guaymas. On landing on the Mexican west coast from a sailing boat which had been chartered to carry mining machinery, Hammond found that the Apache Indians were on the war path and that the long journey to the interior by stage would have to be done under cover of darkness. The first night out the drunken driver upset the coach; one man sitting opposite Hammond was killed and another so hurt that he died next morning.

Finally reaching the mines, Hammond found that the natives were systematically stealing the best ores. So he had himself appointed a special officer with power to arrest and soon terrorized the thieves, who did not relish either imprisonment or the alternative decree, enlistment in the army.

Conditions improved sufficiently to warrant Mrs. Hammond's joining her husband. The second day after she arrived at Guaymas, with a young baby, a revolution broke out. Hammond promptly commandeered a small house, barricaded it, and prepared to defend the fort, which was besieged by brigands; but he had learned in California to use a gun with the best of them, and the besiegers, discerning this, departed after a few days. During the long journey to the interior the party came upon a village which the Indians had cleaned out completely, the only living things in sight being a few chickens in place of the 200 population which Hammond had found on his journey coastwise. How near the Indians might be or how soon they might appear on the scene, no one could guess. If the Indians found the little American party, it meant its annihilation.

Fifty miles of dangerous territory had to be covered. Armed to the teeth, Hammond rode a mile or two ahead, signalling to the team. Mrs. Hammond had a pistol with which to commit suicide rather than submit to capture. However, the destination, Alamos, southern Sonora, was reached safely.

Mrs. Hammond stayed until the poor food began to undermine the health of the child. Mr. Hammond remained until he had the mine on a profitable basis and everything working smoothly. Before he was ready to depart, revolutionists seized the mint at Alamos, the only one on the western coast, and began to rob and cheat the company shamefully, refusing to pay the full amount for the bullion deposited. Hammond conceived the plan of accumulating the silver and then slipping away with it, to deliver it to the American Consul at Guaymas.

He had trained ten Yaqui Indians to shoot, and by their loyal assistance had been able to resist attacks by ten times as many Mexicans at critical times. Loading picked mules with 150 pounds of silver each, and taking the trusted Yaqui Indians into his confidence, Hammond bolted one night in a terrible thunder-storm, when no Mexicans were about. A relay of mules was in readiness seventy miles away, and, by travelling all that night and next day, Hammond got a good start of his pursuers—who, of course, took up the chase as soon as they found what had happened. When about 100 miles from Alamos, Hammond learned that the Yaqui Indians of the neighbourhood were on the war path against the Mexicans and that the Apache Indians were up in arms against the Americans. There were Apaches to the right, Yaqui Indians to the left, and Mexicans in the rear, all on the rampage, thirsting for the blood and the plunder of the North American intruder, the only white man of the company. The famous "Light Brigade" was in little worse plight than the hunted Hammond party. The ten faithful Yaquis could easily have betrayed their master and received big rewards for delivering so much booty. But they stood by him, guided him through the enemy-ridden territory, and landed him safely at Guaymas.

Incidentally, after the Diaz revolution, and when Madero was in power, Hammond offered to go, singlehanded, into the fastnesses of the Yaquis, bring them down to property controlled by Hammond and his associates and pay them sufficient wages to enable them to build homes and raise families if the Mexican Government would grant them amnesty, Hammond pledging his company to make good any damage thereafter done by the Yaquis. Madero was murdered, however, before he had opportunity to carry through the arrangement. Had Hammond's plan been carried out, the subsequent uprising of the Yaquis would doubtless have been avoided and the damage done averted.

"The Yaquis were the most honourable and honest tribe I ever met, far more so than white people, when treated fairly," Mr. Hammond declares.

Even more exciting were some of Mr. Hammond's experiences in the little-known region of the Andes. Accompanied by only two natives, he travelled over the third range of the Andes, between the headwaters of the Orinoco and the Amazon. Gold was being brought down by natives from that region and Hammond went to investigate. His guides' plans miscarried, and the three found themselves stranded in the jungle. For three days they were without food. After that the natives unearthed some beans, which looked like coffee, and this sustained life until relief came.

The final stage of the journey had to be made without horses or transportation of any kind. There were no trails. The trio followed the creeks, wading through one after another the whole day.

In this remote spot Hammond discovered a little mining community where the mining was done by the Negro women. The woman who was the boss and who brought gold for the visitor to test disappeared for two days. When she returned, the third day, her husband disappeared. Much cross-questioning revealed that the woman had had a child and that the primitive custom of *couvade* was still being practised there; that is, the father took the place of the mother in bed, was regaled with delicacies, received visits and congratulations from all the neighbours, and was treated in every way as mothers are in more civilized communities!

Cannibals also were encountered by Mr. Hammond during this sojourn in South America, but they made no attempt to molest him.

In his own country, too, the mining engineer and manager has had his full share of the rough-and-tumble life of pioneer mining. Serious labour troubles broke out in the Bunker Hill and Sullivan mine in the Coeur d'Alene district of Idaho. Strikers were led by such firebrands as Haywood and Moyer. Hammond was determined to keep the mine going. Collecting a trainload of men, he mounted the engine and rushed through the danger zone at the peril of running on to dynamited bridges, being shot by incensed strikers, etc. In riots which followed shortly thereafter quite a number were killed.

It was during those bloody days that Hammond, a marked man, on learning that the rioters were accusing him of being afraid to venture out, coolly announced one evening that he would walk down the street next noon. Armed with two revolvers, he started off entirely unaccompanied. Great excitement stirred. Rioters followed him, and one or two got directly in his path, but a significant little movement of the hand proved an effective passport. Reaching the end of the street he crossed to the other side and walked the whole way back. After that the miners had a healthy respect for the young Californian.

By the early nineties Hammond had won a reputation as a spotter of paying propositions. Before his day mining "experts" were mostly of the home-made, pick-and-shovel, rule-of-thumb variety, knowing little or nothing of geology or metallurgy or any other scientific aids. Numbers of the first university-trained mining engineers brought the new profession into more or less disrepute by their dilettante ways, their aversion to incurring hardships entailed in penetrating remote spots and living the crude life of on-the-ground pioneers. Hammond, on the other hand, had proved his ability to go anywhere, civilized or uncivilized, on an hour's warning.

The greatest goldfields in the world were then, as now, in the Transvaal. A famous South African magnate, Barney Barnato, in 1893, secured the services of the brilliant American engineer. Hammond lost no time in investigating the geological formations of the gold reef at Johannesburg. His study convinced him that, though only outcrop properties were then being worked, vast quantities of rich ore would be found at deep levels. When Barnato would not venture upon so dubious and costly a venture, Hammond, convinced of the soundness and the value of his plan, quit.

Within a few hours of this news becoming known, the American received a telegram from Cecil Rhodes, the greatest figure in British Colonial history and one of the most notable men of the nineteenth century. When Hammond arrived at Groot Schuur, the quaint residence of Rhodes, near Cape Town, the Empire Builder opened their business interview thus:

"I don't suppose you came to Africa for your health?"

"No, the climate of California is better," Hammond replied smilingly.

"Name your salary. Don't be modest," Rhodes commanded.

Hammond obeyed. A salary of $100,000 a year was a secondary item in his terms; he stipulated for a share of profits. Also, that Rhodes and not any board of directors should be his sole boss.

Rhodes had such faith in Hammond's ability that when the latter urged that the Colossus sell many million dollars' worth of shares in outcrop mines and stake his fortune on the development of deep levels, then purchasable for a song, the scheme was immediately taken up. Hammond became the father of the deep-level mining on the Rand, which is adding to the world's stock of gold many million dollars a year in the Transvaal alone, to say nothing of what the example then set has meant for mining throughout the world.

Another thing that appealed to the imagination of the founder of Rhodesia was the tradition that King Solomon's mines, of Biblical fame, were located in Mashonaland, now Rhodesia, and he proposed an exploration. He and Doctor Jameson accompanied Hammond and his party hundreds of miles through fever-saturated country. The last lap was undertaken by the engineer and a few sturdy natives. They found the 3,000-year-old El Dorado. Hammond decided it could be re-opened profitably, and the mines are now producing $20,000,000 a year.

"Rhodes," said Mr. Hammond, "was by far the greatest man I have ever met. He had unlimited vision, extraordinary perception, unbounded courage. He always insisted on looking at every business transaction from the other side's point of view and scorned to take advantage of anyone. Had Britain heeded his early advice there would have been no Boer War. He cared nothing for money except as an instrument to achieve great, worthy ends. Had money been his aim, he could have left $200,000,000 or $300,000,000 instead of $20,000,000."

Into the details of the abortive Jameson Raid which brought the death sentence to Hammond and three others, I cannot here enter; but from first-hand knowledge gathered on the spot I can state briefly the part played by the American leader of the Reform Committee. The Uitlanders, as the non-Boer residents of the Transvaal were called, were paying nine-tenths of the Republic's taxes, yet were denied not only representation but the most elementary civic liberties. Kruger kept promising but never granting reforms. Finally, when he realized that an uprising was planned, he offered to grant all the Reformers' demands if they would leave the Jews and the Catholics outside the pale. This treachery Hammond and his colleagues would not countenance. The revolution was not a movement to annex the Boer Republic to the British Empire. When somebody suggested hoisting a British flag over the meeting place of the Reform Committee the Boer flag was at once raised and Hammond proclaimed that he would shoot any man who dared lower the national emblem.

Doctor Jameson, then Commissioner of Rhodesia and a man of overwhelming ambition, had raised troops which were not to cross the Transvaal border until summoned by the Johannesburg Reformers to aid them in overcoming any Boer resistance that might be offered. Jameson, however, invaded the Transvaal Republic before the Reformers were ready to rise and he was surrounded and compelled to surrender. The British High Commissioner at Cape Town induced the Reformers to lay down arms, promising them, after he had communicated with Kruger, safety and reasonable reforms.

No sooner had the Uitlanders given up their arms than sixty or seventy of the Reformers were arrested. This created the utmost indignation but, virtually deserted by the British Government, the Uitlanders could do nothing. The trial of the Reformers is a matter of history.

What may not be generally known is that John Hays Hammond, while awaiting sentence, was allowed to journey to Cape Town in what appeared to be a forlorn attempt to prevent his death from illness. While at the British port he had abundant opportunity to flee the country, but he scorned to decamp. He elected rather to undertake a three days' return railway journey, lying helpless on his back, and to run the gauntlet of hostile Boers, who were planning to waylay the train avowedly with the intention of killing him. His bravery, however, captivated the Boers. The courage and devotion, also, of Mrs. Hammond in sticking by her husband's side in Johannesburg and Pretoria and through the upheaval, won the admiration of "Oom Paul." Kruger likewise believed in the sincerity of Hammond's motives; he realized that what this American wanted was to set up a republic where all would have equal rights, a republic after the pattern of the United States.

As a matter of fact, after Hammond, along with his three associates, had been released by paying a ransom of $125,000 each, Kruger used to tell the Uitlanders when they had grievances that he wanted to deal with "this Republican Hammond." Hammond subsequently, at Kruger's request, became a mediator in the negotiations which preceded the Boer War in 1900.

After the war, John Hays Hammond, at a notable banquet in London, pleaded with the highest British authorities for magnanimous treatment of the Boers. He urged a policy of conciliation which in time would make possible the confederation of South Africa. He pointed out that, owing to their numerical strength, the Dutch would inevitably gain the upper hand at the polls and it would be the part of statesmanship to grant voluntarily and wholeheartedly that which would have to be granted *nolens volens* sooner or later. "He gives twice who gives quickly," was the pith of Mr. Hammond's exhortation.

How abundantly successful this policy has proved history, particularly the part played by the Boers during the present war, has demonstrated.

The most gripping account of this chapter of John Hays Hammond's career is contained in a little volume, "A Woman's Part in a Revolution," written by Mrs. Hammond.

After the outbreak of the Boer War Mr. Hammond returned to the United States, in 1900. He made investigations for English interests and attracted millions of capital here. At his say-so a town would spring up on some spot almost overnight. Of course, Hammond's judgment was not then or at any earlier period infallible. He sometimes made mistakes, but his successes were so notable that the Guggenheims, in 1903, engaged him at reputedly the highest remuneration paid any employee in the world.

Among the projects with which he has been identified are the Guggenheim Exploration Company, the Utah Copper Company, Nevada Consolidated, Tonopah Mining Company, lead mines in Missouri, the Esperanza Gold Mine and various silver mines in Mexico and, in short, mining enterprises in many parts of the world.

Twice the Russian Government engaged him to investigate that empire's mineral and industrial resources and its irrigation possibilities.

Since he left the Guggenheims, Mr. Hammond has become deeply interested in irrigation. With associates, he is carrying out around the mouth of the Yaqui River, in Sonora, Mexico, the development of some 1,000 square miles of land, the largest irrigation project on the American continent. Already 30,000 acres are under cultivation. Another ambitious irrigation project which is bringing thousands of acres of orchards into existence is being carried out by the Mt. Whitney Power Company, California, the water in this case having to be pumped, by means of a system invented by Hammond. Among his various Mexican activities was the formation of the important Guanajuato Power Company.

Much of Mr. Hammond's time is now devoted to the public interest. He is particularly active in education, and delivers many lectures before students and other bodies. For some time he acted as Professor of Mining Engineering at Yale, which university he presented with a mining and metallurgical laboratory. Several honorary degrees have been conferred upon him. He is chairman of the Economics Department of the National Civic Federation, and has laboured assiduously to bring labour and capital to a better mutual understanding. He takes active participation in and is a generous supporter of hospital work. He is a notable advocate of international coöperation for the insuring of peace.

His political work won for him the presidency of the National League of Republican Clubs, and President Taft offered him the post of Minister to China, regarded by Taft as one of the most important of all diplomatic posts. As president of the Commission Extraordinary of the Panama Exposition, Mr. Hammond visited most of the capitals of Europe, interviewed rulers and foreign ministers, and greatly helped to bring about the success of the Exposition. Mr. Hammond was selected as representative of the United States at the coronation of King George V.

Both in business and in politics Mr. Hammond advocates publicity. One of his contentions is that corporations protected by tariff should be compelled to publish the fullest information concerning their profits.

Not many Americans have so wide an acquaintanceship among all classes and in all countries—his gallery of autographed photographs of men he has personally known is probably the largest in the United States; it runs the whole gamut from those of the principal European rulers to labour heads, one of whom, Samuel Gompers, appends to his picture these words: "To John Hays Hammond, the most constructive, practical, radically democratic millionaire I have ever met."

The time may soon come when America will have need of the services of business-statesmen of Hammond's calibre and experience. His knowledge—practical, technical, gathered at first hand—of foreign countries' resources, industries, and commerce fit him to become an important and valuable figure in the momentous deliberations which must follow the restoration of peace. What America will then need is not parochial, untravelled politicians, but hard-headed, sophisticated business giants, familiar with the whole world and its economic workings.

Mr. Hammond, who declares that "character is the real foundation of all worth-while success," can truthfully say, in the words of his intimate friend and correspondent, Kipling:

"Whate'er may come, thank God I have lived and toiled with men."

Postscriptally, Mr. Hammond attributes no small share of his success to his intrepid wife who has never hesitated to share his hardships and perils.

Any "Men Who Are Making America" series of articles written ten years from now promises to include another John Hays Hammond. The son's achievements in directing torpedoes at sea by wireless from land has already made him famous, and just what the effect of young Hammond's inventions may have in America's waging of war cannot be foretold. And this, it is declared, is not by any means the only important one of his many inventions. Few famous men are blessed with famous sons.

AUGUST HECKSCHER

WHEN a youth unable to speak the English language can come to the United States and attain marked success in half-a-dozen different fields, surely few native Americans ought to complain of lack of opportunities.

The career of August Heckscher illustrates better than any other in this series the abundance of channels open in this country for the exercise of intelligent and profitable industry. After thirty years of rigorous toil, first in coal mining and then in the zinc field, during which, after an abnormal amount of opposition, Mr. Heckscher earned a comfortable fortune, he became interested in real estate development and became a very important factor in this line of enterprise. Not satisfied with this achievement, he branched out—very successfully—into copper mining, steel manufacturing, iron ore properties, and such diverse activities as grape-fruit culture in Cuba, the manufacture of fire engines for most of the country's cities and towns, a paper company, large foundries, silver mining, and financial institutions.

I asked Mr. Heckscher to what he attributed his diversified success, to what particular qualities he attached special importance, and what, in his opinion, was the most common weakness in the make-up or training of American-born youths who failed to attain their ambitions.

As Mr. Heckscher has been a citizen and a voter for a longer period than most native Americans—forty-three years—and has rounded out a half century's residence here, he may be regarded as qualified to discuss the subject.

"Thoroughness and perseverance are cardinal requisites," he replied. "The trouble with most Americans who fail to succeed is not that they are not brilliant enough, but because they have not laid the proper foundation. They are not thorough enough. They do not master their subject from the ground up. They dislike the tediousness, the study, and the labour involved in laying foundations. They do not want to begin at the bottom—they seem to forget that men like Lincoln and Washington did not start at the top and that Napoleon began as an obscure artillery officer.

"You must learn to obey before you are fit to command.

"Opportunities are boundless in this country. You mentioned that I have made some success in a number of different undertakings.

If I have, it is because I set myself to learning each one of them painstakingly and applied myself to it perseveringly until I knew it well.

"How did I do it? Well, I am an omnivorous reader and my memory is a little like what Mr. Roosevelt once said to me when I asked him how he could remember so many things. 'I can't forget,' Mr. Roosevelt replied. I am not impatient; I have been blessed with a faculty for perseverance no matter what happens. I do not give in."

Some of the most powerful financial interests in the country learned from experience that August Heckscher possesses bulldog tenacity. They fought him and he fought them in the courts for ten solid years over title to the great New Jersey Zinc Mines which Mr. Heckscher had acquired. The records of this case, famous in jurisprudence, form a small library. From court to court the case was carried. Even when the Court of Appeals of New Jersey ruled against Mr. Heckscher he did not give up. Instead he redoubled his efforts. He even went and ransacked Europe for specimens of ore to substantiate his contentions.

He kept ten lawyers busy. Finally he presented such an array of facts, exhibits, and testimony that the Court of Appeals actually reversed itself, admitting that its previous decision had been based on insufficient data. During the thick of this battle Mr. Heckscher lost every penny of his fortune through the failure of the financial institution which did his business. One night he went to bed a moderately rich man, and woke up next day to find himself worth less than nothing. A friend had sufficient faith in him to lend him $50,000 to meet the more pressing of his debts, and Mr. Heckscher had to start all over again. That was in 1890, the year of the Baring Brothers memorable failure, which shook not only London but every other great financial centre.

His tenacity, his unwavering courage, his aptitude for arduous exertion stood him in good stead. Although he had lost his money, he did not lose heart. The combined opposition of influential financial, railroad, and industrial interests in New York and in New Jersey could not defeat or discourage him. Had he been a man of only moderate self-confidence, a man of mediocre ability, a man of only half-hearted determination, he never would have withstood the pressure for ten long years.

Perhaps Mr. Heckscher inherited his fighting qualities. His father fought in the battle of Leipzig against Napoleon the First as long ago as 1813, when a boy of only sixteen. In later life his father became Prime Minister of Germany. Heckscher, who was born in Hamburg on August 26, 1848, received a typically thorough education in Germany and Switzerland.

When nineteen, he decided to strike out for the United States.

He was given $500 in gold, which he strapped about his waist, and thus early manifested his faith in himself by giving his mother an assurance that under no circumstances would he call upon her for the gift of another penny. Nor did he. He landed in New York in 1867, and, through relatives, obtained employment in the anthracite coal-mining regions of Pennsylvania. All that he knew about coal was that it was black, but the manager falling ill, young Heckscher was placed in charge of the whole property.

"Running a coal mine in the 70's was not the pleasantest of occupations, for the Mollie Maguire gangs were then on the warpath," Mr. Heckscher recalled. "The miners' unions came and tried to lay down the law as to what the operators must do and must not do. The riots and the bloodshed in the coal districts during that reign of terror formed a dark chapter in American industry. However, my experiences, I suppose, tended to develop self-reliance. It was a rough but a salutary school for a young man in my position. I managed to fight my way through somehow or other."

A town having been built on top of the mine, rendering its continued development dangerous, the whole property was sold in 1881. By this time the anthracite coal trade was being corralled by the railroad companies, who, because of their control of transportation, were in a position to make it extremely difficult for private coal companies to stay in business. The Philadelphia & Reading Coal and Iron Company bought out the mine in which Heckscher was interested.

On looking around for a new opportunity, Mr. Heckscher, along with an older cousin, bought control of a zinc plant at Bethlehem, Pa., now forming part of the Bethlehem Steel Works. Although the concern had sunk into bankruptcy and was purchased by the Heckschers at practically sheriff's sale, they developed it aggressively and so successfully that, within a few years, it paid dividends regularly of 2 per cent. monthly. Mr. Heckscher became convinced that the zinc industry had vast possibilities and he resolved to extend his operations.

Accordingly, he took the lead in forming the New Jersey Zinc Company. Certain intrenched capitalistic interests did not relish the advent of this outsider, who was not of their number, and an attack upon the Heckscher interests was instituted. As already told, Heckscher lost all his money in 1890 and also at one stage had his title to the zinc property declared invalid, yet fought on until he attained ultimate victory at the end of ten trying years. He continued as manager of the zinc company until 1905, when he resigned.

Although he had now sufficient wealth to satisfy all his needs for the remainder of his life, he found he could not remain simply an inactive investor. He had been appointed by the courts to the receivership of several railroads, forming what is now the Kansas City Southern. He had also been receiver of a large steel plant. At each step he made it his business to master the industry or business which he took up, so that, in course of time, he acquired exhaustive knowledge of various lines of activity.

Then he was tempted to enter a field with which he had not first made himself thoroughly familiar. He purchased the Whitney property at 57th Street and Fifth Avenue, New York, as an investment, but soon discovered that it could not be made to pay. Having once taken up real estate, however, Heckscher, unaccustomed to doing things by halves, began to analyze conditions throughout the city with a view to more extensive operations. The Whitney property was then too far up-town to be turned to profitable account; in other words, Mr. Heckscher found he had bought prematurely—he was too early. He therefore decided to build merely a taxpaying structure on that site and to devote his attention to the 42nd Street district as being more immediately in the line of enhancement in value.

Having now a reasonably good knowledge of real estate, his activities became distinctly profitable. Among the buildings Mr. Heckscher now owns or controls are the twenty-five-story office building at 50 East 42nd Street, the Manhattan Hotel, the Tiffany Studios property, the former Havemeyer residence at 38th Street and Madison Avenue, the whole block fronting on Fifth Avenue, at 104th Street, another large property at 45th Street and Vanderbilt Avenue, and a business building at 622 Fifth Avenue, formerly used by Mr. Heckscher as his residence.

And the probabilities are that this list will be steadily lengthened, for he is as active to-day as he was thirty years ago.

The variety and extent of his activities may be gathered from the following partial list of his executive positions and directorships:

Owner of the Vermont Copper Company, director of the New Jersey Zinc Company, vice-president and director of the Eastern Steel Company, member of the executive committee of the Central Foundry Company, chairman of the Union Bag & Paper Company, director of the Central Iron & Coal Company, president and director of the Benson Mines Company (iron ore), director of the Canada Copper Company, director of the Nipissing Mines, chairman of the American-La France Fire Engine Company, director of the Ray Hercules Copper Company, member of the executive committee of the Empire Trust Company, director of the Lawyers' Title & Trust Company, and director of the Cuba Grape Fruit Company.

Yet, with all his multifarious business affairs, Mr. Heckscher has taken time to live. To his friends he is "Commodore," having been commodore of the Seawanhaka-Corinthian Yacht Club—yachting is his favourite recreation. His intense love of good pictures is revealed by the great number of meritorious paintings which adorn his office walls and also his home at Huntington, L. I. He has also taken time to discharge a full share of civic duties. A believer in good roads, he served as commissioner of highways at Huntington for two years, having been elected by a decisive majority, notwithstanding opposition by some of the working people on the score that he was a capitalist and had no business to take the $3 a day salary away from some workman in need of it. This little objection Mr. Heckscher handsomely overcame, not only by adding the $3 to the salary of his chief assistant, but by engaging at his own cost a capable engineer to carry out many improvements.

Huntington has since received a gift of a beautiful park upon which Mr. Heckscher spent much labour, to say nothing of money, beautifying and equipping it for the use of the townspeople and particularly the children, who occupy a specially warm spot in his heart. The park is amply endowed to meet all upkeep charges, so that it may not at any time impose the slightest burden upon the taxpayers.

"Oh, it is hardly worth mentioning, but, do you know, I had no end of real pleasure out of planning and laying out that little park, with its rustic home for the caretaker, its fountains, and other attractions," replied Mr. Heckscher, almost apologetically when I brought up this subject. "It is a nice place for the kids and the birds."

Mr. Heckscher married Miss Atkins in Pottsville, Pa. They have one married daughter who lives in England, while the nationally known polo player, G. Maurice Heckscher, now of the Meadowbrook Polo Team, which defeated the best team England could produce, is a son of Mr. and Mrs. Heckscher.

In view of Mr. Heckscher's own record, it is not surprising that he should regard America as a land of unequalled opportunities for those who will undergo the necessary preparation to fit themselves to seize them. He firmly believes that responsibilities seek only shoulders able to bear them, and that the idle and the ignorant are apt to reap just what they sow. Knowledge is power and hard work is the only dynamo that can generate success.

His career proves that to the man with seeing eyes, a well-trained mind and willing hands, Opportunity comes many times in a lifetime, not once, as sang the poet who put these words into the mouth of "Opportunity":

> Master of human destinies am I!
> Fame, love, and fortune on my footsteps wait.
> Cities and fields I walk; I penetrate
> Deserts and seas remote, and passing by
> Hovel and mart and palace, soon or late

> I knock unbidden once at every gate!
> If sleeping, wake; if feasting, rise before
> I turn away. It is the hour of fate,
> And they who follow me reach every state
> Mortals desire, and conquer every foe
> Save death; but those who doubt or hesitate
> Condemned to failure, penury, and woe,
> Seek me in vain and uselessly implore,
> I answer not, and I return no more!

Opportunity may not constantly come knocking at the door; it may be necessary to set forth and diligently search for her. But she *is* to be found by those who look forward and go forward equipped to see her and seize her.

A. BARTON HEPBURN

"I HAVE always been lucky."

That was the frank admission made by A. Barton Hepburn, usually described simply as a banker. His career, however, has been one of many-sided success. He has made his mark as an educator, as a lawyer, as a legislator, as a government official, as an author, and as a big-game hunter—of which last he is perhaps most proud.

The Chase National Bank eighteen years ago, when Mr. Hepburn took hold as president, had deposits of $27,000,000 and capital, surplus, and undivided profits of only $2,500,000. Now it has over $300,000,000 deposits and $22,000,000 of capital, surplus, and undivided profits. Also, there is an allied Chase Securities Corporation, young but vigorous.

The experience I am about to tell sounds like a page from the pen of an over-imaginative novelist.

Mr. Hepburn had just taken his seat as an Assemblyman at Albany, thirty-seven years ago, as a Republican under a Democratic house and senate, a position apparently offering little scope for recognition. He was writing letters in the house thanking some of his friends for the support they had given him, when he became conscious that someone had sat down beside him. He turned to find a giant of a man occupying the adjoining chair.

"I believe I have the honour of addressing Mr. Hepburn?" said the giant with a Scottish accent.

"Yes, I am Mr. Hepburn, but I am quite sure I never met you before, for I surely would remember you," was the reply.

"Mr. Hepburn, I have called upon you for your name's sake. I hope in future to call for your own sake. I am John F. Smythe, Chairman of the State Republican Committee and Postmaster of Albany, and this is why I came to meet you.

"A great many years ago I was a student in college in Scotland and in hazing the freshmen we went to great lengths, committing what undoubtedly were criminal acts. We were arrested, indicted, and —despite the intercession of many family friends—arraigned for trial, and it appeared certain that we should all be disgraced for life.

"There was great excitement the day of the trial. The court was crowded with parents, relatives, friends of the students, and local people. When the case was called a patriarchal-looking old man of the neighbourhood, Sir Andrew Hepburn, begged leave to address the court. 'You are about to commit a very serious and a very grave wrong,' he began. 'You have here a number of young men of excellent families indicted for alleged crimes, whom you propose to punish and disgrace for life. What they did was wrong, but what they did the class before them did, and the class before them, and the class before them, even going back to the class in which your Honour and I and the prosecuting attorney were members. We all did the same thing, and if we had been indicted we would have been placed behind prison bars.'

"The aged man's appeal made such an impression that the whole proceedings were dropped.

"I came to America. I made up my mind that, while there was nothing I could do for Sir Andrew Hepburn, if I ever had opportunity to do anything for anyone having the name of Hepburn, I would not neglect to do it. Here I am. I know all about you. If there is anything I can do, I shall feel privileged in being allowed to do it. If there is ever anything you want, call on me."

Smythe was then perhaps the greatest political power in Albany and he saw to it that his young friend Hepburn was placed on important committees, thus giving him a standing in the legislature which ordinarily would have taken years to attain. Governor Tilden sent for him, complimented him on his independence of mind, and asked his coöperation in carrying through reform measures which the Governor was championing. As there was a Democratic majority of only five in the Assembly, every vote counted. Hepburn was an ardent reformer and he pledged his enthusiastic support.

Alas, the very next bill that the Administration submitted called for a commission of four members whose reform proceedings were to be conducted *in secret*. The measure was railroaded through to its third reading in five minutes.

Up jumped Hepburn and made a rousing protest against the proposed star-chamber methods of the commission. He thundered against secret, hole-and-corner legislative doings, although not long before he had promised the Governor whole-hearted support.

Next morning the New York *Tribune* and the New York *Herald* printed the name of Mr. Hepburn and five others with black, mourning borders around them, charged them with being lackeys of the "canal ring," and gave them a terrible editorial trouncing.

Hepburn got mad. He raised the question of privilege, had the articles read, and then delivered a masterpiece, quoting, from Blackstone down, against star-chamber proceedings. Speaker Jerry McGuire left the chair, came along the centre aisle, and sat down beside

A. BARTON HEPBURN

Hepburn. "I like you," he cried, shaking Hepburn's hand. "You are right, and we can work together." Opposition to the secret proceedings was spreading over the State.

Tilden sent for him again. Hepburn expected a lambasting. Instead, the Governor greeted him with: "I have read what you said in regard to this bill. You were right. We want to turn on the light. The bill will be amended to meet your views and I trust it will get your support."

The Governor gave a dinner to William Cullen Bryant, and Republican Assemblyman Hepburn was honoured with an invitation. With one bound he had sprung into prominence. In later years Mr. Hepburn became chairman of a legislative investigation the New York Chamber of Commerce inspired to expose discrimination by the railroads against the City of New York by giving special rates to Philadelphia and Boston and other seaboard cities and also to individuals. As a result of this investigation Mr. Hepburn drew up a bill providing for a State Railroad Commission and was able to have it passed in the face of the opposition of the all-powerful railroad interests. It is this Commission law which exists to-day. Four other important measures he brought forward and carried through.

"How did you do it?" I asked Mr. Hepburn.

"I found most of the members did not know how to work or to study up a subject and that the most formidable weapon to use was a volley of facts," he replied. "Facts which could not be disputed when fired at them always awed them. Having won a reputation for being right, it was easy enough to become a factor in any debate. Of course, I had to work very hard."

Five years' effective work in the Assembly won him the appointment of superintendent of the State Banking Department.

But let us get back to the beginning of our story. The founder of the Cleveland *Plain Dealer*, a successful railroad contractor in Ohio, and a literary-oratorical light—all three of good education—were among the uncles of Alonzo Barton Hepburn, but his father, a farmer in Colton, N. Y., objected to giving him a college education on the ground that it would unfit him for the work of a farmer. Three older brothers had gone off as privates in the Civil War—each came out with a commission—but Barton was too young, having been born on July 24, 1846. No boy had ever gone from Colton to college and one citizen who was not at all proud of this tradition offered to lend Barton $1,000 if he would take insurance and join the Masons. Barton did. To eke out his slender resources he taught district school between terms and also became clerk in a Colton store.

This job cut his wisdom teeth. The store bought everything the community produced and sold everything it consumed. The town had a tannery which used 10,000 cars of hemlock bark a year, two saw mills, two grist mills, a tub factory, etc. The yeomanry were slick—and their wives slicker. Because he was well educated, young Hepburn was given the job of measuring and computing the value of loads of bark, wood, hay, etc. Often his measurements and his weights, taken at the store, did not tally with those of the mills when the stuff was unloaded—the loads, it was discovered, had been weighted with stones, iron, etc. Colton, lying at the foothills of the Adirondacks on the banks of the Raquette River, at the entrance of the lumber industry, was then the most flourishing place in St. Lawrence County, with 1,800 permanent inhabitants and many transients. The young clerk learned to handle and appraise the value of all sorts of materials raised by the farmers as well as the supplies needed for the lumber camps up the mountains.

On graduating with an A. B. degree from Middlebury College, the town where his father was born, he became instructor of mathematics at St. Lawrence Academy, and, later principal of Ogdensburg Educational Institute at a salary of $1,200 a year. This enabled him to pay off all his debts. He next studied law, was admitted to the bar, and returned to Colton to rest.

So many people swarmed to him for legal advice that he decided to stay there and practise. He could pick whichever side he wanted in almost every suit. Business boomed. His clients included the King estate of Boston and others owning extensive tracts of land. Then the State of New York engaged him to look after overdue taxes, etc. Plenty of timber land could be picked up by merely paying back taxes.

Hepburn saw his opportunity. He bought 30,000 acres at 50 cents an acre, sold some timber off it, joined several others in building a saw-mill which cut 25,000,000 feet per year, put money into wing dams, and made the river navigable for logs. He was, however, "land poor."

Governor Cleveland offered to re-appoint him State Bank superintendent, but as his lumber interests were harassing him, he quit. In addition to his domestic expenses, he had to pay interest and taxes on his land, build a new mill, and meet other obligations far beyond the salary paid by the Banking Department. For several years he worked hard to clear his feet—and then sold out at a profit of $200,000. This when forty.

His liking for law had not been eradicated by his political experiences, but the banking field easily overshadowed the legal arena. His first banking position in New York was as United States bank examiner. His work here attracted notice, and he was called to Washington as Comptroller of the Currency. This proved the stepping stone to that aim of nearly all bankers, the presidency of a New York bank, the Third National. When it was taken over by the National City Bank, Mr. Hepburn went along, as a vice-president.

"Come over and help us or we perish," was the gist of a message he received from the directors of the Chase National Bank two years later.

Having been Federal bank examiner, he knew the whole situation. The field was broad, with inviting opportunity. So he accepted, with results that constitute a remarkable chapter of successful American banking.

"How have I succeeded?" Mr. Hepburn repeated. "Simply by hard, systematic work directed by every ounce of intelligence in me. To my mind it is true that 'genius is 95 per cent. perspiration and only 5 per cent. inspiration.'"

Then he gave this pointer for winning success:

"Whenever I have studied any subject or dug out any information I have always carefully compiled the data in a form that would be instantly available. I have kept a memorandum of all facts I gathered.

"Thus, my book on 'The Artificial Waterways of the World' contains many figures I secured when in the legislature and when chairman of the Committee on Transportation in the Chamber of Commerce. My 'History of Currency' embodies much information I gathered as secretary and treasurer of the Sound Money League which opposed free silver all through the Bryan campaign, in the work of which I was constantly engaged.

"By keeping a proper record of facts and figures you can turn to them and use them to help you whenever occasion arises."

Mr. Hepburn has lived. He has achieved as much out of business as in business and has had many honours showered upon him. He rivals his friend Andrew Carnegie in the number of honorary degrees conferred upon him by colleges—LL.D's. from Middlebury, Columbia, Williams, and Vermont; D.C.L. from St. Lawrence University, etc. Commerce elected him to its highest office, president of the Chamber of Commerce. Finance, not to be outdone, made him Chairman of the Currency Commission of the American Bankers' Association on its formation a decade ago and has kept him in that place ever since, while he has been president of the New York Clearing House and the National Currency Association as well as chairman of two State Commissions to Revise the Banking Laws. He has held the presidency of the St. Andrews Society, the New England Society, the Bankers' Club, and other social organizations. France made him an Officer of the Legion of Honour.

His philanthropies have been notable. He donated Hepburn Hall to his Alma Mater, Middlebury College, in 1915. It consists of two elaborate buildings, a five-story dormitory to accommodate 100 students, and a three-story commons building. Ogdensburg in 1916 announced a $130,000 gift from him for hospital purposes there, and the A. Barton Hepburn Hospital was erected for the use of St. Lawrence County, the scene of his early struggles and triumphs. He is also active in the work of the Rockefeller Foundation, of which he is a trustee.

His books have commanded the attention of the thoughtful. They include "History of Coinage and Currency," "A History of Currency in the United States," "Artificial Waterways and Commercial Development," "Artificial Waterways of the World," and "Story of an Outing." He was one of the founders of the Academy of Political Science.

His services as a director are in wide demand. He sits on a score of financial, industrial, and mercantile boards dealing with such diverse things as five-and-ten-cent articles (Woolworth), insurance (N. Y. Life), automobiles (Studebaker), manure (American Agricultural Chemical) and gasoline (Texas Co.).

Mr. Hepburn is as much at home among big game as among big business. By way of celebrating his seventieth birthday, Mr. Hepburn travelled 5,000 miles to hunt for the famous brown bears which are to be found—sometimes—on Kadiak Island, Alaska. After an exciting hunt he bagged two—no one is allowed to kill more than three. A few years ago he also journeyed several thousand miles to search for big game in British East Africa and had the sensation of meeting and the satisfaction of killing the best game of that country, including two lions in the open.

He can wield a golf stick as expertly as he handles his gun. Fishing is another of his hobbies. So is swimming.

Independence is one of Mr. Hepburn's outstanding traits. Whether in politics or in finance he will not bend the knee to anybody acting questionably. He has always insisted on doing his own thinking and travelling his own road. His great learning, first as a student and teacher, and then as a lawyer, rendered him fit to form his own conclusions and he has all along reserved the right to do so.

Intense energy is another of his characteristics. He burns much midnight oil in searching for knowledge—sometimes for knowledge's sake, more often to fit him to grapple more effectively with practical problems of social, political, financial, and industrial life.

He believes in orderliness, and practises it. He hates chaos and avoids it—his desk is always just so.

Mr. Hepburn has one son living, Charles Fisher, whose mother died in 1881. In 1887 Mr. Hepburn married Emily L. Eaton, of Montpelier, Vt., and they have two daughters, Beulah Eaton, wife of

Lieut. Robert R. M. Emmet, of the U. S. Navy, and Cordelia Susan. Because of his fondness for the country, Mr. Hepburn maintains a residence at Ridgefield, Conn., in addition to his city home in 57th Street, New York City.

Although past the seventieth mile-post, Barton Hepburn is as alert in body and mind as he was a quarter of a century ago. He attributes his wonderful condition to love of Nature. "The outdoor life," he recently wrote, "sweetens all existence; it cultivates the pure and wholesome in one's life and aspirations; it lures from the manmade attractions that pander to sensation, to God-made attractions that sustain the source of being; in advancing years it enables one to exclaim:

> "'Though I look old, yet I am strong and lusty,
> For in my youth I never did apply
> Hot and rebellious liquors in my blood,
> Nor did not with unbashful forehead woo
> The means of weakness and debility.'"

SAMUEL INSULL

ONE bleak November evening a poor but ambitious young London clerk, who in his spare moments had contrived to learn shorthand, stood on the dingy underground railway platform at King's Cross waiting for a train to take him to the home of Thomas Gibson Bowles, proprietor and editor of *Vanity Fair*, where the youth eked out his two-dollars-a-week salary by earning a few shillings as stenographer after his regular day's work was done.

To while away the time during the drab ride in London's "Sewer," the lad resolved to buy something to read, and his choice fell upon an American magazine, the old *Scribner's*, now the *Century Magazine*. It chanced to contain an article on the electrical experiences and achievements of one Thomas A. Edison, then hardly known in Europe. The writer was Francis R. Upton, one of Mr. Edison's aides, and the story he told was fascinating.

Not very long after this the real estate agent and auctioneer for whom the clerk worked decided that he could cut expenses by engaging an "articled" clerk—an apprentice who would serve for nothing. So the paid clerk answered a "Situations Vacant" advertisement in the London *Times*.

The advertiser turned out to be Colonel George E. Gouraud, the English representative of Edison and the resident director in London of the Mercantile Trust Company of New York, then owned by the Equitable Life. Colonel Gouraud was favourably impressed by the youth's enterprise and experience, for in addition to his daily task and his shorthand writing for the famous Bowles, he had found time to do secretarial work for Sir George Campbell, a noted member of Parliament.

He was engaged as Colonel Gouraud's secretary—and then resolved to strive to become secretary to Edison himself, the wonder-working hero of the magazine story.

In his new position with Colonel Gouraud, he not only did his full day's work but, as a possible stepping-stone toward his goal, made himself useful at night to Edison's technical representative in England, E. H. Johnson, who was then assisting in the formation of the Edison Telephone Company in London. To Mr. Johnson he confided his ambition.

The abilities, the enthusiasm, and the inordinate energy of the young secretary began to be noted by Americans visiting the Edison headquarters, and before long he received an attractive offer from the most prominent international banking house in America to come to New York. Acceptance would have diverted him from his purpose; so he refused the proffered position.

One day the cable brought the message he had waited for and worked for. *Thomas A. Edison wanted him as his private secretary.*

The youth was Samuel Insull, the early secretary, associate, confidant, financial manager and *alter ego* of Edison and now the creator and head of the largest power plant in the world producing electricity by steam, a plant supplying more customers and more power than any in New York, London, Berlin, or Paris—the Commonwealth Edison Company of Chicago. Mr. Insull has also won his way to the head of Chicago's elevated railways and the city's entire gas business, while, in addition, he has built up and dominates enterprises which supply 350 different communities with gas and electric light, power for industries, and current for numerous urban and interurban railways.

But we are getting ahead of our story. We left Mr. Insull, then twenty-one, jubilant over the receipt of the Edison summons. He had equipped himself for the job. He had already imbibed much knowledge concerning electricity and had been given the honour of acting for the first half hour as the telephone operator in the first experimental telephone exchange erected in Europe. He had done his work well—better than one of his colleagues did on an eventful occasion.

A celebration of one of the royal societies was being held at the Burlington House, Piccadilly, and a telephone had been installed for the entertainment and edification of the guests—and also with a view to bringing it to public notice. Mr. and Mrs. Gladstone came along and showed much curiosity. Mrs. Gladstone asked Mr. Insull, who was in charge of that end of the wire, to let her use the instrument. The wife of the famous statesman asked the Edison employee at the other end whether he knew if a man or a woman was speaking. In loud tones came back the reply: "A man!"

Full of rosy hopes, Mr. Edison's new private secretary set foot on American soil on February 28, 1881.

Although it was between five and six in the evening, he was taken, by Mr. Johnson, direct to Mr. Edison's office at 65 Fifth Avenue.

At first glance both employer and secretary felt disappointed. Edison had not expected so boyish-looking a person; the hero's appearance did not tally with the worshipper's imagination.

"With my strict ideas as to the class of clothes to be worn by a prominent man," Mr. Insull declares, "there was nothing in Edison's dress to impress me. He wore a rather seedy black diagonal Prince Albert coat and waist-coat, with trousers of a dark material, and a white silk handkerchief around his neck, tied in a careless knot falling over the stiff bosom of a white shirt somewhat the worse for wear. He had a large 'wideawake' hat of the sombrero pattern, then generally used in this country. His hair was worn quite long, and hung carelessly over his fine forehead. What struck me above everything else were the wonderful intelligence and magnetism of his expression, and the extreme brightness of his eyes. He was far more modest than in my youthful picture of him. I had expected to find a man of distinction. His appearance, as a whole, was not what you would call 'slovenly'; it is best expressed by the word 'careless.'"

The new secretary very quickly learned of Edison's contempt for the clock. He was asked to report for duty after dinner—and his first day's work finished between four and five o'clock in the morning!

Mr. Insull immediately fell a victim to the wizard's magnetic spell. He forgot that Edison lacked a collar, that his shirt was frayed, that his hair was frowzy, and that his trousers were not creased to a razor-edge. One night's association was sufficient to create unbounded admiration for what was in his hero's head.

"Next evening," Mr. Insull recalls, "I was taken out to Menlo Park by Mr. Edison and I well remember how surprised I was to see the fields around his laboratory, the houses of himself and his assistants all illuminated by this wonderful new light, using a carbon-filament lamp—a decided improvement on the paper-filament one which I had seen in London. I recall that I was quite impatient on that occasion to run down to the railroad station from the laboratory, about half a mile away, to send a cable to my friends in London, telling them that I had seen Edison's system in operation. About ten or twelve days later I received an acknowledgment from the man to whom I cabled in which he said he supposed I had been in America just about long enough to be able to draw the long-bow as well as any of those Yankees with whom I had been associating!"

The secretary soon found that he must perform little duties not called for in the bond. Among other things, he had to buy clothes for Edison in order to keep him looking half respectable, for Edison himself was too much engrossed with the things that were in him to be fastidious about what was *on* him. Edison "took to" the young man at once. Within a few months Mr. Insull was given an interest in every Edison enterprise. He had to take entire charge of Mr. Edison's finances and looked after all sorts of personal and company affairs for his chief.

"I used to open the correspondence and answer it all," Mr. Insull recalls, "sometimes signing Edison's name with my initial, and sometimes signing my own name. If the latter course was pursued, and I was addressing a stranger, I would sign as Edison's private secretary. I held his power of attorney, and signed his checks. It was seldom that Edison signed a letter or check at this time. If he wanted personally to send a communication to anybody, if it was one of his close associates, it would probably be a pencil memorandum, signed 'Edison.' I seldom took down from Edison's dictation, unless it was on some technical subject that I did not understand. I was expected to clean up the correspondence with Edison's laconic comments as a guide as to the character of answer to make. It was a very common thing for Edison to write the words 'Yes' or 'No,' and this would be all I had on which to base my answer. Edison marginalized documents extensively. He had a wonderful ability in pointing out the weak points of an agreement or a balance-sheet, all the while protesting he was no lawyer or accountant; and his views were expressed in very few words, but in a characteristic and emphatic manner."

"How many hours a day might you have worked in those times?" I asked Mr. Insull.

"I had to work in the office all day, look after the financial and business end, and then very often I would be with Mr. Edison at his laboratory most of the night," replied Mr. Insull. "We usually worked about four nights in seven. We seldom worked on Sunday nights but, as a rule, we were at it during most of Monday night and Tuesday night. By Wednesday night we were so exhausted through lack of sleep that we usually spent that night in bed.

"Thursday and Friday nights saw us busy again until well into the morning. I have known Edison to work night and day ten days on end. He seemed to be able to do without sleep as long as a camel can go without water."

These were busy days. Writing to an English friend two months after his arrival in New York, Mr. Insull expressed exuberant confidence in the prospects for electricity. He recited how he had seen 700 lights burn the current generated from one electric machine for them all and supplied through mains of "no less than eight miles in length." He explained that the first district to be lighted up in New York would have about 15,650 lights and added: "I suppose that this district will be all lighted up in from three to four months and then you will see what you will see. You will witness the amazing sight of those English scientists eating that unpalatable crow of which Johnson used to speak in his letters to me when I was in the old country. . . . A great difficulty is to get our machinery manufactured."

The first central power station was opened in Pearl Street, in lower New York, in September, 1882. Mr. Edison had completed the invention of his incandescent lamp but encountered enormous difficulties in having supplies of the necessary materials manufactured, in inaugurating proper methods of distribution, in reducing the amount of copper required for the conductors, etc., etc. Mr. Edison had sold out for large sums his telephone and telegraph inventions and interests both in Europe and at home and this money he had freely poured into his various manufacturing companies for making lamps, electrical generators and motors, electric tubes and fixtures, and miscellaneous appliances. Although Edison spent his last penny, he could scarcely cope with the situation.

"At one time everything looked so blue and so hopeless," Mr. Insull told me, "that Edison said to me one night in all seriousness: 'If we cannot pull through, I can go back to earning my living as a telegraph operator and I suppose you could get along as a shorthand writer.'

"For six months things were so involved and money so scarce that I was compelled to get a friend, who had been a little more thoughtful of the rainy day than the rest of us, to lend me money to pay for my meals and my room.

"Mr. Edison, and I as his financial man, were harassed at every turn by creditors. Looking back from this long distance, I must confess that our troubles then were really very serious.

"However, we stuck to it and finally managed to get on our feet. About the only people who were willing to assist us in those early days were J. P. Morgan and Henry Villard."

Other veterans have told me that they question whether Mr. Edison would have been able to surmount the obstacles that met him at every turn had it not been for the heroic fight made by Sam Insull. What the world would have lost, how much of the progress of the last generation would have been forfeited, had Edison succumbed and retired to oblivion, who can guess? For the loyal assistance and encouragement he then lent Edison day and night, the American people owe Mr. Insull a meed of gratitude.

To escape incessant labour troubles at their machine shop on Goerck Street, N. Y., and at other points, it was decided to build works at Schenectady, N. Y., where there was an ample supply of workers and where the Schenectady Locomotive Works (now part of the American Locomotive Company) had established a great reputation. Mr. Insull took charge of this epochal enterprise, and as its general manager built it up from a plant employing 250 men to one employing 6,000. It was this plant which later formed the nucleus for the great General Electric Company. His close association with the wizard had enabled Mr. Insull to gain a thorough practical knowledge of every phase of the business and he also developed ability to handle men.

Apropos of this, Edison was once asked to give particulars of Samuel Insull's collegiate education in connection with the latter's application for membership in a learned society. Edison wrote down this reply:

"Samuel Insull's education has been obtained in the college of experience."

Recognition of Mr. Insull's yeoman service came in 1889. Various Edison manufacturing companies and the Edison Light Company were consolidated into the Edison General Electric Company. He became vice-president in charge of the entire manufacturing and selling ends of the business. He continued in this responsible position until shortly after June, 1892, when the Edison General Electric Company amalgamated with the Thomson-Houston Company to form the present General Electric Company. In the fall of that year Mr. Insull resigned to accept the presidency of the Chicago Edison Company.

He found this concern had a total capital of only $883,000, that it was not the largest concern in the city, and that it had almost a score of competitors. It employed only a handful of men and had a capacity of only 4,000 horse-power.

Few men have done more creative, constructive work, conceived more productive developments, or overcome more technical and sociological difficulties in the last twenty-five years than Samuel Insull.

Instead of less than $1,000,000 of capital, Mr. Insull's Chicago company (now the Commonwealth Edison) has actual assets of $85,000,000.

Instead of 4,000 horse-power, it has 500,000 horse-power.

Instead of consuming a few hundred tons of coal a week, the company now uses as much as 300 tons of coal in a single hour.

He is head of the People's Gas Company and of the Elevated Railways of Chicago which, together with the electric company, have a turnover of $1,000,000 *every week* and represent the investment of $275,000,000.

Through the Middle West Utilities Company and other organizations brought into being and controlled by him, Mr. Insull supplies 350 communities spread over thirteen or fourteen states with electric light and power, bringing the total annual revenue of his various companies up to $75,000,000 a year and making the total investment capital between $400,000,000 and $450,000,000 for all the Insull companies.

His 1892 force of a few men has grown to an army of over 25,000.

Customers have increased from hundreds to hundreds of thousands—and are still constantly increasing.

MEN WHO ARE MAKING AMERICA

The value of Commonwealth Edison has multiplied 100 times in the twenty-five years.

Mr. Insull several years ago demonstrated in black and white that he could supply the elevated railroads of Chicago with current at a lower rate than they themselves could generate it, and his company now turns every elevated wheel throughout the city.

Instead of several central stations peddling electric current, Chicago now has only one great station, the baby of 1892, now a giant of greater proportions than any other metropolis in the world can boast.

Perhaps the best and briefest way to convey some idea of what Samuel Insull has achieved will be to present a list of the enterprises of which he is head either as chairman or president, and the concerns in whose management he has a voice as director:

Chair. of Bd. & Dir.	People's Gas Light & Coke Company
President & Director	Commonwealth Edison Company
" " "	Public Service Company of Northern Illinois
" " "	Middle West Utilities Company
" " "	Illinois Northern Utilities Company
" " "	Twin State Gas & Electric Company
" " "	Sterling, Dixon & Eastern Railway Co.
Chair. of Bd. & Dir.	Central Illinois Public Service Company
" " "	Kentucky Utilities Company
" " "	Missouri Gas & Electric Service Co.
Director	Interstate Public Service Company
"	Public Service Company of Oklahoma
"	Electric Transmission Co. of Virginia
Chair. of Bd. & Dir.	Federal Sign System (Electric)
" " "	Northwestern Elevated Railroad Company
" " "	South Side Elevated Railroad Company
" " "	The Metropolitan West Side Elevated Railway Co.
Receiver	Chicago & Oak Park Elevated Railroad Co.
Chair. Exec. Comm.	Chicago Elevated Railways Collateral Trust
Director	American Water Works & Electric Co.
President & Director	West Penn Traction & Water Power Co.
" " "	West Penn Traction Company
" " "	West Penn Railways Company
" " "	West Penn Power Company
" " "	Great Lakes Power Co., Ltd.
Director	International Transit Company
"	Central Power Company
"	Illinois Midland Coal Company
"	Midland Counties Coal Company
"	The Chicago & Alton Railroad Co.
"	Electrical Testing Laboratories
Member of Comm.	Chicago City & Connecting Railways Collateral Trust
Chair. of Bd. & Dir.	Chicago North Shore & Milwaukee Railroad
" " "	Chicago & Interurban Traction Co.

His policy in dealing with the public—and the politicians—has been "Publicity." From the start he has advocated regulated monopoly of the public services, since duplicate plants mean waste investment and therefore higher costs to consumers. He has not hesitated to reveal the minutest details of his costs, the return on the capital invested, and everything else connected with the business. His theory has been that by securing an enormous volume of business, distributed as evenly as possible throughout the twenty-four hours, electric light and power could be sold at a lower figure than would be possible under any other conditions.

As a matter of incontrovertible fact, Chicago, thanks to Mr. Insull's tremendously aggressive policy, enjoys the lowest rates for electric current of any large city at home or abroad.

He has been a pioneer in installing new devices, especially the more recent high-power, costly machinery designed for large-scale production at lower costs.

But while ceaselessly seeking to improve the production end, he has devoted even more attention to developing the selling end of the business. He has been a great believer in advertising, in making the public acquainted with what electricity can do for the housewife, the storekeeper, the manufacturer, the railways. While others sought to antagonize the investigation mania that swept over the country a decade ago, Mr. Insull willingly volunteered to put all his cards on the table. He also spent much time in giving private and public advice (through addresses, etc.) to other corporations to deal with the public frankly, fairly, and cheerfully.

Mr. Insull believes that the age of electricity is only dawning, that developments of a magnitude not yet imagined are even now on the way, and that by and by the greater part of the world's work will be performed by the harnessing of the mysterious vital fluid in a thousand ways which even Edison has not yet had opportunity to tackle.

He believes, for instance, that properly conducted central electric stations should and will furnish the power to run all the railroads in the country, the railroad people attending to the operation of their systems and the electrical people attending to the supplying of the motive power. To Mr. Insull, Germany's dream of dividing the whole country into a number of zones within which every house and factory and railway will be supplied by electric power from one huge plant in each zone, is not so extremely fantastic as many imagine. A similar scheme for the United Kingdom was proposed by a very famous British engineer, S. Z. de Ferranti, years ago. If Mr. Insull lives long enough I rather think he may do something along this line in the United States—indeed, he has already made a substantial start in Illinois and in a dozen or more Middle Western states, although so far he has not been able to do much with the steam railroads.

"What has been the hardest part of your battle—obtaining franchises, satisfying the people, or what?" I asked Mr. Insull.

"Raising the money," was the emphatic reply. "The public are usually fair when they are fully and properly acquainted with the facts."

"And your greatest pleasure?"

"The pleasure of achievement—of doing things, of building up, of creating something constructive."

"What are the principal requisites for a successful career?" I next asked.

"Good health, imagination, persistency, and a good memory—and, of course, keeping everlastingly at it."

"How can a man acquire a good memory?" I pursued.

"The way to cultivate a memory is to exercise it. The man who takes a great interest in his business has little or no trouble to remember the main facts connected with it. You usually remember the people you like; in the same way, if you like your business, you can easily remember the facts governing it without even making any special effort. Don't carry a notebook in your hand all the time."

"Why do so many young men and even older men fail to succeed?" was my next question.

"Because they are not willing to make the necessary sacrifices. As Edison used to say, 'A man should never look at the clock except to be sure he gets to work early enough in the morning.'"

Mr. Insull has always been an early riser—he is still about the first man to reach the office in the morning.

"You often," Mr. Insull continued, "hear fellows in different companies and institutions remark: 'Oh, So and So is solid with the Old Man.' If you take the trouble to investigate, you will invariably find that the employee who is 'solid with the Old Man' is a real worker, one who is always on the job, one who is ready to do things at any hour and to go anywhere, whereas the complainer is likely to be more concerned about how he can find entertainment for himself in the evening than how he can increase his usefulness during the day.

"Then, non-success is often due to inability to see things, to note intelligently what other people are doing, to learn what is what and to grasp new opportunities. They don't seem to keep their eye on the ball."

Mr. Insull is entitled to talk on such matters. He had to leave school shortly after he was fourteen—he was born on November 11, 1859—and began life as an office-boy at $1.25 a week, a sum which he had to supplement by finding other duties in the evenings. He taught himself shorthand when still a boy—and the rest I have tried to tell in the foregoing brief sketch.

His favourite hobby is farming. He has a 3,500-acre farm in Lake County, Ill., about thirty miles from Chicago, where he is rendering invaluable service to the State by raising, and showing other farmers how to raise, high-class cattle, horses, sheep, and hogs and how to introduce improved methods of agriculture.

OTTO H. KAHN

MANY American mushroom millionaires affect art but few understand it or really love it. Quite a number of the *nouveaux riches* become enamoured of grand opera—ostensibly. Others develop a consuming passion for the collection of rare books and manuscripts—the contents of which they cannot appreciate. America has one notable financier who does not need a tutor when he goes picture-hunting, not even when he spends $500,000 for a Franz Hals masterpiece. Nor when he attends the opera does he need an interpreter, be the production in French or Italian or German. He knows more about the fundamentals of grand opera and its production than most professionals.

While he has won a place second to none among modern financiers, he has made an even greater impress and achieved even more valuable ends in the realm of art and music and culture. He is Otto H. Kahn.

He is a banker—plus. He is an art connoisseur—plus. No man has come more prominently to the front in finance during the last dozen years and no man has done so much as he, not only to give America the finest operatic fare in the world, but also to bring art—not only operatic art—within reach of the public. Though engaged during these years in the reorganization of more transportation systems than any other man in America, yet he has found time to reorganize the Metropolitan Opera House from top to bottom, to provide opera of the highest quality for other leading American cities, to take a leading part in the Society of Friends of Young Artists, to arrange for excellent summer concerts at nominal prices, to be the main factor in the French Theatre of America, to be at the head of the Shakespeare Tercentenary Committee, and to bring into being what was destined to be a model playhouse where people of small means but artistic tastes could enjoy wholesome dramatic food.

Though an aristocrat by birth and breeding and association, Mr. Kahn's non-business activities have been inspired, not by a wish to tickle the whims and the jaded appetites of those of his own social standing, but by an inborn desire to furnish for the masses the mental and spiritual nourishment afforded by genuine art and beauty and culture. "For," as he said in a recent speech, "art is democracy, art is equality of opportunity, not the false democracy which, misunderstanding or misinterpreting the purpose and meaning of the democratic conception, seeks or tends to establish a common level of mediocrity, but the true democracy which, guided by the star of the ideal and firm in its faith, strives to lead us all onward and upward to an ever higher plane."

When first these promptings took possession of him, shortly after his settling in New York and before he had made his mark in the financial world, he revealed his longing to his friend and confidant, the late Edward H. Harriman, half expecting that the railroad wizard, himself engrossed in business, would frown upon the ambition to mix music and art with money-making, the beautiful with the mundane, the ideal with the practical. In those days only dilettanti busied themselves in the production of opera or took an active part in matters of art in general. To spend time over such frills and frivolities was interpreted as reflecting a lack of seriousness of purpose, of only half-hearted interest in the stern realities of life and fortune-making.

"Go ahead and do it," Mr. Harriman replied unequivocally. "If you don't let it interfere with your application to business, if you keep it in its place, it will do you not harm, but good. It will be exercise and practice for imagination. Don't you ever let your imagination get rusty."

It was not long before Otto H. Kahn made his influence felt in things operatic. He took hold of the Metropolitan Opera House and reorganized it as he would have reorganized a railroad, purging it of deadwood, introducing valuable reforms, infusing new life into it, and setting up as its goal artistic achievement in place of mere monetary success, an operation that entailed the solving of many problems, the vanquishing of much opposition, and, incidentally, considerable cost to himself and the few kindred spirits who sympathized with his unselfish aims. But his wisdom was justified by its fruits, not only in New York but also in Boston, Chicago, and Philadelphia.

To Kahn, music, beautiful paintings, artistic statuary, literature, and other things often regarded lightly are meat and drink and religion, the very essentials of a full life, indispensable food for both body and soul. He believes, with Carlyle, that "music is the speech of angels."

"Art," declares Mr. Kahn, "can be as educational as universities. It has elements which, to a great part of our population, can make it as nourishing as soup kitchens, as healing as hospitals, as stimulating as any medicinal tonic. Mæcenases are needed for the dramatic stage, the operatic stage, the concert stage; for conservatories and art academies; for the encouragement and support of American writers, painters, sculptors, decorators—in fact, for all those things which in Europe are done by princes, governments, and communities. There is vast opportunity here for cultural and helpful work. To strive toward fostering the art life of the country, toward counteracting harsh materialism, toward relieving the monotony and strain of the people's every-day life by helping to awaken or foster in them the love and the understanding of that which is beautiful and inspiring, and aversion and contempt for that which is vulgar, cheap, and degrading—this is a humanitarian effort eminently worth making."

How came Mr. Kahn to take the graces of life so seriously?

Briefly, he imbibed it at his mother's knee, was raised on it during the boyhood years spent in his own home, and had it parentally impressed upon him that, whatever the world might have in store for him, whatever his fate or fortune in things material, he must hold fast to the priceless, intangible things which alone could enrich the mind and the soul and give to life its savour.

This home of Otto Hermann Kahn was in Mannheim, Germany. He was one of eight children. His father was a prosperous banker, and the Kahn home was a centre for artists, musicians, singers, sculptors, and writers. Young Otto's earliest ambition was to be a musician, and before he graduated from high school he had learned to play several instruments. His father, however, had other plans for him. One brother was allowed to follow Apollo, and became Professor of Music at the Royal Academy of Music of Berlin.

When Otto was seventeen—he was born on February 21, 1867—he was placed in a bank at Karlsruhe, near Mannheim, where he received an unceremonious baptism into the financial cult, his principal duties for some time being cleaning the inkwells of the other clerks, running out to buy sausages, beer, and other victuals for their lunch and being generally kicked around in a manner calculated to cure any symptoms of swell-headedness at the prospect of being installed as a "banker." Incidentally, it is difficult to picture the immaculate, dignified, polished Otto H. Kahn of to-day toting the beer can and wiping out inkwells!

"Yes, it is true," Mr. Kahn admitted when I asked him if what I had been told about this was the truth. "And it was a useful, salutary training, for it taught discipline and order. One must learn to obey before he is fit to command. It instilled a proper sense of one's place and emphasized that the most humble duties must be performed conscientiously and without any loss of self-respect. I suppose I must have wiped the inkwells fairly satisfactorily, for it was not long before I was promoted and had another novitiate to clean my inkwell and fetch my lunch."

During these apprenticeship years he attended lectures on art, continued to study and practise music, and in other ways fulfilled the parental injunction not to neglect this side of his development lest he contract a wrong perspective of life and of the relative value of the materialistic and the idealistic. After three years' service in Karlsruhe he went into the army as a hussar for a year, an experience which has left its traces to this day: Mr. Kahn is straight of back, invariably correct in posture, precise and snappy in deportment.

The young banker's training was to be Teutonically thorough. Mere domestic experience was not enough; he must needs be broadened by international travel and service. His next step, therefore, was to enter the important London agency of the Deutsche Bank. Here he displayed unusual talents and rapidly rose to be second-in-command.

Although he had not gone to London with any settled purpose to make his home there permanently, he developed so intense a liking and admiration for the English mode of life, both political and social, with its unbounded freedom, breadth, opportunity, and inspiring traditions, that he renounced his German citizenship and became naturalized as an Englishman. Comparison between life in England and that in Germany moved him to choose the former. He became an "Englishman from conviction."

This same spirit of democracy, coupled with a desire to enhance and diversify his knowledge of banking, impelled Mr. Kahn to seize an opportunity to gain first-hand insight into the functioning of the greatest republic under the sun. His talents had attracted the notice of the Speyers in London, and they offered him a position in their New York house. Mr. Kahn came to the United States in 1893, intending to remain here only temporarily.

But he found his task here of absorbing and arresting interest, and life and the people very congenial. Particularly did he find one American congenial. In 1896 he married Miss Addie Wolff, daughter of Abraham Wolff, one of the early upbuilders of Kuhn, Loeb & Company. It was on January 1, 1897, that Mr. Kahn joined the firm whose prestige and influence, already great, he was destined to enhance extraordinarily. He had the good fortune to be thrown into immediate contact with Harriman—and Harriman had the good fortune to be thrown into contact with Kahn. The two, notwithstanding sharply defined differences in temperament and method, became as brothers. Harriman in business was gruff, truculent, domineering, almost spoiling for a fight. As Mr. Kahn, with true insight and praiseworthy candour says in his excellent study of Mr. Harriman—the only serious appraisement published of the great railroad gladiator: "Smooth diplomacy, the talent of leading men almost without their knowing that they were being led, skilful achievement by winning compromise, were not his methods. His genius was the genius of a Bismarck, of a Roman Cæsar. His dominion was based on rugged strength, iron will and tenacity, irresistible determination, indomitable courage, tireless toil, marvellous ability, foresight almost prophetic, and, last but not least, upon those qualities of character which command men's trust and confidence; his rule was frankly the rule of the conqueror. He was constitutionally unable either to cajole or dissemble. He was stiffnecked to a fault."

Mr. Kahn, the travelled, cultured banker and diplomat, although not possessed of the *bonhomie* or the captivating smile of a Schwab, had learned the value of suavity, of covering the iron fist with a velvet glove, of cultivating the coöperation and good-will of others rather than rousing their combativeness and their ill-will. Often he reasoned with Harriman to use more gentle methods, but Harriman would invariably reply: "You may be right that these things could be so accomplished, but not by *me*. I can work only in my own way. I cannot make myself different nor act in a way foreign to me. This is not arrogance on my part. I simply cannot achieve anything if I try to compromise with my nature and to follow the notions of others."

Although only thirty years of age, Mr. Kahn almost immediately became Harriman's right-hand man in the gigantic task of reorganizing the Union Pacific, a task which in its early stages had been handled by the head of Kuhn, Loeb & Company, Jacob H. Schiff, with a skill and effectiveness for which Mr. Schiff did not receive adequate credit. Harriman discovered in the young banker a mind as quick and fertile as his own, a depth and breadth of vision astonishing in a man so young, ability to analyze mathematically and scientifically, not only financial, but railroad problems with a thoroughness and accuracy which captivated the railroad wizard. That Mr. Kahn owes something of his subsequent success in railroad finance to his intimate association with Harriman, he would be the last to deny. Indeed, he has preserved for the memory of his great friend the most profound affection and reverence.

To-day Otto H. Kahn is recognized as perhaps the ablest reorganizer of railroads in the United States. The systems which have been or are being treated by him, in addition to the Union Pacific, include the Baltimore & Ohio, Missouri Pacific, Wabash, Chicago & Eastern Illinois, and the Texas & Pacific, not to mention other similar operations to which he has been called in as a consulting financial physician.

"Reorganizations," remarked Mr. Kahn, "embody a certain element of romance; they call for constructive imagination. To take a broken-down property, a few streaks of rails, and aid in working a transformation which will bring into being a great transportation system to serve the country and, incidentally, to rehabilitate the owners, is a species of creative work which fascinates me. It yields the joy of creation.

"Taking hold of the Metropolitan Opera House when it had ceased to do full justice to its functions and was living largely on its reputation and on the splendour of a few big stars, neglecting the other attributes of a great opera house, such as a chorus, stage setting, orchestra, and ensemble work, also appealed to this desire to create something. Just like a broken-down railroad, it did not have the necessary equipment to make it a complete, well-rounded organization. To take a hand in remodelling this institution and making of it a great symmetrical, artistic organization with its appointments and equipment functioning effectively, was an irresistible task and one well worth doing, both for the creative joy it carried with it and the valuable public service thereby attained."

It was Kahn who, after all efforts to cure by conciliatory methods the inveterate mismanagement of the great Missouri Pacific system had failed to bring results, finally resorted to steel and gave the Gould dominion the *coup de grâce*.

It was Kahn, also, who saved the financial world from what threatened to be a disaster of very dangerous potentialities by jumping forward and rescuing from collapse the famous Pearson-Farquhar syndicate which, with more ambition than judgment, had overextended itself in a daring attempt to weld together a transcontinental system out of a combination of existing lines controlled by powerful interests.

It was Kahn, too, who played a leading rôle in the intricate, delicate negotiations which led to the opening of the doors of the Paris Bourse to American securities and the listing there of $50,000,000 Pennsylvania bonds, in 1906—the first official listing of an American security in Paris. And it may be suspected that he had no small share in the negotiations which resulted in the issue by Kuhn, Loeb & Company of $50,000,000 of City of Paris bonds and $60,000,000 Bordeaux, Lyons and Marseilles bonds during the war.

To come down to another recent instance, Mr. Kahn has taken so valuable a part in the formation and conduct of the $50,000,000 American International Corporation with its vast potentialities for furthering America's world position in trade and finance that its president, Charles A. Stone, remarked to me: "I don't know what we would have done without the counsel and practical assistance of Mr. Kahn. He is a wonder. His understanding of international affairs is amazing."

Mr. Kahn has more than fulfilled the prediction made years ago by Thomas F. Ryan when discussing informally the coming financial giants; as he walked and talked Mr. Ryan espied Mr. Kahn coming along the street and remarked: "Here comes a man who will be among the first in the list."

It was Kahn who finally succeeded in persuading Harriman to abandon his cast-iron mask of secrecy; to reveal himself, his methods, and his aims with great frankness during the last two years of his life. Harriman had followed the methods of the mole, burrowing here, there and everywhere, allowing the public to catch a glimpse of his activities only when the fruits of his burrowing came to the surface. Kahn, having early realized the potency of democracy and clearly foreseeing the trend of events, urged Harriman to take the public into his confidence, to cease dodging the representatives of the press, and thus have the public with him rather than against him in his many plans for the development of the nation's transportation facilities, plans which both Harriman and Kahn earnestly believed were conducive to the enlargement of the country's prosperity and efficiency, agriculturally as well as industrially. Even in the short time Harriman lived after his change of attitude he accomplished wonders in disarming and winning over public opinion, and had he lived a few years longer he probably would have become a national hero.

In an address on "High Finance," Mr. Kahn made this statement: "One of the characteristics of finance heretofore has been the cult of silence; some of its rites have been almost those of an occult science. Finance, instead of avoiding publicity in all of its aspects, should welcome and seek it. Publicity won't hurt its dignity. A dignity which can be preserved only by seclusion, which cannot hold its own in the market place, is neither merited nor worth having. We must more and more get out of the seclusion of our offices, out into the rough and tumble of democracy, out to get to know the people and get known by them. The eminently successful man should beware of that insidious tendency of wealth to chill and isolate. He should never forget that the social edifice in which he occupies so desirable quarters has been erected by human hands, the result of infinite effort, sacrifice, and compromise, the aim being the greatest good of society; and that if that aim is clearly shown to be no longer served by the present structure; if the successful man arrogates to himself too large or too choice a part; if, selfishly, he crowds out others; then, what human hands have built up by the patient work of many centuries, human hands can pull down in one hour of passion."

For his own part Mr. Kahn is doing much to make finance and financiers understood by the people. He is attaining no mean reputation as a writer on financial and economic subjects and as a public speaker. Moreover, while he does not court the limelight from day to day, he is invariably willing to see financial reporters and others and to give them all reasonable information as well as sane views on current happenings.

Incidentally, while on this phase of his character, I might add that

Mr. Kahn may frequently be seen sitting in the low-priced seats in the Metropolitan Opera House and mingling freely with the audience there, with those real lovers of art who are willing to wait in line for hours to gain admission and who go to hear, not to be seen.

In conceiving the New Theatre it was Mr. Kahn's idea to supply wholesome plays, presented with as near an approach to perfection as attainable, at moderate prices for the benefit of people of ordinary means, and to set an example to professional theatrical producers to the end that the whole theatrical business might be elevated to a higher plane. In this movement Mr. Kahn and those associated with him were ahead of the times, hence the project, as originally planned, had to be abandoned. The New Theatre has now been transformed into the Century Theatre, which differs little from other New York playhouses. However, another movement along somewhat similar lines was inaugurated by Mr. Kahn and others in connection with the Shakespeare Tercentenary and something permanent may be evolved.

Greater success promises to attend the foundation here of the French Theatre, of which Mr. Kahn is chairman. In many other ways Mr. Kahn has contributed and is contributing continually to the support of things dramatic and artistic and to the encouragement of the artistic world and its people, including genuine young talent.

His activities are not confined to New York. In addition to being chairman of the Metropolitan Opera Company, he was chairman of the Century Opera Company (founded to give opera at popular prices), treasurer of the New Theatre, vice-president and the principal founder of the Chicago Grand Opera Company, and director of the Boston Opera Company. He is also honorary director of the Royal Opera, Covent Garden, London, and is equally well known in French operatic circles. As a matter of fact, Otto H. Kahn is the foremost figure of the world in grand opera, known in Europe as well as in America for his understanding and appreciation of all art and his helpfulness to art and artists.

I asked Mr. Kahn what advice he had to offer to ambitious young men.

"*Think*," he flashed back. "The young man who applies himself seriously to thinking will by and by be amazed to find how much there is to think about. He should never be content simply to take things as they are. Nor should he be satisfied with the accomplishing of one task, no matter how worthy or important, but should continue thinking and thinking and he will find many channels opening up for his activities.

"Doing—acting—is the second stage. Sufficient depth and comprehensiveness of thought leads to a corresponding depth, degree, and quality of action.

"The young men—and their elders—in this country now have an opportunity such as has come to no other nation since the middle of the seventeenth century, when England rose to conspicuous greatness. It is preëminently a time for fundamental thinking and wise, broad-gauge action on the part alike of statesmen, business men, labour, and every other element of the nation. Every great privilege carries with it a corresponding duty and obligation. In the present emergency, we must first of all clarify our collective mind by serious thought and study."

Several years ago, a little weary of the drudgery of business and of the tremendous stress and strain of his activities in America, and tempted by the vision of a quieter and more settled life, Mr. Kahn planned to return and enter British public life. He was cordially welcomed and was duly accepted as a parliamentary candidate. It was characteristic of him that he chose for his constituency a district almost wholly populated by working people. Not very long after, however, the cables brought the news that Mr. Kahn had abandoned his political ambitions and had decided to return to America.

"I discovered," Mr. Kahn told me, "that my roots had gone too deeply into American soil ever to be transplanted. The microbe of America had entered my blood and could not be dislodged. I found I had been mistaken in thinking that I could forsake America for England. A little taste of a life of leisure there convinced me that I wanted to and was bound to return to the strenuous life I lead here, to my work and associates, my duties, responsibilities, and aspirations and do what little might be in my power to aid in constructive development, both in a financial and a cultural way. Work is infinitely preferable to loafing."

Having reached the final conclusion that his place and his heart were in America, Mr. Kahn became an American citizen.

The palatial, historic home, St. Dunstan's, which Mr. Kahn acquired from the Earl of Londesborough, in 1913, when he had visions of settling there, was turned over by him, when the war broke out, as a hospital and home for blinded soldiers and is still in use for that purpose. Mr. Kahn, of course, was from the start intensely pro-Ally. But, also of course, he is not against the German people at large. He considers this war not as a mere conflict between nations in which the call of blood or race or former affiliations and relations may be heeded, but as a fundamental conflict between civilization, governmental methods, ideals and ethical conceptions. His eldest daughter —he has two daughters and two sons—was for some time a Red Cross nurse in France.

Notwithstanding all that he does for art and artists, Mr. Kahn takes an active interest in a number of other worthy institutions, including the Boys' Club at Avenue A and 10th Street, New York City, founded by the late Mr. Harriman, and the Neurological Institute, which Mr. Kahn helped to establish to study and seek a cure for that characteristic American malady, nervousness born of the strenuous life.

When he cannot find anything big to do in finance or in art, Mr. Kahn manages to fill in the time driving a four-in-hand, riding, autoing, golfing, sailing, playing the violin or 'cello (of which he is a master) or reading—he makes it an inviolable rule to read for one hour every night before going to bed, no matter how late the hour. His wide reading, extensive knowledge, and diversified experiences have enabled him to come to the front lately in authorship.

One of his most notable contributions to the discussion of public questions was made at the annual dinner of the Association of Stock Exchange Brokers in January, 1917. "The New York Stock Exchange and Public Opinion" was the title of his address and it contained so much sane thought that the Stock Exchange authorities published it in pamphlet form and it reached a circulation rivalling that of the "best sellers." Among the points Mr. Kahn covered were: Should the Exchange Be Regulated? Is the Exchange Merely a Private Institution? Short Selling—Is It Justifiable? Does the Public Get "Fleeced"? Do "Big Men" Put the Market Up or Down? The Responsibility of Members of the Exchange.

Another article by Mr. Kahn on "Some Comments on War Taxation," originally written before the first draft of the war tax bill was laid before Congress in the spring of 1917, also excited widespread interest because of its breadth of view, its concrete constructive suggestions, and its patriotism—he advocated, for example, a high tax on all excess profits over the pre-war average, saying: "It is absolutely right that no man, as far as it is possible to prevent it, shall make money out of a war in which his country is engaged." Mr. Kahn also "did his bit" in arousing the country to the need for subscribing liberally to the Liberty Bonds.

MINOR C. KEITH

ONE American could have a crown for the asking. He is the uncrowned king of the tropics, the Cecil Rhodes of Central America, a demigod in the eyes of half a dozen republics.

He sits daily in an unpretentious office at Battery Place, New York, a silent Hercules transforming the American tropics from a jungle to a fruit garden; creating prosperity, health, and peace where only poverty, disease, and revolutions formerly luxuriated; steel-rail linking Central American republics to one another as a necessary preliminary to their union into one powerful commonwealth; and plodding, also, to make it possible to travel from New York, Chicago, or San Francisco all the way by rail to Panama or even to Rio de Janeiro.

"When Mistah Keith comes here de country has a holiday. You can't get within blocks of de station. He is de greatest man ever live—an' de best-hearted. De poor know dat."

That was the tribute paid Minor C. Keith by a coloured waiter in the San José Hotel in Costa Rica's capital when I mentioned the great civilizer's name.

Minor C. Keith was a Brooklyn lad who, at sixteen, started in a men's furnishing store on Broadway, New York, at $3 a week; didn't care for selling collars, socks, and neckties; and quit in six months to become a lumber surveyor. He made $3,000 in the first year and then went into the lumber business on his own account, his father having been in that industry.

Before old enough to vote he was raising cattle and hogs on a bleak, uninhabited island called Padre Island (as long as Long Island) near the mouth of the Rio Grande. He had looked over the country after the Civil War and decided to settle on this forsaken territory. Only one other family lived on the island.

Here young Keith trained for the battle of life, under rough, nerve-trying circumstances, with two revolvers never unhitched from his belt and with cattle-thieves and other care-free gentlemen all about him when he crossed to Texas and the Mexican border to buy cattle. He rose at four every morning, roughed it for sixteen hours daily, often slept outside—and prospered.

He reared and bought cattle all over the surrounding territory to kill for their hide and tallow. The beef, not worth anything in Texas in those days, was fed to swine! He amassed a herd of 4,000 stock cattle and 2,000 pigs. Stock cattle were then worth $2.50 to $3.00 and steers brought $1.00 for each year of their age. (To-day, alas! we city folk pay 35 cents a pound or more for the choicest parts of such steers!)

Once a hurricane blew fully a thousand cattle over the edge of the island into the sea. They swam to the mainland, five miles distant. After the hurricane they were rounded up and driven back across the shallowest part, where the water ordinarily reached the pommel of the cowboy's saddle. A count revealed that not more than a dozen had been drowned.

Then something happened to change the course of Keith's career. His uncle, Henry Meiggs, was the famous builder of the first railway over the Andes and of other epochal South American lines. Minor's eldest brother, Henry Meiggs Keith, had joined his uncle in Peru and had taken over a contract from his uncle to build a railroad in Costa Rica for the Government. One day, in 1871, Minor received a letter from his brother asking him to come to Costa Rica.

"He told me," said Mr. Keith, "that I would make more money in Costa Rica in three years than I could make in Texas all my life. Perhaps there was a railroad tinge in the family blood. I went."

Little did he dream that his migration was destined to shape Central American history.

The whole Atlantic Coast from Mexico to Panama was then a dense, unexplored, formidable jungle, with only a few Caribs and Creoles here and there who eked out an existence by fishing for hawksbill turtle, gathering sarsaparilla, vanilla beans, and wild rubber. There was no steamship service to any port in Central America on the Atlantic side.

Minor's job was to run the commissariat of the railway. His brother subsequently died and the constriction of the railway was suspended through the Government not being able to supply the money. In order to carry out his brother's undertaking he re-contracted the coast line of the railway with the Government. Also, to make possible the building of the mountain section for which the Government had not the needful $6,000,000, he made a contract with the Costa Rican Government to settle their external debt which had been defaulted for thirteen years. He proceeded to London and after many difficulties arranged a settlement of the debt and all arrears of interest, and obtained $6,000,000 for the construction of the railway.

Before the railroad was begun the journey from San José down to the coast, about 100 miles, took, during bad weather, about two weeks' trudging through woods, bogs, and jungles infested with reptiles. The Costa Ricans had a saying: "The man who makes the journey once is a hero; the one who makes it twice is a fool."

Puerto Limón was the name given the coastal starting-point of the railroad. Not one house marked the spot. Not one pound of fresh beef was to be had, not a single fresh vegetable, not an ounce of ice to combat the satanic heat. All was jungle, snakes, scorpions, monkeys, mosquitoes.

The construction of the railway on the coast commenced in a jungle and ended in a jungle, which was entirely devoid of population. Many of the rivers had no name. Subsistence for two or three years was principally on salt codfish and a sprinkling of canned goods.

The surveying over, the real troubles began. Labour could not be enticed to such a graveyard. The natives abjured the fever-soaked coast as they would a plague.

But Minor C. Keith had undertaken to build this railroad for the Costa Rican Government and he meant to do it.

Off he went to New Orleans and began engaging labourers—cut-throats, robbers, thieves, and other riff-raff. He rounded up 700 of them. The Police Commissioner warned Keith that his collection was more dangerous than dynamite.

Such was the cargo of the *first* steamer in history to sail from New Orleans for Central American Atlantic ports, the *Juan G. Meiggs*, owned by the Keiths. The voyage was eventful.

The boat struck a coral reef north of Belize, Honduras, and began to pound—pound—pound upon the jagged rocks. The captain lost his head—the pandemonium was terrific. A barrel of liquor fell into the hands of the 700 ruffians and scores of them promptly got drunk! Then they mutinied and became threatening. But Keith was not white-livered. He armed his foremen, issued peremptory orders and succeeded in cowing the 700.

The ship finally backed off, Port Limón was eventually reached and the men set to work, at a dollar a day. Of the 700 not more than twenty-five ever returned. The deadly jungle claimed the rest.

Subsequently De Lesseps was struggling to cut the Panama Canal and labour was not to be had, as the higher wages paid in Panama enticed the labourers away. Yet Keith would not give in, although hundreds died around him, including first one and then another of his own brothers. Fever also overtook him often, but he fought on— fought and planned.

On account of the difficulty in obtaining labour 2,000 labourers were brought from Italy. At the cost of $200,000 for transportation, food, and drink acceptable to the Italians, wages, etc., he brought them—and fondly imagined he had solved his labour problem. Alas! blackhand letters quickly began to bombard him; disease—of course —broke out, and the digging of so many graves unnerved the whole squad.

One night the entire gang disappeared into the woods! And the first thing Keith knew, a ship sailed along and took away the last man of them to Italy! Their leaders had slyly chartered the vessel.

What was the cost in life of the first twenty-five miles of that Costa Rican line?

Four thousand lives, including three of Minor's own brothers. Yet the average working force was only 1,500.

Civilization was advancing through blood and bleached bones.

Another tragedy happened. The Government ran short of money. It could not pay the monthly estimates except by notes. The enterprise on which the country had set its heart would have to be abandoned.

Costa Rica did not know Minor C. Keith as well then as it does to-day. He determined to spend his own last cent in prosecuting the work. But the financial panic of 1873, as bad as any in American history, upset all calculations, and his resources gave out.

Even then he did not succumb.

He had in his employ about 1,500 Jamaican Negroes. Summoning them, he explained the circumstances and offered to repatriate those who were sick or who wanted to go home. Such was their faith in "Mistah Keith" that a decision to stand by him was carried by acclamation. For *nine months* those 1,500 black men worked loyally for Minor C. Keith without a pay-day.

"That incident gives me as much satisfaction as any in my whole life," Mr. Keith admitted. "I pensioned many of the Jamaicans who had worked with me and had risked their life with me times without number."

When the financial skies cleared and the Costa Rican Government was in funds, the full nine months' wages were paid, and the Government paid all its obligations to Keith, including his large losses caused by the want of funds.

But fever, reptiles, labour, and money were not the only things the pioneer railroad-builders had to contend with. In Costa Rica when it rains it rains. Port Limón had a fall of over 20 feet—250 inches—in one year. The rivers became leaping torrents.

Washout after washout occurred. Temporary bridges were swept away time after time until permanent steel structures were erected. One, on the Matina River, was destroyed thirty-one times!

"The narrowest escape I ever had was on that bridge after the permanent one was erected," Mr. Keith remarked reminiscently. "I've had so many close shaves that I've forgotten about most of them. I've been shipwrecked three times, been upset in the surf and rivers many times, had tropical fevers of all varieties, and encountered all kinds of difficulties. But that day sticks in my mind!

"My superintendent wired me to come and inspect the bridge at Matina River. When I got there the river had risen twenty-five feet. The superintendent and a mason were standing on the bridge and a white man and four Negroes were working on it. I saw that the only thing that was supporting the cylinders (on which the bridge rested) was a steel cable they had fastened to a tree on the shore. Before I could order all hands off the cable snapped and the structure collapsed.

"I made one desperate leap toward the shore span, the base of which rested on an offset of the cylinder. This span did not collapse, but stood out over the river like a bracket. I caught the end of a tie with my left hand and gripped it as I had never gripped anything before. I was athletic and didn't slip. But I didn't hang there over that boiling torrent very long! The superintendent and the mason saved themselves somehow, but the other five were pitched into the river and drowned."

In the midst of his arduous railroad building the pioneer conceived other projects.

This jungle road had no traffic, nor would it have any until it reached the 5,000-feet mountain-tops. But he leased the uninviting coast road from the Government. Shortly after landing he had brought a few banana plants from Colon, and the *Juan G. Meiggs* took 250 bunches to New Orleans from Colon on her first voyage, these being the first bananas taken by steamship to the New Orleans market. Year in, year out he expanded his banana plantations, and the hauling of the fruit kept his road busy. In 1915 over 7,000,000 bunches of bananas—say, 1,000,000,000 bananas, or ten for every man, woman, and child in the United States—were shipped from Port Limón! Mr. Keith also built up large interests in Panama, Colombia, and Nicaragua.

Ever on the alert for opportunities, he early set up as a storekeeper. Commissaries in Costa Rica were followed, in 1873, with a store in Bluefields, Nicaragua, the first there, and various other points on the Central American coast as far north as Belize, Honduras, for the purchase of rubber, sarsaparilla, and tortoise shell.

His experience in growing bananas, his knowledge of soil and jungle, his familiarity with transportation by water and land, his ability to attract and satisfy Jamaican labour, his reputation for trustworthiness, his adamantine physique, his irrepressible energy, his unconquerable will—all these qualities contributed to his success.

He became the largest grower of bananas in Central America. His shipping facilities developed apace. His store and commissary operations alone ran into millions of dollars. And he finished his Costa Rican railroad after seventeen years' building.

All this brought him wealth.

Then disaster came.

His United States agents, to whom he consigned all his bananas, failed. Over $1,500,000 paper bearing his name and drawn upon this firm was outstanding.

Keith had saved Costa Rica. Costa Rica, to its eternal credit, sprang to save Keith. Within a few days $1,200,000 was offered to him by the Government, the Costa Rican banks and individuals. In two weeks he reached New York and met every dollar of his debts.

Without delay he had to find new distributing agents for his bananas as his whole international machinery was out of gear.

Andrew W. Preston was then the greatest factor in the banana industry in New England and the North, just as Mr. Keith was in the South. The Preston fruit came from Jamaica, Cuba, and San Domingo and did not compete in the Southern markets.

The two giants joined forces. They formed the United Fruit Company, destined to become the greatest single force in developing Central America, in bringing the United States into commercial and social touch with her Latin neighbours, in conquering the tropics—and in keeping down the cost of living in this country.

Mr. Keith's fruit properties were valued at over $4,000,000 on going into the United. His hardships had not been suffered in vain!

The record of the Preston-Keith enterprise—embracing Cuba, Jamaica, Colombia, Panama, Guatemala, Costa Rica, Nicaragua, Salvador, and the Canary Islands—forms one of America's most romantic commercial chapters. The United Fruit Company has spent over $200,000,000 in cultivating the tropics; it gives employment to 60,000 men at wages several times the rate they formerly received; it has built and operates over 1,000 miles of railway and tramways; it has spent millions of dollars in fighting fever and in building hospitals. Its "Great White Fleet" constitutes the best and largest array of ships America can boast—some forty-five steamers are owned outright and nearly as many more are under long charter. The United has knit together every republic and every island in the tropics by its huge wireless stations. It has built many lighthouses on the coast of Central America.

It is the biggest farmer, and almost the biggest grocer, on earth. It owns upward of 1,200,000 acres, equal to half the State of Delaware. Over 250,000 acres are actually under cultivation. Its livestock includes 20,000 cattle and 6,000 horses and mules!

Its tropical plantations and equipment are valued at over $50,000,000 and its steamships at $17,000,000. Its total assets foot up to $90,000,000.

But Keith is first, last, and all the time a railroad builder. His heart is in that. Two steel rails run through all his dreams.

Like Cecil Rhodes, the far-seeing founder of the Cape-to-Cairo railroad, Minor C. Keith "thinks in continents." Also like Cecil Rhodes, he has conceived an international railroad that stirs the imagination, a railroad, as already told, that will join North America's transportation system with that of Central America and later with South America, a steel highway that one day may run from one end of the New World to the other. The advance of civilization, the welding of peoples together, the abolition of racial misunderstanding—these are the inspiring aims and end sought.

To dream and not do, avails little. Keith has laboured with unbelievable success to make his dream come true.

The International Railways of Central America—the "Pan-American Railway"—is not a mere paper railroad. Half of it is already built. Connection has been made, on the Pacific side, with the National Railways of Mexico, at the Guatemala boundary. The road runs down the Guatemala coast and then cuts clear across the continent, to Puerto Barrios, on the Atlantic side; this transcontinental line is now in profitable operation. From mid-continent the line is being built straight through the little republic of Salvador to La Union, on the Pacific. Next it will pass through Honduras and join the Nicaraguan road. The Costa Rica system will then be reached, and from Port Limón to the Panama Canal will be the final link on the northern side of the "great divide." The South American extension, Mr. Keith is confident, will follow.

Some 600 miles of the International Railways are actually operating—and making money. And the daring project is daily creeping toward completion.

"I have heard, Mr. Keith, that you hope to bring about the union of the five Central American republics—Guatemala, Salvador, Nicaragua, Costa Rica, and Panama. Is that your ambition?" I asked. He gazed into space. Then:

"I believe that will come. It will be a great thing for them all. But only railroads can bring it about. The people of Costa Rica are still strangers to the people of Nicaragua although their countries adjoin. There must first be commercial and social intercourse. The railroad will make that possible."

When you travel in Central America you learn that Minor C. Keith can have anything he wants *because the people regard him as their biggest friend, their "father," their leader, one of themselves.* Mr. Keith married the daughter of one of Costa Rica's early presidents, José Maria Castro, lived there continuously for twenty-seven years, spent millions in relieving disease in the tropics, and feels in a sense responsible for the welfare of these undeveloped little nations. Not once has he or his companies had the slightest rupture with any Latin government.

So if Keith by and by decides that the time is ripe for the creation of a Central American Commonwealth the chances are that it will be established.

DARWIN P. KINGSLEY

HERE is a New England idyl. From such rustic scenes and surroundings, from such rocky soil have sprung many of the men whose names are writ large in the annals of American achievement.

The speaker in this instance is Darwin P. Kingsley, president of the New York Life Insurance Company with $2,500,000,000 insurance in force and assets of $900,000,000, a figure not approached by any other insurance company in the world:

"On the 40-acre farm, in Vermont, where I was born, everything we wore and everything we ate was grown on the farm, except a little sugar once in a while in place of the maple sugar, which was indigenous, and a little tea. From a dozen sheep came wool which was first spun and then woven by hand into winter clothing. Our garden supplied flax which was made into summer garments. Even the thread we used was manufactured in our home. The sound of the spinning and flax wheels was rarely silent from morning till night, for five children, in addition to our parents, had to be clothed. What we called coffee was made from parched wheat or corn. I well remember the first time my father took his wool and swapped it for fulled cloth. We all regarded that as an epochal advance into a higher state of civilization.

"At Alburg, where I was born, there were not then (1857) enough houses to form even a hamlet. In the summer I attended the old 'deestrict' school, a primitive affair, innocent of any suggestion of higher education. In our home were very few books. Life there was clean through and through, self-respecting, and full of moral and religious discipline. But it was extremely narrow, uninspiring, and unimaginative. There was little or nothing to fire a boy with ambition or enthusiasm or to acquaint him with the world that lay beyond his 'cabined, cribbed and confined' sphere. At first I had no larger vision than any of the other folk there.

"But one day something happened. It was only a little talk with our family doctor, yet it changed the whole course of my life. He said to me, 'You ought to go to school.' I told him I was going to school. He said, 'Oh, yes; but I mean you ought to go on and study Latin.' I asked him, 'What is Latin?' He told me: 'You cannot understand your own language unless you know Latin. What does subtraction mean? What does it come from?' I told him it meant just subtraction. Then he explained to me that the word came from two Latin words, *sub* meaning 'from' and *trahere*, meaning 'to draw'—to draw from under.

"A whole new world flashed into my vision at that instant. There was a world, I realized, that I had known nothing about. This glimpse of it made me resolve there and then that I would study hard and learn all about it. Before I was twelve I had finished Greenleaf's Common School Arithmetic, but though the little school had nothing much beyond that to offer I continued to work on the farm in summer and to go to school in winter until I was seventeen. I was sent to Swanton Academy for one winter term and to Barre (Vt.) Academy for one spring term. Dr. J. S. Spaulding, head of the academy, was a very noted man, and under his guidance I became determined not to quit school, as had been intended, but to work my way through both academy and college.

"Between terms I worked as a day labourer in the fields, swinging a scythe all day or tilling the fields. I got through the academy before I was twenty, and without knowing where the money was to come from, I went to the University of Vermont, at Burlington, and took the entrance examination. This was in the spring.

"During the summer I saved $45 working on a farm, and the farmer agreed to lend me additional money to go to college if I could give him security in case I died—he was not afraid of his money if I lived. Dr. Spaulding was an ardent believer in life insurance and used to impress upon his students the many advantages of a good policy, emphasizing, among other things, that it could be used on occasion as security. I took out $1,000, in the Metropolitan Life, although the cost, $20 a year, was a tremendous drain upon my resources. I handed the policy to my farmer benefactor. This incident, doubtless, is responsible for my being president of the New York Life Insurance Company to-day.

"Off I went to Burlington, some forty miles from home. My expenses for the first year at college totalled exactly $165. How could I live on that? Well, my mother used to send a roast turkey and a few other things that would keep. I lived chiefly on boiled potatoes, bread, and milk. After a while, even though I had had my fill of boiled potatoes, I felt ravenously hungry for some kind of meat. I fought against this gnawing appetite as long as I could, but succumbed one day and bought a little box of chipped beef. I reasoned that by nibbling at it I could drive away this hunger for quite a few days. The moment I got out of the store I opened the box to have just a tiny slice, but the instant I got a taste of the meat I devoured it, to the last scrap, right there on the street.

"I paid all my college bills by ringing the college bell seven times a day, calling the chapel and all the classes. If I rang that bell five seconds ahead of time I got 'Jessy' from the boys, and if I was a second late the professors jumped on me. This drilling in punctuality was one of the best things I derived from my college course. I don't think I have ever been late in my life since."

The day labourer, bell-ringer, and semi-starved youth became the prize orator of the University, a Phi Beta Kappa man, and a notable scholar in Greek, Latin, and mathematics. His struggles did not end with the winning of his A.B. degree, however. Hard as the climbing of the hill of learning had been, a still rougher road lay ahead.

"What was your ambition on finishing college?" I asked Mr. Kingsley.

"The height of my ambition was to get a position as a teacher at $1,000 a year. In my eye that was the acme of success—and opulence. I had a vague longing to become a lawyer, but as I was in debt, I felt I must get to work right away. At that time almost every ambitious young man had an irresistible desire to go West. The cosmic urge struck me, and I went along, going first to a sister who lived on a ranch in Wyoming. It did not take me long to realize, however, that baling hay, tending cattle, and riding bronchos would not get me very far toward my goal. So off I set for Cheyenne.

"There, in that far-off town, without a friend, without work, and possessing only $15, I became terribly homesick for the first and last time in my life. I was so bad that I would go to the station and watch with intense envy the brakeman on the rear end of a train going East! My loneliness almost drove me insane.

"But I had to buckle to and find something to do. I could not afford to sit and mope. An old fellow I met in the second-rate hotel I stopped at befriended me and put me in the way of starting to peddle books. I tramped all over northern Colorado until I fell ill at Longmont. The kindness then shown me by strangers is one of my happiest memories; although I was nothing but a travelling book agent, the people took as good care of me as if I had been one of their own kin.

"After I recovered I was selling a book to an old milkman who told me he hailed from Vermont. We got to chatting, and I told him I was going to Denver. 'What are you going to do there?' he asked. 'I don't know, but I think that is the best place for me to strike,' I replied. He finished by recommending me to a lawyer friend of his in Denver, also from the Green Mountain State. This lawyer became one of my dearest friends and continued so until the day he died. As it was not feasible for me to read law, I found a position as a teacher at $70 a month—but of this I had to pay $45 every month for my room and board. I remained for a year at this circumscribed job.

"The old impulse to go West again seized me, and as the Ute Indians were then being removed from the valley of the Grand River, preparatory to opening it up for irrigation, I migrated to Grand Junction, then a place of tents, log huts, saloons, dance halls, and other characteristics of a rough-and-tumble frontier town. Before the irrigation scheme was completed no more vegetation grew in that valley than on Broadway.

"With $500 which I managed to borrow from a friend at Oshkosh, I bought a half interest in the Grand Junction *News*, then a struggling weekly, but now an influential daily. I was then twenty-six. But being editor of a frontier-town paper was no picnic. Graft was rife and I showed up the grafters. Things became so lively that I often had an armed guard in my room while I slept. At one period I never went on the street without my hand clutched on a six-shooter in my coat pocket, ready for business."

"Did you have any fisticuffs or gun battles?" I asked. Mr. Kingsley's reply was evasive. Finally I persuaded him to tell what manifestly was in his mind.

"Well," he began, "I was a Republican, and when the Democratic governor appointed a gang of disreputable carpet-baggers to the local offices, we wanted our own people. The fellow appointed County Commissioner was particularly objectionable, and I made fun of him in the paper over some silly thing he did. My partner warned me that there would be trouble. Sure enough, the morning the paper appeared, as soon as I went on the street, he came straight toward me. I was not anxious for trouble—indeed, my aversion to street rows had begun to create an impression that I was more courageous with my pen than with my right arm.

"White with rage, he struck at me. I was no boxer, but it dawned on me that he didn't seem to know much about the game either; so I parried his blows, and when he saw that he could not get me that way he kicked me in the stomach with his heavy ranch boot. I caught enough of the blow to make me mad, and I struck him on the chin with such force that I lifted him off his feet. He landed on the sidewalk.

"After that I had less trouble. The funniest immediate effect was that a big Irishman who had been anxious to lick the Commissioner, but didn't quite have the nerve, came to my house that evening with a bumper basket of strawberries and presented them as a sort of thank offering!"

Shortly after that Mr. Kingsley was named a member of the delegation from Colorado to the Republican National Convention at Chicago, and in the following year, 1886, he was elected State Auditor and

Superintendent of Insurance, with headquarters, of course, in Denver. There he found it necessary to go after fake insurance companies and to give insurance much study. Dr. Spaulding's preachings about the value of life insurance became very real to him, and the more he studied insurance the more deeply convinced he became of its value, both to individuals and to society. In short, he became a whole-hearted insurance convert.

Therefore, when George W. Perkins went to Denver and offered him the post of Inspector of Agencies for the whole of the New England territory of the New York Life, Mr. Kingsley gladly accepted.

"I took up my headquarters at Boston in the beginning of 1889," said Mr. Kingsley, "and remained there until 1892. And here I am."

That sounds very simple—"And here I am." But when he came he was merely superintendent of agents, whereas now he is president. The intervening years have been filled with constructive, aggressive, clear-sighted work. They have covered the years of trials and crises for the insurance companies, years during which the weak and the unworthy have gone to the wall and the strong and worthy have forged to the front.

It was, as a matter of fact, the first onslaught upon the New York Life and its president, William H. Beers, that was directly responsible for Kingsley's coming to headquarters. Both Mr. Perkins and he, on being summoned to New York at that time, at once took up the cudgels on behalf of the company and its head. Both could wield a pointed pen; both could rally and stimulate despairing agents; both could ably meet the newspaper attacks. Although President Beers was reëlected by the board, he resigned rather than have the company's interests injured, and when John A. McCall was elected to the presidency both the young Western gladiators were promoted.

Then when the historical insurance investigations of the Armstrong Committee began in 1905, Darwin P. Kingsley came to the front as a man of unusual calibre, unquestioned character, and farsighted statesmanship. By this time he had mastered not only the insurance business but had cultivated a thorough grasp of its collateral financial and investment problems. After the smoke of battle cleared away only one man stood out as conspicuously fit for the presidency. When Alexander E. Orr, elected temporarily to succeed Mr. McCall, stepped out in 1907, Mr. Kingsley, without contest or question, was elevated to the presidency.

The company had not then a dollar invested in farm mortgages, but Mr. Kingsley's Western experiences had taught him that here was a safe and profitable field for the investment of insurance funds. To-day the company has $30,000,000 out on loans to farmers, of which $17,000,000 was supplied in 1916, every dollar representing a soldier fighting against the high cost of living through facilitating the development of agricultural production. Similarly, Mr. Kingsley introduced the innovation of investing in trustworthy municipal bonds.

His aim, as he impressed upon the whole force, was not necessarily to have the New York Life the largest insurance company in the world, but to have it the best and strongest. While, therefore, its $2,500,000,000 insurance in force is exceeded by two other companies, both doing "industrial" insurance, no competitor can show, within two or three hundred million dollars as much assets. Of course, Mr. Kingsley is a believer in healthy growth, and the amendments which have been secured in the original law limiting the amount of new business undertaken have been largely the result of his exertions by pen and speech.

For years the most serious insurance office problem was the delay and congestion occasioned by the necessity of keeping thousands of records in very ponderous volumes. While one clerk was writing data from one page of the tome, scores of other clerks were waiting to get at other pages. No solution was found until Mr. Kingsley tackled it personally; he overcame the whole difficulty by introducing a card system from which blue prints were made by the Cooper-Hewitt photographic process. The value of this innovation cannot be grasped by the layman.

Tradition has it that prize orators at school never shine as speakers in later life. D. P. Kingsley, of the Vermont University class of '81, has broken this rule. Not only is he the author of more than one book on insurance, its fundamental principles and universal ramifications, but he is a brilliant orator and is in constant demand to address business associations, educational institutions, and all sorts of banquets—one of his neatest addresses, although he is not a stickler for creeds and doctrines, was recently delivered to a large body of Episcopal clergymen on "The Sin of the Church."

Mr. Kingsley is a man of big ideas. As head of an organization which does business in every civilized country of the world and which finds the people of one country ready to pay their money into a central fund to be used for the benefit of the people of all other nations in common, he has a consuming conviction that this same principle of coöperation between nations could and should be extended to the general affairs of life throughout the world, thus evolving one colossal democracy recognizing and founded on the brotherhood of man. We have outgrown tribe life and clan life; on more than one continent we have progressed from independent and isolated states to commonwealths and federations. Why not, asks Mr. Kingsley, carry this development across national boundaries?

War, he contends, is the logical and inevitable fruit of the doctrine of sovereignty. How can democracy supplant sovereignty and remove the war-breeding friction which rule by sovereigns begets? Here is Mr. Kingsley's answer, delivered in a recent address:

"Ultimately through the federation of the democratic world, but, as a first step, through the re-union of the Anglo-Saxon world. This re-union must be accomplished not to over-awe any other people, not to pile up force with which to meet force, not to eliminate small nationalities or make great ones afraid, but primarily to make the Anglo-Saxon world really democratic—democratic, inter-state as well as intra-state—democratic as our forty-eight States are internally democratic. Such a federation (not confederation) would almost certainly come to include—perhaps before its completion—France, Holland, Switzerland, probably the Scandinavian countries and Spain, and possibly some of the republics of South America. 'The Parliament of Man' would then be something more substantial than a poet's dream. . . . What an opportunity! What a glorious opportunity! After the hideous ruin of 1914-15-16, after seeing Europe do what our States would certainly have done but for Alexander Hamilton and the great Federalists who drove the Federal Constitution through in 1787-8, after seeing the Southern States fearfully attempt its ruin in 1861-5, after coming ourselves up out of the world of littleness and jealousy and fear, after feeling the pride that citizenship in this great Republic justifies—can we not now see a nobler picture, do we not get a wider vision, do we not hear the call of a still more majestic citizenship? . . . The Anglo-Saxon Republic: The United English Nations. Who shall estimate its significance?"

Insurance knows no national boundaries. After the war began the New York Life maintained offices and met claims in Germany as well as in France and Austria, Russia and England. Each people has paid into one common fund and from that common fund, composed of the moneys drawn from all nations, receives succour according to contract.

"I look upon life insurance as an international evangel preaching the gospel of internationalism and brotherhood with a force and cogency equalled by no other agency," Mr. Kingsley impressed upon me with all the earnestness of a Moody or a Beecher.

Of Mr. Kingsley's qualities, perhaps the most notable is his squareness. He hews to the straight line and will tolerate no deviation therefrom by any one representing the company. He insists likewise upon a square deal *for* the company. His social friends, when playing pranks, often take advantage of his guilelessness, I am told. Mr. Kingsley has childlike faith in his fellowmen—the world appears to us largely as a reflex of our own make-up.

At first glance he gives the impression of seriousness almost to the point of gruffness, but when he starts to speak all this melts. An intimate told me that he once remarked to Mr. Kingsley: "If your face could only reflect your heart, people would warm up to you more the moment they come in contact with you."

Neither his tremendous business responsibilities nor his activities as a scholar, a writer, and an orator, consume his whole energies. Until recently he was president of the unique Hobby Club, each member of which must have a hobby and a creditable collection; Mr. Kingsley's is Shakespeariana, and as the foundation of his collection he was fortunate in securing the four folios more than twenty years ago. He is president of the Seniors' Golf Association, another novel body whose annual tournament at Apawamis attracts veterans from all over the country. He is also an enthusiastic disciple of Izaak Walton. He took a leading part in organizing the Safety First Federation and became its president. The American Museum of Natural History numbers him among its life members.

His philosophy of life has led him to subscribe unreservedly to the creed of his favourite poet: "The merry heart goes all the day, the sad one tires in a mile a'." In his journey through life he seems to radiate good cheer.

His eldest son, Walton P. Kingsley, graduated from his father's Alma Mater in 1910 and is now assiduously climbing the insurance ladder. His other sons are Darwin P., Jr., and John M., both students at Groton. Mr. and Mrs. Kingsley—the latter, Mr. Kingsley's second wife, was Josephine I. McCall, daughter of the late John A. McCall—also have two daughters.

I have made the discovery that the ambition of nearly every successful man is to receive an honorary degree from his Alma Mater. Mr. Kingsley won this honour at forty-four.

CYRUS H. McCORMICK

CARNEGIE once expressed pity for millionaires' sons. He declared that their fond parents, who had travelled a hard, stormy road, were fearful lest a puff of cold wind touch the cheek of their precious offspring. Mollycoddles, not men, were thus bred, poor, pampered, dependent weaklings, unable to stand on their own feet, to fight their own battles, or make a place for themselves in the world.

"It is a handicap, being the son of a rich man," complained the heir of one of America's foremost financiers the other day. "If you simply go in for sport and pleasure and never amount to anything, people remark: 'That's all you can expect of a rich man's son.' If you apply yourself seriously to study and then to business, work hard, and think hard, and succeed in accomplishing really important things, you get no credit whatever. People then say: 'Why shouldn't he amount to something? Look at all the advantages he had; everything came his way.' You are damned either way."

There is truth in both these statements. Many millionaires do rear dainty, hothouse sons who are of less worth than ciphers since they consume much and produce nothing. Other millionaires bring up, not pleasure-chasing ornaments, but young men, strong, self-reliant, well-disciplined, well-trained, and inculcated with the principle that they must use their talents and their possessions diligently and worthily and so win an honourable place in the world.

"I want my sons to know how to endure hardship," was the rule laid down by the brainy, capable mother of Cyrus H. McCormick, the present president of the International Harvester Company, an organization whose plants and appliances and ramifications far transcend those of the more loudly advertised Ford motor factory.

Let me relate how the boy Cyrus earned his first money, since it illustrates the character of his upbringing. Twenty-two tons of coal had been dumped on the side of the roadway a hundred yards from the cellar of the McCormick home to be loaded into a wheelbarrow, trundled across the grounds, and emptied into the coal bin. The twelve-year-old Cyrus volunteered to do the job if his mother would pay him the regular rate of fifty cents a ton allowed for this work. She readily consented, and for several days the schoolboy kept loading and pushing and emptying that wheelbarrow until the last pound of the twenty-two tons had been deposited in the cellar. His back was nearly broken and his hands were badly blistered, but when the work was done he placed $11 in his bank and resolved to set about earning $100 as fast as he could.

There was a sad sequel.

By doing many other jobs about the house and never missing an opportunity to earn a few cents or a few dollars, he accumulated in three years his $100 and deposited it in a savings bank. He had attained his first financial ambition. By his own efforts he had become a capitalist. His achievement gave him intense satisfaction.

One month later the bank failed! Carlyle could not have felt worse when he discovered that the maid had burned the manuscript of his "French Revolution"; De Lesseps could not have suffered more through the collapse of his Panama Canal venture; nor could Jay Cooke have been more poignantly chagrined over the loss of his millions than was young Cyrus McCormick over the loss of his hard-earned savings.

"It was a terrible blow," he told me not long ago, "and it took me some time to accept philosophically the consoling words of my mother that the experience of toiling industriously for the money was worth much more to me than the money itself. But," he added with a laugh, "I now believe she was right."

In gathering material for this character sketch I asked one of Mr. McCormick's Princeton classmates, who has remained intimate with him ever since, what were some of Mr. McCormick's predominant qualities.

"He is the personification of 'John Halifax, Gentleman.' He might well stand, also," he replied, "for the man in that well-known anecdote about the new footman who was engaged during his master's absence and who, on being told to go to the station to meet his master, asked his mistress how he would be able to recognize him. 'He is a tall man and you will be sure to see him helping some one,' she told him. That's Cyrus McCormick—a tall, robust man who is constantly helping some one. Even when at college he regarded the inheritance that was to come to him in the nature of a responsibility, a stewardship, something entailing upon him a great duty rather than bringing him any privileges or mere pleasure. He had inherited a name which he must honourably uphold and would inherit a vast business which he must administer creditably for the sake of its founder, for the sake of the thousands dependent upon it for a livelihood, and for the sake of its farmer customers all over the world who looked to it for dependable machinery."

Few sons have more worthily administered their heritage. Not only as a business man, as head of an enterprise that distributes its agricultural implements in every civilized country throughout the world has Cyrus H. McCormick amply fulfilled parental hopes; but he has attained equally noteworthy success as a public-spirited citizen, as an employer considerate of his workers, as a helper of his fellowmen. Were all wealthy men of his type, millionaires would not be held in such suspicious regard by the people.

It is trite to say of a man that he is democratic. Cyrus McCormick is democratic; but he is something more than that. During the Columbian Exposition in 1892 there was a dearth of men to push the roller chairs while Mr. and Mrs. McCormick were showing a friend and his mother the sights, and without any fuss Mr. McCormick put his wife in one chair and the friend put his mother in another and they pushed the chairs for a couple of hours. Other men might do a thing like that; but there are not many men of Mr. McCormick's resources who live as simply and indulge in as inexpensive pleasures and recreation as he does. Instead of maintaining a fleet of yachts or a string of race-horses, his favourite diversions are tramping in forests or over mountainous country, camping in remote spots amid the beauties of nature, canoeing in little-explored streams, felling trees, chopping wood and other activities demanding physical exertion but affording healthful mental relaxation "far from the madding crowd."

"A man cannot work successfully and work hard unless he loves it and unless he keeps in sound physical condition," declared Mr. McCormick. "A man who simply sits continuously at his desk without taking exercise to keep him in trim will not do his best work. The best tonic and restorative for a tired man is to get next to Nature. Tramping and camping in the woods is the best thing I know of for developing, not only a man's physique, but his mentality and his soul."

It is not surprising, rather is it natural, that Cyrus H. McCormick should be a man of both physical and mental power, of sustained industry, of broad vision, of large heart, of rational tastes, sensible of his responsibilities in the world. He was born of such stock. From a combination of these qualities sprang the reaper, one of the half-dozen greatest blessings the nineteenth century brought to mankind, since it virtually abolished famine and gave bread even to the poorest of civilized peoples.

The reaper was not born without travail nor nurtured without struggle and stress, pinching and plodding. No laurels were immediately placed upon the brow of the young inventor in 1832, the first Cyrus H. McCormick. No grateful acclaim greeted his discovery. No fortunes were laid at his feet for his epochal invention. Instead, he ran the whole gamut of ridicule and penury and hardship; of blasted hopes and blighted ambitions. But through it all, though at one time he lost every penny, he at no time lost faith. He exhibited unconquerable courage, unwavering tenacity, and indomitable optimism. And he won. Indeed he afforded the world one of the few instances of an inventor personally becoming a manufacturer on an international scale and garnering a large fortune from the universal adoption of his idea.

Even before the first Cyrus H. McCormick was born, in 1809, a McCormick, his father, had sweated and struggled to construct a machine that would cut grain. In his workshop on his farm under the Blue Ridge Mountains of Virginia, Robert McCormick, grandfather of the subject of this sketch, worked constantly for years to invent a workable reaper. Early in 1831 Robert McCormick brought a machine from his smithy, hitched horses to it, and tried to cut a field of wheat. His experiment was a flat failure and he gave up his quest.

Not so the son, however. He started on an entirely new track, evolved the reciprocating blade and in a few weeks he built a reaper containing the basic principles of one that the world now knows. On its first tryout it cut six acres of oats. Its first public trial in the following year was on hilly, uneven ground, and as it did not instantly work satisfactorily it was jeered at and laughed to scorn until a prominent neighbour, a member of the State Legislature, arrived on the scene and ordered that one of his fences be torn down and the machine given a fair chance on an adjoining field owned by him. Here it worked smoothly and successfully.

The world before then had been dependent on the sickle, the scythe, and the flail for its bread. Mankind then had no steel plows, no sewing machines, no telegraph or telephone, no photography, no postage stamps, and no railroads to speak of. In the little log workshop on that remote Virginia farm had been created a machine that was destined to drive hunger from the world. It was destined to enable the North to preserve the Union by freeing its able-bodied men from the hand-harvesting of the fields. It was destined, moreover, to lead the western march of civilization. The reaper likewise was to put men upon the soil, to transform the United States from a wheat-importing to a great wheat-exporting nation, and was to draw hundreds of millions of dollars to this country from the pockets of foreign buyers.

But success was not to be won at once. It took nine years to find the first buyer of a reaper!

From 1831 to 1840 not one machine could be disposed of—not even with the aid of an advertisement offering the reaper at $50. Meanwhile the young inventor had taken to digging ore from the ground and smelting it, a business he thought would give him working capital.

The terrible panic of 1837 swept him into bankruptcy. No creditor cared to attach his grotesque machine—nobody thought it worth having. The sale of two machines in 1840 helped a little, but 1841 was a blank. The next year brought seven orders, the next twenty-nine, and the next fifty.

The Virginia farm was far removed from transportation facilities and remote also from the developing wheat centres of the Middle West. So in 1846, when thirty-seven years of age, McCormick set out to survey the country for an ideal location for his works. With characteristic shrewdness he chose a straggling village, untouched by railroads, on the shores of Lake Michigan. It could not even boast of one public building and it had a queer name, Chicago. There he found a partner willing to pay $25,000 for a half interest in the business and began to manufacture the McCormick reaper on a sizeable scale. He established agencies at over a score of central points and adopted the then novel method of advertising "Money back if not satisfied." He offered to send a reaper to any farmer, let him use it, and, if not pleased with the results, return it at the maker's expense.

Then came constant harassment from competitors, a mass of legal suits and other worries and difficulties. Yet McCormick found time to plan and do big and still bigger things. In 1851 he sent an exhibit to the London Exposition, and although its appearance drew forth the ponderous wit of staid British journals, the London *Times*, after the reaper had been put to a practical test, retracted all its previous abuse and declared, "It is worth the whole cost of the Exposition."

The great Chicago fire of 1871 wiped out the McCormick works, the most extensive in the city. McCormick was then sixty-two years of age, had accumulated a fortune of several million dollars, and measured by ordinary standards, had done more than his share of the world's work. Would he retire? He put the question up to Mrs. McCormick.

"Re-build at once," was her immediate and emphatic verdict.

She had in mind not only the welfare of their army of workmen, but also the future of another Cyrus H. McCormick, by this time twelve years of age. She did not want her boy to become an idler, or a mere society ornament. She was an intellectual, devout, painstaking, capable woman, zealously training her son to be a useful, upright citizen.

I had the good fortune to meet one of little Cyrus's boyhood playmates who told me that, even when a mere lad, Cyrus was kept constantly informed about the business of the family, usually from his parents. The other boys used to wonder at his knowledge of a world about which they knew nothing. They pitied him because business discussions often caused an interference with his play, but they had a vague sort of admiration for the attention he was called upon to give to the general business affairs of the family.

It was characteristic of the McCormicks that they sent their son to the public school in Chicago—"the best in the world, better than any private school," remarked Mr. McCormick in discussing his schooldays. "There were sixty-five boys and girls in my class, and the poorest children usually were nearest the head of the class, so that it took real, hard study to hold one's own." Later he entered Princeton, but was brought back to enter the business after two years' study, as his father was then (1879) seventy years old.

"My father taught me that I must work, and must work out my own salvation, that I was to have no favouritism, that I must apply my whole energy to learning every phase of the business," Mr. McCormick told me. "He impressed upon me that constant industry must be combined with intelligent thinking in order to attain success. No amount of inherited money, he explained, could gain for me or any one else a high and honourable place in the world, but each man must carve his own way, and by the sweat of his brow and brain earn his own station in business and the world.

"Under such conditions and counsel I began my apprenticeship. I am as thorough a believer in such a policy as my father was, and am applying it to my own sons, one of whom began in overalls on leaving college, at the lowest round of the ladder in the branch house of the International Harvester Sales Department at Wichita, Kansas, preliminary to starting in at headquarters in Chicago. My other son is at Princeton."

In 1884 the inventor of the reaper died, and the present Cyrus H. McCormick became the head of the McCormick Harvesting Machine Company, the largest industry of its kind in the world. It was a tremendous responsibility for a man of twenty-five years of age to shoulder.

"I was really carried along at first by the tide of the organization," Mr. McCormick modestly explained. "There were able, trusted managers who supervised things until I found myself and became as much of a real president as I could. It was, I confess, a somewhat staggering responsibility, for our business practically covered the world. We were at home in every wheat field on the globe. We had agencies in many lands and had to keep in touch with agricultural, business, and financial conditions all over."

How well Mr. McCormick measured up to his responsibilities was demonstrated sixteen years later, in 1902, for when the great International Harvester Company was organized by J. P. Morgan & Company, he was selected as president of the company.

And here let me set down the truth about how this merger came into existence, for more fiction—picturesque fiction, most of it—has been printed on this subject than on almost any other industrial episode in America.

Under Cyrus H. McCormick, the McCormick Harvesting Machine Company was expanding aggressively, even in face of the cut-throat competition which had raged for years, and one day Mr. McCormick came to New York and visited Morgan & Company with a view of having them raise additional capital to take care of the growing business. The alert George W. Perkins, then a Morgan partner, immediately the matter was broached asked, "Why not form a large and new company with capital much greater than anything which now exists?" He had had an active hand in forming the billion-dollar Steel Corporation in the previous year and saw an opportunity to bring off another gigantic coup. Negotiations were promptly started with the leading harvester concerns. There were bitter rivalries and jealousies to handle, but the problem was solved by buying each company outright and leaving J. P. Morgan & Company to organize the new corporation exactly as they saw fit, not only fixing its capital, but choosing the executives. There were no stipulations that this man or that man must be engaged for this position or the next position. Morgan & Company, as sole organizers, had an absolutely free hand.

Their choice of Cyrus H. McCormick as president was dictated solely because they saw in him the best man for the job. He was strong physically and mentally, he was a glutton for work, he had so managed his own company that it was the foremost in the field; he was young, forceful, enterprising, long-visioned, and had earned the fullest confidence of the farmers here and abroad.

Mr. McCormick is no ornamental executive. For several years after the International was formed, Charles Deering, as chairman, shared the burdens, but for the last half-dozen years Mr. McCormick has been the sole executive head of the organization. He has spent a great deal of time in the different countries of Europe, especially Russia, developing demand for the corporation's products —and was selected by the United States Government as a member of the Root Commission to Russia, where "McCormick" is a name to conjure with.

I cannot refrain from relating here an incident that brought McCormick into notice abroad. He had been commissioned by his father to take a binder, then quite a novelty, across to the great show of the Royal Agricultural Society of London to be held in that city. On the voyage the boat carrying the machine was wrecked and it lay in salt water for several weeks, but was rescued just in time to rush it to London for the field test. The other machines appeared on the scene

CYRUS H. McCORMICK

beautifully painted and drawn by the finest of horses. Young McCormick conceived the idea of entering his rusty, dilapidated-looking machine without giving it even one daub of paint and of having it pulled by a couple of disreputable-looking nags. The "exhibit" tickled the risibility of all the spectators, who made it the butt of a constant volley of jokes and squibs. The shining, speckless competing machines, with their exquisitely groomed steeds, did their work more or less satisfactorily. Then the pitiable McCormick entry was lined up while everybody waited to see the fun. Lo! Off went the shaggy horses, click-click went the blade, and in thirty seconds the ridicule gave way to admiration, for not one of the gaily-caparisoned exhibits had cut down and bound grain with the speed and efficiency of this queer contraption rescued from a salt-water grave. It won, hands down.

The Harvester's activities are not confined to reapers and binders; it manufactures some thirty different machines for farmers. The invention of the reaper in 1831 was followed in the 70's by the invention of the wire binder, the twine binder and, more recently, by the wonderful machine that also stacks the grain, while the principal problem now under solution is the development of a tractor which will mechanically displace horses in drawing the modern powerful binders, plows, and other implements used on a large scale by progressive farmers.

Here are figures which illustrate the enormous extent and the wide diversity of the International Harvester's operations:

Harvesting Machines (Grain, Grass, and Corn)	975,000
Tillage and Seeding Machines	525,000
Engines, Tractors, and Motor Trucks	105,000
Wagons and Manure Spreaders	90,000
Cream Separators	35,000
Gray Iron Castings—Pieces	45,000,000
Malleable Iron Castings—Pieces	75,000,000
Malleable Chain Links	75,000,000
Bolts	95,000,000
Nuts	150,000,000
Twine—tons	125,000
Cars shipped from all Works (1916)	60,054
Lumber requirements 1916 (board feet)	120,000,000
Steel requirements (tons) 1916	267,000

Amazing as production figures of the International are, there is still 40 per cent. of the world's grain cut, not by machinery, but by hand. Cyrus McCormick is directing much of his energy and the energy of his organization to remedying this. The largest untapped market for American farm machinery is in Russia, where millions and millions of acres still know nothing but the hand sickle and the scythe.

"If the revolution is as successful as is expected," said Mr. McCormick in reply to my questions before President Wilson selected him as a commissioner to Russia, "the tremendous potential resources of Russia should be developed more rapidly than in the past. Russia's latent power, its vastness, and its possibilities impress one more than those of any other country in the world."

Notwithstanding all his business duties, Mr. McCormick has found time to be a human, humane being. One thing impressed me: no man I have ever written about has been quite so admiringly spoken of by his friends as Mr. McCormick.

"He is absolutely the best man I know," declared a prominent man of affairs who has met and mingled with most of the leading figures in America. "His constant thought is: 'What is right? what is my duty? what ought I to do?' His success as a business man is well known, but no one but himself knows half the good he has done in aiding worthy individuals and worthy causes. He has inherited the teachings of his Calvinistic forefathers, but is without the severe, almost harsh traits that often accompany the followers of Calvin and Knox. His treatment of his employees has been noble, thoughtful, and generous, and I understand that he maintains personally a bureau to look after his own individual philanthropies. He also has a close relation to the McCormick Theological Seminary for the education of preachers. He has always been personally interested in and a contributor to Princeton, of which he is a trustee. The Elizabeth McCormick fund—founded by him in memory of his little daughter who died when a girl of twelve years, and dedicated to the welfare of children in the United States—is doing a work of national importance in bringing open-air schools into existence for the education and benefit of weak and defective children. He has given generously to the Y. M. C. A. and I personally know of instance after instance where he put his hand into his pocket to aid persons overtaken by misfortune."

Over 20,000 Harvester employees participate in the profits through ownership of profit-sharing certificates subscribed for by them, and pensions are paid to old and incapacitated employees. An elaborate medical and hospital service is maintained with special provision for treating victims of tuberculosis; an Employees' Mutual Benefit Association is liberally supported by the company, and in every way care is taken to insure the comfort and safety of the employees.

Under Mr. McCormick's inspiration the International is now spending hundreds of thousands of dollars in educating American farmers, by means of lectures and demonstrations and other means, to improve and extend their methods of cultivation and thus become more capable and more successful crop-growers. The results are proving gratifying beyond expectation. This broadly conceived, patriotic work brings no immediate pecuniary reward to the company, but it tends to make farming more profitable and therefore more attractive, so that in the end there will be a wider demand for farm machinery. Also, this commonsense campaign is doing something to retard the soaring cost of foodstuffs.

In his philanthropic endeavours Mr. McCormick is enthusiastically supported by Mrs. McCormick, who is active along many civic and social welfare lines. She is also warmly interested in woman suffrage but has no sympathy with the militant element of the suffrage movement. Especially in the cause of child welfare has Mrs. McCormick enthusiastically enlisted with personal effort and pecuniary support.

There are few American families who deserve better at the hands of their country than the McCormicks.

J. P. MORGAN

"WHAT kind of a man is J. P. Morgan?"
That question is often asked but seldom answered comprehensively; so instead of writing an account of Mr. Morgan's career, I shall attempt to analyze his character, to present a study of his characteristics, to diagnose his ideas, and to dissect his ideals. In trying to portray the personality of this international figure, I am able to write without the bias that intimate friendship is apt to beget, and without any aid or suggestion or countenance from the subject himself. Yet I feel that my deductions are not open to the charge of ignorance of Morgan the man and financier, for circumstances have compelled me to follow his activities and delve into his motives and quiz his friends and associates for more than a decade.

Had Mr. Morgan the power he would forbid the writing of one line, favourable or unfavourable. But, fortunately, I am under no obligation to conform to his wishes. I am free to set down the truth as faithfully as my knowledge and impressions permit.

Let us start off with a few questions, typical of the many constantly asked about the heir of the greatest financier America ever produced.

Is Jack Morgan a second J. P.?
He is not.
Is he a very able man?
Able, yes; transcendentally able, no.
Does he aspire to fill his father's shoes, to sit on the throne set up by his father and rule the financial world?

J. P. Morgan the Second is not ambitious to become a great dominating force over the whole Kingdom of Finance. He possesses neither the will nor the qualities to become a Napoleon. He is obsessed by no lust of power. While far from being a figurehead in the activities of J. P. Morgan & Company, he is content to let his trusted associates, particularly Henry P. Davison, bear the brunt of the actual executive work, conscious that it is in capable hands. Mr. Morgan prefers to live a rational, unfevered life; for no honours or emoluments would he sacrifice his home life, forego the satisfying pleasures of his domestic hearth, or permit himself to become more of a money-making machine than a man, a husband, a father. He is infinitely more zealous that the reputation of his firm shall not be tarnished in the slightest degree than he is over winning additional millions.

What kind of a personality has he?

He is the most undiplomatic man of importance in America. He is the product of his heredity, a veritable Bourbon. He would consider it beneath his dignity, he would regard it as weak, contemptible, mugwumpish to go out of his way one inch to placate the public or enable it to understand his motives—or even to remove a single false conception that any of his acts may have created.

"He understands the public and can put himself in its place as little as you or I understand royalty or could put ourselves in its place," one of his associates, a staunch admirer, told me; and this unquestionably is the truth. His father did not have to reckon with the sovereignty of public opinion during the greater part of his life, and his attitude toward the common people cost him, before the end, more than can be recorded. His son has not yet learned the lesson. Morgan the younger is as punctilious as any man living that his acts shall be honest and in every way above reproach, according to his lights; but he has wofully failed to realize that, next to doing the right thing, the most important consideration is to do it in the right way, that the public may see that it is right.

He is seriously lacking in statesmanship, a fact that more than once has occasioned the financial community, especially its more responsible members, grave concern, for Mr. Morgan typifies High Finance in the eyes of the people, and when he assumes a cavalier, I-don't-care-a-snap-of-my-fingers attitude—as he did, not without provocation, when a witness before the Walsh Industrial Relations Commission—the effect upon the public, upon public sentiment, upon citizens and voters, as well as upon lawmakers, is incalculably injurious not merely to financiers as a class, but to the welfare of all. This hauteur constitutes perhaps his most regrettable defect

Is Morgan domineering?

No. His apparently lordly attitude toward the public is due to a mistaken idea of his place in the financial structure. He does not look upon himself as the most dominant figure in the financial world, as powerful enough to defy anybody and everybody, as beyond the reach of criticism or control; he sees himself merely a private banker doing a large, valuable, constructive business, beneficial for the development of the nation's resources, honest and straightforward beyond cavil, scrupulously fair to his clients—and not accountable to any one else, since it is nobody else's business. Modesty thus blends with his Bourbonism.

Is he developing?

Yes, responsibility has broadened him, and it may be that experience will in time teach him the necessity for cultivating some of the qualities he now scorns. More than one event of the last three years has been calculated to bring home to him the commonsense wisdom of striving honourably to gain the good will of his fellowmen and the shortsightedness, not to say folly, of antagonizing and irritating them by ignoring or flouting them. If J. P. Morgan would only reveal himself to the public as he reveals himself to his friends he could and would, without any sacrifice of self-respect, become one of the most popular financiers in the country. His intimates find him a large-hearted, red-blooded, democratic, considerate, jovial, humane, likeable, companionable fellow, not a bit purse-proud or arrogant or selfish or small, above doing anything mean, petty, or underhanded.

"I would trust Jack Morgan behind my back as far as any man living," was the ringing declaration of a prominent banker not of the Morgan group. "I don't think any amount of money, which would be a small consideration, or any amount of prestige, which would be a strong consideration, would for a moment tempt him to do what he knew would be unfair or unjust. He may not always analyze things exactly right; in the very nature of things he could not be expected to have a broad social view, for his environment has always been that of the most powerful financiers, friends of his own and of his father. He is inexperienced in many matters; but he lives up to the highest standard he knows."

Cynics declared, after the 1907 panic, that there was only one man in Wall Street that all Wall Street felt could be trusted, the original J. P. Morgan. The truth is that the late Mr. Morgan was not the most brilliant banker in America or the best judge of financial propositions; his analyses and conclusions often were faulty. What enabled him, then, to become the financial Moses of the New World? Simply and solely his unimpeachable trustworthiness, his innate fairness, his inability to take advantage of any one. Now the son has inherited these same virtues. The strict maintenance of the reputation of the house of Morgan is with him a fetich. Rather than lower it one iota, he would wipe the dust of the financial district off his feet forever.

It was widely rumoured that, when his father died, the son began by assuming a dictatorial policy toward other financial interests, that he adopted his father's brusque manner, and that he felt he was privileged to act exactly as the previous head of the house, but that he was soon given to understand by those whom he essayed to boss that they were willing to coöperate with him, but not to be coerced by him, that they would gladly work with him on a basis of equality but would have nothing to do with him if he fancied he could lay down the law to them. There was very little, if any, truth in this. Mr. Morgan's lack of diplomacy was probably responsible for the creation of any such impression.

J. P. MORGAN

The inheritance to which Mr. Morgan fell heir, in 1913, was not all roses. The bald truth is that he found himself in a trying position. He was bitterly assailed for hurriedly selling important parts of his father's art collection for which a special "Morgan Wing" was added to the Metropolitan Museum of Art; and in the inner circles a good deal of indignation was felt when it became known that the person in charge of the collection first learned the news of the sale from reporters and not from Mr. Morgan himself. This latter fact illustrates Mr. Morgan's inherent tactlessness. But the disposal of the priceless pictures for which New York City had erected a special home was not prompted solely by want of public spirit on the son's part. He did not sell them for the fun of the thing. His father in the later years of his life had devoted the bulk of his income to buying art objects, the upkeep of which entailed inordinate expense. The Morgan will revealed that the popular belief that Mr. Morgan was fabulously wealthy was wrong. Outside of his collections and other property which constituted a liability rather than an asset, he left comparatively little realizable wealth. His security holdings, apart from several millions (par value) that were classed as worthless or of nominal value, aggregated only $19,000,000, while of cash he, of course, left only an inconsiderable amount.

To carry on an international banking firm requires a vast amount of capital and, in blunt language, the younger Morgan needed the money to run his business, to pay the $3,000,000 inheritance tax, and to take care of the various provisions in the will. His sales of pictures, etc., were prompted more by necessity than by choice, although I understand that some of the newspaper comments on his father had stirred him into a somewhat resentful frame of mind. It was characteristic of his makeup, however, that he allowed his fellow-citizens to interpret his conduct in any way they saw fit.

A recent incident is illuminating in this connection. Since the European war began J. P. Morgan & Company, as fiscal agents for the Allies, have occupied a unique and most profitable position, the duties of which, incidentally, it has discharged with conspicuous ability—did not Jacob H. Schiff, head of Kuhn, Loeb & Co., Morgan's most powerful rivals in private international banking, describe Morgan & Co., in a speech on the Liberty Loan, as "the house which has done more than any other in this country to make the world safe for democracy?" Mr. Morgan, no longer under the necessity of counting his dollars, notified the American Academy in Rome that he would cancel one dollar of its indebtedness to him (as his father's legatee) for every dollar contributed to its endowment fund. He also made a handsome money gift recently to Trinity College, Hartford. His firm's subscription for no less than $50,000,000 Liberty

Bonds is worth recording. These acts give a truer insight to the man than did his disposal of the pictures.

I want to give the inside explanation of another matter which caused widespread criticism, namely, Mr. Morgan's apparently supercilious replies to questions put to him by members of the Walsh Commission appointed by Congress.

It was the presence of moving-picture machines that upset the banker's equilibrium.

While Mr. Morgan, in common with almost every one else, viewed Walsh as a notoriety-seeking mountebank, he did not proceed to the examination room with battle in his eye. He was prepared to answer all legitimate questions and to give not only facts, but, if necessary, his views, on matters coming directly within his sphere. The moment he took the witness chair, however, "movie" machines began to click-click all around him. The nozzle of one machine was levelled at him within a few feet of his face, and every time he opened his mouth or moved an eyelash the machine opened up full fire.

This riled Morgan. He felt that he had been summoned, not to help the work of the Commission, but to provide a public exhibition, to attract sensational attention to Walsh's doings and to give yellow newspapers material for illustrated front-page stories. So Morgan balked. He considered that the Commission was subjecting him to unfair, unnecessary, and undignified treatment and that, therefore, he was not obligated to lend himself more than he could avoid to its far-from-judicial tactics.

Hence, when he was asked if he considered $10 a week a proper wage for a longshoreman and replied, under pressure, "If that's all he can get and he takes it, I should say that is enough," the public was not afforded a picture of the real Morgan, but of a citizen righteously indignant and angry. Of course, a man of the suavity and broad-mindedness of the late J. J. Hill or Charles M. Schwab would have retained his poise and avoided giving the public the impression of utter indifference to the social welfare of the masses. But how many of us would have kept cool and collected under such circumstances?

Morgan's attitude was at least human—and understandable.

J. P. Morgan does not know fear. Though detectives are alert during these disturbed times it is not uncommon to see Mr. Morgan elbowing his way through the curb market mêlée or swinging along Wall Street unescorted and unshadowed. He has braved Germany's submarines several times, crossing and re-crossing the Atlantic whenever business has demanded. His fearlessness, in a sense, is responsible for his indifference to what the masses may think of anything he does in the financial or industrial field.

No man ever gave a finer exhibition of physical courage and chivalry than Mr. Morgan when an assassin entered his country home at Glen Cove on Long Island and pointed a pistol at him. Instead of attempting to save himself, which, according to all accounts, he might have done by darting under cover, Mr. Morgan, fearful lest the maniac injure his wife or children, sprang at the mouth of the upraised gun and, though wounded, grappled with the would-be murderer and overpowered him. Like H. C. Frick, under somewhat similar circumstances, Morgan kept his head and acted throughout with the utmost bravery.

Nor could he understand why the newspapers made such a hubbub about the incident. When Rudyard Kipling was at death's door during a long illness contracted at the height of his fame the newspapers published bulletins and columns about the course of his illness day by day, but Kipling, on regaining consciousness and rallying somewhat, asked innocently: "Did any one call?" Morgan was a bit like that.

An incident significant of Mr. Morgan's conception of his position and personal rights occurred the first time he was able to leave his house. As he and a companion approached his yacht, tied up at its pier, they saw a photographer in a small boat manifestly waiting to snap the banker. He was furious. The idea of a photographer or any one else invading his property and infringing upon his privacy was to him not only a gross insult, but an utterly unwarranted intrusion upon his freedom and liberty as a private individual. Hadn't he an indisputable right to be left alone on his own property? He was no public character, no statesman, no officeholder elected by public vote. He was merely an ordinary person, a *private* banker.

When the photographer made overtures to Morgan he was met with an oral volley. Meanwhile, Mr. Morgan's companion, seeing the effect the encounter was having, began to explain that this man was only trying to carry out orders given him by his employer and that if he had refused to do his best he would doubtless have lost his job.

Just as Mr. Morgan was stepping on board the yacht his hat blew into the water. The photographer rescued it, and as he handed it up he remarked that, though Mr. Morgan would not let him take a picture, he (the photographer) was a good sport "and here's your hat."

Like a flash Mr. Morgan's anger gave place to a broad smile. He saw things in a new light. The photographer became, not an interloper on an offensive mission, but a fellow-mortal trying to do his best to earn his pay. Morgan immediately posed, not once, but several times in order that the photographer might get exactly the kind of picture he wanted.

There you have two sides of the Morgan character—intolerance of public curiosity and interest in him, but, beneath it all, a large heart.

One more incident will suffice to emphasize the human sympathy that lies beneath Morgan's ostensible callousness where the rank and file are concerned. Some time ago the newspapers reported how money had been stolen from the Morgan offices and a boy arrested for the theft. While Mr. Morgan's sense of justice and discipline would not allow him to let the offender go unpunished, he at once sent for the boy's mother, assured her that the lad would be given a chance to make good in another place, and arranged that she should not suffer financially. "He could not have treated that mother more kindly if she had been his own sister," one of his friends, familiar with the facts, informed me.

Mr. Morgan's beautiful affection for his mother and his unremitting attention to her comfort and happiness, as well as his intense fondness of his own domestic circle are matters of general knowledge. For his father he had—there is only one word to use—reverence. For years the son was constantly his father's companion at the exclusive card parties, composed of some half-a-score of the aged banker's most intimate friends, as well as at other functions, while in business matters the same close association prevailed during the last decade.

Yet when the Morgan mantle fell upon the son the public and the press knew little or nothing of his character or calibre. This was because Jack Morgan had scrupulously remained in the background. He had no thirst for fame. He was not ambitious to become recognized as the sole factor in guiding the destinies of the house of Morgan. Even now Mr. Morgan consistently dodges the limelight. His name is rarely attached to any statement; he elects to have Mr. Davison or some other partner attend to all matters calling for public announcement.

Banking was in Jack Morgan's blood when he was born, in New York, on September 7, 1867. "Morgan" was even then a name known the world over. Junius Spencer Morgan, the grandfather, comparatively early earned the reputation of being "the best business man in Boston," and was selected by George Peabody, the foremost American international banker of that day, as a partner. He went to London, the Peabody headquarters. When Mr. Peabody died, ten years later, the firm of J. S. Morgan & Co. was organized. Its head, who was a mathematical genius, soon became recognized as a financial giant. He startled conservative Europe by undertaking, in 1870, to float a loan of $50,000,000 for the provisional French Government, then crumbling to defeat, its Emperor already a prisoner of the Germans. Junius Morgan boldly formed a "syndicate,"—then a novelty to Anglo-Saxon finance—handled the daring transaction with masterly skill, and cleaned up several millions of profit in eighteen months.

Meanwhile a second Morgan, John Pierpont, after beginning his career with Mr. Peabody's New York correspondents, had become the Peabody representative and later formed the firm of Dabney, Morgan & Co. In 1871 he joined the powerful Drexels of Philadelphia, the house then becoming known as Drexel, Morgan & Co. Its chief rival was Jay Cooke & Co., and when that meteoric firm failed in 1873, the Drexel-Morgan house, along with August Belmont, the Rothschilds' representative, became the Government's mainstay in underwriting and refunding its enormous war debts—using the syndicate as its chief instrument. In this work J. P. Morgan played an active part; but his greatest achievements were to come later, in organizing and financing railroad and industrial corporations more colossal than any the world had known.

The third Morgan, "Jack," emerged from Harvard with an A.B. degree in 1889, by which time his father was the recognized leader of American finance. At college young Morgan, a strong, muscular six-footer, had exhibited several inherited traits; he had a will of his own, pronounced determination, an admixture of brusqueness and jollity, was normally fond of recreation, and possessed an average amount of brains. His father lost no time in breaking him into financial harness. After a sound preliminary training, under paternal tuition, at the New York office of Drexel, Morgan & Co., Jack was sent to London to broaden his vision and his experience. Both he and his wife—he married Miss Jane Norton Grew in 1890—"took to" English life, made many friends there, and have ever since had a hankering for English ways and customs. While in London, where he kept also in close touch with the Paris branch of the firm, young Morgan developed notably as a banker. He remained there until 1905. Long before then—in 1894, in fact—he had become a partner of J. P. Morgan & Co., "Drexel" having been dropped from the firm name.

Curiously, the first notable work undertaken by J. P. the Second, within eighteen months of his father's death, was for his English and French friends. On his accession he had notified his partners that the amalgamation and concentration of banking institutions and resources had gone far enough and that the house would confine itself strictly to attending to its regular business. He outlined a conservative policy.

But he was destined to become the child of Fate—or Fortune. The sudden declaration of war by Germany, followed immediately by Britain's entrance into the conflict, threw New York into a financial panic. The Municipality of New York owed London scores of millions and London insisted upon payment in gold. Sterling exchange went skyrocketing to $7—that is, the English pound, normally worth $4.65, could not be procured here under $7. There was a deadlock. And, as in 1907, the financial community, as well as the New York City government, turned to the Corner House, to Morgan, for succour. The crisis, as every one knows, was met successfully.

When the Allies, thrown into confusion by the tragic events in the first stages of the war, found themselves in desperate need of hundreds of millions' worth of military supplies, they turned to J. P. Morgan & Co. as the only concern capable of enabling them to cope with the situation. The firm was appointed fiscal agents of both Britain and France and was commissioned to purchase all war materials required here, its remuneration being one per cent. on everything bought and all expenses paid.

No other banking house ever conducted operations of a magnitude such as those undertaken and successfully carried through by J. P. Morgan & Co. during the last three years, operations not confined to banking, not confined to raising for Europe loans approximating $1,500,000,000, not confined to importing $1,000,000,000 in gold metal, not confined to marketing for the Allies untold millions of American securities, not confined to keeping the foreign exchanges on a workable basis, but operations entirely outside the purlieu of bankers, the placing of contracts for three billion dollars' worth of merchandise of every conceivable description, the passing upon the responsibility and ability of scores of concerns to turn out satisfactory munitions, the financing or extension of numerous enterprises designed to meet the dire needs of half-a-dozen European nations in the throes of a life-or-death struggle.

All that Morgan & Co. have done probably will never be known—when he lent the Army Department $1,000,000 without security to help it out of a hole he was chagrined when the incident found its way into the newspapers. In the historic achievement of Morgan & Co. during the war Mr. Morgan has been no idle onlooker. On his shoulders and on the shoulders of H. P. Davison, T. W. Lamont, and E. R. Stettinius have fallen the brunt of the burden. It is a work into which Mr. Morgan has thrown his whole heart and soul, for he feels that in so doing he has been aiding in the preservation of civilization, in making "the world safe for democracy."

My opinion is that Mr. Morgan will not remain in active harness as long as his father did, but that by and by he will spend a goodly part of his time in semi-leisure either here or in England. He is interested in various things besides banking, particularly the domestic circle. It may astonish most people to learn that he is a student of the Bible and constantly quotes passages from it. He is also a devoted Shakespearian scholar. He likes to read good literature. Then he is an enthusiastic yachtsman, the owner of a number of fast boats and vice-commodore of the New York Yacht Club. He is more of a tennis player than a golfer.

Incidentally, all unknown to the multitude, Jack Morgan has been the inspiration of more than one of the profit-sharing, stock-ownership and other schemes for the benefit of the employees of concerns with which the house have been financially associated.

The notion promulgated by muckrakers that J. P. Morgan is a rapacious, money-thirsty, unprincipled capitalist, bent only on self-aggrandizement regardless of the consequences to others, is false through and through. For the prevalence of this idea he himself is partly to blame. He could do much to remedy matters by taking a leaf out of young John D. Rockefeller's book and adopting a less I-don't-care attitude in his dealings with the public, for, after all, we are all—rich and poor, high and humble—members of one human brotherhood.

As a P.S. let me add that another Morgan is in the making, Junius Spencer, a Harvard graduate who was learning the ropes in his father's firm but, immediately war was declared by President Wilson, became a naval gunner. Before then he could have been seen almost any night making for the subway with a not-aristocratic pipe in his mouth and mayhap carrying a parcel of a size and style that the average ten-dollar-a-week bank clerk would scorn to be seen with. He puts on no airs. The other fellows in the office claim him as one of themselves.

Mr. Morgan's two daughters, Jane Norton and Frances Tracy, were recently married. He has another son, Henry Sturgis Morgan.

America can at least feel that at the head of our greatest banking house there is an honest man.

WILLIAM H. NICHOLS

AMERICA has tardily awakened to the necessity for the domestic production of chemicals. One American realized the opportunities and importance of the chemical industry nearly fifty years ago and has produced possibly a greater quantity of heavy chemicals than any other man in the world.

From a humble business employing one helper, William H. Nichols has built up an organization owning and operating over thirty chemical manufacturing plants in the United States and Canada and employing tens of thousands of workmen. The General Chemical Company possesses assets of $50,000,000, earns profits of millions yearly, pays handsome dividends to its stockholders, and brings to America millions of dollars from oversea buyers of its products.

When William H. Nichols took up the scientific manufacture of chemicals there were only a few, relatively small, chemical plants in this country, run for the most part by men of little or no technical or scientific education in chemistry. Rule-of-thumb, rough-and-ready methods were in vogue. How Nichols, as a youth, came to study for and enter the chemical industry is worth recording for the benefit of others.

"Every young man when he is in the formative stage of his youth should consider carefully and seriously what he wants to be or do. When I was quite a young lad, before I entered college, I looked over the whole situation and tried to study out what field offered the most attractive opportunities," Mr. Nichols told me. "I found that in the chemical business there were few who had been thoroughly educated for it, few who had had scientific training at college. I concluded that if I took a scientific course and applied myself diligently there would be a chance to attain at least a fair measure of success. So I enrolled under Dr. John W. Draper and his two sons at New York University although the few scientific students of that day were looked down upon by students in other branches and considered of lower rank.

"I was very much in earnest. Even as a youth I realized that I had only one life to live, and I was determined to make it count as much as possible. Any fellow who has a chance to acquire a proper education and neglects his opportunity is foolish.

"As soon as I had graduated, in 1870, I went into business on my own account, but as I was not of age—I was only a little over eighteen—I could not use my own name. Along with a man named Walter, I formed the firm of Walter & Nichols, my father lending me his name until I reached twenty-one, when the name was changed to Nichols, Walter & Nichols. When more than one pair of hands was needed to do a job I had to supply those hands—that is, I had to stop my laboratory work and help to turn out the stuff, mostly acids.

"Walter's untimely death in an accident knocked my entire plans on the head, as he had looked after all the office work and all the business end. I was strictly a scientific man, with no practical experience in handling business problems. I tried to get along by getting up very early every morning, doing the factory and the laboratory work in the forenoon, taking a horse car from our place on Newtown Creek to New York, and then hustling for orders and attending to other matters in the afternoon, returning to clean up the office duties after the day's work was over.

"I soon realized, however, that I could not accomplish very much alone, so I engaged the now-celebrated Dr. J. B. F. Herreshoff, at what then appeared to be the staggering salary of $2,000, to be my factory man. We were producing chiefly sulphuric acid, muriatic acid, nitric acid and tin crystals. The veteran rule-of-thumb men in the business, my competitors, thought I was crazy to employ a scientific chemist like Herreshoff, but I had my own ideas about the value of a sound education and scientific knowledge. I was not spending anything like $2,000 on my own living expenses. I put every penny I could, not into expensive clothes or any other luxuries, but into the works, and also borrowed additional sums from my father to enable me to branch out. For a second time, after I had things going, I was suddenly landed in a hole.

"There was a gentleman's agreement in the trade regarding the price of sulphuric acid. Without giving me a hint of warning all the others cut their prices, booked up every available order and contract, and left me without a single customer. This bolt from a clear sky naturally upset everything.

"Not long after that we were pushing the sale of our sulphuric acid when a strange incident occurred." Mr. Nichols stopped, looked straight into my face very earnestly and then resumed: "What is the secret of success? is a question often asked.

"Looking back over my life I can now see clearly that there were two or three crucial points in it and that in each instance the successful outcome was due to the practice of strict honesty, just doing the plain, simple, right thing, and refusing to deviate under any circumstances from the ordinary path of fairness and integrity.

"My experience and observation convince me that great cleverness is not necessary; in fact, that smart tricks to take advantage of either competitors or customers or the public cannot build up a solid, lasting, worth-while success. The Golden Rule is as applicable in business as in the church.

"If any young man will study hard, think hard, keep his eyes always open for opportunities, exercise all the foresight he can cultivate by painstaking effort, at the same time observing the strictest honesty and prudence in all his doings, he cannot prove a failure."

"What was the sulphuric acid incident you were to tell me about?" I asked.

"When I began making this acid," said Mr. Nichols, "I found that, although all the sulphuric acid on the market was labelled as 66 degrees, much of it was under strength, usually only 65 degrees. I made mine 66 degrees and marked it accordingly. Before long I was waited on by a body of my competitors who declared to me: 'You are making a fool of yourself. You are only a young man and new at the business and perhaps that's why you don't seem to know that you are incurring unnecessary expense to yourself by making your sulphuric acid 66 degrees when 65 degrees is just as good.' I told them that if I made 65-degree acid I must put '65 degrees' on the package and that if I put '66' on the package I must make 66-degree acid. They went off very much dissatisfied and disgruntled.

"About this time the process of refining oil was discovered and orders for sulphuric poured in to us faster than we could fill them. But though we were swamped with demands for our product, our competitors were not. Of course they set about finding out the reason why and they discovered, as the oil refiners had already discovered, that 65-degree acid was not strong enough for refining oil, whereas 66-degree acid met every requirement."

What the world would have done without electrolytic copper is hard to conceive. Moreover, the electrolytic process has enabled mining companies to redeem scores of millions of dollars' worth of silver and gold which formerly ran to waste in the smelting and refining of copper. How many people know how the electrolytic process was born?

Let William H. Nichols tell the story.

"I was sitting in my office one day when a man named Davis came in with a piece of ore which he asked me to examine. Having studied metallurgy, I saw it was sulphide of iron containing copper pyrites. 'Are you interested?' he asked. 'Yes,' I replied. 'Thank heaven,' he said, 'for I have been to every other chemical works and couldn't interest any of them in it.'

"We bought his mine, at Capelton, across the Canadian border. We turned our attention to utilizing our by-product of copper cinder and Dr. Herreshoff invented a water-jacket furnace for smelting it into copper matte. This process was very successful and we sent to England and Wales, where most of the refining had been done, to see if we could not introduce our new style of furnace there at Swansea. They ridiculed us, asking if we, who had been smelting copper for a year, imagined we could do it better than they could do it after 200 years' experience. To-day we turn out more copper in a month than they do in Swansea in a year.

"The copper industry at that time did not know how to analyze copper correctly. Many laboratories had wrestled with the problem and as we were now interested in copper we also took it up. Thanks chiefly to Herreshoff, we evolved what we called the electrolytic process, which, as every one now knows, not only reveals the exact amount of copper in matte or in anything else, but liberates all the gold and silver that used to be thrown away and produces a quality of copper that has made possible the great advance in electricity."

As notable progress was made in the copper field as in the chemical field by Dr. Nichols and his associates. Their revolutionary processes for smelting, refining, and analyzing the metal brought them a great deal of custom from existing mines. They thus became important factors in the selling of the finished product.

The entrance of the Nichols interests into the refining of copper came about in a peculiar way. They had been content before to dispose of their product in the form of matte and had not considered the advisability of invading the smelting branch of the business. Curiously, this eventful step in Mr. Nichols's career was likewise the result of his refusal to join others in what he regarded as unfair or unwise tactics.

One day a very influential New York magnate beckoned to Mr. Nichols in a downtown club and rather emphatically told him: "You are not charging enough for your copper." Mr. Nichols replied that the price he was charging satisfied him. "You are not charging the price others are getting," the magnate declared and after some further parley presented this ultimatum: "I see I will have to speak to you rather strongly. We have an agreement on the price of copper and unless you will agree to adhere to this price I will have to tell you, very regretfully, that I will not be able to refine any more of your matte."

The gentlemen had miscalculated the timbre and the temperament of William H. Nichols. "You have a perfect right to say you will do no more refining for me," he replied, "but you haven't the slightest right to tell me what I must charge for my copper. I won't ask you to refine another pound."

Dr. Nichols walked over to the newly-installed telephone, called

Herreshoff, told him to come over to the office and, on his way, to think about plans for building a little copper refinery. Before the sun went down they had designed a modest refinery on lines which are being followed to this day.

From that conversation sprang the Nichols Copper Refining business which is now running at the rate of 500,000,000 pounds of copper annually.

"You are not a believer, then, in gentlemen's price-fixing agreements?" I asked.

"No. I had had my lesson at the very outstart of my business career in price agreements and even were there no law against it you could not drag me into a price-fixing agreement of any kind. I don't think such agreements are wise. It is better for each one to use his own brains and exercise his own intelligence and commonsense in conducting business in his own way. It is better also for the public."

So rapidly did the Nichols copper activities expand that they overshadowed the original chemical enterprise as the latter had ceased to be pushed ahead with the old-time vigour. But Dr. Nichols, at heart a chemist and a scientist, determined, while enjoying the solitude and leisure of a vacation at his place in The Thousand Islands, to formulate plans that would enable him to do full justice in the sphere which, as a lad, he had chosen.

The General Chemical Company was then conceived. So, too, was the Nichols Copper Company. By separating his chemical and his copper interests, organizations could be built up to handle both with greater vigour, greater efficiency, and on a greater scale. The plan has worked out admirably.

The General Chemical Company is the largest of its kind here or abroad. Its products are heavy chemicals; fuming sulphuric, muriatic, and nitric acids, sodas of many varieties including sulphite, bisulphite, and phosphates, as well as alum in vast quantity. Chemicals enter into the very warp and woof of our industrial fabric—into textiles, silk, paper, water filtration, and every industry.

Mr. Nichols was the first in this country to tackle the manufacture of aniline oils. During a visit to Germany, where coal-tar dyes were being manufactured in large quantity, he decided to experiment, on his return home, but was assured by his German friends that by-products of American coke ovens could not be utilized for this purpose, as our coal was not of the right kind. Mr. Nichols persisted, and built a plant which produced a thousand tons a year of excellent aniline oil. But the Germans cut the price so drastically that it was impossible to compete with them. Congress did not then realize the astuteness and far-sightedness of the German manœuvre. Germany well knew that no stable smokeless powder could be made without the product of an aniline oil plant. The deficiency has since been well remedied, America having become not only self-supporting, but an exporter of aniline oil and other chemicals won from by-products of coal.

Mr. Nichols is a staunch believer in coöperation, not with competitors, but with his own workers. Many of his men have been with him a full generation—some for almost forty years. Many years ago he became a pioneer in sharing profits with his employees. In 1916 over $1,500,000 was distributed as "extra compensation to workmen and staff based upon profits." Mr. Nichols's attitude toward workers has always been inspired as much by his sense of humanity, his belief in the essential brotherhood of man, as by cool, calculating business considerations, although, of course, his experience has taught him, as it has taught other employers, that it is profitable to treat employees generously and thoughtfully. A small corps of picked men do nothing but look after the well-being of the workers.

All the activities for betterment of the condition of the workers are handled by the men themselves. They make their own rules and by-laws for their associations, conduct their own clubs, arrange their own interworks baseball, football, and other matches. Boxing bouts and wrestling contests between champions in the different plants excite the keenest of interest. The same spirit of healthy, stimulating rivalry enters into the constant campaign for greater safety. The company awards annually a very substantial sum to the force which keeps its plant going with the least loss of time through accidents— it was won in 1917 by a Canadian plant and the men donated a large part of the money prize to a national war relief fund. The spirit of patriotism is inculcated consistently into all the workmen, who salute each morning the Stars and Stripes which floats over every plant of the General Chemical Company.

His kindness to his men once placed Dr. Nichols in a predicament which caused him deep mortification. The head of one of the concern's largest customers came to him and complained that he had been systematically cheated by short-weighing of carboys containing acid. Dr. Nichols could not believe the allegation, but on going to the consumer's plant fifty carboys were weighed and each was found ten pounds short. He promised to make an immediate investigation.

An Irishman was pointed out to Dr. Nichols as the man responsible for seeing that every carboy contained the proper quantity of acid. This employee Dr. Nichols would have trusted with his own money. But, when questioned, he coloured up and stammered. Finally he blurted out:

"Mr. Nichols, the boys is very fond of you and we wanted to help you."

That anecdote will obviate the necessity for entering into details of all that the General Chemical and the Nichols Copper Company do for their workers.

There are some Americans better known abroad than among their own countrymen. These are men of real achievement, men who have accomplished things of international importance but who have not advertised themselves by brass-band methods. Dr. Nichols is such a man. I recently read in a French paper a reference to him as "the scientist and chemist known all over the world." And it is even so. Honours have been conferred upon him by royalty, by great scientific and chemical organizations, and by universities. He was elected president, in 1912, of the International Congress of Applied Chemistry, the largest congress of chemistry in the world, while the Society of Chemical Industry of Great Britain paid him a similar honour. He is a charter member of the American Chemical Society which now has 9,000 members in New York and which was founded with only fifty members, of which only two others survive. King Emmanuel decorated him with the Order of Commendatore of the Crown of Italy, an honour enjoyed by only one or two other Americans. He is an honorary LL.D. of Lafayette College and an Sc.D. of Columbia University.

Unlike many busy business leaders, Dr. Nichols has found time to render many years of constructive service in church and educational fields. As chairman of the trustees of the Clinton Avenue Congregational Church of Brooklyn and as president of the Congregational Church Extension Society, he has been an invaluable force in forwarding religious and benevolent movements. The Polytechnic Institute of Brooklyn, from which Mr. Nichols graduated in 1868—he was born in Brooklyn on January 9, 1852—owes its present robustness to him more than to any other individual. It was a small, struggling, moribund organization when he accepted the chairmanship, whereas it now has between 800 and 900 students and is preparing to double its capacity. Also, it is now self-supporting.

Mr. Nichols began life with the advantages of a superb physique inherited from ancestors first of Norman and then English stock until the earliest days of America, an excellent home training from a Quaker mother and a well-to-do father of high business standing and a thorough education. On leaving Brooklyn "Poly." he entered Cornell, then just founded as a semi-military institution. Young Nichols soon became captain of a company of students but was implicated in the hazing of a youth for ungentlemanly conduct. The authorities offered him full immunity if he would reveal the names of the others taking part, a suggestion he indignantly scorned. He was expelled, of course, but the train on which he departed was held until

WILLIAM H. NICHOLS

every student of the university could file past and shake hands with him!

Dr. Nichols married Miss Hannah W. Bensel in 1873 and they have a daughter, Mrs. M. O. Forster of London, and two sons who are making their mark in the industrial world. William H. Nichols, Jr., is president of the General Chemical Company (his father being now chairman of the Board) while C. Walter Nichols is president of the Nichols Copper Company. In handling men and in conducting business, both are exhibiting inherited qualities of generalship.

JOHN H. PATTERSON

JOHN H. PATTERSON devotes his life to building cash registers and making workers happy.

Few employers who have made millions have chosen to spend the best part of these millions on their own employees. Many build themselves palaces, line them with costly pictures and bric-à-brac, spend money lavishly and ostentatiously for their own diversion, doing little for the benefit of any one but themselves. Even philanthropically inclined millionaires have rarely given first consideration to those who helped them to make their riches. It is more spectacular to build halls, to proclaim large gifts to this or that organization, to strut into the limelight and do something calculated to win plaudits from the public than to do worth-while things inside one's own factory and give one's self to the daily task of brightening the lives of labourers, artisans, stenographers, and other unromantic employees.

John H. Patterson has chosen the more prosaic course. He has made of a factory and its environment a thing of beauty. He has put joy into work. He has made the earning of a living harmonize with the earning of happiness.

The workshop of the National Cash Register Company, at Dayton, O., is a glass palace flooded with light. Through its thousands of windows the workers can feast their eyes on exquisite views. The air throughout all the buildings is changed every fifteen minutes. Hundreds of shower baths are provided, and every worker is allowed to enjoy them in the company's time. Of course, there is a hospital with a doctor and trained nurses in attendance; employees receive electric massage treatment free of cost; there are numerous rest rooms for women employees. To avoid the overcrowding of street cars and elevators and to save the women from having to mingle unceremoniously with the men, the former are allowed to start work half-an-hour after the men and to finish fifteen minutes before them. At ten every forenoon and at three every afternoon recesses are granted the women workers. The commodious dining rooms furnish midday meals at cost and an orchestra regales the diners with sprightly music.

Every noon hour a moving picture or other entertainment is provided in a hall which seats 1,250, and here those who bring their own lunches may sit and eat while enjoying the pictures, the music, and, occasionally, short talks. The men are given the privilege of smoking.

JOHN H. PATTERSON

By an arrangement with high schools and colleges, vocation training is provided promising youths.

Not one acre of Mr. Patterson's extensive estate, Hills and Dales, is reserved for his exclusive use; every square yard of it is thrown wide open to his employees and to the public. There is not a fence or a locked gate on the whole place. Instead, it is dotted with quaint, rustic camps where all sorts of paraphernalia is provided free for picnic parties—cooking utensils, tables, benches, even flour and waffle machines and distilled water.

A golf course, tennis courts, baseball field, and other facilities for recreation are provided, while a large club house permits of dances being held on Saturday evenings and all sorts of concerts, lectures, and entertainments throughout the week. There is another club house in the city for the use of employees, and here largely attended educational classes are held in the winter months.

Mr. Patterson is a sunshine worshipper. He enjoys nature—enjoys it so much that he wants every one around him to enjoy it also.

Any worker who offers a feasible suggestion for improving anything at the factory or elsewhere is rewarded, "Suggestion Boxes" having been in use for many years.

When he started, over twenty years ago, to treat workers like human beings, other employers called him a fool, a fanatic, a socialist, a dreamer. They warned him that coddling labour would bring him nothing but discontent and disaster, but he contended that, unless employers showed the working people greater consideration, grave trouble would arise sooner or later.

How he came to adopt the revolutionary plan of coöperating with instead of coercing labour is interesting.

His action was originally prompted more by business necessity than by sentiment. Previously he had followed the universal rule of getting from his employees the greatest amount of work for the least amount of money, and they had reciprocated by giving the least amount of work for the greatest amount of money they could obtain.

Let us first trace briefly the record of John H. Patterson and the making of cash registers before this turning point was reached.

There were no cash registers when John Henry Patterson was born —December 13, 1844. His forbears were Scots-Irish, the first to come to America (about 1728) having been his great-grandfather, whose son fought as a colonel in the Revolutionary War, founded the city of Lexington, Ky., became one of the three original owners of the land now covered by Cincinnati, and finally located on a 2,000-acre farm near Dayton. Here John Henry was born, almost on the spot now occupied by the National Cash Register Company. As a lad, one of eight children, he had to work hard on the farm. He received a good education, first in the Dayton schools and later at Miami University and Dartmouth College, where he graduated B.A. in 1867, having previously served in the Civil War as a Hundred Day Man, although then only a stripling.

Farm labour had little attraction for the Bachelor of Arts. Commerce appealed to him most, but he could not pick and choose jobs. Collecting tolls on the Miami & Erie Canal, on duty night and day, Sundays and holidays, was the best he could land. But this was not commerce. He wanted to buy and sell things. Having saved a little money, he succeeded in borrowing a little more and set up as a retail coal dealer in Dayton. From selling coal he gravitated to mining coal and iron ore, in partnership with his brother, Frank, in Jackson County, some eighty miles from Dayton.

To enable their miners to obtain supplies, the Pattersons, in conjunction with two other mining concerns, opened a store. Business was plentiful but profits were nil. At the end of two years the store had not netted a cent, notwithstanding that all goods were supposed to be sold on a reasonable margin of profit. There was a leak somewhere.

From his militant grandfather, who by profession was a civil engineer, Mr. Patterson had inherited a mania for doing things with scrupulous accuracy and precision; nothing slipshod, nothing faulty, nothing careless could be tolerated. Everything must be done just so. The mysterious mismanagement of the store worried him. It must be run down and eliminated.

Hearing that a merchant in Dayton had invented a contrivance to keep a record of all sales, Mr. Patterson immediately telegraphed for two of the novel machines. The idea of the cash register had taken birth in 1879, in the brain of Jacob Ritty, a Dayton merchant who, suffering from a breakdown due to overwork and worry in attempting to keep tabs on the details of his business, had started on a voyage to Europe. While in the engine room of the ship one day, he noticed a device that recorded the number of revolutions of the propeller shaft. Why not construct a machine that would record each coin put in the till? Hurrying back, he set to work with his brother, a skilled mechanic, and evolved the first cash register.

Mr. Patterson's was the first order filled. Crude and clumsy though it was, the machine immediately turned the store's loss into a substantial profit. Mr. Patterson's commercial instinct told him that the new invention had unlimited possibilities. "What is good for our store is good for every store in the world," he told himself. At the first opportunity he went to Dayton, investigated the situation thoroughly and, although only a few machines had been turned out, he was so certain of the outlook that in 1884 he bought out the Ritty business and changed the name from the National Manufacturing Company to the National Cash Register Company.

The acorn did not at once grow into an oak. Troubles and obstacles were met at every turn. Construction of the cash registers demanded highly skilled and scrupulously careful workmanship of a novel kind. It was difficult first to teach the workers and then to retain them, as their expert services were sought by others. The factory was located in an unsavoury section of Dayton called Slidertown—everybody and everything on the down grade had a habit of sliding into this section. To work at "The Cash" did not bring a high social rating; in plain language, the better class of young men and particularly young women preferred to earn a living in more respectable surroundings.

John H. Patterson was partly to blame for this unsatisfactory state of affairs. He was not then a model employer. He was neither better nor worse than other factory owners. His interest in his employees was confined to what he could get out of them. And they repaid him in kind. Poor working conditions begot a poor product.

So bad, indeed, did things become that in one year $50,000 worth of machines was thrown back on the hands of the company as faulty.

Then John H. Patterson woke up.

He experienced not only a change of viewpoint, but he underwent a change of heart. Adversity had taught him humanity. Why should workers treat him with more consideration than he was treating them? Why should they interest themselves in his welfare if he was not interested in theirs? He would adopt a new policy. Also, he installed his own desk in the centre of the factory floor.

With this new spirit in his heart, he went to the factory to study conditions. He saw a woman engaged, as he thought, in mixing glue in a very unscientific way. He spoke to her. "It's not glue, it's coffee," she told him. Leavings from the previous day were being reconcocted.

Mr. Patterson immediately ordered the manager to arrange to have the women supplied with good coffee every day. He next looked around for other things needing correction. Not noticing any provision for the proper serving of the coffee, he summoned the manager, who gave him a dozen reasons why the factory could not be turned into a coffee house. Mr. Patterson ordered him to rent a house across the street for the purpose. Again there was delay. This time the manager and his assistants were told that dismissal would follow were the reform not instituted forthwith.

The serving of the coffee had an instantaneous effect upon the output of the women. Patterson learned that kindness paid in dollars as well as in disposition. From that day on he never wavered in his determination to improve the lot of his people. One thoughtful innovation after another was introduced and a systematic effort was made to raise the quality and tone of the working force.

Better workmanship and better product brought increased business. Sales increased from a few thousand a year to several score thousands. Larger buildings became necessary. Slidertown had been cleaned up somewhat under Mr. Patterson's influence, but it was still no Newport or Tuxedo. Mr. Patterson next bought up much of the property in the neighbourhood and resolved to spend both money and time in revolutionizing the whole neighbourhood.

Most important of all, he engaged the leading firm of architects in America to design a factory building which would be the very antithesis of the ordinary factory. He wanted it to contain every conceivable appointment conducive to the comfort and safety of the workers. He wanted, also, halls for noonday entertainment, for the holding of classes, for illustrated lessons and lectures on the different phases of manufacturing the cash register, and on salesmanship.

When the glass and steel palace began to be erected Dayton shook its head. Among other things, Patterson was told that the boys of Slidertown would not leave one whole window overnight, that new glass would cost him more than his profits. Patterson took the boys in hand and began to transform embryonic gangsters into young gardeners and young gentlemen. The boys were given individual gardens, received instruction from a head gardener, were shown how to organize themselves into a stock company, were inspired to interest themselves in the work, received prizes and, at the end of the year, were paid dividends from products sold. The company was run entirely by the boys themselves. Also, a club was formed to send city lads to work on farms during summer vacations. This solved the window-breaking problem—and solved, also, problems of more vital importance to the boys and to society.

Patterson's "coddling" of labour was bitterly resented by other employers. They reasoned that the best type of workers would prefer to secure positions with the Cash Register Company. They also feared that labour would become discontented, not to say obstreperous. Still he went ahead, convinced that he was on the right track and that one day his example would have to be followed. The more he did for the happiness of those around him the more fun he got out of it.

His enormous new plant, however, was costing a mint of money. So were grounds he had bought for the use of his workers and others. The rapid expansion of his business—in two years he sold as many machines as he had sold in the previous twenty-two years—necessitated the tying up of extensive capital.

Like a thunderbolt came the announcement from the bankers that he must pay off loans. Not a dollar could he obtain from any bank in Dayton. This, Patterson's critics and enemies chuckled, would put a quietus to his welfare capers.

It almost did. Patterson, however, was a born fighter. He also was a philosopher. "Thrice armed is he who hath his quarrel just," he reassured himself. It was a time of tight money, and outside banks were indifferent or worse. Finally, however, a New England financier sent a representative to Dayton to analyze conditions. He learned the cause of the trouble and he learned also that the Patterson brothers were men of unimpeachable character, of indefatigable industry, of indomitable will, and that they were conducting a growing, profitable business. All this appealed to him and he offered to lend them several times the amount they had asked. Had the character of the Pattersons not withstood the searching test, the history of the National Cash Register Company might have ended disastrously.

Mr. Patterson's activities on behalf of his employees multiplied. Slidertown began to blossom. Besides the boy club gardeners, grown-ups in the neighbourhood became so greatly enamoured of the beautiful that, under consistent encouragement, they began to spruce up their homes and to surround them with flowers and lawns.

Mr. Patterson also worked laboriously and against much discouragement to arouse the citizens of Dayton to make of it "The City Beautiful." He threw himself enthusiastically into reforming the administration of the city, then politics-ridden, not to say corrupted. Like most reformers, he made enemies.

Nor did he wholly escape the trouble with workers which other employers had predicted. During a period of acute labour unrest throughout the country, whisperings began to be heard that a section of the Cash Register workmen were to strike. Mr. Patterson's kindness had been misinterpreted as weakness. Some of the men wanted to become masters of the establishment. They imagined they could do as they pleased, that Mr. Patterson would submit to anything. He had made one mistake in the treatment of his workers; some of the privileges, such as taking baths and attending certain of the entertainments provided, were made compulsory. This form of paternalism, naturally, was resented. Mr. Patterson, however, saw his mistake and rectified it.

On learning that a strike was to be called by a part of the workmen, he assembled the whole force, explained that he understood some of them were dissatisfied, told them he himself was not wholly pleased with the way things were going, and announced that a rest would probably do them and him good. He closed the whole works without intimating when they would be re-opened and then went travelling.

At first the prospective strikers were jubilant over their "victory." Within a fortnight, however, other classes of employees began to criticise the malcontents. Another week passed, and still no intimation of re-opening. Inquiries began to be made as to when work would be resumed. No comforting information was forthcoming. At the end of a month things began to be made unpleasant for those responsible for the shut-down. Petitions began to be sent Mr. Patterson to come back and open the gates. But not until two months had passed did he announce that he would return to Dayton although he let it be known that he had been invited to locate his works at other more convenient points.

The whole city prepared to give Mr. Patterson a welcome home with brass bands, public receptions, complimentary dinners, and laudatory speeches. Sober reflection had convinced the citizens that Dayton could not afford to lose Patterson.

He would have none of their joyful reception. Instead, he replied by outlining a long list of things Dayton citizens ought to do to make their city more attractive, more efficient, and more healthful.

He re-opened the works and there was not another murmur of a strike, and since then he has had no trouble with labour. The true worth of his work for his employees and for Dayton was grasped during the period there were fears that Dayton would lose both him and his plant, thus emptying thousands of pay envelopes weekly.

When operations were resumed the demand for National Cash Registers increased enormously. Mr. Patterson's system of training salesmen was bearing fruit. Every employee was filled with ambition to do his or her best. National Registers, pushed with redoubled energy, were driving others from the field. The enthusiasm of the salesmen sometimes outran their discretion.

When the national mania for trust busting swept across the land the Government did not overlook the National Cash Register Company. Was it not rapidly becoming almost a monopoly? Patterson's reply to that was that he owned the basic patents for cash registers and that he was entitled to fight competitors both legally and commercially. Fight them he did without mercy. Into the rights and wrongs of the Government's prosecution I cannot here enter. A lower court sentenced a number of the officers and responsible employees of the company to a year's imprisonment, but this verdict was quashed by the higher court. The Government did not drop the matter, but started to prosecute the company under the civil section of the Sherman Law, and rather than continue at loggerheads with the Administration for another year or two, demoralizing the whole organization, Mr. Patterson was induced to plead guilty to the technical charge of "conspiring" to build up a monopoly, a business policy

JOHN H. PATTERSON

which Mr. Patterson had all along contended he was entitled to follow by reason of his exclusive patent rights.

Mr. Patterson declared to me that only the consciousness that he was doing constructive work and setting an example to other employers in the treatment of workmen impelled him to struggle on against both labour and governmental obstacles after he had all the money he needed for his personal and family requirements.

To the American public the crowning achievement of John H. Patterson was that which won him the title "The Saviour of Dayton," on that memorable day and night of March 25-26, 1913, when the greater part of the city was floodswept and laid under as much as seventeen feet of water.

It was Patterson who, hours before the flood came, by telephone, by telegraph, by horseback, by automobile, by foot messenger, by every means of communication that could be impressed, aroused the whole city to its impending danger and gave instructions how to prepare for the coming avalanche of water. It was Patterson, too, who summoned his executive and other force to Industrial Hall, mounted the stage, and showing his famous pyramidical chart illustrating the organization of the company, announced: "I declare the National Cash Register Company out of commission and I proclaim the Citizens' Relief Association." With a piece of charcoal he sketched a diagram of the Relief Association, naming a head for each division of the work and instructing them how to proceed.

From the Patterson factory came rafts and boats—constructed of materials taken from his immense lumber yards—*at the rate of one every seven minutes.*

By common assent Patterson became the acknowledged dictator of the whole rescue work. Never did military generals direct forces with more skill, with more rapidity, or to more effect. So brilliantly did he command that when General Wood, commander of the U. S. Army, and Secretary of War Garrison rushed to the scene and viewed the functioning of the Patterson emergency machine they announced: "We can do nothing beyond what you are doing."

A faint glimmer of what Dayton underwent may be derived from the fact that in one improvised maternity hospital twenty-nine children were born during that terrible night.

To describe John H. Patterson's personality would require pages. His business methods and his whole mode of life are novel. His brain works night and day. At his bedside are pencil and pad on which he commits ideas the instant they enter his head. To his secretary he dictates dozens of orders every morning to be transmitted to heads of different departments. These orders are pasted on large charts, one for each department, and not until an instruction has been carried out is a broad red line drawn through it. By turning the charts, constructed like swinging doors, Mr. Patterson can see at a glance any order that has not been obeyed. I noticed one without a red line although it dated back several months. It read: "Make nine-hole golf course into eighteen-hole golf course." I remarked upon it.

"That is now being done," I was informed—an eighteen-hole golf course for the use primarily of Mr. Patterson's employees.

He is an originator and an admirer of mottoes and his whole plant is hung with placards of wisdom and inspiration. These are frequently changed.

Mr. Patterson rises regularly at 6:30, indulges in a glass of hot water for breakfast, works like a battering ram until noon, lunches on some fruit or vegetables, takes a nap for a couple of hours, and spends the remainder of the day as his fancy dictates. For dinner he eats nuts, fruits, and vegetables. For years he has not tasted meat or fish or fowl. His home is a quaint, unpretentious, old-fashioned, delightful place on the top of a hill overlooking the plant and was formerly owned by his ancestors. He has a grown-up son and daughter, who are both interested in their father's activities. Until her recent marriage, the daughter had an office at the factory and directed the welfare work of the women's department.

Almost singlehanded John H. Patterson, following the flood, reorganized the civic administration of Dayton. The City Manager plan instituted there has been notably successful—but how long politics and politicians can be held at arm's length is a question. One indisputable fact is that Dayton is now better governed than ever before and that the taxpayers receive larger value for their money. Mr. Patterson, diplomatically, does not try to dominate or domineer the administration, having learned by experience that able-bodied citizens of a free republic abhor even the most benevolent efforts of that kind. Nevertheless his influence, his example, and his ideals have been a potent factor in elevating the conduct of the city's affairs. Indeed, he has been the thinker and inspirer in all such activities as industrial welfare, public recreation, and coöperative health promotion. To a seer's vision he has wedded the qualities of a doer; his gift of imagination is equalled only by his energy and get-it-doneness. His inborn masterfulness, at times resented by others in earlier days, has been mellowed by experience.

"I feel," he told me, "that I have only a few more years to live and my main object in life now is to influence others, especially employers, to have more consideration for their workers, for after he has a competence, money can do nothing satisfying for a man's own wants. It is useful only in enabling him to do good. I would rather spend money to bring my fellow-beings out into the open, into God's sunshine, and enable them to enjoy the beauties of nature than hoard great wealth for my children."

I cannot even touch upon the extent of the National Cash Register Company's business, with its branches and agents in every part of the world, except to mention that it employs more than 10,000 people thoughout the world, produces some 60,000 machines per annum, and has sold more than 1,800,000 registers to merchants in every civilized country in the world.

I asked Mr. Patterson for some suggestions for the attainment of success, and this is what he laid down:

"Learn to overcome difficulties while young. The farm is the best school, for it teaches the fundamentals of success, namely:

"1. Hard work.
"2. Commonsense.
"3. Good habits.
"4. Practical experience.
"5. The value of a dollar."

GEORGE W. PERKINS

ONLY one man ever refused a partnership in J. P. Morgan & Company.

The partnership was offered the first time the late Mr. Morgan saw the man. It came after only a few moments' conversation on a non-business subject.

More extraordinary still, the man had never had a day's banking experience.

Mr. Morgan's engagement of H. P. Davison, a banker, and known to him personally, was dramatic enough; but his proffer of a partnership to George W. Perkins, as here described for the first time, constitutes perhaps the most dramatic episode in the annals of high finance.

Mr. Perkins, then a vice-president of the New York Life Insurance Company, had been named a member of the Palisades Park Commission and wanted to raise money. A Morgan partner had several times asked Mr. Perkins to come into the office and meet Mr. Morgan, and about this time he again suggested an introduction. Mr. Perkins, with an eye to "touching" the banker for a contribution, agreed. Mr. Morgan greeted him in his private office, separated from the office of his partners merely by a glass partition.

Mr. Perkins at once unfolded his scheme, told the banker that they wanted to raise $125,000 and that Mr. Morgan's name among the contributors would facilitate the raising of the fund.

"I will give you $25,000," Mr. Morgan replied without cavil.

Mr. Perkins thanked him cordially—and asked if Mr. Morgan could suggest others that might be approached.

"Look here," Mr. Morgan immediately countered, "I will give you the whole $125,000 if you will do something for me."

Astonished, Mr. Perkins stammered: "There is nothing I can do for you, Mr. Morgan."

"Yes, there is. You can turn round and take that desk and go to work," said Mr. Morgan very emphatically as he pointed to a large desk at the other side of the glass partition.

Mr. Perkins did not comprehend. He looked at Mr. Morgan quizzically.

"I mean, come in here as a partner," explained Mr. Morgan.

Mr. Perkins, to Mr. Morgan's great astonishment—for he was not in the habit of having young financiers refuse to join his cabinet—

replied: "I can't do that. I am with the New York Life and must spend my days there."

It was not until nearly a year after that Mr. Morgan finally induced Mr. Perkins to join the firm, and then Mr. Perkins consented only on condition that he be allowed to retain his position with the New York Life.

Knowing this story, I asked Mr. Perkins why he did not at once grasp the opportunity to become a member of the greatest international banking house in the country, a position regarded as the Ultima Thule of American banking.

"Because I never have been in this world merely to make money," replied Mr. Perkins in a tone that suggested there should be no amazement over his action. "I early learned that any man who starts out simply to make money never gets very far, for he will ruin his health, or sacrifice his friends, or drive so hard that there is nothing in it. I was brought up in the life insurance business. It is not a charitable institution, but it is a business in which you deal with human beings and where you are doing something for people. You serve in a cause which you believe to be helpful to other people.

"I had worked up from office-boy to the highest salaried insurance position in the world—$75,000. My heart was in the work. I was striving with all my might to put the New York Life in the premier place among the insurance companies of the world. I had spent much time in Europe to induce different countries to give us a license to do business there and we had succeeded in gaining admittance to every civilized country on the face of the earth. It was a big, difficult, but fascinating task, and I did not want to give it up even for the coveted honour and emolument of a partnership in J. P. Morgan's."

Mr. Morgan knew what he was doing when he approached Mr. Perkins, for, although they had never met, New York's leading banker was well aware that a new genius had invaded the financial world. Mr. Perkins, in addition to having revolutionized the conduct of the life-insurance business, had demonstrated unwonted ability as a financier. Confronted in Russia with apparently insuperable barriers, Mr. Perkins resourcefully arranged that his company should handle a large bond issue for the Russian Government if given permission to do insurance business throughout that vast land. Mr. Perkins brought the bonds back, carried the deal through with consummate skill, and won for himself a place on the Finance Committee of the New York Life, a position then keenly coveted by the greatest financial interests in the metropolis.

Mr. Perkins's adroitness and originality as a financier sprouted at a very early age.

One very stormy night, when he was a fledgling insurance solicitor out West, he waded through deep snow to a country flour mill, and tackled the miller, his brother and son.

They were not interested—at first. But they could not run away. Finally, Perkins, finding they would not part with any cash, offered to accept their notes in payment for the first premium. This bait got them. By this time the hour for finishing up the day's business had arrived, and Perkins noticed they were putting quite a snug sum into the safe.

"I suppose you sometimes buy bargains, don't you?" he remarked.

To be sure, they did.

"Well, now, I'll sell you something absolutely good at a bargain price. I'll sell you your own notes at a discount."

And in five minutes Perkins was walking out with his pockets bulging with cash!

"Say, young fellow," the old German miller called after him, "I wish you would let me know what you are doing when you are 40. Will you send me your photograph then?"

At thirty-nine the insurance solicitor was drawing a larger salary than the President of the United States and refusing a partnership in the country's greatest banking house. At forty he was a member of Morgan & Company.

How had he done it? How may others attain similar success?

"The most important thing of all is to look upon your work as play and throw yourself into it with the same zest and relish and determination to excel as when you play baseball or checkers or football," Mr. Perkins emphasized. "By adopting this mental attitude toward your work you can accomplish more and find greater pleasure and satisfaction in the doing of it. Any young man—or older man—having this conception of his duties, will not worry if obliged to stay after five o'clock; he will be eager to achieve the task in hand and will get genuine fun out of attaining his purpose.

"Another valuable lesson I learned from my father, namely, that a change of occupation is almost equal to a vacation. The idea that you must have a certain amount of rest, doing nothing, is all wrong. To keep your red corpuscles red, there is nothing like healthy work enthusiastically performed.

"*My own method has been to live every day as though it was the only day I had to live and to crowd everything possible into that day.* Pay no attention to the clock or what you are paid, but work and live for all there is in it—just as you would play football—and everything else will take care of itself.

"At the head of the table there is always most room. It is the tree that grows and grows until it overtops the others that gets the most air and sunshine. The thing for the young man to do is to strive with all the energy he possesses to excel in actual ability. Pull is not necessary. Nor should a young man bother too much about his wages—I never asked an increase in my life. You can command sooner or later what you are entitled to—if you preëminently deserve it.

"But you have got to be ultra-proficient in some particular thing. You must stand out and do it better than the fellows around you whether you are an office-boy, a stenographer, or an executive. You must use your head as well as your hands. Don't be afraid to do extra work lest it interfere with your theatre-going—I don't go to the theatre half-a-dozen times during the winter, not that I don't like it, but there are other things more worth doing."

As I have always regarded as Mr. Perkins's chief contribution to the improvement of the modern economic system his origination and introduction of profit sharing with employees, I questioned him on how he came to conceive and carry out this idea.

"Necessity was the mother of its invention," he replied. "Also, I realized that profit sharing would add to the zest of work. It is absolutely the only way to solve the problem between capital and labour. I adopted it before ever I entered Morgan's

"It came about in this way: When I took charge of the New York Life agents, I found conditions most unsatisfactory. The company had only a general agent in each state and this agent appointed all the solicitors for his state and had them under him. If one of those general agents resigned he would take away most of his solicitors with him. Moreover, it was a very common thing for solicitors to make all sorts of gross misrepresentations in order to get initial premiums, and once they had 'worked' one particular district they would clear out and start all over again to fool another group of people.

"It was essential, I saw, that there should be something to bind all the agents and solicitors to the company, some strong inducement for them to stay by the company and treat it fairly by not misrepresenting things to people and thus heaping all sorts of troubles and tangles upon the officers to straighten out.

"Most of the agents, too, were an improvident lot, spending everything they made. I organized the much-discussed 'Nylic' to cure all these evils. We explained to the agents that if they would save as much money as they could each year and put it into a common fund, the company would add to it a certain percentage. Then the entire sum would be invested for the benefit of those who subscribed to it and made to earn as much as possible.

"This plan accomplished these valuable results: It taught the agents to save. Automatically it induced them to stay with the

New York Life. Then, when they knew they were to stay with the company, they had to tell the truth; and when they ceased to fool the policy holders, these agents had no longer the reasons they formerly had to quit. The few agents who had been in the habit of saving, often invested their money unwisely and the consequent worry militated against their efficiency. The 'Nylic' money was judiciously invested for these men and increased very markedly.

"When the insurance investigations came along, the forces of the other companies were demoralized whereas ours stood by us like a stone wall.

"We did away with the general state agents entirely. They were really nothing but middlemen. The company rented its own offices throughout the country, put a responsible man in charge of each on a salary basis and engaged the agents direct, so that the company knew the name and kept a record of each man representing it in the field. Under this system if any agent left he could not take a whole crowd with him. The arrangement made for efficiency and saved the company—and, therefore, the policy holders—a great deal of money."

The profit-sharing plan thus instituted by Mr. Perkins was later introduced by him into the United States Steel Corporation and the International Harvester Corporation and has since been copied, either in toto or in modified form, by scores of other corporations. This, to my mind, is the best monument raised by Mr. Perkins.

Mr. Perkins has been an enigma to most of the financial community and to a large section of the public. Some of his activities, actual or rumoured, while he was with Morgan & Company, his retirement from that firm at the end of ten years, his announcement that he intended to devote the remainder of his life to aiding in the amelioration of social conditions and the solution of economic and public problems, his extremely unconventional political activities under the Roosevelt Progressive banner—all these things have excited comment, criticism, and even suspicion. For a "Wall Street millionaire" to give up money-making, cast off established political affiliations and announce that he would become an active, practical humanitarian was something the people could not quite fathom. There must be a nigger in the woodpile. It was so unlike the ordained order of things. It was too good to be true.

I hinted at these things and asked Mr. Perkins: "What about it?"

"I know," he nodded. "I suppose my action did seem queer to those unfamiliar with all the facts, but to any one knowing my ancestry and my view of life and of money-making, and knowing, also, how I at first refused the lucrative offer to join Mr. Morgan, my conduct has not been at all illogical. Two of my forbears were David Walbridge and George Walbridge, both prominent men in Michigan, the former being a staunch Congressman from that state. It was this David Walbridge who presided at the meeting at Kalamazoo where the Republican Party was born. By the way, when Mr. Hughes was recently in Kalamazoo they presented him with a cane that Abraham Lincoln had given to this granduncle of mine, David Walbridge. My middle name is Walbridge, as also was my father's. I, therefore, had good Republican blood in me—and also, perhaps, a fair share of independence.

"Then, my father, although not a rich man by any means, was deeply interested in philanthropic and similar work. He was chairman of the Illinois Board of Reformatories and was associated with Dwight L. Moody, about 1860, in organizing the Sands Missionary Sunday School—so called because they had no building and met on the sands. It became the largest in Chicago with an attendance of 1,200 scholars, rivalled only by John Wanamaker's school in Philadelphia. He also organized other mission Sunday Schools and started the Railroad Mission in a box car—until recently I carried the watch the Railroad Sunday-school teachers gave my father, one of the first stem-winding watches in the country.

"Is it not natural, therefore, that I should become, for example, a member of the Prison Commission and be interested in Thomas Mott Osborne's work? My father believed in the honour system fifty years ago and believed, also, in rewarding delinquents for good behaviour, etc. I recall that while I was a lad of only six, George Payson Weston was to pass our home on the south side of Chicago on his first great walk from New England to Chicago and my father, who had supplied the boys of the reform school near our home with instruments, got the superintendent to take more than half the boys out of the school and accompany Weston into Chicago with the reform-school brass band at the head of the procession. Not a single boy tried to run away, yet my father was trounced unmercifully by the newspapers for the danger to which he had exposed the city! He was, you see, something of a progressive!

George Walbridge Perkins, born on January 31, 1862, was ten years old before he was sent to school, his father's theory being that, as he would not ask a child to carry a hod of coal upstairs lest it hurt his spine, it was even more important not to put undue strain upon the brain of a child. At school George often got into trouble for not doing things according to rule; he could get the correct answer quickly by methods of his own, a species of originality that was not encouraged. Graduating from the public school at fifteen he insisted on going to work rather than to high school.

His first job was sorting lemons and oranges in a fruit store in Water Street—"and I have been more or less engaged in sorting lemons from oranges ever since," he commented laughingly in recalling these early days. It was dirty, unremunerative work, affording no outlet for ingenuity or originality. So in a few months he found a place as office-boy with the New York Life Insurance Company. Almost from the start he would go out of an evening, after finishing his day's duties, and hunt for "prospects." Before long he was writing quite a little insurance.

Next he invented an entirely new kind of ledger, which attained quite a reputation under the name of the "Perkins Record." It did away with many unnecessary entries in other books and kept a complete and convenient record of each policy. He did other radical and progressive things—so much so that the first time he went to New York the chief accountant, an old German, to whom all the branch offices reported, snapped, when Mr. Perkins was introduced: "So you are the man who breaks more rules of the company than any other cashier?"

This rebuff from such a dignitary "scared me out of seven years' growth," Mr. Perkins afterward related.

From office-boy in Chicago young Perkins, when seventeen, went to the Cleveland office of the company as assistant bookkeeper, and when twenty-one had been appointed cashier. There was not much room for originality in this position, nor did it afford enough facilities for rubbing shoulders with other people and doing business. When twenty-four he resigned and took a roving commission as solicitor, making Denver his headquarters. Within two years he was made agency director there and soon made $15,000 a year in commissions. Next he was promoted to the responsible position of inspector of agencies in the West, with his office in Chicago, at $15,000 per annum.

This was a man's job. As already explained, the agency system in those days was extremely unsatisfactory. To make matters worse, vicious attacks began to be made by the New York newspapers upon the principal life-insurance companies. The situation called for virile, aggressive action. Perkins rose to the occasion.

His fecund mind hatched a new idea to hearten and stimulate the discouraged agents. With a stroke of genius, he started the "Bulletin," which was destined to become famous throughout the insurance world—and destined, also, to have many imitators. It began as a four-page circular of which three pages carried interesting miscellaneous information, and the first a message each week from the brilliant young inspector of agencies. Perkins's idea would have done credit to the editor of the most up-to-date morning or evening newspaper. The "Bulletin" was mailed to reach every agent at his home on Monday morning.

In Mr. Perkins's mind was the picture of an agent sitting in a chair reading a local newspaper, smoking a cigar, taking things easy. The Perkins message was directed straight to that man and was so constructed as to arouse him to throw away his cigar, put on his coat, and go in search of somebody to insure. It was a clarion call to duty, a ringing message of inspiration. It appealed to the man's manhood. It shamed sloth. It awakened ambition. Also, and importantly, it did the trick.

The New York Life's agents, or most of them, became veritable dynamos. They hustled as never before. Croakers who wrote complainingly that the New York newspaper attacks were killing business received the crushing reply that exact data had been gathered of the number of copies of New York newspapers that went west of Chicago and that the total was infinitesimal contrasted with the number of people to be insured. This little investigation was another idea born in the inspector's fruitful brain.

The inevitable happened. The invaluable work being done by Perkins became the talk of the insurance world and in three years, when exactly thirty, he was elected third vice-president of the New York Life Insurance Company at $25,000 a year. In less than a year he was honoured by election to the Board of Trustees. Promotion to the second vice-presidency, in 1898, at $35,000, was immediately followed by his elevation to the Finance Committee, while in 1900 he was made chairman of the Finance Committee, a post, in some respects, carrying greater responsibilities than even that of the presidency of the company.

It was in this year, 1900, that Mr. Perkins became a Morgan partner. In 1903 he was elected first vice-president of the New York Life.

Mr. Perkins retired from J. P. Morgan & Company on December 31, 1910, "for the purpose of devoting more time to work of a public and semi-public nature, notably profit sharing and other benefit plans."

During his decade's service as a banker perhaps the most notable achievements of Mr. Perkins were his epochal introduction of profit sharing in the United States Steel Corporation, of whose Finance Committee he became a member, his gigantic merger of farm machinery manufacturers into the International Harvester Corporation, and his effective financial piloting of that organization as chairman of the Finance Committee.

Mr. Morgan never had a more active, on-the-jump partner than George W. Perkins, yet, although the two men were totally different in their make-up, they managed to pull together in close harmony for ten years. Wall Street gossip that Mr. Perkins was asked to resign because of certain stock-market operations was widely credited by those ignorant of Mr. Perkins's philosophy of life, for it did seem an extraordinary thing for a man under fifty, full of health and vigour and ambition, to step down from a shining banking pedestal into financial retirement. The most notable characteristic of George Walbridge Perkins, however, is his inherent penchant for doing original, out-of-the-ordinary, not to say startling, things.

Even while in the thick of the game he preached doctrines not then generally subscribed to concerning capital's responsibilities to the public. For example, ten years ago he laid down this dictum in an address on "The Modern Corporation" at Columbia College. "The corporations of the future must be those that are semi-public servants, serving the public, with ownership widespread among the public, and labour so fairly and equitably treated that it will look upon its corporation as its friend and protector rather than as an ever-present enemy; above all, believing in it so thoroughly that it will invest its savings in the corporation's securities and become partners in the business. . . . For business purposes in this country the United States Government is a corporation with fifty subsidiary companies, and the sooner this is realized the sooner we can get the right kind of supervision of semi-public business enterprises and, in this way, give the public the publicity and the protection to which it is entitled in the conduct of business by corporations. In no other way can the public be protected from evils in corporation management."

Mr. Perkins now works harder in the public interest than he ever worked for his own pocket. His most recent activities have been in checkmating the rising cost of foodstuffs, his efforts in this direction having won him official recognition and an official position. While others talked, Perkins did things, bringing food to New York and placing it on the market at low prices. He is a member of thirty-five non-business societies and associations interested in various phases of the public welfare, education, art, etc. Almost singlehanded he has brought within measurable distance of fruition the colossal scheme to create not merely a local Palisades Park across the river from New York but an interstate park running all the way from Fort Lee to Newburgh along the west side of the Hudson River.

Some shallow money-grabbing individuals were at first inclined to scoff and sneer at Mr. Perkins's avowed intention to devote the rest of his life to worthy public or semi-public purposes, but his works have stopped their mouths. I confess to having been prejudiced against Mr. Perkins because of his somewhat brusque, snappish mannerisms, of which I once received an unpalatable taste; yet the fact remains that he is a conspicuous example of a wealthy, active, forceful business man relinquishing money-making at a relatively early age to devote unstinted energy to unselfish, helpful causes.

Europe has many men of somewhat similar type, men of affluence who devote their lives chiefly to the public interest, but this country is, or at least was before the war, so madly engaged in dollar-making that few millionaires have turned from serving mammon to serving their fellowmen with their heads, hearts, and hands—though some have been lavish enough with part of their surplus lucre.

Mr. Perkins married Miss Evelina Ball of Cleveland, in 1899, and has two children, a daughter and a son, the latter, George W. Perkins, Jr., who graduated from Princeton in 1917 and immediately took up Y. M. C. A. war work.

GEORGE M. REYNOLDS

CAN you picture a young bank clerk of to-day rising before daylight, hurrying off to the bank to oil and polish the floors, clean the brass, and then scrape the mud off the street crossings in front of the bank door so as to make the spot the cleanest in the town?

Or, do you know many country lads of twelve having vision enough to subscribe regularly for a dozen newspapers in different parts of the country with a view to learning something of the great world lying beyond the native village and using the knowledge thus gathered as a means of making dreams come true?

The story of the rise of George M. Reynolds from a farm boy, following the plow, to the presidency of the largest bank in the United States outside of New York—the Continental and Commercial National Bank of Chicago and its allied institutions, having $400,000,000 resources—glows with lessons of inspiration for the youth of America. This is the ex-farm boy who was offered the post of Secretary of the Treasury by President Taft. Also, among the honours conferred upon him has been the presidency of the American Bankers' Association, with its 17,000 members. When the famous Aldrich Currency Commission went to Europe, the former plowman was taken along as expert financial adviser.

Determination, incessant work, continuity of purpose, patience, unflagging optimism, never-failing cheerfulness, careful study of human nature, a spirit of democracy and faith in the goodness of human nature are the principal ingredients of success, Mr. Reynolds has learned in the character-testing school of experience through which he has passed.

"In life, as on the farm, you reap what you sow," Mr. Reynolds declared. "The trouble with most young men to-day is that they want to reap the moment they have sown. That is not nature's way. By sowing or planting carefully and tilling the ground intelligently the harvest-time will come in due season—but not before. Patience is not a virtue; it is a necessity."

Mr. Reynolds began his sowing early. His farmer father, however, put him in the wrong field at the start. He wanted George to be a merchant. So he purchased an interest in a store in the neighbouring township of Panora, Iowa, and installed the 15-year-old son behind the counter. The farmers' wives brought butter and eggs, and George's duty, after counting the eggs and weighing the butter, was to dole out, in return, tea, coffee, sugar, tobacco—and calico. It was the calico that upset all papa Reynolds's plans. Every housewife buying calico wanted to make sure beyond doubt that the colours in her new dress were fast and would not run.

The standard method of proving the quality of the dyes was to have the store clerk tear off a small piece of the calico, chew it vigorously, take the ball of calico from his mouth, unravel it in front of the critical customer, and show that each colour had stayed strictly within its own bounds.

George's ambitions persisted in bursting through the walls of the village store—and his teeth were rebelling against calico-chewing. The whole business was too small and petty, he felt; it did not appeal to him.

After a particularly busy Saturday of butter-weighing, egg-counting, grocery-selling, and calico-munching, George went home and told his father he would ten times rather work on the farm, as he knew he was a round peg in a square hole.

On Monday the Reynolds interest in the store was sold.

George became plowman and teamster. In those days Iowa required each farmer to do so many days' work in road-making and repairing. Young Reynolds got a team and did work for neighbours at $2.50 a day instead of the $3 allowed. He was a sturdy, healthy, broad-backed youth and, though not sixteen, he could hold his own with the best of them.

Every spare moment was devoted to reading and gathering information about a broader world than Panora. Whenever he got a chance he hied to the orchard, squatted in the shade of the apple trees, and devoured his newspapers, among them the St. Louis *Globe-Democrat*, New Orleans *Picayune*, Cincinnati *Enquirer*, Atlanta *Constitution*, San Francisco *Chronicle*, Portland *Oregonian*, and *Rocky Mountain News* of Denver.

He found his feet when given a job at $12.50 a month in the Guthrie County Bank, a small local institution in which his father was a stockholder. His foot was now on the right ladder, he knew, and he prepared to climb. The first steps included, as already told, the polishing of the floors and the scraping and sweeping of the street crossings in front of the bank—all duties not called for in his contract; his title, if you please, was that of bookkeeper.

"You liked the banking business from your first day in it?" I asked.

"Yes," he replied, "I liked it so much that social pleasures lost interest for me. I got more fun out of working at the bank in the evenings than I could have got by attending local parties or other social functions. My newspaper and other reading had taught me that nothing worth while could be gained without industry, and I was determined to work hard."

Many a night, after finishing at the bank, between eight and nine o'clock, he hurried to a small grain elevator owned by his father, donned overalls and, with a scoop-shovel, loaded railroad cars in order that the elevator might have space for grain arriving from the farms next morning.

For his intelligence and application to duty at the bank he was soon given opportunity to assist in making loans. Business activities interested him. He wanted to try his own hand at it. His chance came.

One winter day a stranger from northern Iowa stepped off the train and called at the bank to ask where he could buy 2,000 cords of wood to use in burning brick seventy-five miles away. Young Reynolds saw a chance for a profitable deal by turning wood contractor. Quickly ascertaining the freight rate, etc., the embryonic trader agreed to furnish the wood at a price which he calculated would net him a profit of $2 per cord, or $4,000 on the transaction.

Alas, the business novice overlooked the fact that the surrounding black loam roads became impassable for a wagon after a spring thaw. Consequently, those from whom he had purchased supplies were unable to make delivery when the frost left the ground. The brickmaker clamoured for his wood, urging that failure to send it would ruin several kilns of brick, in which event he would sue Reynolds for the loss!

Reynolds hustled here, there, and everywhere, scouring the near-by country for small quantities which, by paying extra, would and could be dragged over the bad roads. His $4,000 was dwindling sadly!

But fate, he was determined, should not cheat him of his entire profit. He would save all loading charges by doing the work himself!

After finishing at the bank, he took a lantern night after night, went to the railway side track, piled in as much wood as he could get through the car door, then climbed into the car, carried the wood back and stacked it up until the car was filled. Early next morning he would repeat the performance. In sixty days he finished the loading and shipping of the full 2,000 cords—a cord of wood is a large wagon-load eight feet long, four feet high, and four feet in width, so you can guess what the handling and rehandling of the 2,000 wagon-loads with his own hands meant to Reynolds.

The whole community guyed him about his famous wood contract. But as he had actually cleared $2,500 profit for his 60 days' work Reynolds was not quite sure whom the joke was on!

"I was no worse for the wear except that I had lacerated hands and the bank books suffered a little from bad writing," he declared in recounting the incident.

The larger world still kept a-callin'. Panora had several citizens clearsighted enough to see that young Reynolds possessed qualities likely to carry him far. To celebrate his majority—he was born on January 15, 1865—he set out to seek a larger sphere. Two well-to-do citizens furnished enough capital to increase his own savings to $40,000, and, with drafts in his inside pocket, he first looked over Kansas, and then Nebraska, where he opened a farm loan business, in Hastings. By buckboard, horseback and every other available means of transportation he traversed southern Nebraska and northern Kansas. He kept his ears and eyes open, and drew maps locating all creeks and rivers, alkali pits, etc. He granted mortgages to farmers and disposed of farm loans wherever he could find a market. He was now for the first time seeing the world and rubbing shoulders with the people in it. He took up the study of human nature in earnest, believing that a knowledge of this science would prove a key to success.

Much against his inclination, he consented to return to Panora two years later when his father purchased the controlling interest in the Guthrie County National Bank. This time he entered it as cashier and manager—only eight years after his first entry into the institution. It was not long before he doubled the bank's resources. Though only in his early twenties, he was already one of Panora's most prominent citizens.

He wanted Panora to spruce up. Other towns, his journeyings taught him, had electric light and water works; why not Panora? True, it had only 1,000 inhabitants, but what of that? Reynolds laid his idea before the mayor but he, staid citizen, squelched the ambitious project. Reynolds quietly canvassed the town, found the majority of the voters were with him, and then coolly told the Mayor it would expedite matters if he would resign. He did so, and "Mayor Reynolds" was his successor.

When twenty-eight he accepted the cashiership of the Des Moines National Bank, where the field was broader, the opportunities more plentiful and the competition keener. He proved his mettle. In less than two years he was elevated to the presidency of the bank. At thirty he had thus risen to a place of prominence and influence in the world.

He had and has a memory that is almost uncanny. He can recall probably more names and faces than any other banker in America, and this, with his years of active work in the American Bankers' Association, his wide travel, his approachability, and his genuine interest in all classes of mankind, has enabled him to build up perhaps the widest circle of friends of any man in his profession.

His reputation having become more than local, he received numbers of flattering offers from institutions in other cities, but refused them all until the powerful Continental National Bank of Chicago, backed by the prestige and millions of the Armours, asked him to join it as cashier.

On December 1, 1897, when he entered the institution, it had a capital of $2,000,000 and deposits of $14,000,000. Now the institution and the two offshoots formed by it have a combined capital and surplus of over $40,000,000 and deposits approximating $400,000,000.

From cashier, Mr. Reynolds stepped first to vice-presidency and later (in 1906) to the presidency of the Continental Bank. Here his restless energy, his inordinate capacity for hard work, his aggressiveness and his ambitions had full play. First the Continental took over two small institutions, the International Bank and the Globe National Bank, in 1898, and followed this up by acquiring the National Bank of North America, with over $10,000,000 deposits, in 1904; the American Trust & Savings Bank, with $34,000,000 deposits, in 1909; the Commercial National Bank, with nearly $72,000,000 deposits, in 1910; and the Hibernian Banking Association, with $26,000,000 deposits, in 1911.

Mr. Reynolds's bank has fully 50 per cent. more deposits than the total deposits of all Chicago banks when he went there twenty years ago. Of Chicago's increase from $240,000,000 to about $1,500,000,000 the Continental and Commercial has been responsible for nearly 30 per cent.

Mr. Reynolds is president also of the Continental and Commercial Trust and Savings Bank and the Hibernian Banking Association, both owned outright by the parent company.

One of Mr. Reynolds's dreams was to have not only the largest Bank in Chicago, but the finest bank building in the country. It cost $12,000,000 to turn this dream into a reality. The bank building covers a larger ground area than any office building in the world and the main floor of the bank, measuring 160 x 324 feet, with ceilings seventy feet in height in the centre, has no equal in this or any other country. Its "windows" number ninety-two. The building has three miles of corridors. Incidentally, the building earned on the bank's investment $8\frac{1}{2}$ per cent. in the second year and has been unqualifiedly successful ever since.

Some idea of the extent of the business done may be gathered from the fact that over 1,100 clerks are employed and that the national bank alone handles 100,000 outside checks every day, while its clearing and over-the-counter business brings the aggregate number of checks up to from 200,000 to 350,000 per day. The Reynolds institutions have a combined total of well over 100,000 accounts, including more than 5,000 bank depositors. No commercial bank, even in New York, can eclipse such totals.

When Reynolds came to Chicago as cashier of the Continental he was at his desk and well into the day's work before the doors were open for business. He perused nearly all the mail that came into the bank in order to familiarize himself thoroughly with the business and he actually signed practically 75 per cent. of all the outgoing letters. He worked with lightning speed. He could size up situations at a glance. Also, his industry became infectious; all around him were inspired to do faster and better work.

There was little "luck" in his rise.

Here was this man, born in an obscure little town in a then undeveloped part of the country, surrounded by only puny enterprises and having little direct connection with great centres of financial, commercial, and industrial activity. Yet, when only twelve, he cast off the provincial fetters. His acumen in subscribing for newspapers from all parts of the country; his readiness to do the work of a charwoman and a scavenger in order to help the little bank he entered; his willingness to jump in and help his father to load grain cars after having worked a round of the clock in the bank; the resourcefulness and pluck he exhibited in carrying out his first business deal, in lumber; his perception of the value of studying human nature and of making many friends—all these things and the spirit behind them meant that Reynolds could not fail to make his mark in the world.

What was his philosophy? What were his propelling ideas and ideals? What things did he find helpful in attaining success?

I cornered Mr. Reynolds for half an hour at his desk one very busy day and fired these questions at him. With characteristic promptness and directness he replied:

"A wide acquaintance is a great asset. I attended my first bankers' convention while I was still a youth at Panora. I have noticed bankers making up their golf matches before starting for a convention. When I attend conventions I play the business game, not golf.

"Studying the science of human nature has helped me greatly. If you know human nature you know how to handle human beings.

"I have never aspired to become a tremendously rich man. The best reward is consciousness of duty well done. This consciousness enables a man to sleep at the end of the day.

"The average boy wants to become vice-president in a year or two. Patience is indispensable. But if a young man always strives to be agreeable and to do his full duty without spending any time watching the clock, he is certain to have a fair measure of success. The man who makes a great success is the one who does the task a little better than the other fellows and who shows a little keener insight into men and things.

"If a man elects to play poker five or six times a week and to shine in society, he must not complain if he does not shine in his business. The man, on the other hand, who makes riches his all-consuming consideration and ambition must not be surprised if people turn their backs on him because his finer instincts have become blunted and stunted.

"You cannot undertake to develop certain qualities in others without unconsciously developing the same qualities in yourself.

"One of the greatest forms of satisfaction comes from doing something for other people.

"To sum up, it is personality that counts. Personality embraces many qualities, such as neatness, cheerfulness, courtesy, alertness, intelligence, and a sound knowledge of human nature. These qualities spell efficiency and efficiency spells success. The 'all-round' man is the highest type of human product, higher than the specialist, because the 'all-round' man must be able to handle specialists as well as others."

Mr. Reynolds has been erroneously accredited with having taken no vacation for many years, whereas the opposite is the case, for he firmly believes in the efficacy of recreation and diversion in the open air, with plenty of sunshine and exercise. He not only takes frequent vacations himself, but sees to it that his associate officers have generous and regular vacations, and, furthermore, that they are given a full day off each week throughout the year.

Discussing banking, Mr. Reynolds said: "Candour and frankness will carry a man farther than subterfuge. If a banker feels he must refuse a loan he should explain frankly his reasons. A borrower should never be made to feel that he is under any obligations to a banker outside of the repayment of the loan. Borrowers are as necessary to the success of a bank as depositors. In panic times the best policy is to help customers in every possible way, not to squeeze them. Confidence is the greatest asset in banking."

Incidentally, Mr. Reynolds does not own a share of stock in any railroad or industrial company doing business with his bank. He feels he can serve his stockholders better if he has no "entangling alliances" which might warp his judgment in deciding questions affecting his bank and its customers. He is, however, a director in the home bank where he started.

Mr. Reynolds for many years has given away one-tenth of his income annually—that is, he and his wife together. He married very young. "It was the best day's business I ever did," he says of this step in his career. Indeed, Mr. Reynolds attributes more than half his success to Mrs. Reynolds. She is noted for her activities on behalf of crippled children and homeless waifs. She is a talented musician.

Their only child, Earle H. Reynolds, is old enough to be a chum of his parents. Earle is duplicating the success of his father. He refused to work in his father's institution and struck out for himself. He is already, though only twenty-nine, president of the People's Trust and Savings Bank, with deposits running into eight figures.

JOHN D. ROCKEFELLER

JOHN D. ROCKEFELLER is the most impressive, the broadest-visioned, the most fundamental-thinking man I have ever met. Napoleon "thought in Empires," Cecil Rhodes "thought in Continents." John D. Rockefeller thinks universally; his yard-stick is the world, the whole human family. His invariable test is: How will it affect mankind? He looks and acts beyond parochialism, beyond provincialism, even beyond nationalism.

For example:

"The support of a hospital is a local duty and ought to be regarded by local people as a privilege," he told me; "the hospital serves only its own locality. But if a body of earnest, brainy, resourceful, scientifically minded medical men can be enabled to conduct researches that may evolve new knowledge which can be placed at the service of all, then something is accomplished for the whole human family. That is a duty and a privilege beyond any one locality. That is something a rich man can properly aid."

"What has given you the greatest satisfaction in having been able to do?" I asked.

We were playing golf, and Mr. Rockefeller played one of his characteristically straight iron shots before replying. Then he replied only indirectly.

"If in all our giving we had never done more than has been achieved by the fine, able, modest men of the Medical Institute, it would have justified all the money and all the effort we have spent. Only a day or two ago I received a report that we have discovered a cure for the terrible war condition known as gas gangrene. The tests convince these scientists that the new serum will prevent in large measure that destructive disease which has already maimed for life or killed thousands of young men. Isn't that a splendid and timely work these men have just done?"

Mr. Rockefeller will converse a whole day without using the word "I" half-a-dozen times. He always says "We"—unless telling a joke at his own expense. Once, before I knew Mr. Rockefeller well, when he said "we" in reply to a question I asked about an early incident of his career, I was puzzled as to whom he meant. "But who were the 'we?'" I asked. He was embarrassed. He alone had done it, I had gathered from the records. "Oh—well—my brother William came in with us—later," was the halting, evasive reply born of modesty.

Another time I had cornered him into admitting that it was he and not "we" that had done a certain thing. Mr. Rockefeller didn't quite like it.

"You must be careful," he cautioned, "if you write anything about me, not to make me out as having done anything more than the other men you write about."

I mention these incidents to illustrate the trait that first strikes one in Mr. Rockefeller, his innate, unassumed modesty, his unobtrusiveness, his utter lack of ostentatious self-assertion. Pressure was brought to bear upon Mr. Rockefeller several years ago to have him assist in preparing a full biography of his life and work.

"No," said Mr. Rockefeller in all sincerity, "I have never done anything worth writing a book about." And no biography was written.

I count myself exceedingly fortunate in having been able to induce Mr. Rockefeller to recount some of his early struggles and experiences, to emit occasional flashes of his philosophy of life, and to express his views on the ever-fresh and timely subject of the attainment of success. "Don't make me preach," was another of Mr. Rockefeller's modesty-inspired injunctions to me; he simply abjures the idea of being represented as posing as an authority or a self-appointed dictator on any subject. "Don't take my son's say-so about me—he's biased," was another of Mr. Rockefeller's exhortations, given laughingly in front of John D. Rockefeller, Jr.

Here are some of the pointed sentences dropped informally—at golf or automobiling or at the table—by the most remarkable man the world of business has ever produced:

"The most important thing for a young man starting life is to establish a credit—a reputation, character. He must inspire the complete confidence of others.

"The hardest problem all through my business career was to obtain enough capital to do all the business I wanted to do and could do given the necessary amount of money. You must establish a credit (character) before you can hope to have people lend you money.

"The first large bank loan I received—it was $2,000, a big sum in those days—was granted me only because the head of the bank made himself familiar with my mode of life, my habits, my industry, and learned from my former employers that I was a young man who could be trusted.

"Nowadays young men—and others—want to have too much done for them. They want to be presented with bonuses and to receive all sorts of concessions.

"To get on, young men should study their business thoroughly; work carefully, accurately, and industriously; save their money, and then either become partners by buying a share of the business or go out and form a business of their own.

"They must be self-reliant. They must not expect to have things handed them for nothing. They must make themselves strong by becoming able, brainy workers, by establishing a credit and by accumulating every dollar they can save after doing their full duty to society.

"The way business is conducted now, it is easy for a man to buy shares in it and thus participate in the profits.

"As for opportunities, there are ten to-day for every one there was sixty years ago. There were then few opportunities and very scanty means of taking advantage of them. Now large opportunities constantly spring up everywhere and we have a wonderful currency and credit system for enabling people to take hold of them."

I asked Mr. Rockefeller how he came to conceive the idea of forming the Standard Oil Company, the first large-scale industrial combination in modern times. His scrupulous care to give credit to others and to minimize his own efforts again obtruded.

"We were not really the first to adopt the combination idea," he corrected me. (It was this "we" that tripped me up.) "The Western Union Telegraph people had begun to buy up two or three small telegraph lines and add them to their system. The Standard Oil Company was less the fruit of an idea than an outgrowth of necessity. The oil business was so demoralized that nearly every refinery was threatened with bankruptcy. Prices were below cost of production. Competition had been very keen, not to say cruel. There were many bitternesses. Conditions had become impossible. Something had to be done if the industry was to be saved.

"I wrote our largest competitor asking if he would meet me at a certain time and place. Although we had not spoken for a year—as I told you, there were keen bitternesses at that time—he agreed. We talked over the whole oil situation. He realized that heroic measures would be necessary to prevent general ruin. He then agreed to sell his property at a fair valuation and to come in with us. After that other properties were acquired in the same way."

"Where did you get the capital, Mr. Rockefeller?" I asked. "You told me that capital was chronically scarce."

The veteran founder of the most wonderful business enterprise ever created by the brain of man smiled and, with a twinkle, remarked: "That had its funny sides. After we had had a property appraised, and a price satisfactory to all had been agreed upon, we offered either shares in the Standard Oil Company, or cash." Mr. Rockefeller laughed. He hesitated, as if undecided about telling more. I hinted that he must have something interesting in his mind.

"Yes, it does seem amusing now, although it was a matter of grave concern to us then. I would whip out our check book with rather a lordly air and remark, as if it were a matter of entire indifference to us: 'Shall I write a check or would you prefer payment in Standard Oil shares?' Most of them took the shares—very wisely, as it turned out. In some cases where the sellers were not very well up in business matters we persuaded them that it would be better for them to take at least part of their payment in shares because we ourselves felt very strongly that this would be more profitable for them in the end."

"What did you do when cash was demanded instead of stock—you were always short of capital?" I asked.

"We managed to scramble through somehow. By this time we had learned fairly well how to get banks to lend us money," was Mr. Rockefeller's reply.

"To what do you attribute the phenomenal success of the Standard Oil Company?" I next asked.

"To others," was Mr. Rockefeller's lightning rejoinder.

I begged to question the accuracy of this explanation. We were walking from a teeing ground after two good drives. Mr. Rockefeller stopped, leaned his head toward me, and said in a sort of confidential tone:

"I will tell you something. People persist in thinking that I was a tremendous worker, always at it early and late, summer and winter. The real truth is that I was what would now be called a "slacker" after I reached my middle thirties. I used to take long vacations at my Cleveland home every summer and spent my time planting and transplanting trees, building roads, doing landscape gardening, driving horses, and enjoying myself with my family, keeping in touch with business by private telegraph wire. I never, from the time I first entered an office, let business engross all my time and attention; I always took an active interest in Sunday-school and Church work, in children, and, if I might say so, in doing little things for friendless and lonely and poor people. I feel sincerely sorry for some of the business men who occasionally come to see me; they have allowed their business affairs to take such complete possession of them that they have no thought for anything else and have no time to really live as rational human beings.

"Our success was largely due to our having been able to gather together a group of the brainiest men in the business, men of great business aptitude, earnest and hardworking, forceful and honest men who, although possessing strong individualities, yet worked together for the one common aim, the building up of a sound, successful business.

Sometimes there were differences in views, but our policy was 'All hands above the table,' and we would sit two whole days, if necessary, fighting a proposition out until an agreement was reached. We never could get too many men of great brains to join us; there were no fears, no jealousies on this score."

As an afterthought, Mr. Rockefeller added: "When you think of the calibre and the character of the men who worked together for so many years isn't it ridiculous to think that they could have done so were they engaged in anything dishonest or doing anything which must be kept secret? Had these men not been engaged in honourable work how could they have stayed together and pulled together without a rupture so many years?"

No American business man has ever been the target of more vituperation than John D. Rockefeller. When I ventured to mention this matter I expected Mr. Rockefeller to drop his mild, kindly tone and the note of charitableness which had run through all his conversation. Instead, my remark served but as an occasion for the revealing of another phase of Mr. Rockefeller's bigness, broadness, tolerance, and charitableness.

"Yes, we have been misrepresented a great deal and accused of many things we never did and would not dream of doing," he replied in even voice. "But while I won't deny that some of the things written and said hurt very keenly and deeply indeed, I never allowed myself to harbour resentment or bitterness, for I did not forget that it was natural that some who had not succeeded in the measure we had should feel disappointed and aggrieved. That was what we had to expect and be prepared to bear. I never for a moment doubted that, when the people understood things as they really were, they would be fair in their judgment. The whole record may not be made plain for years, but I am satisfied that twenty-five years from now the people will understand and will judge us according to the truth and not by the misrepresentations. I have no doubt as to the justice of the verdict."

When I turned the conversation one day to the subject of giving, Mr. Rockefeller manifested keen interest. I mentioned to him that in course of my association with the most notable financial and business leaders in the country they had emphasized even more than his business achievements the efficacy of his philanthropies—instead of trying to mitigate evils, he had gone to the very roots of the causes of human ills and evils and had striven to effect fundamental remedies for their eradication.

"Giving is not a thing of to-day or yesterday with me, as some people seem to think," Mr. Rockefeller replied with unusual earnestness. "I began to give away a part of my income regularly from the time I earned $25 a month, and I never ceased that practice. My mother taught me to help others, and I was extremely fortunate in having the heartiest coöperation of my wife and, later, my children, particularly my son, in this work. Without the sympathetic encouragement and assistance of the whole family we might not have been able to do what little we have done. We all felt that the giving of money demanded just as careful study and as painstaking attention as the making of money.

"Just as when I entered business I reasoned that the best and biggest field to get into was one which would supply something useful having the whole world as a potential market, so we reasoned that in our giving we should also aim at doing something which might benefit the world in general—the people as a whole. This has been our guiding principle, to benefit as many people as possible. Instead of giving alms to beggars, if anything can be done to remove the causes which lead to the existence of beggars then something deeper and broader and more worth while will have been accomplished. In the same way, if the best doctors in the world can be given facilities to conduct experiments and researches year after year, going to any part of the world and spending whatever sums are necessary in their work; if by means of such scientific efforts new knowledge is acquired and new cures are devised for the elimination of diseases, then the benefits of this work become valuable for the whole human race."

Education Mr. Rockefeller regards as a panacea for many of the world's troubles. Since ignorance is responsible for most of the world's misery, by doing away with ignorance and substituting therefor knowledge a long step is taken toward the abolition of misery. Hence Mr. Rockefeller's colossal donations for the furtherance of education.

I touched upon the furore which has been created by the experiment in eliminating Greek and Latin from the college curriculum, which the General Education Board is planning to make.

"It *has* stirred things up," Mr. Rockefeller replied spiritedly; "but this alone will do good. It will bring out all sides of the question and from it all something should be gained. I myself did not have any Greek or Latin, but one of my sons-in-law is very fond of Latin and always corresponds in Latin with one of his boys. I mention this to let you understand that I am not prejudiced one way or the other."

"Who is the greatest of all the business men you have known?" I once asked Mr. Rockefeller when a blow-out stopped the automobile in which we were riding and thus gave an excellent opportunity for talking. It was at the side of a wood, and Mr. Rockefeller became interested in his favourite hobby, trees. I suggested one or two names. He still kept looking at some fine forest specimens.

"Did you read a little article that was printed the other day about Mr. Gates?" he finally remarked. I had. "Well, now, in anything you may write about me, don't forget to explain that Mr. Gates has been the guiding genius in all our giving. He came to us first to undertake certain business matters requiring talent of a high order and he showed phenomenal business ability. He combined with this the rare quality—born, no doubt, because he had the right kind of heart —of being able to direct the distribution of money with great wisdom. We all owe much to Mr. Gates, and his helpfulness should be generously recognized. He combines business skill and philanthropic aptitude to a higher degree than any other man I have ever known."

From which I would deduce that Frederick T. Gates—the man who was instrumental in negotiating Mr. Rockefeller's first gift to the University of Chicago and has for many years shared with John D. Rockefeller, Jr., the supervision of the Rockefeller philanthropies— has been Mr. Rockefeller's most valuable personal aide.

On the subject of men Mr. Rockefeller said: "Men, not machinery or plants, make an organization. The right kind of business men will build up an organization capable of producing a large volume of a good product at a low price, the three things essential to success. These men will introduce the right kind of appliances for the handling of their business; they will carefully conserve and utilize all byproducts so as to prevent waste; they will know how to market their products in the largest and most economical way. They will also be big enough to know how to handle workers successfully."

I brought up the subject of speculation. Mr. Rockefeller had emphatic views and expressed them with unusual animation.

"We used to be accused of speculating in everything known to Wall Street. It was not true," declared Mr. Rockefeller. "The Standard Oil Company never owned or controlled a single bank or trust company or railroad or any other corporation not directly connected with its own business. Certain personal investments of mine did not turn out satisfactory and instead of leaving the sinking ship, we, as individuals, tried to save them by putting in more money and improving the management. That was how I came to be interested in certain mining properties and, as an outgrowth of them, in ore-carrying ships.

"The success of the Standard Oil Company was largely due to the fact that for many years those connected with it concentrated all their energies to developing it and extending its ramifications to other countries. I kept denying the charges that the Standard Oil Company was speculating in the stock market time and time again until I became tired. The charges, no doubt, were based on the unfortunate fact that certain interests connected with the company entered into more or less speculative operations. The company never did.

"I always opposed putting Standard Oil shares on the Stock Exchange because I did not want to have them become the playthings of speculators. It was better that all our people should concentrate their attention on developing the business rather than be distracted in any way by the stock ticker. The oil business, you know, is liable to sudden and violent fluctuations, new fields are discovered which sometimes send down prices very sharply while at other times and places sources of supply give out. If our shares had been listed in the stock market they might have become favourite objects of speculation and gambling. To this day our shares are not listed on the New York Stock Exchange."

No matter what phase of life—whether social, religious, financial, or business—was under discussion, I found Mr. Rockefeller always taking a world-wide view, always broad, always tolerant, never condemning others, insistent upon minimizing his own achievements. He actually does not think of himself as having been the architect of the most efficient business organization in history. He does not think of himself as the richest man in the world—indeed, he takes so detached a view of his wealth that he speaks as if it did not belong to him at all, but was merely something to be devoted solely for the progress and betterment of mankind. He will speak of "those rich men" as if he did not belong to that class at all: as he views it, his money is not his in any real sense, but is a trust to be used according to the best judgment of the ablest men that can be brought together to study its use so as to further the greatest good of the greatest number.

The Rockefeller homes, those of both father and son, have been on a strict war-ration basis for many months. The meals served by the richest family in the world are more simple and less expensive than those indulged in by the average American. The Rockefellers do not take the view that because they have the money, they are entitled to buy and consume as much as their fancy might choose. Three courses is their maximum. "We must all do what we can to save food for the millions who are suffering starvation," remarked Mr. Rockefeller at one meal.

And may I here digress to explode the popular fallacy that John D. Rockefeller eats only bread and milk. I have dined oftener than once with him and he ate as much as I did.

I am tempted to go on and on quoting replies given by Mr. Rockefeller to my questions on all sorts of subjects, but I must here confine myself to merely a brief outline of his career.

John Davison Rockefeller is come of old French (Norman)

stock. The first Rockefeller to migrate to America came from Holland in 1650. Mr. Rockefeller's grandfather married Lucy Avery, of a famous Connecticut family which traced its ancestry back to Egbert, the first king of England. Their eldest son, William Avery Rockefeller, married Eliza Davison, and John Davison Rockefeller was their oldest son, the second of six children.

The Rockefeller children were taught the value of thrift, the necessity for working industriously, and the wisdom of managing their affairs carefully and thoughtfully. They were encouraged by rewards for work well done and very early John Davison exhibited business acumen by electing to raise a brood of turkeys which could fend for themselves for the most part, so that when he sold them the amount realized was very much net profit. The proceeds he lent at 7 per cent. The systematically kept records of this first business venture are among Mr. Rockefeller's cherished possessions. He was then not more than nine years old. He learned also how to milk cows, tend cattle, work in the field, and do general chores.

The family removed from Richford, Tioga County, New York, where John Davison was born on July 8, 1839, to a farm on the Owasco Lake, near Moravia, when the lad was some three or four years of age. From here he removed to the valley of the Susquehanna, near Owego, at the age of ten years. At the age of fourteen he removed to Cleveland, Ohio. His elementary schooling was assiduously supplemented by his mother, and he later entered high school, which he left at fifteen, and took a short course at a commercial college in Cleveland.

At sixteen he started to find work. He tried stores, factories, offices, in vain. Finally a firm of forwarding and produce commission merchants, Hewitt & Tuttle, engaged him as office-boy and assistant bookkeeper, on September 26, 1855, a date whose anniversary he celebrates every year. No wages were stipulated for, and for three months he worked without knowing what he was to receive—an arrangement not quite typical of his composition. But the one thing which interested him was a chance to make himself useful to his employer; his compensation was entirely secondary. At the end of the year he was paid $50 for his fourteen weeks and started the new year at $25 a month. In the year following the $2,000-a-year bookkeeper resigned and young Rockefeller took the place at $500 a year. The third year he received $550. The fourth year he asked $800, and when only $700 was offered he decided to resign and to start a business.

He was not yet twenty years old but he had used his time to advantage. "I had learned everything I could about the firm's activities," Mr. Rockefeller recalled to me. "I checked up every bill that came in and made it my business to see that my employers were not cheated. I recall that there was one captain who was always putting in claims for damages to shipments—we handled all kinds of import and export trade in addition to produce—and I decided to investigate. I insisted upon examining all the documents and shipments, and I found that he had been making entirely unwarranted claims. By taking just as keen an interest in everything that went on as the partners themselves, I learned a great deal. I got an insight into how business was handled, into systematic keeping of records, into every phase of office management. I saw, too, how business was financed. Then I also had opportunity to see how customers were treated."

Meanwhile the young man was "establishing a credit" outside his business circle. He had become, first, an enthusiastic member of the Sunday-school. At sixteen he was made clerk of the board of trustees of the struggling mission known as the Erie Street Baptist Church, which is now the Euclid Avenue Baptist Church. Before he was eighteen he was elected a trustee of the church and his younger brother, William, succeeded him as clerk. The little church was threatened with disaster by the imminent closing of a mortgage. John D. Rockefeller decided to save it. He took up a position at the church door and buttonholed every one who came out for a donation or a pledge for the wiping out of the debt, setting an example by donating a substantial amount from his own pocket. Of course he succeeded. He became a leader and later the superintendent of the Sunday-school, was constantly searching out lonely young men and bringing them into church fellowship, and assisted poor people to the limit of his means. The reputation, he was thus conscientiously building up was to stand him in good stead when he entered business on his own account. His industry, his energy, his enthusiasm, his alertness, his ability, and his optimism impressed all with whom he came into touch.

He engaged in the produce business, in 1859, with Morris B. Clark, a man ten years his senior. Mr. Rockefeller had saved $800 and his father lent him $1,000 at 10 per cent. interest to enable him to supply his share of the capital.

"I went out and visited farmers and others all over the adjoining territory, talked with them, told them we would be glad of an opportunity to serve them at any time, did not ask them to change their existing connections, but left a card in case they would like to get in touch with us at some future time," Mr. Rockefeller recounted. "The results of this personal solicitation were far beyond our expectations. Business poured in to us in such volume that we did more than $500,000 worth the first year."

It was before Mr. Rockefeller was twenty-two years of age that he became interested in oil. Several refineries were started in Cleveland to prepare crude oil for illuminating purposes and Mr. Rockefeller, already a shrewd business man, always on the lookout for opportunities, foresaw that this new industry possessed unlimited potentialities. He made investigations and calculations. He grasped the fact that here was a substance which could probably be brought within the use of every household. He lost no time in helping to establish the oil refining firm of Andrews, Clark & Company, in 1862, of which Clark and Rockefeller were the financial and business managers. And three years later he sold out his interest in the commission business to M. B. Clark and bought out the interests of his partners in Andrews, Clark & Company, and joined with Samuel Andrews to continue the business under the firm name of Rockefeller & Andrews.

"We realized then that here was something the whole world would want, but we had no idea that our business would develop into the proportions it did," Mr. Rockefeller modestly confessed. "Indeed, I may say that, while I was always ambitious and always willing to work hard, I had no vision as big as the subsequent realities. Those associated with me and I, myself, simply did our day's work the best we could, doing what seemed wisest, and trying always to plan for a larger and larger future. We did not seek momentary advantages, but tried to build solidly and safely. My father had taught me this lesson by coming to me at the most awkward moments in my early business life and demanding repayment of his loans. He did this, of course, to test my resourcefulness and my ability to meet sudden emergencies. After I had hustled to procure his money he would laugh and hand it back, saying he did not need it but was glad to know I was able to meet my obligations."

How to procure capital and credit to handle the enormous volume of business which Mr. Rockefeller's enterprise attracted was his hardest problem during those creative years. Banking facilities were limited and the maximum his own bank could furnish was entirely insufficient for his rapidly growing needs. In one instance a bank president met Mr. Rockefeller on the street and gravely told him that his borrowings had become so heavy that Mr. Rockefeller must come and talk the situation over with the directors. "I'll be delighted to meet the directors," Mr. Rockefeller replied, "*for I need a great deal more.*" Mr. Rockefeller added: "He never sent for me."

As the business grew, the oil refining firm of William Rockefeller & Company was established, in the year 1866, consisting of William Rockefeller and Rockefeller and Andrews, with a refinery adjoining the works of Rockefeller & Andrews. Later the firm of Rockefeller

& Company was established in New York City to manage the export business of both firms. About the year 1867 H. M. Flagler and S. V. Harkness were brought into a firm, which included all these previously organized firms, under the name of Rockefeller, Andrews & Flagler. Spectacular fortunes had been earned in the oil industry and, as a consequence, the field had become overcrowded. More oil was produced than the market could absorb. Even the pioneer work done by the Rockefeller group in opening up foreign markets could not keep the domestic production within the limits of consumption. The selling price of oil fell below production cost. Grievous losses were incurred and many people went to the wall. Others frantically sold out when buyers could be found. Ruin confronted the whole industry.

In 1869 the firm of Rockefeller, Andrews & Flagler was merged into the Standard Oil Company of Ohio, with $1,000,000 capital, and Mr. Rockefeller became its president. He never once lost faith in the future of the business into which he had entered only after mature deliberation. Fires might sweep away valuable plants; important oil fields might dry up over night, rendering worthless costly apparatus; banks might refuse to risk money in so hazardous a business; prices might fall to disastrous levels; markets might become glutted; foreign oil fields might threaten to dwarf the whole American output, yet never once did John D. Rockefeller waver.

Thirty years before Morgan grasped and acted on the combination method of doing business à la Steel Corporation, Rockefeller, with foresight, courage, and resourcefulness, introduced the combination idea in his sphere. One tottering concern after another was taken over by the new Standard Oil Company; its capital was doubled and then multiplied, its operations were extended east, west, and south, it opened up foreign territories, and, by camel and human transportation, introduced the new illuminant into even the remotest parts of China, where the natives were supplied with oil lamps gratis.

Only a company owning properties in different parts of the country could withstand the risks incidental to the oil business, since fire would wipe out a whole plant in a few hours or the flow at any one point could stop without notice. Only a large company could afford to spend millions in improving facilities, in constantly opening up new territory, and in reducing costs. Only a company such as the Standard Oil could afford to build thousands of miles of pipe lines to do away with costly processes of shipping the fluid in barrels. Only such a company could afford to erect huge refineries which might have to be discarded at any moment. Only such a company could afford to design and build expensive tank steamers for export trade and tank cars for domestic transportation. Only such a company could afford to send agents into every country of the world to create new markets, often against bitter opposition. Only such a company could undertake to supply large quantities with unerring regularity, notwithstanding the sudden disasters to which any and every oil property was liable. Only such a mammoth concern could cover the country with facilities to supply oil direct from the producer to the millions of small consumers.

As Mr. Rockefeller quietly observed: "Our business didn't grow of its own accord. We didn't simply sit still and do nothing but draw in dividends. Our business grew for the same reasons that other successful businesses grow: our basic principles were right; we dealt justly with everybody and met our obligations promptly; we studied facts; we watched for opportunities and also created opportunities; we spared no expense and no effort to manufacture a product of the best grade; we did not shortsightedly curtail our market by charging exorbitant prices but constantly aimed at reducing them to a minimum so as to encourage wider and wider consumption; we allowed neither success nor temporary setbacks to cause us to lose our heads; and always we were careful to keep our financial condition sound and strong, resisting all temptation and all suggestions to put out unwarranted amounts of shares to foster speculation or create inflation. I can speak with more freedom about what was accomplished in later years, when our business grew to unimagined proportions, because I personally took very little active part in the management of it. I retired in the early nineties, before I was fifty-five, and have visited our offices only on rare occasions since."

This is in no sense an attempt to describe the growth or the history of Standard Oil, but is merely a feeble effort to portray the personality of John D. Rockefeller, to bring out the humility of the man; to outline his early struggles, his extraordinary industry and vigilance to seize opportunities, his broad human sympathies, his deep sense of stewardship in the matter of the money that has come under his control, his insight into fundamentals and his clearheadedness in seeking primary causes rather than attempting to assuage evils. I can speak of Mr. Rockefeller only as I have found him. I do not presume to pass judgment on all or any of the acts of the Standard Oil Company or those who followed Mr. Rockefeller in its active direction.

I can say and do say and must say, however, that of all the eminent men abroad and at home that I have met, none has impressed me as possessing such breadth and depth of vision, both business and humanitarian; none has manifested such intense anxiety to use his money and his influence for the permanent benefit of mankind; none has shown more kindliness and humility of heart; none has been so ready to put a charitable interpretation upon the acts and motives of others; none has been more free from everything savouring of arrogance or domination; none has exhibited more unfailing readiness to do kindly little deeds and to say cheering little words to the lowliest and to children.

"The days are not half long enough to do all that I find happiness in doing," Mr. Rockefeller remarked to me on the eve of his seventy-eighth birthday. "I can find happiness and contentment wherever I go, and it is a matter of extreme gratification to me that my son has become so genuinely interested in the things we have been trying to do through the Medical Institute, the Foundation, and other agencies to which some of the noblest men in the country are devoting their best effort, many of them busy business men who are directing this work without thought of reward."

JULIUS ROSENWALD

THE selling of a few watches by mail by a hard-working young station agent in Minnesota was the birth of the greatest modern mercantile wonder of the world. Seventy railroad cars are now needed daily to haul away the merchandize the organization sells.

Its sales for 1916 exceeded $140,000,000, or almost half-a-million dollars every business day, all at retail—one pair of shoes, one suit of clothes, one dress, one sewing machine, one watch, one pound of tea, one piano, etc. The postman brings it in from 70,000 to 140,000 orders every time the sun rises.

It employs directly, at headquarters and in its factories, between 30,000 and 40,000 people and, indirectly, even a larger number.

A half interest in the enterprise was bought twenty-two years ago for $70,000 and although not another dollar of capital has since been invested in it the market value of its stock now is upward of $140,000,000 after the payment in dividends of many millions of dollars.

Not a dollar's worth of goods is sold over the counter; every order, without exception, is sent by mail accompanied by check or post-office order in payment.

This company's publications have a circulation through the United States far transcending those sent out by any other concern, not excluding the annual sales of the Bible publishing houses—the 1916 figure was in excess of 40,000,000 copies.

Speaking of the Bible, I heard a story in Chicago the other day that the teacher of a Sunday-school in Minnesota asked her class: "Where did we get the Ten Commandments?" Whereupon a little Swedish girl answered with great assurance:

"From Sears and Roebuck!"

There! That lets the cat out of the bag. This modern mercantile wonder is Sears, Roebuck and Company, of Chicago.

And the miracle-worker behind it is Julius Rosenwald, its president.

Mr. Rosenwald would resent being called a miracle-worker. He does not feel that he has done anything remarkable. He disclaims in all sincerity any great share of credit for what has been accomplished.

"What one man can do to execute his ideas, or the ideas of others, is very little," Mr. Rosenwald rebuked me when I suggested that he had achieved something extraordinary. "The fellow at the top usually gets too much credit; often he gets credit for ideas that come from the brains of his fellow-workers. What could any one man do if there were not other men to carry out his and their own ideas? It is the able, willing fellows around a man at the top who really do things. I have played only a very small part in the building up of Sears, Roebuck and Company."

A friend was riding home with Mr. Rosenwald one day as the more than 13,000 Chicago employees were pouring out of the principal establishment.

"How does it feel, Mr. Rosenwald, to have so many people working for you?" the friend asked.

"Why, I never think of it in that way," he replied; "I always think of them as just working *with* me."

When the company entered into its present palatial buildings several of the executives felt it was not fitting that their president should have no rug or carpet on his floor. So they clubbed together, bought a magnificent Oriental rug, invaded his office, made a little speech, and presented him with their handsome gift. Greatly confused, he tried to thank them and to appear pleased at their thoughtfulness.

The rug, tightly rolled, stood in a corner week after week and then disappeared! If linoleum-covered floors were good enough for his co-workers, they were good enough for him!

"The finest type of citizen in Chicago," is how one of the most eminent men in the city described Mr. Rosenwald to me.

The most notable thing about Julius Rosenwald is not any superhuman business ability, not any phenomenal smartness in seeing and seizing mercantile opportunities, not any transcendent qualities as a merchant. *The greatest thing about Julius Rosenwald is not his business, but himself, not what he has but what he is*, his character, his personality, his sincerity, his honesty, his democracy, his thoughtfulness, his charity of heart, his catholicity of sympathy, his consuming desire to help the less fortunate of his fellow-creatures, be they black or white, Jews or Gentiles, young or old.

In his business, Mr. Rosenwald takes great care and pride in advocating correct merchandising principles. Every illustration and every description in the Sears-Roebuck catalogue is compared minutely with the actual goods by experts employed for that special purpose. Extensive and expensive laboratories are maintained to analyze scientifically and chemically every consignment of merchandise received, and, if the slightest defect in materials is detected, the goods are immediately rejected and returned—a rule that has taught manufacturers to think twice before trying to make deliveries unfit to pass the severest inspection. Any customer not satisfied with a purchase can return the goods, and have his money refunded, including transportation charges both ways. The seller, you see, must therefore beware. He, not the buyer, takes the risk.

Every conceivable kind of merchandise is handled by Sears, Roebuck and Company, from a button to a bungalow—yes, bungalows are sold by mail.

How has it been done? What is the history of this remarkable institution?

Thirty-five years ago, in Minnesota, R. W. Sears, then a young station agent, conceived the idea of selling watches by mail. He had acumen enough to advertise intelligently. So his business boomed. He promised himself that when he had accumulated $100,000 he would retire. He did. But six months of idleness cured him; the ideal life, he discovered, consisted of doing things, not of doing nothing. He had agreed, however, not to connect his name with any mail-order business for three years. He got over this difficulty by entering into an agreement with a watchmaker friend named Roebuck, and the name A. C. Roebuck & Co. was given the new venture. At the expiration of the three years the name "Roebuck," having been extensively advertised, was not dropped, a change being made to Sears, Roebuck and Company, although Mr. Roebuck was not a partner. Mr. Sears was a keen, progressive business man, and in time moved to Chicago, where he added various new lines, including clothing. All sales continued to be made by mail, however.

Julius Rosenwald, then in the clothing business in Chicago, sold Mr. Sears large quantities of clothing. The mail-order demand for it expanded rapidly, and it was not long before Sears, Roebuck and Company—then consisting of Mr. Sears—had far more business than the capital could swing. He asked Mr. Rosenwald to become financially interested.

Mr. Rosenwald had learned to spot opportunities and to grasp them. From boyhood up he had displayed unusual initiative, enterprise, and industry. Before he was eleven he had taken little excursions on the sea of business. He used to peddle various odds and ends from door to door in his native town, Springfield, Ill., where his father was in the clothing business. He did best with a new species of pictures, chromos, which then sprang into popularity. He turned his hand, however, to other things to earn an honest dime. For example, he used to pump a church organ for a woman organist who wanted to practise.

"I remember as if it were yesterday," said Mr. Rosenwald in discussing those boyhood days, "how I made $2.25 selling a pamphlet programme the day President Lincoln's monument was dedicated in Springfield by President Grant. He was the first President I ever saw—and the first man wearing kid gloves."

Julius evidently was even then not too young to take notice of matters pertaining to clothes. His first real employment was in a fancy-goods store during a summer vacation when he was fifteen.

"What did you do with your money?" I queried.

"I saved it," he replied—hesitatingly, I noted.

"And then what did you do with it?" I persisted.

"I took it all, nearly $25, and bought a tea set for my mother's twentieth anniversary of her wedding."

At sixteen he left school and went to New York to enter the wholesale clothing house of Hammerslough Brothers, his uncles. He lived economically, and by the time he was twenty-one he had saved enough to acquire, with a little financial assistance from his father, a going retail clothing store on Fourth Avenue, a few doors from Brokaw Brothers. It did not prove a gold mine, but through incessant enegry it was made to pay fairly well.

One day Mr. Rosenwald was talking with one of the owners of a business which made a specialty of summer clothing for men. "We have at least sixty telegrams for goods and we cannot begin to fill the orders," remarked this manufacturer.

"This statement made an impression upon me," Mr. Rosenwald relates. "Here was a man getting more orders than he could supply. In the middle of the night I woke up and there and then resolved that that was a business worth getting into. I decided to sell the retail store and take up the manufacture of summer clothing."

He formed a partnership with Julius E. Weil, also from Illinois, and figured out that, as there was no concern in Chicago in this line of business, that would be the best field. Rosenwald & Weil, manufacturers and wholesalers of summer clothing, had to overcome the usual obstacles encountered by beginners, but in a year or two they were doing a large and profitable trade. From 1885 to 1895 Mr. Rosenwald devoted himself exclusively to the growing activities of Rosenwald & Weil, but then withdrew and branched out as a manufacturer of regular clothing under the name of "Rosenwald & Company." By this time Mr. Sears had become his most important customer.

In 1895 Mr. Rosenwald and another man agreed to take a half interest in Sears, Roebuck and Company for $70,000. At first Mr. Rosenwald did not become an active partner but continued to look after his own affairs. The new capital enabled the mail-order enterprise to expand to about $500,000 turnover within a year. Mr. Sears could not possibly look after everything, so in 1896 Mr. Rosenwald took up duty with Sears, Roebuck and Company as vice-president and treasurer, and on Mr. Sears's retirement in 1908 he became the president. Mr. Sears died a few years later.

In the earlier days neither Sears-Roebuck nor any other mail-order house was fastidious about the wording of their advertisements or their catalogues. Illustrations and the articles illustrated did not always jibe. Merchandising morals all over the country were then on a distinctly lower standard than they are now. Mr. Rosenwald addressed himself to raising standards. And his code of ethics began to prove profitable. Honesty abundantly justified itself as the best policy.

The rejuvenated Sears-Roebuck introduced other improved methods of doing business. It rapidly extended its list of goods. It began to open factories of its own—it now has 20,000 employees in them. It engaged the best buyers and gave them almost limitless scope. It lengthened its mailing list, greatly enlarged its annual catalogue, and introduced special and other seasonal catalogues—and all the time kept raising and raising the quality of the merchandise sold. Also, it inaugurated the revolutionary policy "money-back-if-not-satisfied." This courageous step sent sales up with a bound—they went from $11,000,000 in 1900 to over $50,000,000 in 1906, jumped to $100,000,000 in 1914 and have gained about 40 per cent. in the last three years.

Who would have thought, for example, that shoes could be sold by mail? The experiment was tried not very long ago and sales quickly reached over $1,000,000 a month—far ahead of the sales of any retail store in the world. Most of these shoes are made in the company's own factories.

You will recall how Sears-Roebuck took hold of the Encyclopædia Britannica and instituted a selling campaign on a scale the book world had never before known. This one item added over $5,000,000 to the 1916 turnover. This was less the idea of Mr. Rosenwald, I should add, than of Albert H. Loeb, vice-president, another man of extraordinary ability.

The labour-saving devices, the system, the mechanism throughout Sears-Roebuck's eclipse anything I have ever seen, even those of up-to-date automobile plants.

Unlike some short-sighted presidents, Mr. Rosenwald has never sought to arrogate all power to himself. Department heads in Sears-Roebuck are given an amount of leeway unknown in most enterprises. They are encouraged to think up new ideas and are given a free hand to try them out.

"We give opportunity to others to do things," said Mr. Rosenwald. "We place confidence in them, give them plenty of rope to work out their own ideas. Even if they do make mistakes occasionally, the results are better than if we were to dominate them with one person's ideas all the time."

Mr. Rosenwald has very strict ideas about the deportment of employees. He takes a fatherly interest in the thousands of girls in the place and rigidly enforces a cast-iron rule that any man, no matter how important, who attempts to abuse his position, dismisses himself; from this rule there is no appeal. Picnics or other social functions which would encourage familiarity between men and women workers are forbidden, although no concern does more in supplying facilities for wholesome amusement and recreation to its force. Indeed, the first things you see when you approach the Sears-Roebuck property are athletic fields for baseball, tennis courts galore, recreation grounds, and beautiful gardens directly in front of the works. Elaborate facilities are provided for the feeding of thousands of employees at low prices. The women and men have separate tables, but in the same room.

One day a visitor was dining with Mr. Rosenwald—the Sears-Roebuck lunches are good enough for him—when Mr. Rosenwald noticed a man and a girl at the same table. The president immediately investigated. When he found that they were father and daughter, both employees, he ordered the cafeteria manager to set apart a special table so that in such cases the two could lunch together every day without infringing the rules.

Several thousands of the employees availed themselves of the opportunity several years ago to buy Sears-Roebuck stock "on the ground floor," and its market value has more than quadrupled.

Perhaps the crowning achievement of Mr. Rosenwald in connection with his co-workers is the "Employees' Savings and Profit Sharing Fund." Students of the subject have pronounced the plan the best ever conceived. Briefly, the employees who join agree to pay 5 per cent. of their salaries into the fund and thus share in 5 per cent. of the Company's net earnings every year. On the basis of normal profits, the Company's contribution would be two dollars for every dollar the employees paid in. A worker receiving $20 a week, paying $1 weekly into the fund would, in fifteen years, receive for the $780 paid in by him, $3,428. In thirty years, in return for $1,560 paid by him, he would receive $10,556! The conditions covering the working of the fund are extremely favourable to those joining it.

In addition, all employees who earn under $1,500 annually receive an "Anniversary Check," which amounts to 5 per cent. of their *annual* salary on the fifth anniversary of their entering the service, 6 per cent. on the sixth, and so on up to 10 per cent. on the tenth anniversary, and 10 per cent. every year thereafter. For example, a 10-year employee earning $25 a week receives annually a check for

$130. With the first anniversary check goes a gold badge, another badge is given at the end of ten years, another for fifteen years, and another to mark twenty years' service. These badges are given to all regardless of salary and are worn by the officers and long-term employee with as much pride as a British soldier wears a Victoria Cross.

"The besetting sin in America is extravagance," Mr. Rosenwald declared in explaining the introduction of profit sharing. "Our plan will bring home to our people the value of saving part of their earnings. It will encourage them and assist them to accumulate something, and will have a beneficial influence on their characters by stimulating them to deprive themselves, if neceassry, of some things they can get along without. If they want to withdraw their savings after a number of years, they can do so without waiting until they are gray-haired. After five years' service a girl who leaves to be married can withdraw her savings and also her share of the company's contributions. Men are entitled to withdraw their share of profits after ten years' service.

"Don't imagine, however, that anything we do for our people in the way of profit sharing, or enabling them to acquire stock, or providing meals at low rates, medical attention, recreation grounds, vacations, and so forth, is done from philanthropic motives—not in the least. Whatever we do for our employees we do because we think it pays, because it is good business."

That sounds businessy, quite cold-hearted, doesn't it? With all due respect to Mr. Rosenwald, I don't quite believe that those brave words represent the real truth and the whole truth. I suspect these various humane activities come from the heart rather more than from the counting house. In other words, sentiment has something to do with it.

"The happy spirit that seems to pervade the place is part of the magnet that attracts me and keeps me in harness," Mr. Rosenwald admitted.

In going through the Sears-Roebuck plant I was struck with the manifest cheerfulness of the workers. I remarked to one girl who was feeding thousands of sheets of paper into a printing machine that it must be terrible drudgery. "No," she replied with a smile, "it is like playing at work."

"Don't your fingers get sore?" I asked.

"No, I use a thimble, you see."

Any concern that can instill into its workers such an intense spirit of loyalty and satisfaction that even the feeding of printing machines week after week and month after month is regarded as play and done with unqualified contentment has solved at least one phase of the labour problem.

JULIUS ROSENWALD

Let me cite one more instance of Mr. Rosenwald's attitude toward those for whose welfare he feels in some degree responsible. When the company in 1906 moved out to South Chicago, to its huge offices and warehouses there, Mr. Rosenwald was anxious that the place should not be surrounded with saloons. There was some objection, on the ground of "paternalism," to trying to regulate the habits of free-born citizens. Mr. Rosenwald, however, was persistent and finally it was agreed to promulgate a rule that no worker would be permitted to enter a saloon within eight blocks of the plant, a first infraction to be met with a warning and the second to be followed by dismissal.

One saloon, just eight blocks from the plant, tries to catch workers both going and coming, for it has one sign facing the works, "First Chance," and another sign facing the other way, "Last Chance."

Mr. Rosenwald celebrated his fiftieth birthday on August 12, 1912, by making gifts totalling $700,000 to various worthy organizations, including $250,000 to the University of Chicago, $250,000 for a Jewish Charity building on the west side of Chicago, $50,000 for a social workers' country club near Chicago, and $25,000 to Tuskegee Institute offshoots, including rural schools for Negro children. At the beginning of 1911 he offered to contribute $25,000 for a coloured Y. M. C. A. building to every community in the United States which within five years would raise by popular subscription an additional sum of $75,000. More than a dozen cities qualified.

What was described by the newspapers as the largest gift of the kind ever made was announced in March, 1917, by the American Jewish Relief Committee. Mr. Rosenwald agreed to contribute $100,000 for each $1,000,000 raised by the Committee in its campaign to collect $10,000,000, his total offer thus amounting to $1,000,000.

Within the last two or three years he has built 150 small schools in rural communities, principally in very poor districts of the South. His purse knows neither colour nor creed. The late Booker T. Washington found in Mr. Rosenwald, a trustee of Tuskegee Institute, one of his staunchest supporters, not merely financially but in solving various administrative and racial problems.

One incident told me in Chicago is worth narrating as illustrative of Mr. Rosenwald's unostentatious way of doing things. A worthy head of a large Chicago congregation had more duties than he could overtake. A new automobile with chauffeur drove up to the divine's door one morning and the servant was told to inform her employer that his automobile was waiting for him. He told the servant that there was some mistake, that he had not sent for any car. The chauffeur insisted there was no mistake. Investigation brought out that Mr.

Rosenwald had bought the car and had arranged to maintain it solely at his expense.

Mr. Rosenwald is president of the Associated Jewish Charities of Chicago, an active worker in many civic, philanthropic, and educational bodies, president of the Board of Trustees of the Chicago Bureau of Public Efficiency and prominent in the Chicago Peace Society, yet President Wilson selected him as a member of the new Council of National Defence, and he at once began spending most of his time in Washington, toiling early and late to equip America's armed forces to take the field. His exhaustive practical knowledge of various branches of manufacture, especially clothing, has proved of inestimable value to the Government.

Chicago University has a Julius Rosenwald Hall—but not with the consent of Mr. Rosenwald. He never allows his name to be attached to any building or institution that he provides, but the Chicago University authorities took advantage of his absence —he was in Palestine— to name the hall he had contributed toward "Julius Rosenwald Hall."

The name of Sears, Roebuck & Company should really be Rosenwald, Loeb & Co. I suggested this to Mr. Rosenwald.

"No, no," he protested. "I want no monuments either outside of the cemetery or in it. Men are quickly forgotten when they die." After a pause, "And perhaps it is best so."

A beautiful incident occurred while I was in Mr. Rosenwald's office. The telephone rang and his face immediately broke into smiles. Turning to me he said excitedly: "That was my mother. She is coming to see me. She hasn't been here in four years." From this on he kept glancing out of the window, and the moment she appeared he rushed to meet her. After that he ceased to act as president of Sears, Roebuck and Company. He became just "Julius" and all business, so far as he was concerned, was off.

"Every morning in his life," one of his associates confided to me, "Mr. Rosenwald visits his mother before coming to work. And when he returns from out-of-town trips, no matter how we may be clamouring for him at the office, he first visits his mother, who is in her 85th year and active in mind and body. Mr. Rosenwald once remarked to me: 'I regard as a fresh gift from God every day He spares her to me.'"

I know no finer type of American citizen than Julius Rosenwald.

JOHN D. RYAN

POLITICAL corruption was rampant in the state when he took hold; bitter warfare was being waged, not without loss of life, between the two dominating mining factions; rivalries and jealousies were rife; individual companies and labour had become lawless. He first routed the political antagonists, then bought out the entire business interests of the opposition and next harmonized all the internal differences and jealousies among the individual concerns and proceeded to build up what is now not merely the largest copper mining enterprise in the world, with an output of a million pounds of copper a day, but he developed it into a great, integrated industry comprising very important railroad, coal, lumber, and mercantile properties, as well as a producer of lead and zinc on a scale exceeded by few companies in the world."

The man whose achievements were thus summarized is John D. Ryan, president of the Anaconda Copper Company (which supplies almost one-sixth of the world's total production), creator and upbuilder of the Montana Power Company and director of railroad, industrial, and financial organizations, including the great American International Corporation, whose directorate reads like a page from "Who's Who in Big Business."

"After that," went on the business man here quoted, a man who was on the ground all through the transformation in Montana, "he threw himself into creating what is to-day the most efficient water-power enterprise in America, supplying 95 per cent. of all the electrical power used in Montana and, because of its low rates—the lowest charged anywhere—it has greatly advanced the general prosperity of the state.

"And, although the public at large doesn't realize it, he has done more than any other man or any group of men in the United States to bring about the electrification of railroads, for it was the extraordinary success he attained in the complete electrification of his own company's railroad that led the St. Paul to undertake its wonderful project of operating its whole Rocky Mountain division by electricity. This is perhaps his greatest contribution to progress and civilization.

"How did he succeed in doing all this? By tact, nerve, and judgment; by the sheer force of his personality; by his ability to inspire confidence among all classes and factions, including labour; through his undeviating fairness to everybody."

Having had a fairly comprehensive knowledge of his record, I asked Mr. Ryan to tell me something for the inspiration and perhaps guidance of others trying to win their way toward the top.

"No!" replied Mr. Ryan, holding up both hands in protest. "I have not done anything worth talking about by way of an example to the youth of this country. You cannot write any picturesque story about me, picturing me sweating in miner's togs at the bottom of a shaft, for I never did a day's mining in my life. Nor was I a prodigy at school. Nor have I worked any harder than lots of other men."

"Then do you want me to assume that you have got where you are because of influence——"

"Influence!" broke in Mr. Ryan. "Influence is the worst handicap any young man can have. It tends to make him feel he need not exert himself to his full capacity and has a bad effect upon him. When other workmen learn that one of their number has a pull with somebody higher up, they look at him askance and the effect upon these other men is bad. Then the foreman, or whoever is over him, will either show him undue favours and push him into a position for which he is not fitted, or, if the boss is of a different stamp, he will hesitate to promote him even when he deserves it because the boss knows the others will think it is a case of favouritism. The effect, therefore, is bad upon the whole organization. When any young engineer or college graduate or anybody else comes to me asking for a letter to enable him to get a job at our works I say to him just what I have told you."

This character sketch of John D. Ryan is very different from others that have been printed about him. There is a reason. Mr. Ryan has never before outlined his career for publication, with the result that romance and fiction rather than fact have been written about him. Usually he has been pictured as a young giant who began work in the bowels of the earth and gained mining-camp fame for his ability to lick any cowboy or miner in the West, and, because of his prowess, was selected by New York capitalists as the best man to keep order around their turbulent mining properties. He displayed natural aptitude, so the legend runs, and was soon filling the post of mine manager. When the politicians became unruly, Ryan so tamed them that by and by they came and ate out of his hand while, incidentally, he completely routed from the state F. A. Heinze, the quondam copper king of Montana. As a reward, the young Lochinvar was made head of all the so-called Standard Oil mining properties. That is the picturesque John D. Ryan painted by imaginative writers.

It seems almost a pity to have to puncture all this romance. Not that there are not real elements of romance in John D. Ryan's career. Is there not romance in the fact that a young man without money, without technical education, without financial training and with only the experiences of a travelling salesman, by dint of stick-to-itiveness and well-directed intelligence, won his way before middle life to part-ownership of a string of banks, earned the presidency of the foremost copper mining company in the world, built the most remarkable electric power enterprise in the land, was elected to the directorates of a number of gigantic financial, railroad, and industrial organizations, and acquired a fortune running probably into eight figures?

A record of this kind is not simply a freak of Fortune. Results usually have causes.

I mentioned to him how he had been depicted as a veritable man-eater, a Samson who had only to lift his little finger to cow a whole campful of unruly miners, the very personification of courage—Ryan is a splendid example of manhood.

"Rot!" he broke in. "I never had any rows with labour while I was at a mine and I never licked a miner or anybody else in my life."

Mr. Ryan would stand for none of the heroic qualities the magazine writers had invested him with. Here are the facts.

John D. Ryan came of mining stock. His father was the discoverer of what are now the Copper Range Mines of the Lake Superior district. Shortly after John was born, at Hancock, Michigan, on October 10, 1864, the family moved to the Calumet & Hecla mine. Mining, however, had no particular attraction for the boy. His parents wanted him to go to college but he preferred to begin work. When seventeen he entered one of a number of general merchandise stores in the copper district of Michigan which were owned by an uncle. For eight years the future copper magnate weighed sugar, measured calico, and wrapped parcels behind the counter, working, as was then the custom, a full round of the clock daily. From this uncle, who was the leading merchant in that part of the country, he picked up more or less business information and insight, but he had no ambition to become a Marshall Field.

A brother and a sister having been obliged, because of ill health, to live in Denver, young Ryan, at twenty-five, decided to try his luck in that city. Fortune did not immediately smile on him. Month after month he looked in vain for a congenial job.

"I was six months in Denver before I found employment to suit me—and I wasn't hard to suit either," was how he described his discouraging experience at this stage of his life. Then he got a start as a drummer, selling lubricating oil on the road. He travelled all over the Rocky Mountain section from Montana to Mexico, knowing little or nothing of home life for several years.

"Wasn't that a trying, cheerless kind of existence?" I ventured to ask.

"Of course, it wasn't exactly a primrose path or rose-bed life, but I was not married then and it was easier for me than it would have been for most other fellows, because my father was well known among mining people, and, as miners move about a good deal, I met friends of his all over and this helped me in my business.

"Among the good friends I met during that time was Marcus Daly, who was then building up the Anaconda organization. I sold him oils and in that way was thrown in contact with him."

Mr. Ryan, contrary to the popular impression, never did a day's work for Daly in his life, nor did he work for Anaconda during Daly's lifetime. Daly did offer the hustling salesman employment on more than one occasion, but the offers were declined. The truth is that when Ryan was thirty he was not making, and had never made, more than $100 to $150 a month.

When thirty-two he married Miss Nettie Gardner of his native town. After that he apparently developed bigger ambitions, for when Marcus Daly died the oil salesman conceived the idea of obtaining an interest in the Daly chain of banks. He used his own savings and borrowed freely from friends to buy out various minority stockholders in the banks. This gave him general charge.

Ryan's removal to Montana as directing head of the powerful Daly financial institutions brought him into contact with all classes of the community. In the volcanic atmosphere then prevailing he must have handled himself better than he will admit, for within three years Henry H. Rogers, one of John D. Rockefeller's most fearless partners, asked Ryan to take charge of the Amalgamated Copper Company's affairs in that state.

The job was about as uninviting as any in the United States. Amalgamated had several fierce political fights on its hands; it was neck-deep in litigation with Fritz Augustus Heinze; labour conditions were unsettled and warlike; and the whole state was in a ferment, everybody being lined up either for or against one side or the other, Amalgamated or Heinze.

Curiously, all Ryan's activities in the oil business had been in opposition to the Standard Oil people, his employment having been with their rivals.

It was in 1904 that Ryan became managing director of the Amalgamated Copper Company with entire charge of all its subsidiaries. His job was not merely to manage the mines, but to manage men as well. When the first election came after Ryan took charge, the

Heinze faction was so soundly beaten that Ryan concluded Heinze, although no mean fighter, must realize he was completely licked and would, consequently, be in a mood to talk over terms of peace.

So Ryan opened negotiations with Heinze to buy all his properties in Montana. Heinze was anxious to sell, but he wanted the deal arranged so as to create the impression that he was merely effecting a compromise and not selling out. Amalgamated was determined to eliminate Heinze entirely from the situation and would entertain no negotiations which would leave him a loophole to cause any further embarrassment in the conduct of the business. This Heinze-Amalgamated deal forms so notable a chapter in America's mining and financial annals that I prevailed upon Mr. Ryan to tell exactly what happened.

"Because of Heinze's strong objection to have it appear that he had been bought out, and because of his insistence that the deal be represented as a merger, it was very hard to carry on negotiations that would remove Heinze root and branch," said Mr. Ryan. "The situation was relieved at times by a spice of humour. Heinze was mortally afraid that the miners in Butte would learn that he was preparing to sell out, as he was loudly promising to fight their battles for them if they would stand by him. He would never meet me except in the most out-of-the-way places. We never entered a building by the same door. He never came to my office and I never went to his. Instead, we would meet in the offices of one of our lawyers or in the rooms of friends. One of our most important sessions was held in Providence, R. I., because he was then staying at Newport and I was in New York and he did not want to run the risk of our being seen together at either place.

"From the very opening of negotiations Heinze and I were friendly and, though many times we came very near breaking off, we continued to treat with each other in good faith. He never once broke his word to me.

"After six months' negotiating we finally met one night, talked price from nine o'clock to three o'clock in the morning and reached an agreement."

Amalgamated then (1906) bought all the Heinze mining properties in Butte except the Lexington Mines, which, being covered by an outstanding bond issue, could not be delivered by Heinze. The departure of Heinze was followed by the subsidence of political turmoil. This enabled Ryan to wash his hands of political campaigning and to devote his attention to developing the Amalgamated's increased properties.

"How did labour act?" I asked.

"We had threats of labour difficulties, but in all the time I dealt with labour we had no strikes or lockouts. In fact, our mines never lost a day from labour troubles. We paid good wages and we got good service. Our relations with labour were most satisfactory. In fact, I have very little complaint to make over any dealings I have ever had with labour during all my connection with mining."

Later on Montana did have serious labour disturbances, but they arose from a bitter struggle between the I. W. W. and the Western Federation of Miners for control of the Butte Miners' Union. This clash brought grave disorder, during which the Miners' Union Hall was wrecked by dynamite and the militia had to be called out to enforce order. The mining companies were not involved, the row being between the two unions. Amalgamated solved the problem by refusing to recognize either faction and declaring an open shop, for the first time in over thirty-five years.

Mr. Ryan's effective work was rewarded by his selection as president of Anaconda.

John D. Ryan was one of the few business men in America who did not even know in 1907 that there was a panic. He was stricken with typhoid fever in August of that year, was so ill for months that he learned nothing of what was going on, and did not return to duty until March of the following year. About the time this Amalgamated giant recovered a still more powerful Amalgamated giant, H. H. Rogers, began to lose his health. By then Rogers had set such an appraisement upon his western "find" that he induced Mr. Ryan to come to New York to aid him in looking after this important branch of the Rogers activities. When Rogers died in the following year Ryan succeeded him as president of Amalgamated.

One of Ryan's fortes is bringing scattered properties together under one efficient management, with capital enough to develop and expand them. He has a faculty for handling big things. It is both easier and more economical to handle one integrated, strong organization than to keep tabs on half a dozen or more smaller and weaker ones. Mr. Ryan believes that, industrially, in union there is strength.

In Montana there was very special reason for merging numbers of important properties into one large concern, for there had been interminable disputes over encroachments by one company upon the underground ores of another as the mining lands were patchworks of claims held by different companies. While Anaconda had a large interest in several other properties, the stockholders were not the same in each case, so that it was impossible to run things without friction. At one time there were before the courts disputes involving almost $200,000,000.

Ryan's fairness, ability, and personality had impressed themselves upon the whole community by this time, and when he set about evolving order out of all this muddle he was able to bring the various companies under the full ownership of Anaconda, a feat that called for the exercise of the most delicate diplomacy. After he had eliminated Heinze, Ryan had rigidly refrained from seeking revenge upon any former antagonists, and his magnanimous course at that time had won him the respect and the confidence of all factions. Had he proved vindictive or narrow on that occasion he probably never would have been able to bring the various companies together.

In 1910 all the holdings of Amalgamated and all properties of subsidiaries were merged into the Anaconda, and by 1914 it was feasible to dissolve the Amalgamated Copper Company.

To-day Anaconda, in addition to producing 15 per cent. of the world's total output, is the largest producer of silver in the world, and its output of high-grade zinc exceeds that of any other mine in the world. Its metallurgical processes are admittedly the most advanced known, and to them is due in large measure the phenomenal increase in the company's profits during recent years. Anaconda, furthermore, has made large investments in other mining enterprises and is now heavily interested in properties in various parts of the United States as well as in South America, notably Chile. It is also, through subsidiaries, a great industrial and mercantile enterprise.

During one of his shopping expeditions through the Southwest Mr. Ryan, in 1912, was so struck with the Inspiration Copper Mine, then only a fledgling, that he invested extensively in it; already it is the third largest producer of copper in the world, and an idea of how good a bargain Ryan made may be gathered from the fact that in the first twelve months its profits were almost double the total cost of the property and its complete equipment.

What is here recorded by no means adequately indicates Mr. Ryan's responsibilities or ramifications, since he is a power in several other important metal companies.

If the man who makes two blades of grass grow where only one grew before is a public benefactor, surely a man who contributes in a large way to the general progress of the development of a state's resources is no less entitled to public recognition even though in both instances the primary motive has been profit rather than philanthropy or public-spiritedness. Although Mr. Ryan's home is now in New York and he is condemned to live in that city most of the year, his heart is still in Montana. He has derived, perhaps, most satisfaction from his work in bringing into being the Montana Power Company and, in the space of six years, developing it into so efficient and so huge a concern that it can supply power to industries and railroads and general business in Montana at rates which give these interests an advantage over enterprises located in any other state in the Union.

The world has heard a great deal about the electrification of 440 miles of the St. Paul Railroad over the Rockies, but only railroad and electrical men know the genesis of this wonderful feat.

John D. Ryan was its ancestor.

When he had his Montana Power Company in working order he decided to electrify the Butte, Anaconda and Pacific Railroad, between the mines in Butte and the smelters in Anaconda. Although there is only about 100 miles of track all told, this road handles a tremendous tonnage. As it was a system complete in itself, it lent itself ideally for experimental purposes. When the task of electrifying the road was completed, the experiment proved an unqualified success. Cost was cut to a minimum, efficiency reached a maximum. Railroad men and electrical engineers from all parts of the world came and studied the results. The St. Paul Railroad was peculiarly interested because of its almost insurmountable problems in hauling freight up the slopes of the Rockies. It has solved its problems now by having Ryan's company supply it with electric current.

Montana Power now provides current for the operation of no less than 550 miles of railroad. Moreover, practically all the mines of Montana get their power from this project. It also lights most of the state.

Indeed, it has functioned so much better than any similar utility company in the state that a committee of Congress two years ago haled Mr. Ryan before it and ordered him to confess whether or not the Company had a monopoly of the power business throughout the state.

"Yes," Ryan replied to the astonishment of the probers. "It does 95 per cent. of the business in its line in the state. It has a monopoly, not of the water-power resources of the state, but of the market, and it is a monopoly because the service it gives is so good and the charges are so low that there is no possibility of competition from any other water-power company or any other source."

Before they were through, the investigators found that, under the advantageous terms given by the Ryan enterprise, the consumption of electric energy in Montana was greater per capita than in any other state or in any other country.

"Hydro-electric development, the electrification of railroads, the discovery of improved metallurgical processes of one kind or another, are destined to make infinitely greater progress than is even dreamed of to-day," Mr. Ryan impressed upon me enthusiastically, for this is one subject on which he is not averse to talking In his imagination he sees mining, industry, transportation, and civilization as a whole, not so very many years hence, on a plane higher than matter-of-fact business men would dare to predict.

I asked one of the originators of the American International Corporation, which is extending America's influence and achievements in foreign markets, why Mr. Ryan was picked as one of the directors. I wanted to know what his special qualifications were. The reply was: "John D. Ryan is one of the most level-headed fellows we have. He is, of course, one of the foremost men in the mining industry and is accustomed to handling international transactions; but, more than that, he has an unusual amount of business sense. He is not fossilized. He is always on the job, thinking up new things and then going ahead and doing them. He has all the breezy progressiveness and enthusiasm of the typical Westerner, and he combines with this the financial and business experience which he has imbibed here in the East."

When the United States Government, early in 1917, sought to buy many millions of pounds of copper for military purposes, the first man approached, the Government representative later recorded, was John D. Ryan. His attitude was so satisfactory that the representative had to see but one other man, Daniel Guggenheim, before receiving assurance that the War Department would be supplied at less than half the price then current. "Those two men deserve all the credit," was the tribute the Government's representative paid them.

Not a bad record for a mining camp boy who was only an oil drummer on the road at thirty-five and is not yet fifty-three?

JACOB H. SCHIFF

JACOB H. SCHIFF has peculiarities.

He has never had a private secretary; he personally attends to every letter addressed to him, often giving first attention, not to business communications, but to charity mail.

He has never subscribed to a press-clipping bureau and hardly ever looks at articles printed about himself or his activities.

"I would like you to let me have a look at data about yourself, including the best sketches that have been written about your career," I said to Mr. Schiff when I found he had been named as one of America's "Fifty Foremost."

"I have not kept one word printed about myself and I don't think my son or any one else has," replied Mr. Schiff.

I expressed regret on the score that it was easier to make bricks if given some straw.

"You don't need any data or any interview to write an article about me," Mr. Schiff commented. "You have known me very well for many years, you know all about me. And"—this with a twinkle —"if you like, I promise to read what you print."

Mr. Schiff's claim to a place in America's Business Hall of Fame rests on several solid foundations.

For over thirty years he has been head of one of the two most influential private international banking firms in the Western hemisphere, and in this position has powerfully contributed to the building up of America's transportation systems which have done so much for our national development and enrichment.

His house has raised capital for scores of transportation and industrial enterprises, and it is a Wall Street saying—one of Wall Street's rather few true ones—that Kuhn, Loeb & Company have issued more good investments and fewer bad ones than any other banking concern in America.

Mr. Schiff's achievements as a financier, however, have been excelled by his record as a philanthropist. To this work he has contributed not only millions, but a large portion of his life—his mind, his brain, his heart, his days, and probably not a few sleepless nights.

On the day the great Northern Pacific panic in Wall Street reached its height the partners of Kuhn, Loeb & Co. frantically tried to get into touch with Mr. Schiff. He had not come down to his office; he was not at his home; he was not holding a conference with Harriman. Search discovered that he had gone to attend a meeting at the Montefiore Home. When his excited partners pounced upon him remonstratingly, he calmly replied: "I thought the poor people up there needed me more than you people down here."

His fetich is not, as popularly supposed, Judaism, but citizenship. It is his creed that a man must first, last, and always be a good, loyal citizen, intensely zealous in discharging all the responsibilities of citizenship. With him citizenship ranks above sect. He holds that unless a man is a worthy citizen he cannot be either a worthy Jew or a worthy Gentile. Everything is secondary to citizenship. All his public service, all his givings to education, his continuous donations to charities, his endeavours for the promotion of the best literature of his race—all have been prompted by his sense of what citizenship demands.

Another characteristic of Mr. Schiff has been his loyalty to his friends. He is not a fair-weather friend. The giants of transportation, of commerce, of finance, of railroading, once thrown into association with him, have remained staunch, close, confidential friends to the end. Mr. Schiff was the earliest financial sponsor of Edward H. Harriman; James J. Hill became closer and closer to him as the years rolled on; Alexander J. Cassatt, the creator of the Pennsylvania Railroad system as New York now knows it, found in Mr. Schiff a wholehearted supporter; Samuel Rea, Marvin Hughitt, Charles W. Eliot, and James Stillman are other tested-and-tried friends, while in his later years J. P. Morgan, although a rival in banking, came to regard Mr. Schiff as a financier whose tremendous influence could be relied upon for constructive effort whenever financial foundations began to be shaken.

He attends more funerals than any other financier in America. Wherever there is occasion for condolences, Mr. Schiff is among the first to tender them. Also, he never misses opportunity to offer congratulations on joyous occasions.

Although Jacob Henry Schiff is seventy you would never suspect it. He can still pedal a bicycle fast enough to get him into trouble with the speed laws. As a walker, Weston would not find him disappointing. Mr. Schiff does not try to break records or blood vessels on the golf links: he is not a golfer. He attributes his sound, supple physique to moderation, to plenty of fresh air and daily "legomotion."

He was born in Frankfort-on-the-Main, a city famous as the cradle of financiers. His parents, who were neither very rich nor very poor, were not in the banking business; but another branch of the family was, and Jacob Henry was early initiated into the mysteries of finance.

He was a bit restless, however, as he grew toward manhood, and when our Civil War ended he decided to come to the land which promised to offer limitless possibilities. He was eighteen then.

He got a job as a bank clerk but had sense and push enough not to stick long at that cramped calling. He soon became junior partner of the brokerage firm of Budge, Schiff & Co. He worked hard, studied hard, and prospered. Young Schiff, in fact, was then recognized as one of the coming financiers of Wall Street. To broaden his experience, he went to Europe for a stay.

On returning, he joined Kuhn, Loeb & Co., already a banking house of prominence. Shortly after he married Therese Loeb, daughter of Solomon Loeb, the senior partner of the firm. He was then twenty-eight. Ten years later Mr. Loeb retired and his son-in-law, who had developed notably, was the logical successor. For over thirty years Mr. Schiff has piloted Kuhn, Loeb & Co. through fair and foul financial weather, piloted it with a skill, foresight, and honesty that have raised it to the very foremost rank among the private banking houses, not only of the United States, but of the world.

When Edward Harriman, the Stock Exchange broker, began to dabble in railroad properties, he had neither experience nor capital. But he had almost infallible judgment, the vision of a statesman, the enthusiasm of an artist, and the determination of a Spartan. Jacob H. Schiff was one of the first financiers to recognize that a new railroad Napoleon was entering the arena.

Union Pacific in those days was a battered, bankrupt, decrepit stretch of rust. Few capitalists had faith in its possibilities. But Mr. Schiff's confidence in the future of the United States was as strong then as it is to-day and he took up the reorganization of Union Pacific. Harriman came knocking at the door, and, discerning in him a genius, Mr. Schiff extended to him the prestige and resources of Kuhn, Loeb & Co. Without this backing, it is doubtful if Union Pacific or the vast territory it serves would have enjoyed such remarkable prosperity.

U. P. shares were then selling for a song. Both Harriman and his bankers acquired enormous quantities, and within ten years the stock netted a fortune for all its large holders. Indeed, it subsequently paid annually a dividend equal to the entire original cost.

Southern Pacific and other railroads were corralled later. The Harriman-Kuhn-Loeb combination became the most powerful, the most aggressive, and the most successful that America had ever known. A railroad kingdom was being created without a parallel in the history of the world.

Harriman made more than $10,000,000 every year in the later part of his life! When he died, in 1909, he left upward of $70,000,000.

Mr. Schiff is estimated by fellow-bankers to be worth not so very much less, notwithstanding his princely gifts to various causes.

Russia's harsh treatment of Jews had long incurred the ire of Mr. Schiff, so when war broke out with Japan he enthusiastically undertook the raising of loans for the Czar's enemy. Mainly through his efforts over $200,000,000 of Japanese bonds were sold here.

As bankers for the Pennsylvania Railroad, K., L. & Co. have floated as much as $100,000,000 at one time. It was this firm that found the money necessary to enable the Pennsylvania to tunnel its way into New York and to raise that modern world's wonder, the Pennsylvania Railroad station. Mr. Schiff had great admiration for Mr. Cassatt, the bold dreamer who turned his dreams into stone and steel and structures. Incidentally, during all the years of association between the Pennsylvania Railroad and Kuhn, Loeb & Co. never once has there been even a suggestion of improper profits, disastrous financial advice, or questionable manipulation of securities.

It was Mr. Schiff's firm that placed $50,000,000 of Pennsylvania bonds in France and had them listed on the Paris Bourse, a step beset with inordinate difficulties but one which had mutually satisfactory results. After the war broke out an offer was made to repurchase these bonds and a majority of them came back.

Kuhn, Loeb & Co. have done heavyweight financing, also, for such railroads as Baltimore & Ohio, Chicago & North Western, Delaware & Hudson, Illinois Central, Union Pacific, Southern Pacific, etc.

Mr. Schiff has been fortunate in having brainy partners, namely, Otto H. Kahn, Paul M. Warburg (brother-in-law), now of the Federal Reserve Board, Felix M. Warburg (son-in-law), Jerome J. Hanauer, and Mortimer L. Schiff, who is one instance of an able son following an able father.

I have already touched upon Mr. Schiff's philanthropies. The public may be interested to know that, while Mr. Schiff has given away millions, he frowns upon wasting one penny. One of his idiosyncrasies is his habit, when he opens his mail, of carefully preserving all unused pages of letters as a substitute for pads. Doubtless, most young readers will smile at this little foible, but does it not point a moral in these extravagant days? If such economy is not despised by a multi-millionaire, can those less well-off afford to scoff at it? It may be that Mr. Schiff's carefulness in saving pennies has had something to do with his ability to save millions.

Mr. Schiff was the first treasurer of Barnard College. He founded the Semitic Museum at Harvard and the Jewish Theological Seminary in New York. He is vice-president of the Baron de Hirsch fund and a trustee of the American Jewish Committee. He is president of the Montefiore Home for Chronic Invalids.

His sense of civic responsibility influenced him to become a forceful member of the Second Committee of Seventy, the Committee of Fifteen, and the Committee of Nine. In later years he has been chosen frequently by Mayors of New York as a member of special mayoral committees. He was a member of the Board of Education under Mayor Strong. In the work of the Chamber of Commerce he has taken an active part, as vice-president and on committees, for a generation. The establishment of a College of Commerce has been a project very near his heart; if others had come forward with offers of contributions as he did, New York would have had such an institution years ago.

Colleges, hospitals, libraries, charitable organizations, the Red Cross, and the Chamber of Commerce have all benefited from Mr. Schiff's widely bestowed gifts. He does not make a "splash" with his donations; his contributions are very largely to meet current expenses and in many cases are made regularly every year. To commemorate the fiftieth anniversary of his arrival in America he presented a $500,000 building to Barnard in preference to doing anything for one sect.

And now comes a tragic part of the chronicle.

Mr. Schiff does not believe that the Jews in America should seek to hold themselves apart. He condemns everything tending to foster racial separateness. He urges that every Jew must be an American citizen first, a Jew second.

In an impassioned speech in 1916, replying to criticisms by his own people, he declared with feeling: "We hold our Jewry, our flag, as high as our fathers did, but we recognize that we are Americans, and we want our children to be Americans. We want our children to love our religion. We want them to be able to read in the original language our laws and our codes, but we also want them to think in English, to read in English, to adopt American ways."

So hurt was Mr. Schiff by the ingratitude manifested by some of his co-religionists that he felt constrained to announce that henceforth he would "have no part in Zionism, nationalism, the congress movement and Jewish politics in whatever form they may come up."

How deep the stabs have entered Jacob Schiff's heart cannot be fathomed by those who do not know the man. To find himself the object of ingratitude, criticism, and condemnation by some of the very people from whom he had reason to receive gratitude has wounded Mr. Schiff grievously.

His experience is reminiscent of what the late J. P. Morgan underwent when he was indicted for conspiracy in the Grand Trunk-New Haven Railroad case. Mr. Morgan, then, like Mr. Schiff, almost seventy, was heartbroken, inconsolable. He could not leave his bed.

JACOB H. SCHIFF

He wept, and from an aching heart wailed: "To think that after all these years I have been branded by my own Government a criminal, fit only to be thrown into jail!" Had not Charles S. Mellen come forward and shouldered the whole responsibility, it is doubtful if the aged financier would have recovered.

One accusation brought against Mr. Schiff has been that he was "dictating to the Jews of New York what they ought to do." Whether Mr. Schiff, with his peculiar—and, to my mind, not wholly wise—attitude toward the press and the public thought it necessary, when doing the right thing, to be punctilious to do it the right way; whether it ever occurred to him that his enormous power made him vulnerable to charges of autocracy, I cannot say. Perhaps the possibility of being misunderstood never entered his head.

I do know that he is among the best friends the Jews of America have ever had; that for years he has spent as much time in their behalf as in attending to his banking business; that the most eminent Jews of Europe regard Jacob H. Schiff as one of the foremost leaders of their race in the whole world, as something of a modern Moses; that the educational, the charitable, and the social facilities for American Jews would not have reached their present state but for the thought, toil, exhortation, and benefactions of Mr. Schiff; that he has, without blowing of trumpets, helped many a poor Jew and Gentile, black as well as white, out of his own purse, and that he is held in affectionate regard by a large part of the masses familiar with his charitable works.

I do know, in short, that Jacob Schiff is a man whom any race might well be proud to call its own.

In presenting him for the degree of Doctor of Commercial Science at the New York University in June, 1916, Vice-Chancellor Stevenson thus summed up Mr. Schiff's services:

"Jacob Henry Schiff, in this land of your adoption you have won a place of acknowledged leadership in financial and commercial pursuits. For enterprise and breadth of vision, for probity and worth, for the patronage of learning, for fidelity to the best traditions of your race, and for altruistic service that transcends the boundaries of race and religion, New York University bestows upon you the degree of Doctor of Commercial Science and directs that your name be added to the roll of her alumni."

Elaborate preparations were made by Jewish, civic, commercial, and other bodies to do honour to Mr. Schiff on his seventieth birthday, January 10, 1917. But it was characteristic of him that he refused to be fêted in any way. To avoid any fuss being made over him, Mr. Schiff quietly left the city on the eve of the anniversary day!

I happened to call upon him at his office just as he was preparing to slip away. Naturally I asked why he would not let fellow-citizens join in paying him the tributes they desired. Mr. Schiff's reply reveals his personality:

"There are any number of people who would like to do just as much as I have ever done, but who have not had it within their power. Because God has blessed me with the means to do something for others, that is no reason why I should set myself up to be praised or fêted for doing it."

On the day Mr. Schiff reached seventy, checks from him reached an undisclosed number of worthy organizations. How much he thus distributed he would not state, but announcement after announcement came from recipients until a total of $500,000 was revealed, including four gifts of $100,000 each.

Men in all walks of life sent Mr. Schiff birthday congratulations and paid tribute to his worth as a citizen, as a valuable force, to quote Mayor Mitchel's words, "in the forefront of those public movements in the city during the last twenty-five years out of which has evolved its civic progress." Almost an entire issue of the *American Hebrew* was devoted to the publication of appreciations of Mr. Schiff by noted Jews and others both in Europe and here. Israel Zangwill expressed the general sentiment felicitously in these words: "Congratulations on such a birthday fall rather to the world which has still the privilege of Mr. Schiff's presence than to the man himself." Secretary of the Treasury McAdoo described Mr. Schiff as "a rare combination of the financier and the altruist," "at once a philosopher and a philanthropist," "a progressive and a patriot, who never hesitates to put country above party and who never fails to enlist in a worthy cause." Another well said that to make a just estimate of Mr. Schiff as a philanthropist would mean to write the history of Jewish philanthropy for the last forty years.

Grievously as the European war has weighed upon Mr. Schiff, it has brought one compensating event of immeasurable moment. "The Russian revolution is possibly the most important event in Jewish history since the race was brought out of slavery," declared Mr. Schiff. It has caused him to revise some of his views concerning the future of the Jewish people.

"It has come to me," Mr. Schiff told an audience just after the revolution, "while thinking over events of recent weeks—and the statement may surprise many—that the Jewish people should at last have a home land of their own.

"I do not mean by that that there should be a Jewish nation. I am not a believer in a Jewish nation built on all kinds of isms, with egoism as the first, and agnosticism and atheism among the others. But I am a believer in the Jewish people and in the mission of the

Jew, and I believe that somewhere there should be a great reservoir of Jewish learning in which Jewish culture might be furthered and developed, unhampered by the materialism of the world, and might spread its beautiful ideals over the world.

"And naturally that land would be Palestine. If that ever develops—and the present war may bring the development of this ideal nearer—it will not be accomplished in a day or a year, and in the meantime it is our duty to keep the flame of Judaism burning brightly."

When the American Jewish Relief Committee launched its campaign to raise $10,000,000 for Jewish victims of the war, Mr. Schiff invited to dinner several hundred of the most prominent members of the race, made a stirring appeal, announced a personal contribution of $100,000 and so aroused the gathering that over $2,500,000 was pledged on the spot. Mr. Schiff's donation, he specified, would be used in establishing a hospital unit in Russia "in recognition of the emancipation of the Jew, won through the revolution."

In presenting a loving cup to Mr. and Mrs. Schiff at Newport, R. I., in the summer of 1917, the spokesman said:

"Many times has the city of Newport been honoured by the presence of distinguished guests, and it is honoured now by the presence of two persons who have devoted their lives to charity and philanthropy."

That simple final clause forms a fitting close to this brief sketch of Jacob H. Schiff.

CHARLES M. SCHWAB

THERE is only one man in the world who ever tore up a $1,000,000 a year salary contract.
When the United States Steel Corporation took over the Carnegie Company it acquired as one of its obligations—it really was an asset—a contract to pay Charles M. Schwab that unheard-of sum as a minimum annually.

J. P. Morgan didn't know what to do about it. The highest salary on record was $100,000. He was in a quandary.

Finally, he summoned Schwab, showed him the contract and hesitatingly asked what could be done about it.

"This," said Schwab.

He tore it up.

That contract had netted Schwab $1,300,000 the previous year.

"I didn't care what salary they paid me. I was not animated by money motives. I believed in what I was trying to do and I wanted to see it brought about. I cancelled that contract without a moment's hesitation," Mr. Schwab explained to me.

There was a sequel. Morgan later told Carnegie how magnanimously Schwab had acted. Carnegie remarked: "Charlie is the only man I know who would have done that."

And he promptly sent Schwab in bonds the full amount of the unexpired contract.

Carnegie has declared publicly since: "I owe my fortune chiefly to two men, Bill Jones and Charlie Schwab."

Schwab, let me add, for years picked all the Carnegie partners. Indeed, the only man to whom the canny Scot ever gave carte blanche was Schwab.

Although rich beyond his wildest imaginings, Schwab is to-day the hardest-working man in the steel industry. Why? Let him answer:

"Why do I work? What do I work for? I have more money than I can begin to spend. I have no children, nobody to leave it to. My wife is rich enough in her own right. She does not need it. I do not need it. I work just for the pleasure I find in work, the satisfaction there is in developing things, in creating. Also, the associations business begets. The man who does not work for the love of work but only for money is not likely to make money nor to find much fun in life."

Since much foolishness has been printed on the subject, let me—let Mr. Schwab rather—clear up this other point: Why did he give up the Steel Corporation presidency after three years?

Here is the plain truth, as told me by Mr. Schwab, who has never been accused of lying:

"I never had a difference with Mr. Morgan in my life. We were always the closest possible friends. The reason I resigned was because I could not do what I had been doing all my life. I was hampered by directors and other interests who did not give me sufficient play to enable me to be useful. If I thought a mill ought to be built at Pittsburgh I didn't want an important director telling me it ought to be built at Chicago. If I had a strike involving a principle, I didn't want to be told to settle it for fear it might affect the stock market. So I quit."

Fate had greater things in store for him. To-day Schwab is ranked as one of the greatest creative forces in American industry. Also, he is perhaps the most popular business man in the country.

He has had more "titles" conferred upon him than any other living American. For example, "The World's Greatest Steel-Maker," "The Most Successful Salesman Ever Born," "The Million-Dollar-Salary Man," "The Originator of the Steel Trust," "The Boy President," "The Developer of Young Men," "The Creator of the American Krupp's," "The Defender of America," "The Incurable Optimist," "The Man With the Golden Smile," "The Bethlehem Miracle-Worker."

This article might well be called "The Truth About Schwab." His picturesque career has inspired so much fiction that it is gratifying to be able to dissipate the fables and to set the record straight.

The Schwab family moved from Williamsburg, Pa., where Charles Michael was born on February 18, 1862, to the picturesque hamlet of Loretto, Pa., on a crest of the Alleghanies, when the future steel king was a little lad. On leaving the local school he spent two years at St. Francis College. As with many men destined to make a mark, he became enamoured of mathematics. He also found chemistry fascinating. Engineering problems became his hobby.

But, alas, instead of landing in a collar-and-cuff position where he could use his knowledge and talent, he was obliged, at sixteen, to mount the driver's seat of a coach his father ran between Loretto and Cresson Station. Undiscouraged, he cracked jokes as well as his whip.

His first real job was as a grocery-boy in the store at Braddock of A. H. Speigelmire, an old friend of Papa Schwab, who also kept a store. From the first day he donned his apron he had his eye on the great steel mills there, the Edgar Thomson Works, owned by Carnegie Brothers & Company. But meanwhile, although he disliked the work, he contrived to liven up things at the store. He smiled on customers, chatted with them, jumped at chances to please them by carrying parcels or doing little errands, and in the evenings he made things pleasant in the Speigelmire household by playing the piano, singing for them, and teaching the youngsters music. "He's willing and bright and wants to know everything," was his employer's description of him. The mathematician was not above learning how to handle groceries. He well earned his $30 a month (without board).

One day Captain William R. Jones, then superintendent of the steel works, the right-hand man of Andrew Carnegie, and the best-known steel-maker in the country, stepped into the store.

"I asked 'Bill' for a place in the mill," Mr. Schwab relates. "He asked me: 'Can you drive stakes?' I replied: 'I can drive anything!' I started driving stakes next morning, at a dollar a day."

In six years the dollar-a-day stake driver was superintendent of the works, then the foremost steel-making plant in America!

"They say it was your piano-playing that attracted Carnegie?" I probed.

"There's no truth in that at all," replied Mr. Schwab with spirit. "I never played for Mr. Carnegie in my life. It was Captain 'Bill' that took me to Carnegie one day and said: 'Andy, here's a young man who knows as much about this mill as I do.'"

Carnegie, like Captain "Bill," "took to" the young engineer. So did the men. Everybody was happy when "Charlie" was around. His enthusiasm, his joyousness, his industry proved infectious. His ability to overcome difficulties was on every one's tongue. He had continued his study of chemistry and engineering, had conducted innumerable experiments to test the strength and qualities of the metal under different processes, and, as Carnegie later handsomely admitted, "knew more about steel than any other man in the world."

His next step was to the head of the engineering department of the whole Carnegie organization. Here he taught the industry a new wrinkle. He conceived and planned a greater plant than any then in existence, the Homestead Steel Works, on the principle of feeding the raw material at one end, keeping it in continuous motion, and having it come out in the form of finished products at the other end—a system since widely adopted in various industries. At this time he had some 6,000 or 7,000 men under him.

All this at twenty-four!

When the Carnegie management was confronted with the nerve-shaking problem of re-opening the Homestead Works after the terrible strike of 1892, when the successful handling of the men appeared impossible, they turned to young Schwab, appointed him superintendent of the plant, and told him to see what he could do.

Do! Why, there was only one thing for Schwab to do—turn every workman into a rooter and make the plant the most pleasant and profitable in the world. The Schwab smile, the Schwab cordiality, the Schwab radiancy, the Schwab sincerity, the Schwab enthusiasm, plus the Schwab ability amounting to genius, won all hands and all hearts. The younger Pitt never showed greater tact, diplomacy, and statesmanship.

Election to the presidency of the Carnegie Company, the greatest prize in the whole steel industry, was his reward. He had won it in fifteen years from his début as a dollar-a-day stake driver, won it by basic study of the metal and of men, won it by hard work with a will and a smile, won it by sheer achievement in evolving methods of producing steel faster, cheaper, and in greater quantities—and in keeping workmen happy and loyal at their tasks. At thirty-five Schwab stood on the top step of the steel ladder.

His fame was international. Whereas England was master of the world's steel markets when Schwab was stake-driving, he had now done much to change that. His brilliantly conceived Homestead plant, though paying wages thrice those of Europe, could meet the keenest of European competition. The United States, indeed, was now clipping England's wings.

Arthur Keen, the foremost steel manufacturer in Britain, approached the young American genius with an offer of a fabulous salary—greater far than any salary paid any man in any country. Schwab told him nothing could tempt him to leave his friend and benefactor, Carnegie, with whom by this time he was on terms of filial intimacy and affection. To nobody did Schwab mention the offer.

Keen and Carnegie met later at a dinner of the British Iron and Steel Institute and Keen related the incident.

"If Charlie is worth that much to you, he is worth more to me," was, in effect, Carnegie's reply.

The moment he got back he sent for Schwab, told him he loved him all the more for his loyalty—and gave him a long-term contract worth a minimum of $1,000,000 a year!

But Charles Michael Schwab had still greater dreams. Why not make the United States the foremost steel-producing country in the world, able to meet and beat Europe in foreign markets?

In his fertile mind he conjured up a vision such as the world had never known, a vision of the greatest, strongest industrial organization on earth, coördinated, integrated, self-contained, with abundant capital, the best of brains, and ramifications covering the globe.

Fascinated, he began to act. His first overtures were repelled by J. P. Morgan and others. But Schwab, as Carnegie was and is fond of saying, "can hurdle any obstacle." At a dinner given in his honour in December, 1900, he glowingly laid his vision before the greatest financiers and business men in America. He was as one inspired. Donning the mantle of a prophet, he pictured the glorious possibilities of the new steel age.

His entrancing outline of the Steel Trust captivated Morgan. And within a few months the billion-dollar United States Steel Corporation was formed, with Schwab as its president and the owner of $28,000,000 (par value) of its capital stock. This at thirty-nine! He was "The Boy President."

On resigning in impaired health at the end of three strenuous years after the great machine was functioning, he announced publicly: "I propose to devote my whole attention to regaining my strength and won't take any position until it is restored."

He rested, though he was not wholly idle, for two or three years before reëntering the business arena, at South Bethlehem, Pa.

Miracles have been wrought at the Bethlehem Steel Works, all the world knows. The world imagines Charles M. Schwab has wrought them. The world is mistaken. The miracles have been wrought by others—by fifteen young partners. So Mr. Schwab stoutly declares.

"There has really been nothing wonderful about my career," protested Mr. Schwab when I broached the subject. "I am not a believer in genius. I believe Solomon was right when he said: 'The race is not to the swift nor the battle to the strong.' Circumstances, environment, opportunity, have a lot to do with a man's success in life.

"But of course there are qualities that go to make a man really successful. A man must have personality—that is very important. He must have industry, application, and commonsense—no man can do much if he has not been endowed with a reasonable amount of brains. He must earn a reputation for unimpeachable integrity, he must tell the absolute truth, he must cultivate good-fellowship, he must be a man other men will like and trust. Optimism, cheerfulness, readiness to encourage and inspire others also help.

"Any man can learn to do anything that any other man has done if he will apply himself to the doing of it.

"I happened to be fortunate in getting into an industry in its infancy that offered phenomenal opportunities, that's all. *And I took risks.*"

"How?" I asked.

This started Mr. Schwab on the story of Bethlehem's upbuilding. The Bethlehem Steel Company was bankrupt when Schwab took hold of it last time—he bought control once before, when he was with the Steel Corporation, sold out to the ill-fated United States Shipbuilding Company, and took it back when that enterprise collapsed.

"When I took hold of Bethlehem the second time I didn't take one well-known steel man from anywhere. I selected fifteen young men right out of the mill and made them my partners. I believe in profit sharing—I believe it will ultimately settle the labour problem. Andrew Carnegie was the most successful profit-producer in this country and he gave his employees half of his profits in bonuses.

"If you want anything well done in life don't engage a man of great reputation to do it. Get a man who has his reputation to make; he will give you his very best individual, undivided effort.

"Of the fifteen I selected not one has proved a failure. I am proud of that and proud of them. One of them was a crane fellow at $75 a month. He is now earning five times as much as any other steel employee in the United States and is several times a millionaire. This is Eugene G. Grace, president of the Bethlehem Company and the man chiefly responsible for its success. He is fifty times the man I ever was."

I smiled.

"I mean that," Mr. Schwab affirmed.

Mr. Schwab didn't say that he closed up his palatial home on Riverside Drive, migrated to the obscure Pennsylvania village, took off his coat and worked day and night for eight years, often against financial and other discouragements, nursing the bankrupt Bethlehem back to health and strength.

"I backed Bethlehem with every dollar I had and could borrow," Mr. Schwab went on in reference to his having taken risks. "I put my own name to every piece of paper issued. Then, also, I took hold of Gray's invention for making structural steel after every important company in the country had turned it down and, because I was convinced I was right, I spent $15,000,000 for the proving of that one invention. Was that not taking risks? But it gave us the leadership in the structural steel business in the United States and in the world. There had never been a conspicuously successful steel plant in the East. But I believed Bethlehem had all the elements of success. It is some satisfaction to have proved that my judgment was right."

I cannot attempt to describe Mr. Schwab's activities of the last ten years—how he worked at the plant early and late encouraging and enthusing his men; how he evolved the most scientific cost-ascertaining and profit-sharing plan ever adopted by any great enterprise; how he crossed and re-crossed the Atlantic and the Pacific, booking greater orders than any other man ever aspired to secure; how he went straight to Kitchener when the war began, told him a few useful truths, and came back with enough business to boom Bethlehem as it had never boomed before. I can mention merely a few facts about the Bethlehem Steel Corporation and its activities.

Schwab has spent well over $100,000,000 in strengthening and expanding it and in acquiring subsidiaries.

Expenditures totalling $100,000,000 were sanctioned in 1916 to cover the ensuing few years.

The corporation (with subsidiaries) employs 75,000 men all told.

Its annual pay-roll exceeds $80,000,000, or nearly $7,000,000 a month.

It is a greater producer of engines of war than the far-famed German Krupp's.

It is now, in conjunction with its subsidiaries, and its properties in Chile and Cuba, next in size to the United States Steel Corporation.

Its shipbuilding companies on both coasts give it 40 per cent. of America's total shipbuilding facilities.

Its war orders from the Allies are unofficially computed at $500,000,000.

Bethlehem Steel to-day forms a bulwark for the United States. Said Mr. Schwab in June, 1917:

"Bethlehem Steel is to-day putting $20,000,000 into plants entirely for the use of the Government. In peace time such plant will have no value, but there are times when more than the business view is necessary. We know that this work ought to be done, and we are doing it.

"We feel that the plants of the Bethlehem Steel Corporation for ordnance making, for steel manufacture, and for shipbuilding—for we build nearly 40 per cent. of all the tonnage of ships turned out in the United States—constitute a national asset of supreme value at a crisis like this. It is our ambition to make that asset of the greatest possible effectiveness in assuring for our country and for our allies an overwhelming victory in this, the greatest of all wars.

"Business must be profitable if it is to continue to succeed, but the glory of business is to make it so successful that it may do things that are great chiefly because they ought to be done. We at Bethlehem are trying to conduct a profitable business, but, profit or no profit, Bethlehem Steel has volunteered to serve the American Government, and to that service we dedicate every man and every material resource which we can control."

On the same occasion—a talk to a salesmen's congress—Mr. Schwab made this statement, illuminative of his humane qualities:

"I may induce you to buy large quantities of goods from me, but unless I can induce my organization, down to the humblest workman, to want to produce those goods economically and efficiently, my skill in selling you the goods is wasted.

CHARLES M. SCHWAB

"One of our great efforts at Bethlehem is to seek to instil confidence and enthusiasm in our own men.

"Bethlehem has prospered, but the fact about Bethlehem in which I most keenly rejoice is that our men also have prospered. The average earnings of each wage-earner in our employ was in 1915 a little over $900, whereas for 1916 the average earnings were over $1,200 per man, an increase of more than 30 per cent. in one year. Since January 1, 1917, we have increased the wages of our men another 10 per cent.

"These large earnings have been realized because in every instance possible the man obtained a share of the profits which he helped to create. And that is one of the reasons why our men have not only been prosperous, but enthusiastic in their work.

"The labour problem is far from being solved, but if the managers of industry can develop some universal plan which will make labour not only well-paid but happy in doing the work itself, one of the greatest possible boons to mankind will have been realized."

Bethlehem's $15,000,000 common shares rose from $25 before the war to $600 in 1915, making many Schwab followers millionaires and eclipsing the record of all other "war stocks." The company now pays dividends of 30 per cent. a year on its increased common stock, $60,000,000.

Schwab early in the war was offered $53,000,000 for his holdings—said to be approximately 90,000 preferred and 60,000 common—with the choice of remaining at the head of the company for ten years. The offer did not even tempt him. Money is not his goal. His ambition is to build up such an organization as he visioned at that dinner in 1900, an organization that will contribute to raising the United States to first place among the great nations of the earth.

Like Carnegie, Schwab is a lavish philanthropist. A beautiful Catholic Church at Loretto, a convent house at Cresson, a model road in place of the dilapidated one where he used to drive his coach, a church at Braddock, an industrial school at Homestead, a school and an auditorium at Weatherly, all in Pennsylvania, a recreation park and school on Staten Island, are among his recorded benefactions. Not long ago a $2,000,000 endowment for St. Francis College, at Loretto, was reported. His unrecorded benefactions probably outnumber this list.

Mrs. Schwab, who before her marriage in 1883 was Miss Emma Dinkey (sister of A. C. Dinkey, the steel master), is noted for her charities and for her musical and artistic accomplishments. She helped Mr. Schwab with the experiments that aided him in acquiring the knowledge of steel that was the foundation of his earliest successes.

JOHN G. SHEDD

"WHAT have your policies been?" I asked the head of the largest wholesale and retail dry-goods house in the world.

"We have no policies," he replied; "we have certain fixed principles. When your principles are right, you don't have to bother about policies—they will take care of themselves."

Who was the speaker? You probably do not even know his name. That is because his modesty is the only quality that exceeds his foresight.

One day a youth, raised on a backwoods farm of New Hampshire, walked into the greatest store in Chicago and thus addressed its head:

"Mr. Field, I would like to get a job here in your store."

"What can you do?" asked the merchant prince.

"I can sell any goods of any kind or character your store has for sale," was the confident reply.

"Then I can give you a job. You can start at once at $10 a week."

Years later Marshall Field, then everywhere recognized as the greatest merchant in America, was summoned before a Senatorial committee to give evidence on the Dingley Tariff Bill. There was much interest in the appearance of Chicago's great mercantile magnate. On rising, Mr. Field began:

"I am holding in my hand a letter from a man I believe to be the best merchant in the United States."

Everybody opened their eyes. Was not the witness himself admittedly the best merchant in the land? Whom else could he mean?

There was much mental questioning during the reading of the communication as to the name that would be signed at the bottom. The signature was this:

John G. Shedd

For over twenty years the writer of that letter has been the real, active head of Marshall Field & Company. And those who know best unanimously declare that the growth and scientific development of Marshall Field & Company's business has been due chiefly to the extraordinary foresight, the exhaustless initiative, the inordinate practical ability, and rare imagination of John Graves Shedd. Although he did not become the titular head of the business until its founder died, early in 1906, Mr. Shedd was its actual directing head for a dozen years before then. His work was so little trumpeted that few people outside the concern were familiar with the facts.

When the New Hampshire youth first entered the store its sales totalled less than $15,000,000 a year.

To-day, under President Shedd, Marshall Field & Company are doing a business of over $100,000,000 a year. They carry over a million articles and do 25,000,000 transactions a year. On special exposition days more than 300,000 customers have visited the retail store between the hours of 8:30 A.M. and 5:30 P.M. The store's floorspace covers fifty-five acres, calling for over thirty miles of carpet. Its electrical power would serve a city of 150,000 inhabitants. The store's eighty-two elevators carry, on busy days, more passengers in ten hours than are carried in twenty-four hours by both the South Side and the Metropolitan West Side Railways of Chicago. To deliver goods more than 350 motor trucks and motor wagons daily cover 350 square miles, and when the holiday business is at its height fifty additional motor vehicles are added. The retail store alone delivered in one December day, within the territory covered by their own equipment, approximately 100,000 packages.

President Shedd has under him some 20,000 employees, including as many as 12,500 in the retail store at holiday times and an average of 4,000 in the wholesale store.

Then the company owns important factories at Spray and Draper, North Carolina, for the manufacture of cotton and woollen goods; also lace, lace curtain, handkerchief, and bedspread mills at Zion City, Illinois, as well as factories in Chicago for the manufacture of miscellaneous merchandise.

It was Mr. Shedd's ability to foresee mercantile trends that led Marshall Field & Company to take up the production of their own merchandise on a large scale, an innovation that enabled them to expand steadily and healthily while the majority of other huge dry-goods jobbing houses, lacking such foresight, went to the wall.

"Let us adopt 'From cotton mills to consumer' as one of our mottoes," Mr. Shedd propounded years ago when he realized that the heyday of the middleman was passed; and it was probably this stroke of mercantile genius that saved Marshall Field & Company from the common fate. It afforded unlimited scope for creative talent, for originating exclusive designs, for upholding and carrying a step forward the Marshall Field idea of "Better Quality."

Also, it opened up new channels to Mr. Shedd for the exercise of his inventive skill, for to him, a born merchant leader, there was as much genuine pleasure and satisfaction in thinking up and evolving some new "creation" in merchandise as ever artist experienced in painting a masterpiece. I have never seen sculptor or artist handle marble or canvas with more touching enthusiasm and affection than John Shedd handled such commonplace but useful things as ginghams and other cotton fabrics designed and produced under the Marshall Field ægis. To most of us a yard of cotton dress goods is a yard of cotton goods and nothing more; to him it was the embodiment of thought, of art, of creative power—a product of which the workman need not feel ashamed. Manifestly the cotton fibres and the delicate colourings had been mixed with enthusiasm and with brains.

Mr. Shedd is little given to talking, but after a while he became interested in the object of these sketches explaining the rise of notably successful men, and during our conversation he dropped many sage sayings.

"Look at those photographs on that wall"—Mr. Shedd pointed to the wall of his private office hung with a dozen pictures of responsible-looking men. "There you see every one of Mr. Field's partners and not one of them but started with him at the bottom. Two of the most successful department managers began, one at $4 and the other at $2.50 a week. They were all men of limited education, but they were bright, discerning, deserving fellows with initiative, willingness, and a desire to do whatever was necessary, not merely for their own progress, but for the progress of the business. They placed first the welfare of the organization. Their own welfare prospered as a matter of course as the business prospered.

"Too many young men are more concerned about how they start than how they are likely to finish. This is especially true of college students. Most of them would rather begin at a fairly high salary, without considering the goal, than start at a low wage where there is more inducement at the top.

"It is wisely ordained that no one can start at the top but must climb to get there; for it is this necessity for starting at the bottom that gives the right stamp of young man a chance to rise above the common level.

"Any one pitchforked into a place at the top would be certain to fall off and break his neck.

"It is a remarkable fact that almost all the Marshall Field partners have been common or, at the most, high school graduates, not university men. I believe in higher education and would have chosen a college course had it been within my reach, even though it probably would have detracted from my ability to acquire whatever modest business reputation I have attained. The trouble is that your average college student comes along wearing his diploma on the lapel of his coat and proclaims, 'I am a college fellow.' He wants to keep his hands clean. He has no patience to learn the A B C of a business. He looks for the highest paid employment he can find at the start instead of entering the bottom of a business with a future.

"The huge business organizations of to-day afford more opportunities for earning large incomes than did the multitude of small stores of former days. An income of $10,000 a year on a capital of $100,000 would be considered a good return, whereas in large establishments there are now many positions paying from $10,000 to $50,000 a year.

"The very best thing about a business like ours is that it has been in continuous operation for over fifty years, and during that whole period not one old employee has been discharged for either lack of work or because of depressed general conditions. Steady employment at generous wages gives a better opportunity to save money than more or less temporary jobs entailing shifting about.

"There is no lack of opportunity in the world to-day. But there is great lack of efficiency, lack of readiness to seize opportunity when it comes. The organization that maintains a high state of efficiency can usually fill its executive offices from within.

"It is equally true, however, that no store can be better than its management.

"Just as one hot box upsets the proper running of a train, so lack of efficiency in any one spot upsets the whole organization.

"Size alone is of no consequence; the important thing is the standard by which a business grows. If a business is run honestly, efficiently, and fulfills a useful function in the community, it cannot well be too large.

"With us we have had just one central thought, one end toward which we have all worked—what we call the Marshall Field idea. There it is——"

Mr. Shedd pointed to this framed statement hanging on the wall:

The Marshall Field & Company Idea

To do the right thing, at the right time, in the right way; to do some things better than they were ever done before; to eliminate errors; to know both sides of the question; to be courageous; to be an example; to work for love of the work; to anticipate requirements; to develop resources; to recognize no impediments; to master circumstances; to act from reason rather than rule; to be satisfied with nothing short of perfection.

"We try to inculcate that idea upon all employees, and any who cannot absorb it and be guided by it must go elsewhere. The daily application and operation of that idea is as good for each individual as it is for the house. Our whole aim, you thus see, is SERVICE.

"Every large employer worthy of the name is constantly looking for men of the highest efficiency to fill important places. That is his most important duty, the selecting and placing of the right men in the right positions. The employer who can rear and train employees to take the principal positions can thus pave the way for promotion all along the line. This makes every worker feel that he is going to reach the highest point his merits warrant.

"Sometimes it is necessary to reason with a man that his present job is better for him than one higher up would be, since he would probably fail to fill it satisfactorily and thus become a misfit."

The career of John Graves Shedd contains nothing hit-or-miss, nothing haphazard, nothing hinged on chance. From the very outset he formulated plans and principles and moved forward unswervingly toward their consummation. He selected a harbour toward which to sail even before he had put out to sea. Then he steered a straight course.

He was born on July 20, 1850, on a farm at Alstead, New Hampshire, and very early had to perform a man's work in the field and in the barn. This life, with its lack of opportunity for advancement, its isolation from social and intellectual activities, its narrow vision and its semi-poverty, had little fascination for him. There were no automobiles on farms in those days, not even facilities for installing bath tubs and the other modern domestic conveniences which have gone far to revolutionize rural life during more recent years. The country lad did much serious thinking as to what avenue of life he should follow, and finally resolved to become a merchant, as good and as great a merchant as industry and honesty could make him. Before he was seventeen he left his father's farm and entered a grocery store at Bellows Falls, Vermont, at $1.50 a week and his board. From the start he felt at home selling things.

"I saved most of the $75 I received for my first year's work and felt quite a capitalist," Mr. Shedd told me. Then he found work in a general store in his native town at $125 a year, but of this he had to pay $2 a week for board to a New England housewife who looked after him well for this modest sum. A fire in the store, which forced him to find another job, proved a disguised blessing, as he received $175 a year in a rival store.

"I now felt on the highway to prosperity," commented Mr. Shedd. By the time he was twenty his ability had become marked and he accepted what was regarded as a most tempting offer to enter a dry-goods store at Rutland, Vermont. The salary was $300 a year with board.

The best dry-goods store in Rutland, however, was owned by Benjamin H. Burt, a merchant of more than local fame, whose principles and practices were far ahead of those then generally current. His keen eye did not overlook the ability of the newcomer from the Granite State, and to secure his services Mr. Burt offered to double his salary and allow him a commission on sales. The environment here proved most congenial and Shedd found himself developing both mentally and commercially.

His goal, however, was higher than anything Rutland could offer. His aim was not to become a large toad in a small puddle, but to test his mettle in a large centre where he would have to match his wits against the keenest of mercantile intellects. He had diligently studied dry goods; he took such a delight in satisfying customers that he was sure nature had intended him for a salesman; he possessed an adequate measure of self-confidence—and he had saved money.

With great regret he said good-bye to his tutor and benefactor, Mr. Burt—whose picture to this day Mr. Shedd keeps close at his hand in his office. Chicago was his destination.

"I was determined," said Mr. Shedd in recounting this epochal step in his career, "to get a position in the *best* store in the city. I had heard of Field, Leiter & Company and found that it was both the best and the biggest house in Chicago. Well, I got a job in it as stockkeeper and salesman—and I am still here."

Of his climb from the bottom to the top of the world's greatest dry-goods enterprise, Mr. Shedd could not be induced to talk further than to say that five months after he began, on August 7, 1872, his pay was raised, not to $12 which had been stipulated, but to $14, Mr. Field explaining that this was in consideration of his notably good work—"A tribute which pleased me more than any other subsequent advancement in the whole course of my career," added Mr. Shedd.

"It was an inspiration to serve a man like Mr. Field," declared Mr. Shedd, as willing to talk about Mr. Field as he was unwilling to talk about himself.

It was Mr. Shedd's good fortune to be placed directly under Henry J. Willing, one of the ablest partners ever connected with Marshall Field. He was an inspiration for those associated with him; from him they learned the value of high character, ceaseless energy, and progressive methods. Within four years Mr. Shedd became head of the lace and embroidery department—this when only twenty-six years of age. The talent he displayed for analyzing conditions, for reading trends, and for skilful merchandising induced Mr. Field to entrust, not one, but half-a-dozen departments to his care. Before long he was appointed general merchandise manager of the whole business, a position carrying tremendous responsibilities since it entailed oversight of the buying as well as the selling of millions of dollars' worth of goods a year. It took him just twenty-one years to rise from $10 a week to a partnership with the income of a prince.

When the firm was incorporated in 1901, Mr. Shedd was given rank second only to Marshall Field himself, the latter being president and the former vice-president. The bulk of the active work fell upon the vice-president, as Mr. Field by then felt entitled to relax and to indulge his fondness for travel. For years before Mr. Field's death, in 1906, Mr. Shedd had been the real head of the firm, and his election to the presidency followed as a matter of course. Mr. Field's career had been along almost exactly the same lines as his successor's. Both had been farm boys, both had started in country stores in New England, both migrated to Chicago as dry-goods salesmen, and both believed in and followed the same principles. Field used to say that he wanted brains, not money—and as a matter of fact, not one of his partners brought a dollar's worth of outside capital into the business.

"What were and are some of your cardinal principles?" I asked Mr. Shedd. He replied:

"Supply nothing but serviceable merchandise, and when possible, of better quality than furnished elsewhere; always satisfy your customer, no matter at what cost or inconvenience, so that he or she will become one of your best advertisements; conduct business on as near a strictly cash basis as practicable and thus avoid bad debts; try always to read coming developments and adjust your activities accordingly; and, not least important, treat employees with the greatest consideration and thus evoke their loyalty."

Mr. Shedd was the first merchant in Chicago to introduce the Saturday half-holiday. He is an advocate of healthful recreation for both employers and employees. "I regard golf as one of the greatest blessings of modern times," Mr. Shedd remarked to me, "for it has drawn men of responsible affairs away from their tasks into the open air, where they not only reinvigorate their health but form new friendships and cultivate social intercourse. This has tended not only to clear their brains but to develop their humanity."

How well the Marshall Field employees have been provided for may be gathered from these facts: A large portion of one floor is devoted to their exclusive use. Reading rooms are provided for men and for women and a branch of the Chicago Public Library is maintained in the building. There are medical rooms, with nurses, etc.; music and rest rooms, educational motion pictures to show the process of manufacturing textiles, etc.; lunch rooms and cafeterias which serve an average of 3,000 employees daily; a choral society of 150 members; a baseball league, and a gymnasium. Then an academy is provided for boys and girls serving in the store, and its diploma is equivalent to that awarded high school graduates. Every employee receives two weeks' vacation with full pay each summer. The management encourages young men to enter the militia. In short, conditions are such that a position with Marshall Field & Company is a coveted one.

Mr. Shedd is a director of several railroads and financial institutions. Nor has he shirked his civic responsibilities, although on this score he remarked: "It is unfortunate that under modern complex conditions it is so difficult for busy business men to take an adequate part in public and civic affairs. Any business that is left to run itself will run downhill. However, we have tried so to organize things that we have young men capable of relieving the older heads from the necessity of overworking. Whereas twenty years ago it would have been thought almost a crime to take an afternoon off, it is now feasible and not accounted foolish to ride into the country for an occasional game of golf." Incidentally, Mr. Shedd not only plays a good game of golf, but is an expert horseback rider and used to be an ardent cyclist before he took to automobiling.

Mr. Shedd's benefactions to the Chicago Y. M. C. A., to hospitals, and to other worthy causes have been substantial, but conducted so quietly that the general public usually have learned little about them —Mr. Shedd is extraordinarily quiet and unassuming. To his native town, Alstead, he has donated and endowed a library built of New Hampshire granite, a gift partly inspired by the recollection of the difficulty he experienced when a boy in securing good books, of which he was then and is still fond.

Mr. Shedd did not get married until he had made his way in the world and until he had wisdom enough to select a suitable life-partner. He married Miss Mary R. Porter of his home town of Alstead, in 1878, and although they have no sons, they have what they call "the next best thing," two sons-in-law, their two daughters being now Mrs. Laura Shedd Schweppe of Chicago and Lake Forest, Illinois, and Mrs. Helen Shedd Reed of Chicago. The Shedd home in Chicago is greatly admired by students of architecture.

"I have often wondered why you have never sought to connect your name with the title of the firm," I told Mr. Shedd.

He replied: "I have always considered that any long-established institution such as our own, with a strong asset of good will, if continuously well managed, adds strength to its business each year by the continuity of style of its firm name, though the personnel of its ownership may have changed completely."

Have you not noticed that the men who have done most are often the least vain-glorious?

EDWARD C. SIMMONS

"DON'T you want a boy?"
"What can you do, my lad?"
"I can do as much as any other boy of my age—where shall I hang my hat?"
"Well, my boy, if you work as quickly as you talk, we can use you."

The boy was Edward C. Simmons; the place, a hardware store in St. Louis; the time, the last day of 1855.

The boy *did* work—worked so effectively that he made St. Louis the greatest hardware centre on earth, doing more business than New York, Chicago, Philadelphia, and Boston combined; worked so successfully that his house now sells three axes, two pocket knives, and several saws *every minute* of the year, supplying not only the United States with hardware and cutlery formerly almost wholly imported from Europe, but in peace times disposing annually of thousands of dollars' worth in cutlery-manufacturing Britain, as well as in France, Germany, Russia, the Orient, Australia, South Africa, South America, and other civilized and semi-civilized parts of the globe; worked so intelligently that before many years passed he was employing more travelling salesmen than any other man in America; worked so efficiently that, to handle his output, there was erected, at his chief establishment, the greatest railroad traffic station of the kind ever conceived, capable of loading sixty cars at once.

The Bethlehem Steel Company is not more exclusively the product of Charles M. Schwab's energy and genius, and the Standard Oil Company is much less the fruit of John D. Rockefeller's individual efforts than the Simmons Hardware Company is the creation of one man, E. C. Simmons.

How did he do it?

He put himself—his personality—into the nursing and developing of the business. He infused humanness into all his activities and into all his salesmen. Among his co-workers he inspired love; among his customers, something beyond respect—affection, even.

Then, too, he had vision half a century ago, when vision was rare among American business men. He was clear-eyed enough to see the buyer's side of a transaction as well as the seller's, and to grasp the now-commonplace idea that a satisfied customer is the best asset. He was the first to teach the salesman not to let his interest in a customer stop with the question, "How many goods can I sell him?" but to do everything possible to contribute to that merchant's success and prosperity. Often Simmons men render invaluable services to retailers, especially those just starting in business. He originated the epigram: "A jobber's first duty is to help his customers to prosper," which has become a recognized principle of trade. He could foresee trends and tendencies of the future, and he was optimistic enough, alert enough, progressive enough to become a pioneer in blazing the new trails called for by the never-ceasing evolution of mankind and of business.

When I asked Mr. Simmons who could give me an insight into his early business methods—the laying of the foundation is always the part that most interests me, since it is usually the most illuminating—he referred me to, whom do you think?

A man who served in his employ for many years, *and then became one of his most aggressive and successful competitors!*

Any man who, near the close of life's day, can intrust the describing of his character, his methods, and his reputation to an old competitor, must surely have a clear conscience and a clean record.

Mr. Simmons has.

But don't jump at the idea that in the early days business morals and business practices were on as high a plane as they are to-day, or that Mr. Simmons was too sanctimonious, too punctilious, too highminded to enter the rough-and-tumble of the business fray, and play the game according to the rules then in force.

He was no mollycoddle. "Catch-as-catch-can" was the only motto or mode business then knew. Truthfulness, money-back-if-you're-not-satisfied, fair prices—such refinements of trade are modern. Mr. Simmons did his share in ushering them in a generation ago. His career covers both the old and the new era.

He was born in Frederick, Maryland, on September 21, 1839, of Philadelphia ancestors, and trekked to St. Louis when a young lad. He had a mania for pocket knives, and no friend or acquaintance had one that he had not examined minutely. So, when he was turned into the world, at sixteen, to look for a job, it was natural that he should apply at a store where they sold knives—that of Child, Pratt & Co.—where the colloquy which opens this article occurred. It was the largest wholesale hardware store in St. Louis, and his first weeks were devoted to taking all the goods from the shelves, dusting them, and putting them back again. His pay was $3 a week, or, to be exact, he served under a three-year agreement, calling for a salary of $150 the first year, $200 the second, and $300 the third. He did the dusting so thoroughly that the boss complimented him, and promoted him to be an errand boy. Every opportunity found him familiarizing himself with the stock. His love for pocket knives in particular, and cutlery in general, had thus early begun to pave the way for the Simmons Hardware Company, owners and operators of the largest pocket knife factory in the world.

By the time his apprenticeship ended he was able to command a better position with another firm, Wilson, Levering & Waters, his theory being that with this smaller house he could make his work and personality tell sooner and more effectively. He had not been there many weeks when this conservation occurred:

"Mr. Levering, will you please let me carry the store key?" This key, by the way, was one of the old-fashioned sort, nearly a foot long.

"What do you want to carry the key for?" demanded the boss gruffly.

"Because the porter doesn't come down early enough. I want to do more work."

"What time does the porter get down?"

"Half-past seven."

"What time do you want to get down?"

"Half-past six."

"Well, if you feel that way about it, you may carry the key—but you will soon get tired of it."

He didn't. Young Simmons had already sensed Opportunity. There were no salesmen in those days to go to buyers; buyers had to go to the sellers. Nor were there railroads. The boats on which merchants came to town landed at night, and the four principal hotels in St. Louis were all within three blocks of the store. The wide-awake young clerk, a very early riser himself, had noticed that country merchants, unable to sleep because of the city noises, often got up between five and six o'clock and walked around sight-seeing. Simmons figured that if he had the store open, some of them might drop in—and the early bird would catch the worm.

The very first morning a Missourian stopped to look at a pile of grindstones at the front door. Simmons went out and greeted him with an affable "Good-morning!" The Missourian was not averse to talking, and the enterprising young clerk diplomatically told him how this was the first morning of an experiment he had conceived and how anxious he was to make it a success.

Before the porter or any one else came to start work, Wilson, Levering & Waters had sold a sizable bill of goods to the Missourian—and they continued to sell him regularly for many years.

The sign over the door soon was changed to read: "Waters, Simmons & Company." From this grew the Simmons Hardware Company.

How the Simmons hardware business, starting humbly, has been built up to its present proportions, with buildings totalling enough to swallow up the great Singer Building of New York, is the main theme of this story.

Mr. Simmons early learned to handle both hardware and human hearts. He knew how to grapple both co-workers and customers to his heart "with hooks of steel." It was he who first introduced travelling salesmen in the business and for years he employed more than any other enterprise in the country—he now has over 500. How he has taught those salesmen; how he has fathered them, enthused them, developed them, and rewarded them, reflects his character and his genius.

He was and is an Optimist—with a capital O. He continually writes and sends out letters of encouragement and every week sends out a long personal chat to the whole force—the Simmons weekly letter was in reality the first "house magazine" in our annals. It breathes optimism; it sparkles with wit and wisdom; it provides "small talk" for salesmen to use when meeting buyers; it supplies selling arguments; it gives the men helpful advice on life and morals without ever savouring of goody-goodyism; it is never a cold business document, but a delightful letter from home, a welcome, cheering message from a large-hearted father who is seeking to aid his sons in making their way in the world.

"How we used to look forward to that weekly letter," one of the veteran ex-salesmen told me. "It did more than Mr. Simmons can ever know to keep some of us straight when we were away from home for six months or even a year at a stretch. A lot of us stopped drinking because of his advice to us. He also taught us that trickiness wouldn't last, and that honesty would win out every time.

"He stimulated us wonderfully. After the 1873 panic, trade went to pieces. We salesmen were disheartened; we felt like giving up trying to do business. I well remember how Mr. Simmons, in his letters, related to us the old story of the two frogs that fell into a basin of milk and couldn't climb out, and how one gave up trying and was drowned, but the other kept on kicking and trying until its efforts churned the milk into butter and enabled it to jump up without any more difficulty! That put heart into every one of us.

"Every Christmas he had us all at dinner at his home—there were nearer fifty than 500 of us then—and this also helped to bind us close to him. He never did the 'boss' act; he was just one of us, our elder brother, anxious to help us to get on."

His salesmen keep Mr. Simmons informed of what is going on among customers. A death has always brought from him a letter that was not a formality, but a genuine message straight from the heart, Mr. Simmons being one of the best of letter-writers. He has always found time for acts of thoughtfulness, largely because he has been, as he says, "an early riser," a pointer that he would pass on with cordial endorsement to all who aspire to success in any field.

In former times, when it was the custom of merchants to go to St. Louis regularly to buy their season's supplies, Mr. Simmons personally welcomed them to the Simmons Hardware Company, and always showed them appropriate kindnesses. His desk was kept full of acceptable little gifts, often novelties brought from Paris and other European cities. On rising to go, a visitor was often handed a souvenir—and on opening it when he got home would be astounded to find his name engraved on it. Mr. Simmons had quietly written the visitor's name on a slip of paper, with other necessary instructions, and the work was done while the conversation was going on. That never failed to make a hit. To this day he spends much thought on the art of how best to entertain visiting merchants; he knows the likes, the tastes, and the interests of most of them, and he sees to it that their stay is made congenial, helpful, and in a sense, educative. They enjoy "a feast of reason and a flow of soul" rather than the kind of feasts and flows buyers are too often treated to. He is, incidentally, a good listener.

Profit sharing was introduced, too, by Mr. Simmons long before it was thought of by others. Every salesman brought his record to him at the end of each year, and a generous percentage of the total sales was awarded him. Every salesman's record is carefully gone over at the end of the year with a view to finding in his results something to warrant extra compensation, "Velvet," as the salesmen call it. "My Velvet was nearly as much as my salary for the first year on the road," one old employee confided to me. "I was flabbergasted —but more than ever determined to deserve the Chief's generosity."

To facilitate his profit-sharing system, Mr. Simmons incorporated his business in 1874. It was *the first mercantile firm in the United States to incorporate*. Employees were given opportunity to acquire stock and this proved extraordinarily profitable. The original capital of $200,000 was increased to $4,500,000, and later to $6,000,000, wholly from earnings—a record which even the strongest bank in the country might envy.

Mr. Simmons's solicitude for the welfare of his men and his customers also led him to become a pioneer in another direction. He was the first to develop the system of having travelling salesmen live in their territory, settle there, and become a part of the community, instead of spending year after year as nomads. Merchants had more confidence in dealing with a fellow-citizen than with a salesman whom they could not know well and who was there to-day and gone to-morrow.

From this evolved the Simmons system of to-day, the most elaborate and efficient ever devised, of dividing the whole country into districts, and having in each of them resident salesmen acquainted intimately with conditions. At headquarters is a sales manager for each district, a man who knows the needs of the merchants in his section and who speaks their language. He is there ready to extend them a personal welcome when they come to market and to take care of their orders which come in by mail.

So familiar are the Simmons salesmen with agricultural, industrial, and social conditions in their territory that their periodic reports on crops, trade, political trends, etc., when summarized, give the very best cue obtainable anywhere of just what is what throughout the country.

In the office of the president in St. Louis hangs a huge map of the United States, dotted with coloured disks; in the centre of each is the photograph of the salesman, the position of the disk indicating where the salesman is travelling, the colour of the disk indicating which one of the Simmons houses he travels from, and an arrow back of the disk indicates by its colour and direction what that salesman is accomplishing by comparison with his previous record. This map thus tells the whole story at a glance. System has been developed by this organization to the *nth* power.

Initiative is persistently encouraged. The founder often allowed men to try out ideas which he himself didn't think would work. "I don't quite agree with you, but go ahead; you may be right and I wrong," he would tell them and would then loyally coöperate to make the innovation a success. And he never failed to pay well for results.

Thirty-seven years ago Mr. Simmons had the courage to spend $30,000 in bringing out the first complete hardware catalogue ever compiled, and as a result added $1,000,000 to his sales forthwith. Now the house issues annually a catalogue of 2,500 pages, 22,000 illustrations, and 70,000 items, with minute specifications, descriptions, and prices, so that every retailer in the land can provide his patrons with any article from the whole line on short notice.

Promptness is such a fetich with Mr. Simmons that he wants all orders billed and shipped the day they are received, and to that end every available modern contrivance and device is utilized, from machines for opening and sealing envelopes down to mechanical conveyers for transferring the cases of merchandise from the packing room to the railroad freight station within the building. Indeed, it was primarily to insure expeditious deliveries, and thus enable their customers to compete successfully with the mail order houses, that the Simmons Hardware Company established complete wholesale houses, similar to that in St. Louis, in such distributing centres as Philadelphia, Minneapolis, Sioux City, Toledo, and Wichita.

Finding that he could not buy certain goods of the high quality he desired, Mr. Simmons, in 1870, inaugurated the idea of manufacturing a complete line of tools of the highest quality, all under one brand, adopting as his trade-mark, "*Keen Kutter*," now known over the whole earth.

Before then there was much flim-flamming in the hardware business, articles of inferior quality being more common than those of merit. The step Mr. Simmons then took was epochal; it led to the revolutionizing of the whole trade and instilled confidence in honest merchandising.

A manufacturer offered Mr. Simmons axes which were not of top-notch quality, but objections were met with the curt reply: "You'll have to buy them; you can't get anything else." Mr. Simmons didn't relish being cornered. He had, and has, a habit of doing much of his thinking in bed.

"That night," he relates, "I got out of bed, whittled a nice model axe-head out of wood, and wrote on it in pencil: 'E. C. Simmons Keen Kutter.' That was the origin of our trade-mark and our quality policy—the ideas on which our house has been built."

The registered motto, as most of us now know, is: "The Recollection of *Quality* Remains Long After the *Price* Is Forgotten." It took courage and unflagging determination to introduce such a high-grade and necessarily higher-priced line of goods, but Mr. Simmons won out. "Wisdom is justified of her children," as he sometimes remarks. He decided to build on a rock, not on sand.

I had hoped to give many of Mr. Simmons's business epigrams and mottoes, since they throw light on his successful methods. There is space for only a few:

"Business is the execution of ideas."

"Promptness is the essence of all good business."

"The difference between failure and success is doing a thing nearly right and doing it exactly right."

"Concentration means strength. Scatteration means weakness. Having chosen one line of work or business, stick to it."

"Spend fifteen minutes every night recounting your day's doings and planning to do better next morning."

"Always put yourself in your customer's place."

"An ounce of industry is worth a pound of brains."

"Character is the decisive force in business."

"My favourite pleasure has been to take hold of a poor salesman and make him a 'Cracker-Jack,' a 'Star.'"

"I am a great believer in the business philosophy of encouragement."

"Settle claims promptly. The merchant who does not permit himself to be imposed upon occasionally will never get far."

"If any of your men, or any customer, gets into a hole, always leave him a loophole to get out easily."

"Quality of goods, confidence in your business and in yourself, ability and readiness to anticipate conditions and to adapt yourself to them—these are some of the essentials of business success."

Most of our self-made men who have sons following them in the business remain as head of their business as long as they are physically and mentally able to do it. Not so with E. C. Simmons, who retired from the active management of his great organization in 1897, handing it over to his three capable sons—Wallace D. Simmons, who succeeded him as president, Edward H. Simmons and George W. Simmons, vice-presidents—while he was yet in his prime and able to give them his advice and coöperation. However, he is still very much "on the job," in an advisory capacity, for, as he recently remarked:

"I love to work and I work because I love it, and because it gives me an opportunity to teach others to learn quickly what it has taken me sixty years to learn."

Edward C. Simmons started, and his sons are still building, a monument to him which has done and is doing much for the country and its development. While the cost of living has soared, the cost of hardware within his time has been greatly reduced. He has done more than any other living man to bring this about, thus benefiting all the people and particularly thousands of his friends among the retail hardware merchants who look upon his counsel and advice as upon a guiding star.

They are using daily in the conduct of their business the principles which he has taught them as well as the facilities which he has created for the better and more economical handling of a complicated line of goods, the benefit of it all inuring, of course, to the ultimate users of them, including the ordinary householder.

His love of humanity and desire to help others he has put into practical form and we are all benefiting by it in our daily life.

JAMES SPEYER

THE toastmaster was presenting James Speyer, the international banker and public-spirited citizen of New York. He dwelt upon the courageous part played by the firm of Speyer & Company, their European houses, and the young financier in supplying Collis P. Huntington with many millions of dollars to fructify our Western Empire by traversing it with the daring Central Pacific and Southern Pacific railroads. He recalled how Speyer and his associates had loosened European purse-strings and poured capital into the development of this youthful country. He commented upon the Speyers' century-old reputation for protecting clients. He eulogized Mr. Speyer's civic and public welfare activities, and finished with an eloquent peroration on Mr. Speyer's innate democracy and human sympathy.

"Your toastmaster, though he gave me far more credit than I deserve, forgot to mention the wisest thing I ever did," Mr. Speyer, on rising, protested.

Everybody stared. Most of them thought the introduction had covered the ground fairly well.

"The wisest thing I ever did," Mr. Speyer resumed with a twinkle, "was to choose New York for my birthplace."

Then Mr. Speyer went on to tell the story of an American from the West travelling for the first time in Europe, who was riding on a coach to Versailles with a number of Englishmen and who was so anxious to let everybody know he was an American that he pulled an American flag from his pocket and spread it over his knees. A peppery Englishman sitting opposite became so annoyed that he caustically remarked, loud enough for every one to hear: "Some people seem to be awfully proud because they happen to have been born in a particular country." Quick as a flash the American answered: "I am not particularly proud because I was born in the United States, but I am mighty sorry for anybody that ain't."

Concerns in this country begin to boast of their venerable age when they reach the quarter-century mark. The Speyers began to make a reputation in Frankfort-on-Main generations ago. By the seventeenth century one of James Speyer's great-grandfathers was quite a figure, while in the following century history records that the Imperial Court Banker Isaac Michael Speyer was seized by the French as a hostage to guarantee the payment of a war tax levied on the people of the free city of Frankfort-on-Main.

The Speyers caught the philanthropic spirit before the founding of the American Republic. Frankfort still has charitable establishments which were named after Speyers of the eighteenth century. This long record has not been broken; recently members of the Speyer family left several million dollars for educational and scientific purposes. Finance and philanthropy were thus bred in James Speyer's bones and blood.

"Does money insure happiness? Is the life of a philanthropist a happy one?" I asked Mr. Speyer.

"Whatever you do, don't call me a 'philanthropist' or any such name," Mr. Speyer replied vigorously. "There are millions of men and women in this country who are doing just as much, indeed a great deal more, proportionately, than we are, and I am sure they get as much happiness and satisfaction out of it. One great—perhaps the greatest—advantage possessed by people who have a competence and who have more money than they care to spend on themselves, is that they have the spare time and money to devote to other purposes. Whatever I may have done in this respect is largely due to the inspiration and example of my wife."

Mrs. Speyer, as all the world knows, gives not only money, but herself freely to worthy causes. Her sympathies and activities go out, not only to children, to the poor, to the unemployed, and other unfortunate human beings, but extend to dumb animals, for which, as President of the New York Women's League for Animals, she was instrumental in founding an Animal Hospital, where many a poor man has had doctored the horse that meant the main source of his family's bread and butter.

James Speyer has the most democratic ideals of any man of hereditary wealth I have ever known. He abhors everything savouring of pretense and cant and hypocrisy. His championship of labour at times has shocked some Wall Street magnates. His outspoken attitude toward autocratically inclined, narrow-minded leaders has often elicited frowns.

But events have abundantly justified the wisdom of his stand. His convictions were born, not of any cheap desire to pose as a friend of labour, but of deep insight and unusual foresight; he can understand and gauge human nature better than some of his fellows; his vision is broad enough to see both sides of a question, and his inborn sense of justice has impelled him to come out boldly for what he has seen to be right and fair. For example, he urged the railroads not to fight Federal supervision when the Interstate Commerce Commission was being formed. He favoured postal savings banks and also the parcel post, as he believed both would benefit the whole country and every one in it.

In 1915 he gave a practical demonstration of his democracy, of his readiness to rub shoulders with all classes of his fellow-citizens, by doing military duty at Plattsburg as a plain trooper—at the cost of not a little sweat, as the newspaper correspondents were fond of recording after Speyer returned at nightfall from some particularly arduous day's work. He believes in universal military service as a great unifying force for our citizenship and endorses General Wood's statement that "equality of opportunity means equality of obligation."

Mr. Speyer does not believe in American High Finance holding itself in icy isolation, for in his conception the banker is a semi-public servant. Nor does he believe that publicity, of which he was an early and ardent advocate, is enough. He believes, above everything else, in drawing the so-called masses and the so-called classes together, in promoting mutual understanding by mingling with one another, getting to know one another and learning one another's point of view. Almost every one of his endeavours has been inspired by this central, dominating idea of drawing together the rich and the poor, the educated and the uneducated, foreigners and Americans.

"People need to know and understand one another to be able to see correctly and sympathize with one another's conditions and aims," said Mr. Speyer in an address at the University Settlement. "A famous Frenchman has said *"Tout comprendre c'est tout pardonner,"* meaning that to understand everything is to forgive everything. When you fully understand another person's mind, and the circumstances and conditions that led to the moulding of his opinions, you are less likely to condemn him than you are to sympathize with his feelings, even though you may have to differ from some of his conclusions. Strife is usually based on misunderstanding."

New Yorkers, especially New York financiers, have kept themselves aloof from the people too much, Mr. Speyer feels. He thinks that railroad directors, for example, should make a point of visiting the territories covered by the roads. When the Baltimore & Ohio directors met in Baltimore not so long ago they were entertained by prominent citizens at dinner and, when called upon to speak, Mr. Speyer said, among other things:

"We realize that we who live in New York are in a sense provincial because we do not travel enough and do not see enough for ourselves of our country and of the men and women who live in it. Unhappily there exists an erroneous impression about New York and there is ignorance among New Yorkers about other parts of the country. This can best be dispelled by visits such as we are paying you. With all due modesty I feel that when Americans outside of New York know us better by personal acquaintance, they will find we have no horns or hoofs and that even that much-maligned animal, the New York banker, has very much the same aspirations, the same heart and feeling as every other American has."

The Speyer School, presented to Teachers' College in 1902, was the first practical plan in this country to link up settlement work with teaching and make the schoolhouse the social centre of its neighbourhood. The University Settlement Society, which Mr. Speyer helped to organize in 1891, was the very first settlement established here—its aim, of course, was to draw together different classes so as to help all. The same idea underlay the organization of the Provident Loan Society in 1894. Mr. Speyer helped to raise the first $100,000 for it and is now its president. This society has a working capital of over $11,000,000 and has made loans, averaging $33, to more than 5,500,000 people, the total amount loaned reaching $185,000,000 since its foundation.

It was Mr. Speyer who founded the Roosevelt exchange professorship with Germany twelve years ago, also with a view to furthering international amity and comprehension. Later he provided funds to maintain the American Institute in Berlin to act as guide, philosopher, and friend to American students in Germany and German students in the United States.

Mr. Speyer's active interest in such organizations as the American Museum of Safety, the National Civic Federation and the Economic Club (of which he was president) is prompted by the usefulness of such bodies in drawing labour and capital closer, thus enabling each to get a more adequate conception of the other.

James Speyer did not find his wife in the gilded halls of plutocratic aristocracy; he married Ellin L. Lowery, *née* Prince, of old American stock, who at that time was conducting a tea room in New York. A niece of William R. Travis, the celebrated wit, her brilliancy, her ready humour, and her kind heart for all, won Mr. Speyer. Before then she had, among other social services, taken a foremost part in organizing and helping working girls' clubs. For years Mrs. Speyer has been one of the most popular women in New York.

It was the larger measure of freedom, the freer play of democracy, and the greater degree of opportunity and equality to be found in the United States than in Germany which determined Mr. Speyer to return to this republic and spend his life here after having been brought up in Germany from his third to his twenty-fourth year. The founder of the Speyer banking house in the United States was Phillip Speyer, who came to New York in 1837 and was later joined by his brother Gustavus Speyer, father of James Speyer. When the war between the States broke out and dire need arose for raising war funds, Phillip Speyer & Company, unlike the Rothschilds, enthusiastically threw in their lot with the North and rendered invaluable service in opening up a market in Europe for United States Government bonds, a stroke which combined patriotism with great profit to the firm and to its large following of clients abroad—the firm purchased bonds at as low as thirty-six cents on the dollar (allowing for the depreciated currency) which were later redeemed at par. It was at this time, 1861, that James Speyer was born, in New York City. He was educated in Frankfort and thereafter received a thorough training in international banking in both London and Paris as well as in the historic banking house of the Speyer family in his ancestral town.

Although his parents had returned to Germany and it was taken for granted that James would remain at home, he made up his mind that he would rather live under the Stars and Stripes, as his father had been a staunch American till his end. When twenty-three he set sail for America, joined Speyer & Company in New York and, soon became its head.

He brought his nerve with him. At first New York's heavyweight financiers took little or no note of the beardless youth. They regarded him merely as a rich man's son, under no necessity to work to add to his fortune, and unacquainted with the intricacies of American finances. The principal figures then in the financial limelight were J. P. Morgan and Jay Gould, with James J. Hill and Collis P. Huntington, the great railroad builders, forging toward the front, although the latter had no general financial backing.

Jay Gould was astonished one morning by a visit from one who looked a mere boy. The visitor, however, had painstakingly drawn up a plan for the reorganization of the St. Louis & Southwestern, then in trouble. Jay Gould controlled the junior securities, but Speyer & Company had been selected as members of a committee to protect the first mortgage bonds held in Germany. The doughty veteran had more respect for his youthful visitor before the interview was over. To make a long story short, Speyer's plan was taken up and finally adopted, the terms, incidentally, being entirely satisfactory to the young banker's clients.

Huntington quickly recognized the young man's ability and industry. The newcomer meanwhile had concluded that Huntington personally and his Southern Pacific and Central Pacific railroads were well worthy of continued financial and moral support. The two men became close friends and co-workers. Millions of dollars were brought by the Speyers not only from Germany, but from their Amsterdam and London affiliations, to be poured into the Huntington properties to put them on a solid financial footing and to meet their indebtedness to the Government in full, a piece of financing that was regarded as remarkable at that time. Union Pacific was then apparently trying to compromise its debt to the U. S. Government, but the Speyers and C. P. Huntington were determined that Central Pacific should pay in full.

President McKinley had been placed by Congress at the head of a commission to settle these railroad debts, and Speyer assured him that the Central Pacific would arrange a full settlement. So many threads had to be taken up in America and Europe that the agreement, which had to get the formal signature of the President by a certain date, was not ready until the last moment. Mr. Speyer, the instant everything was finished, started for Washington with the papers—he was taking no chances of a slip-up. A snow storm burst with great fury while he was on the way and his train was stalled for what seemed to him an eternity. After overcoming considerable difficulties, he reached the capital in the nick of time.

To his courage Mr. Speyer linked judgment. His command of foreign capital enabled him to do so much for the development of American transportation facilities that Speyer & Company soon became recognized as one of the three most influential international banking firms in the country.

"Stand by your clients," Mr. Speyer had had inculcated into him as the family motto. When B. & O. defaulted in 1896, Speyer & Company introduced a new policy in American banking by offering to buy the coupons on an issue they had sold, an example since followed by other high-grade issuing houses. In later times, when, partly because of hasty legislation and regulation, misfortune after misfortune overtook American railroads, driving one-sixth of the country's entire mileage into bankruptcy, Speyer & Company left no stone unturned to safeguard the interests of those who had entrusted them with investment funds and finally secured successful results.

"Jimmy" Speyer, as he is called by his friends, is an optimist. He believes in his fellowmen and in the future of his country. At times when many of his brother-bankers—on account of such things as the free silver agitation and hostile legislation and rulings against railroad and other corporations—were depressed and despairing of the future, Mr. Speyer remained confident. As president of the Economic Club, in 1912, in a debate on "Are Our Railroads Fairly Treated?" he said:

"The American peoople love fair play and want to be fair. Let them know all the facts, and I am convinced we can safely trust their judgment and sense of honour to do the right and fair thing in the end. They always have done it, and they will also do so in this case."

When occasion arose, he was eager to do his share in putting the facts before the public and its representatives.

For instance, when the St. Louis & San Francisco Railroad joined the nation-wide procession to the bankruptcy court, Mr. Speyer was so bent upon receiving fair treatment for investors that he abandoned his annual holiday and personally appeared before the Missouri Railroad Commission and fought for a square deal—fought so successfully that his bondholders have emerged from the trouble unscathed. Also, when reflections were cast upon certain actions of Speyer & Company in connection with the Rock Island case, Mr. Speyer went direct to Washington, insisted on appearing before the Interstate Commerce Commission, and disproved convincingly all aspersions concerning his firm.

Mr. Speyer does not look for, but is not afraid of, a fight, no matter how powerful his antagonist, when the interests of his clients are at stake. He holds that it is most unwise for bankers or others in a position of trust not to repudiate unjust attacks even though "dignity" might sometimes suggest remaining silent. But while he takes his responsibilities and duties very seriously, he is noted for his good humour and for his knack of overcoming threatened deadlocks or squabbles by cracking a joke or dropping some pointed witticism.

It is recorded that at one very important conference over a proposed deal, much was being said by the other side regarding the desirability of "harmony." The terms outlined, however, were not favourable to the interests of Speyer's clients. So when he was asked for his opinion he replied that he would favour "harmony" only after the "harm" had been taken out of it!

Speyer & Company have been and are international bankers in the fullest sense of the term. They took a lead in financing South American projects, both in Bolivia and Ecuador; they provided the Mexican Government, when under Diaz and Limantour, with many millions of dollars to build railroads in that potentially rich but politically unfortunate country; they financed the Philippine Railway construction in 1906 when Mr. Roosevelt was President and Mr. Taft Secretary of War, and later carried through the sale of these railways to the Philippine Government. They also took the first $35,000,000 loan to establish the credit of the new Republic of Cuba.

It was with capital raised by the Speyers that London's underground railway system has been revolutionized. Sir Edgar Speyer, brother of the American head of the family, was the financial power behind this colossal undertaking and became chairman of the whole enterprise. When the problem arose of finding a practical man of sufficient calibre to handle so intricate and extensive a project, James Speyer cabled that he, through one of his Cleveland friends, knew the right man.

JAMES SPEYER

This man was finally accepted by the London directors. He was none other than Albert Stanley, formerly manager of the Detroit Street Railways and subsequently manager of the New Jersey Public Service Corporation, who is now Sir Albert Stanley and one of Lloyd George's right-hand aides as Minister of Commerce and President of the Board of Trade in the British Cabinet. Mr. Speyer is proud of this "find."

As in his charity Mr. Speyer knows no difference in race, creed, or colour, so in politics he is distinctly non-partisan, independent. He was vice-president and treasurer of the German-American Reform Union in the Cleveland campaign of 1892, was a Chamber of Commerce delegate to the Indianapolis Sound Money Conference in 1898, was a charter member of the Citizens' Union, was an active member of the Executive Committee of Seventy which routed Tammany Hall, and was a member of the Board of Education in New York City under Mayor Strong.

For the last twenty years he has held no political office, but has preferred to devote much of his time to educational and other semi-public work. At their modest but beautifully situated country home, near Scarborough-on-the-Hudson, Mr. and Mrs. Speyer frequently entertain groups of working girls, educational associations and others active in the service of humanity—Mrs. Speyer's interest in such work having been redoubled by her illuminating experience as chairman of the Women's Section of Mayor Mitchel's Unemployment Committee in the winter of 1914-1915.

Speyer & Company was the first private banking house in New York to adopt a pension fund for its employees. To get into the Speyer office is the ambition of half the workers in the financial district—especially in these days of high living cost. Perhaps the fact that Mr. Speyer sits in the same chair that was used by his father has something to do with his consideration for his workers! The Speyer building, the first low office building in New York, is an architectural gem; it is modelled after the old Pandolfini Palace in Florence, designed by Raphael.

In the Speyer home on Fifth Avenue are some fine paintings. But there is one, perhaps the least artistic of them all, which is held in special regard. It is a portrait of Mr. Speyer painted, not by a great master, but by an East Side boy who was attending the art class at the Eldridge Street University Settlement, and presented to Mr. Speyer in commemoration of the rounding out of twenty years' service by him on behalf of the institution and its humble aspirants for knowledge.

JAMES STILLMAN

"MONSIEUR BONBON" is known by many children in Europe, especially in Southern France. He is the children's friend. His mission is to make children happy.

He is an ardent motorist. But his enjoyment in motoring is greatly enhanced by scattering joy among juvenile hearts as he rides along. His car is especially fitted up for this purpose. It has a stand on which is a large basket. This is daily filled with specially made Parisian bonbons of the purest quality. There is also room for other little gifts and many of them.

When "Monsieur Bonbon's" automobile is espied coming along the road, the village children on the Riviera shout with glee. The car stops, and Monsieur Bonbon lavishes upon them his good things —"*papillotes*," the little ones call the candy.

Sometimes children in remote parts, to whom "Monsieur Bonbon's" automobile is not familiar, do not understand when the stranger stops and hands them pretty gifts. They cannot analyze the motives of a stranger in lavishing upon them *papillotes* and other gifts. They receive a glimpse, wonderingly, of a new phase of life.

The curés, the school teachers, and the parents of many hamlets know "Monsieur Bonbon" and seek occasion to express their gratitude for the sunshine he brings into so many sombre young lives.

"Monsieur Bonbon" is not a Frenchman; he is an American. "Monsieur Bonbon" is James Stillman, for years the most powerful national banker in America, the builder of the City Bank's Gibraltar-like foundations, the coöperator with Morgan in ushering in a new era of big business and a power second only to Morgan in shaping the financial destinies of the United States during the last years of the nineteenth and the first decade of the twentieth century.

The American public have never looked upon James Stillman as a man of sentiment, as a man given to finding his chief delight in making thousands of little children happy, or even as a man planning and plodding mainly for patriotic motives to raise his bank and his native country to the very forefront of the financial and commercial nations of the earth. Mr. Stillman has been regarded by those not knowing him personally as cold, austere, unbending, uninterested in social activities, unnoted for philanthropy, bent solely on money-making.

But the truth is I have rarely met a man more animated and moved

JAMES STILLMAN

by sentiment, by a desire to achieve things less for the sake of his own pocket than for the upbuilding of his country and her institutions. I know no one who has sought so assiduously to efface self and give credit to those about him.

Indeed, the public's misconception of Mr. Stillman has been born largely by this policy of shunning the limelight, of evading publicity of every sort, and working always unostentatiously, unspectacularly, silently. That was his policy all through his active career and he has not modified it since he handed over the presidency of the National City Bank in 1909 to Frank A. Vanderlip, selected by Mr. Stillman as a vice-president several years before.

"Mr. Stillman wore a shell during business hours," declares one of his veteran associates. "His austerity, his apparent coldness, his reserve, his exclusiveness then seemed necessary. If he had kept open door and open house he would not have had time for the great constructive work in which he was engaged. The real Stillman was a very different being. He was a delightful companion. When off the business chain, he would unbend like a schoolboy. Instead of being stony-hearted as some of the public imagined, he was continually doing thoughtful things for others. He was always helping young people, but he did it so quietly that nobody knew anything about it."

It seemed such a pity that a man of Mr. Stillman's extraordinary achievements should be content to close his business career without affording the public some adequate opportunity of becoming acquainted with his real self and his real character, the heart that beats beneath the shell which it was considered necessary to wear for business purposes.

When I sought to persuade Mr. Stillman that he ought to throw off this business mask and let the public know him as I know him, he replied:

"I am willing to let my work speak for itself. I died, in a business sense, eight years ago and now am no longer an object of public interest. The men to write about are those who are in the thick of the fight. I am no longer an active worker; my sole desire is to give those who are following me the benefit of my experience whenever they feel they want my advice."

Finally I persuaded Mr. Stillman to talk a little.

"My conception of banking is that a bank's resources should be handled as a general handles his soldiers," he replied to my questioning. "You must be strong in reserves. You must be ready to send reinforcements wherever needed. You must send your soldier-dollars wherever they can do most good.

"A bank is to a country what the heart is to the body. It must pump the money through the commercial arteries, causing the whole body to function effectively. As the body depends on the proper working of the heart, so the business of a country depends upon the proper working of the banks.

"I do not regard banking lightly. I do not regard it solely as a mere means of making money. I regard it as something essential to the well-being of the people and the prosperity of the country."

The great industrial developments of the last quarter century and the place the United States was destined to fill in international financial and commercial affairs were foreseen by Mr. Stillman. He inaugurated a new era in banking.

When other important banks were reducing their capitals, President Stillman boldly increased the National City's capital, first from $1,000,000 to $10,000,000, in 1900, and then to $25,000,000 two years later. Without big banks there could be no big business. Banks with trifling capitals were not in keeping with billion-dollar corporations.

Stillman's daring action startled the banking community. Other bankers could not see that an industrial and financial revolution was coming. Stillman had prescience, vision, and judgment beyond any banking competitor. He discerned that gigantic business organizations demanded banks of commensurate size. There must be bank pillars strong enough to support the industrial structure.

The Stillman lead was, of course, followed by others. Instead of reducing their capitals, first one bank and then another increased them.

Stillman's master-stroke, combined with his unmatched capitalistic and business connections, placed his institution far in the forefront. Whereas it was not half the size of several other banks when Mr. Stillman took hold—its deposits in 1891 being only $12,000,000—in two years it was the largest bank in New York with over $30,000,000 deposits. The 1893 panic, in common with every other panic, sent many depositors to the City Bank, for in times of storm business interests felt it would be wise to have money there rather than in some institution of less standing and stability. Mr. Stillman had his own clear-cut, well-matured ideas of how a bank should be conducted. One basic idea was that a bank should, above all else, be strong; that it should carry, not the minimum reserve prescribed by law, but a stock of gold that would make it impregnable.

"A bank is nothing but a bundle of debts," he used to impress upon his colleagues. As soon as he had time to find himself in the presidential chair he began filling the bank's vault with gold. When other institutions were shipping gold to London in 1893, the City Bank paid a premium to bring gold across the Atlantic. In one year he increased the institution's stock of the yellow metal from less than

$2,000,000 to above $8,000,000. The 1893 panic, therefore, found the City Bank strong as a rock. By 1897 its deposits had reached $90,000,000, a new high record for the United States.

Mr. Stillman was developing into a banker-statesman. Not content to handle the most important transactions of his own country, he cast his eyes abroad. Why not have the National City Bank extend its activities to other lands? Branches could not be established because of the provisions of the National Bank Act, but influential connections could be made in the important countries of the world.

"What we now see taking concrete shape was foreseen and planned by Mr. Stillman in the late nineties," one of his veteran colleagues informed me. "He foresaw that this great country, with its vast resources, its matchless energy, and its unlimited ambitions, was destined to become one of the greatest financial centres on the face of the earth. He saw that commerce was to become more and more international. The foundation was then laid for the enormous international superstructure now being erected by the City Bank and its allied organizations.

"He also realized that the day of huge combinations and corporations was at hand, and that larger banks than any then existing would be necessary to cope with the evolution."

Hence Mr. Stillman's decision to increase the bank's capital beyond anything previously conceived. Hence, also, his policy of maintaining a gold reserve as high as 40 per cent. at times, despite protests that the carrying of so enormous a mass of idle money inordinately reduced profits and dividends, for metal locked in a vault, instead of increasing earnings, was carried at a loss. Mr. Stillman, however, was building for the future. His duty, as he saw it, was to lay foundations whereon could be built the structure he foresaw. His motto was not "Make money," but "Build safely and strongly; look always to the future."

One of Wall Street's sayings is, "Stillman refused more loans than any other banker who ever lived." He could conscientiously refuse to help other concerns to go deeper into debt since he had set an admirable example by raising the capital and surplus of his own institution to $40,000,000.

"What you need is more capital, not more debts," he told many a merchant and manufacturer who wanted to over-extend.

During his active banking career Stillman more than upheld the traditions of the old-fashioned banking type—not only in his social and professional deportment, but in the matter of brain-power, for the City Bank of to-day is largely a Vanderlip lighthouse built on strong rocks carefully selected and cemented by Stillman. In later years, however, Mr. Stillman has mellowed. Whereas he formerly inspired the respect of the bank's force, he now has won their affection. In commemoration of the bank's 100th anniversary, in 1912, he presented the City Bank Club with $100,000 and the directors added another $100,000.

Mr. Stillman was fitted for college with the expectation of studying medicine and following this as a profession, but his father's serious illness at the time obliged him to abandon the career of his choice, and he thereupon entered the mercantile office of his father's agents in New York City and rapidly became acquainted with his business affairs. In a very short time he and William Woodward, the junior partner in the firm, succeeded to the business. Before Mr. Woodward's death, in 1889, he and Mr. Stillman had agreed to retire from active business in the following year and Mr. Stillman carried out this resolution.

How Mr. Stillman came to be president of the City Bank is interesting.

Moses Taylor, in his day the foremost American shipowner and commercial power in New York, was president of the National City Bank, and he and Mr. Stillman's father had long been friends. The Stillman children very often used to hear the name "City Bank," and it filled them with wonder. When they wanted to play at keeping a "City Bank" their father had an ample assortment of toy City Bank money made for them. This money, which did duty for many juvenile storekeeping transactions, was withdrawn from circulation many, many years ago, but is still held as a reserve more precious than gold. The tin box, marked "City Bank," with its contents, is now one of the cherished possessions of James Stillman. Although the coins in it are only worth their weight in iron, they could not be bought for their weight in gold.

One of the biggest resolutions made by the boy Stillman was that one day when he was a man he would become a director of the City Bank. Not only did he attain this ambition before he was forty, but when forty-one he was made president of the bank.

Moses Taylor had been succeeded by his son-in-law, Percy R. Pyne, who soon found that in James Stillman the bank had secured a director of rare ability. When Mr. Pyne's health gave way, Mr. Stillman was prevailed upon to take an interest in the management of the bank. His fitness for this work was so conspicuous that, when Mr. Pyne died, the directors insisted that there was only one man to take the place.

Mr. Stillman had no aspirations to become a money king. He wanted rather to have leisure for travel, for art, and for the refinements and graces of life. He wanted to have time to live. As a strictly business proposition, the presidency of the National City Bank was a small thing for Mr. Stillman. He had already had a successful career as a merchant and possessed ample wealth.

But sentiment played its part. The boy Stillman loved to play with toy City Bank money and now the institution needed some one to guide its destinies and handle its real money. Both Mr. Taylor and Mr. Pyne had been almost like a father to him. So James Stillman, at personal cost and inconvenience, responded to sentiment.

His handling of National City Bank money has made history.

But it has not engrossed his whole time and attention. It is now fashionable for bankers to be farmers. Mr. Stillman is not a mushroom banker-farmer; a full generation ago he established a large dairy farm and has continued to run it ever since.

He was also a pioneer in yachting in this country. When some of those now most prominent in the New York Yacht Club were still in short trousers, Mr. Stillman was vice-commodore of the club, was captaining speedy yachts and was handling them with the skill of a veteran "salt." He is now among the senior members of a number of yacht clubs.

When bicycles appeared, Mr. Stillman became a devotee of that sport. Now he is an equally enthusiastic motorist.

Mr. Stillman's name never figures in society columns. Yet probably no living American banker has a larger circle of friends at home and abroad. His counsel is sought by prominent foreigners more often than the public could imagine.

Although he now spends part of each year in Europe, Mr. Stillman is intensely American. He is a loyal member of the Society of Cincinnati, both his paternal and maternal ancestors having served as officers in the War of the Revolution, a record of which he is proud.

Since the outbreak of the European war "Monsieur Bonbon" has not forsaken his little French friends. Instead of bonbons, he, in coöperation with the French authorities, instituted an elaborate plan whereby thousands of needy families have been helped financially. In 1917, President Poincaré announced that he had received a check from Mr. Stillman for a million francs ($200,000), to be used for the relief of children of members of the Legion of Honour claimed by the war. A little later Mr. Stillman headed, with a large check, a movement to raise another fund for the succour of war victims. He spent many months in France during 1917 doing everything within his power to aid the gallant Republic. On returning to New York he said of the French: "They will never be beaten. Such superb gallantry and *esprit de corps* can never be crushed."

"When you see what is being done in France," said Mr. Stillman, "you forget about yourself, you forget everything in a consuming desire to help, help, help."

But Mr. Stillman would not be drawn into any statement about his activities as "Monsieur Bonbon." When I questioned him he simply smiled and said:

"If I have ever neglected my business, it has been because of my love for children."

This is not all Mr. Stillman has done for France and its youth. Feeling that American architects had become the best in the world for modern requirements largely through the unlimited opportunities afforded them to study in Paris, Mr. Stillman, as a token of American appreciation and reciprocity, donated 500,000 francs as a fund for annual prizes for French students of architecture displaying the most promising genius. This little international act did not fail to reach the hearts of the French people. The name "James Stillman" has been engraved on the walls of the École des Beaux-Arts to go down to future generations.

Home students have not been forgotten by Mr. Stillman. Impressed by the fact that Harvard had no hospital accommodation for its thousands of students, years ago he gave the university an adequate hospital.

I asked Mr. Stillman what his many-sided career and his leisure for reflection had taught him of the philosophy of life.

"The elimination of self," he replied, "is one of the finest forms of philosophy and one of the greatest secrets of happiness."

THEODORE N. VAIL

THEODORE NEWTON VAIL is the man who has put all Americans—North, South, East, and West—on speaking terms.

It has cost much brain-sweat, foresight, imagination, enthusiasm, courage—and a billion dollars.

Nearly forty years ago, when Alexander Graham Bell's crude invention was but a toy, Vail conceived a picture of America cobwebbed with telephones, every citizen in telephonic communication with every other citizen no matter how remote.

In 1916 a great engineering association, instead of calling a national convention in one city, conducted its proceedings by telephone in a score of cities at once, a motion being proposed by one city, seconded by another, and adopted by all simultaneously!

Was ever youthful vision more gloriously fulfilled?

"Compared with what could have been achieved, very little has been achieved," was Mr. Vail's own comment when I remarked that his dream had come true. He doubtless had in mind the governmental shattering of one scheme referred to later.

"But *you* have accomplished a lot more than any other man in your line," I argued. "How did you succeed in doing so much more than the average man attains?"

"By never being unwilling, when young, to do another man's work, and then, when older, by never doing anything somebody else could do better for me. I was always fond enough of detail to master thoroughly what I was undertaking—and then hated detail enough not to bother with it when I got to the treatment of the general subject."

The United States has twice as many telephones as all the rest of the world. Our farmers alone have more than the entire population of England, France, or Germany.

Just what is the extent of the telephone business in this country?

To-day there are some 10,000,000 Bell telephones in the United States, or, roughly, one for every two families throughout the length and breadth of the land.

Between 26,000,000 and 27,000,000 telephone talks are held *every day*, or at the rate of 9,000,000,000—nine billion—a year.

The "American Tel. & Tel." has some 19,000,000 miles of wire, enough to stretch from the earth to the moon eighty times, enough to circle the earth 760 times, enough to string 5,500 wires between New York and San Francisco.

It has assets of over $1,000,000,000, making it one of America's two "billion-dollar" industrial corporations.

Its receipts pour in at the rate of $5,000,000 every week.

It pays dividends of well over half a million dollars weekly to over 100,000 stockholders, of whom one-third are Bell employees and one-half are women.

It has more than 150,000 employees and, with growing business, is swelling the number by one thousand a month.

The story of how Theodore N. Vail came to "enter into partnership with electricity" is inspiring to young America.

A father of Quaker descent and a mother of Dutch descent, both born in New Jersey, for generations the home of their ancestors, were temporarily residing in Carroll County, Ohio, when (July 16, 1845) a son was born to them. They called him Theodore Newton, his last name being Vail. Two years later they moved to their native state and lived there until 1866, when they settled in Iowa. Before leaving New Jersey the boy Vail had studied medicine with an uncle. After opening the farm in Iowa he left it to his brothers and followed Horace Greeley's "Go West, young man" advice. He wanted a bit of adventure and world knowledge. He had not as yet settled down to the hard realities of life.

While in Morristown, N. J., he had picked up telegraphy, an uncle, Alfred Vail, having been associated with and having financed F. S. B. Morse in the practical and mechanical development of the telegraph. The Union Pacific gave young Vail a start as agent and operator at a box-car station.

Before long he entered the railway mail service. It was not much of a "service" in those days. There was no real sorting system on the trains, no attempt to route letters direct to any but the larger cities, no schedule for making advantageous train connections. Sacks were dumped out unceremoniously here, there, and everywhere.

Vail set himself to devising a better system. He collected every time-table fact, studied every railroad connection, figured out the quickest routes to reach each place from every other place, and compiled a sort of railway mail guide. This enabled him to handle mail with a celerity never before known.

Incidents illumine characters and careers. A snowslide once blocked the line, and train after train had to pull up on either side. The order was given to transfer all passengers, baggage, and mail from one side of the barrier to the other, so that the trains could return, thus, in effect, overcoming the blockade. There were hundreds of mail sacks to pull or carry over the snow. It was technically the railroad men's duty to do the work. But they had their hands more than full. Vail suggested that the thirty or more mail clerks should get busy. They refused; it wasn't their job to tussle with cold, icy sacks over snow-piles. Vail started in and, with two or three willing helpers, did the whole work.

Washington spotted the young reformer. If he could so reorganize his local mail delivery, why couldn't he do as much for other parts of the country? To Washington he was summoned, as assistant superintendent of mail service, and so valuable did his work prove that, although the youngest officer in the service, he was shortly made general superintendent.

He recast the delivery service of the whole country. His reforms, however, cut into the revenues of certain railroads and the politicians got on his track. They wanted him to alter his schedules for the benefit of special interests. He told them he was working, not for the railroads, but for the Government and for the benefit of the public. This brought trouble.

Senator Beck of Kentucky, a strong-willed old Scot, had been particularly insistent in trying to browbeat Vail into altering his plans. But Vail stood by his guns. By and by an attempt was made in Congress to cut down the troublesome superintendent's travelling expenses and a bitter debate arose. Much to Vail's surprise, Senator Beck acknowledged that he had had an encounter with the young man, but had found him inflexible in doing his duty—and he voted in Vail's favour, helping to win the day.

Meanwhile, Inventor Bell and his chief sponsor, Gardiner G. Hubbard, his father-in-law, were meeting the fate of most pioneers. Their "toy" had been exhibited at the Centennial Exposition in Philadelphia and had afforded novel amusement; but when they sought to introduce it commercially they were ridiculed—the London *Times* called it "the latest American humbug." To make matters worse, the Western Union Telegraph Company, then one of the most powerful organizations in the country, began to fight them and thwart them at every turn, even going the length, finally, of establishing a rival telephone enterprise with the aid of an improved transmitter invented by Edison.

Hubbard wanted a fighter, a man of force, nerve, and brains. He knew Vail, and knew that Vail was the man he wanted.

"I gave up a $3,500 salary for no salary," Mr. Vail dryly remarked later. As general manager of the American Bell Telephone Company he was to get $5,000 when he could collect it—*which was seldom!*

Vail, an expert telegrapher, had unbounded faith in the telephone. He *knew* it could not only be used for local purposes, but that it would one day cover the entire Union. And he at once started working toward that end.

He early induced Charlie Glidden, of balloon fame, to build a line from Lowell to Boston.

"Let's build a line from Boston to Providence," he next suggested to his company. They laughed at him. It was a terrible struggle, but he went ahead.

The treasurer's records show such items as: "Lent Bell 50c; lent Vail 25c."

Alas! the line, when finally completed, would not, at first, work!

"Did you become discouraged?" I recently asked Mr. Vail, referring to those days.

"If I did," he replied with a significant smile, "I never let anybody know it."

Here is a sample of the spirit and foresight then animating the general manager of the Bell Telephone:

> "Tell our agents that we have a proposition on foot to connect the different cities for the purpose of personal communication and in other ways to organize a *grand telephone system*."

"Real difficulties can be overcome; it is only the imaginary ones that are unconquerable," he used to admonish faint-hearted colleagues.

A line from Boston to New York was Vail's next venture. A company, called the Governors' Company, was organized. It was composed of five governors and two laymen, but they became discouraged and the company took the line over. But it proved a success after the public realized just what the new venture meant in the way of convenience.

Before Vail took hold with his bulldog grip, the Bell people, in despair, had offered to sell out to the Western Union for $100,000. Now the Western Union were willing to pay $100,000 a year to get rid of Vail! They pulled wires to have alluring positions offered him by influential railroad companies. Vail, however, fought on. He stayed by the Bell Company until it conquered all obstacles, inspired confidence in itself and the usefulness of its service, and could command capital on reasonable terms to expand from city to city.

In 1887, having fought his fight and won, he bought a 200-acre farm in northern Vermont, where he planned to live when not enjoying travel, to which he looked forward.

His business career was to have ended then. But Mr. Vail's life was to consist of three chapters.

On a tour through South America he visited Buenos Aires, was struck with the possibilities of transforming its horse-car street railways into electric lines by utilizing water-power from newly constructed reservoirs, bought a broken-down but strategic line (one of a dozen then in operation), transformed it into a road as fine as anything in the States, bought in outdistanced lines at his own price, built up an elaborate traction system with the aid of American and, later, British capital—and made money.

As a side line he installed electric lighting and telephone systems in various cities.

His activities took him to Europe frequently. At one time he had business headquarters in London, although he contrived to spend many months in Paris and in Italy, both of which he found fascinating.

But rock-ribbed Vermont kept a-calling him. So he sold out his foreign interests for a handsome sum and, a second time, returned to Speedwell Farm (so named after his maternal ancestors), determined to devote the remainder of his days to scientific agriculture.

He added to his 200-acre farm until it became 6,000 acres and conducted his farming with all the zeal he had thrown into fighting the Bell telephone battles. He bred the finest horses, cattle, sheep, pigs, and poultry. He went in for the proper rotation of crops. He used fertilizers. In short, he became a model farmer on a huge scale, demonstrating that farming in the Green Mountain State could be made to pay.

Of greater moment, he taught other farmers how to get the most out of their soil. To aid in this work, he donated land to the State, reorganized the Lyndon Institute and organized the Lyndon School of Agriculture, supervised their equipment, took a very active part in developing them, and spent a large part of his time in furthering the welfare of the pupils and their parents. The purpose was and is to make good housewives of the girls and skilful farmers of the boys; also, to stimulate, by example, scientific, profitable farming.

To this tranquil, useful life, with his wife and only son, Theodore N. Vail retired.

Chapter III opened in May, 1907.

Financial rumblings were frightening bankers and business men in the spring of that fateful year. Capital was pulling into its shell, scenting over-expansion of credit. Stocks and bonds crumbled. New securities could not be sold. Public sentiment was antagonistic to Big Business.

The American Telephone & Telegraph Company was in a worse plight than most enterprises. Less competent rivals had raised such a noise that State legislatures were considering harassing laws, the Courts were inimical, and the Federal Government was being urged to either "bust" or take over the "Telephone Trust."

Where—to whom—could the directors turn?

There was one man, of course, who could deliver them out of all their troubles, but he had retired, was past sixty, did not need any more money, and was enjoying the peaceful life of a farmer.

They looked around everywhere. Nobody else was in sight.

In desperation a delegation of directors journeyed to Lyndon, Vt. They found a modern Cincinnatus engrossed in his spring plowing. They appealed to him to come and save the company he had given his best years to build up. The welfare of the nation was likewise at stake, they urged.

The veteran telephone wizard could not bear the idea of the great system conceived and nurtured by him going down, or, if it was destined to go under, he was prepared to go down with it.

Their appeal to his loyalty and his patriotism struck a responsive chord. His life's companion had died two years before and his only son, a stalwart Harvard athlete, had been carried off by typhoid a year later. Life on the farm since then had had its lonely spells.

"I'll come," Vail consented.

He straightway raised $21,000,000 new capital—and raised a quarter of a billion in the next six years with remarkable skill. Through his timely action the corporation weathered the terrible panic of October-November, 1907, without a tremor.

He disarmed public and legislative antagonisms by frankly coming out for "one system" and demonstrating the uselessness of two or more vital systems, by openly proclaiming himself in favour of regulation of all public utilities and offering to coöperate loyally with Public Service Commissions.

He mollified rivals by granting exchange facilities to some, selling Bell instruments to others, and offering to pay a fair price to those who wanted to sell out.

He gained the enthusiastic support of employees by treating them with increased generosity and by setting aside millions for old age pensions, sickness, and accident benefits.

He won the encomiums of subscribers by improving and extending the Bell service with a rapidity and on a scale never before known. His motto then and always has been: "Build ahead of the public demand. Lead, don't lag."

Vail proved himself not merely the master of intercommunication but a business statesman.

Still greater ambitions, however, possessed him. He had, a generation before, mail-mapped America. Now he conceived something greater, something in harmony with the spirit of the twentieth century—Speed.

Theodore N. Vail believes that most wars are bred of misunderstanding, and that if nations and individuals learned to know one another, to understand one another, to fraternize with one another, they would lose all desire to murder one another. His mission in life has been to put people in closer touch, to bring them together no matter how far separated, to annihilate distance and delay.

The telephone had done much toward this end, but his genius gave birth to a wider idea.

"Twentieth Century Limiteds" and other famous railroad fliers were, to his mind, too slow for transporting mails. They travelled less than a hundred miles an hour; Vail favoured thousands of miles a minute.

Why not have tel-letters? Why not have all important letters from city to city telegraphed over the wires at the cost of only a few postage stamps?

As a preliminary step, Vail one day in 1910 signed a $30,000,000 check which bought control of the Western Union Telegraph Company. Radical reforms were at once introduced—cheap night letters, lower rates for deferred messages, cable tolls within the reach of all, telephoned telegrams, etc., etc.

Meanwhile, the revolutionary tel-letter was being worked out. But the telegraph-telephone combine was held by the Attorney-General of the United States Government to be contrary to the law, and by its dissolution was lost to America and Americans a system of communication that would have revolutionized letter-writing.

Briefly, Mr. Vail was perfecting plans to use his vast network of wires, always idle at night, for the telegraphing of letters overnight by a new, time-saving apparatus, the receiving office to put the tel-letter in an envelope and drop it in the mail so that the local recipient would have it on his desk in the morning. Thus, New York or near-by business houses could either deliver tel-letters to a local Western Union-American Telegraph office or send them by mail after business hours. The letters would be telegraphed on to Chicago, St. Louis, San Francisco, or elsewhere overnight at the rate of thousands of words per hour, and re-mailed at the other end.

By eliminating all collection and delivery charges—except the two-cent stamp—and by using wires which would otherwise be lying "dead," the cost of a tel-letter would have been almost nominal.

And it would have put every city in the United States within overnight *mailing* distance of every other city!

But the Department of Justice was obdurate, and thus was lost a boon which would have been as great to America as the blighting of it was a disappointment to its originator.

Mr. Vail, however, is too much of a philosopher to let anything sour him—he drops epigrammatic philosophy with all the readiness and richness of the late James J. Hill.

"The most amazing thing about Vail," said one of his friends, "is that he has all the enthusiasm, imagination, and daring of a man of twenty-four and can blend and combine them with the ripe experience of his seventy-odd years. The result is a remarkable— what shall I say? The result is—well, Theodore N. Vail."

While Mr. Vail loves work he also loves play. He rides; drives a spanking team through Vermont's mountains and valleys; lives partly on his yacht in summer. He took part in securing grand opera for Boston. And to quote one of his chums, "He can order a dinner better than any one I know."

"I have always contrived to enjoy life as I went along," admitted Mr. Vail. One of his axioms is: "Make the best of everything rather than fret over what you can't get." Another is: "Success is measured, not by material gains, but by doing work well and faithfully."

The result is that he is a fine specimen of septuagenarian, his massive forehead crowned with a rich crop of white hair, his eye clear and keen, his face often given to smiling.

New York University signalized the esteem in which Mr. Vail is held by conferring on him, in June, 1917, the honorary degree of Doctor of Commercial Science.

He has the satisfying knowledge that he has contributed much to enhancing the amenities of life in America. His faith in the future is such that he believes the time is near when it will be possible to speak from one end of the earth to the other as easily as we now speak from house to house.

CORNELIUS VANDERBILT III

CORNELIUS VANDERBILT III could say with the man of no illustrious family who was being quizzed as to his fitness for admission to a society whose members prided themselves upon their blue blood: "Gentlemen, I am an ancestor."

This member of the Vanderbilt dynasty is no ordinary rich man's son. He has demonstrated his ability to stand on his own feet, to carve his own path through life, to build his own monument.

Early in life he manifested self-reliance, courage, and independence of wealth. He proved his manliness by marrying the woman of his choice, even at the cost of his inheritance. Instead of indulging in the lazy life of leisure typical of many gilded youths, he donned overalls and went to work among the grime, the heat, and the hurry of railroad machine shops, used both his brains and his hands to such purpose that he not only earned from Yale the degree of Mechanical Engineer in addition to his A.B., but evolved inventions so valuable that they were adopted by leading railroads. He became, too, a volunteer soldier, not of the armchair, fireside species, but a soldier ready on every occasion to discharge his full duties whether in the armory, in manœuvres, in the field on the Mexican border, or, more recently, in active service in the European war, at all times sharing the common lot. He is a sailor, also, and has piloted his own craft across the Atlantic, into every nook and corner of the Mediterranean and along the coast of Europe, meeting and mixing with crowned heads and commoners alike.

In business his technical knowledge, combined with his industry and his financial ability, enabled him early to make his mark. To Cornelius Vanderbilt, New York, in considerable measure, owes its subways, for he undertook an exhaustive investigation of under-the-ground transportation in London, Paris, and elsewhere and then joined forces with August Belmont in organizing the Interborough Rapid Transit Company, of which he is still an influential director.

Yet this inventor, engineer, soldier, sailor, financier, patriot, and millionaire member of a millionaire family is the most unobtrusive, self-effacing figure of the younger generation of "doers."

"I always had my own workshop as a boy as early as I can remember," was his modest statement when I pressed him to explain how he came to be an inventor. "I must have been born with a liking for mechanics, as I constantly played and later worked with tools and machinery. After my graduation from Yale it was logical for me to take up a post-graduate course in engineering. In the course of my studies I spent a good deal of time in the motive-power and engineering department of the New York Central, trying to acquire practical knowledge."

"Yes, but thousands of other young men have studied engineering and worked in machine shops without inventing anything. What diverted your mind into this channel, what led you to think up new devices and to become an inventor?" I persisted. Mr. Vanderbilt manifestly was discomfited by my cross-questioning. An assault was being made upon his modesty and his reserve.

"I had not then taken on business responsibilities or interests. My mind was occupied with engineering problems and my study of them led me, as it would lead any one else, to investigate whether improved methods or appliances could not be devised."

"What was the first patent you took out?" I asked.

"The first thing I patented was a new kind of tender, a cylindrical tender which saved weight and expense." Mr. Vanderbilt might have added, but he didn't, that the Vanderbilt road, the New York Central, did not show him partiality by adopting his money-saving invention; the Union Pacific and Southern Pacific were the first important railroads to adopt the Vanderbilt tender as standard.

What heights Cornelius Vanderbilt might have reached as an inventor, had not a turn of the wheel of fortune changed the course of his life, may only be guessed. At this stage he was drawn into the financial and business arena by reason of having acquired investments totalling millions in various enterprises which demanded his personal supervision.

As early as when he was attending St. Paul's School in New York, Cornelius Vanderbilt displayed individualistic traits. He did not feel that his rank conferred on him any little or big privileges over the other boys. Not only was he essentially democratic, but his skill in his workshop, his ability to fix up any juvenile possession that needed repair, made him very popular. At the same time, although small in stature—even to-day he weighs less than 140 pounds—young Cornelius was no mollycoddle, no easy mark, no doormat. He had a will of his own and courage to maintain it. As he grew a little older his mechanical ingenuity made him something of a hero in the eyes of his playmates.

He entered college in 1891 when seventeen years old and was graduated from Yale in 1895 but enrolled in the Sheffield Scientific School as a student of mechanical engineering. Most of his spare time was spent in the New York Central office, where he worked as intently as any apprentice.

Then romance entered the young inventor's life. He became engaged to Miss Grace Wilson, a young woman of the highest character. His father, Cornelius Vanderbilt, objected, however, to the choice of his eldest son. The young man revealed all the grit, determination, and resolution of his noted namesake, the founder of the Vanderbilt fortune. Instead of giving up his fiancée he elected rather to give up his inheritance. His father, as the phrase went at the time, "cut him off with a million," leaving the rest of his enormous fortune to the other children, the largest share going to Alfred, the younger brother of Cornelius. Cornelius went on his way studying and working and inventing. He won his Ph.B. in 1898 and was graduated with the M.E. degree in the following year. By that time his genius was widely recognized.

A re-alignment of the family fortune was brought about, and Cornelius's holdings now demanded so much of his time and attention that his career as an inventor was sacrificed, although, as a matter of fact, even to this day Mr. Vanderbilt's office suggests the engineer and inventor more than the financier. In his very unpretentious offices in the financial district are all sorts of charts and plans, blue-prints and novel mechanical paraphernalia. He became in time a director of the Illinois Central R. R., the Delaware & Hudson, the Missouri Pacific, the American Express Company, Lackawanna Steel Co., National Park Bank, Harriman National Bank, U. S. Mortgage & Trust Co., Provident Loan Society, Interborough Rapid Transit Co., and a trustee of the Mutual Life Insurance Co.

"Yes, I am a thorough believer in insurance and the thrift that it stimulates," Mr. Vanderbilt told me.

It is well known throughout the financial district that Cornelius Vanderbilt is not an ornamental director. He will not lend his name to any board unless he means to give its affairs serious and sustained personal attention. One financier associated with him in various enterprises remarked to me: "Colonel Vanderbilt is a director who directs. He is no dummy. He insists upon receiving full reports and analyzes them closely. When any special committee is to be elected to do real hard work, Colonel Vanderbilt is invariably named for it. He is a worker."

You will often notice the name of Cornelius Vanderbilt on citizens' committees elected by the Mayor of New York. It is notorious that on such committees half the members do nothing. But Mr. Vanderbilt is not of this type. As chairman of the reception to the Atlantic Fleet in 1915, for example, he toiled day and night to insure the success of the various functions. He was also chairman of the great reception to ex-President Roosevelt on his return from Africa. Like another scion of a notable American family, Vincent Astor, he is always prepared to discharge his share of civic responsibilities.

But it is as a volunteer soldier that Cornelius Vanderbilt is best known to the public. No other civilian, of either high or low degree, has worked more conscientiously or more zealously than Colonel Vanderbilt to arouse interest in strengthening the military position of this country. He is not in the service for glory; he has been actuated solely by a desire to do all within his power to protect his native land from danger from whatever source. He regards this as one of the cardinal duties of citizenship.

There have been many recent converts to "preparedness." Cornelius Vanderbilt is not of this class. As long ago as 1901 he joined the 12th New York Infantry, threw himself into the work with characteristic zeal, and rose to the rank of captain after eight years' service. Major-General Roe, who then commanded the State National Guard, appointed him an aide and when General Roe was succeeded in 1912 by Major-General O'Ryan as commander of the Guard, Cornelius Vanderbilt was promoted to be one of the inspector-generals of the state with the rank of lieutenant-colonel.

When the President's call came for Mexican service, in 1916, Colonel Vanderbilt at once responded. To meet Federal regulations the rank of all Guard staff officers was lowered a step, and Colonel Vanderbilt then became Major Vanderbilt, Inspector of the Sixth Division. In the field, under all the discomforts and difficulties that beset actual service, on the dusty, scorching border, Cornelius Vanderbilt was seen at his best. He was no kid-glove soldier. He scorned to pamper himself by setting up *a ménage* beyond reach of unwealthy comrades. When Kitchener went to South Africa to fight the Boers he discovered that not a few aristocratic officers had pianos and all sorts of paraphernalia trailed after them so that these Johnnies could enjoy themselves thoroughly. Had Cornelius Vanderbilt been on service in Africa Kitchener would have had no occasion to reprimand him for the amount of his impedimenta.

It is Colonel Vanderbilt's creed that men who voluntarily devote themselves to become capable defenders of the nation deserve well at the nation's hands. When, therefore, the many thousands of guardsmen on duty on the Mexican border were to lose their vote at the Presidential election because of their absence from their home states, he had a test case made of his application for an order permitting him to register—and won. This incident is significant of his whole conception of soldiering and citizenship.

"I am a staunch believer in the National Guard. It develops men, it develops their character, it develops their physique," he declared very earnestly to me. "The country ought to be prepared to defend itself."

By common consent, Cornelius Vanderbilt was made chairman of the Mayor's Committee on National Defense organized in New York in 1915, simultaneously with the creation of similar committees throughout the country. At the Convention of Mayors and Mayors' Committees on National Defense, held at St. Louis in March, 1916, he made a rousing address.

"Colonel Vanderbilt would rather have faced a charge of Germans than stand on that platform to make a speech," one of his friends assured me. "Without doubt it was the most trying ordeal of his life, he is so averse to anything savouring of strutting or posing or thrusting himself into the limelight. Only his deep sense of responsibility and the urgency for action impelled him to make that public address."

In his speech, "The Navy, Our First Line of Defense," he showed his contempt for mere lip-patriots by declaring with great force that "the nation cannot be preserved merely by displaying the American flag over the door."

"The decision of our forefathers at the first crisis created this nation," he said; "the decision of their sons at the second crisis preserved the Union from internal disruption, and our decision in this third crisis is to determine whether this nation shall be preserved from external domination.

"Is the American of to-day ready to perform this duty; is he less patriotic, less willing to sacrifice than his forbears; has a lip-loyalty replaced that spirit of valour and devotion which gave us our inheritance? It sometimes appears that prosperity and good fortune have blunted our sense of duty to our country, and that we have come to expect favours from, rather than to render service to, our Government.

"The War of the Revolution was won only after eight years of strife in which 395,000 men were enrolled in the American Army to fight forces which at no time exceeded one-tenth of that number; in the War of 1812 over 500,000 men were called out to fight, generally unsuccessfully, a total force that never equalled 10 per cent. of that number.

"It is impossible to conceive of any better proof of the incompetence of an army of untrained citizens with no other military qualification than bravery.

"When we realize that the largest navy the world has ever known has only 250,000 men, it is absurd to suppose that any navy this country is likely to have—even if as large as the largest—will be sufficient in size to corrupt or overawe a population of over a hundred millions, or will incur an expense large enough to imperil our budget.

"Great Britain, though but a few miles from her enemy, relies on her ships, and no foe as yet has set foot upon her soil. Huge armies have not saved Russia or France from invasion; Italian troops are in Austrian territory; France occupies part of German Alsace; in short, armies have not saved their countries from invasions; navies have—and still do.

"Whatever the final lessons may be, we have not only to build those types of vessels chosen by our possible enemies, but we should steadily construct at least four ships of each type to their three.

"This is what we should recommend to our representatives in Congress and thus insist on a return as soon as possible to our position of at least second naval power. We should also recommend a corresponding increase in the officers and men to man these vessels.

"Let us realize and remember that the nation cannot be preserved merely by displaying the American flag over the door."

Announcement of Cornelius Vanderbilt's promotion in December, 1916, to the Colonelcy of the 22nd New York Engineers was everywhere hailed as a just recognition of his fifteen years' active service as a volunteer soldier. It is interesting to know that his military career has exerted a marked influence on other men and boys in his family and to-day four Vanderbilts are enrolled in their country's service. When, in August, 1917, Colonel Vanderbilt rode through New York at the head of his regiment on its departure for training preparatory to service in Europe, this reception testified to his popularity.

While Mr. Vanderbilt could not be called a politician, he has all along taken a rational interest in public affairs. He was a delegate to the Republican State Convention in Saratoga in 1900 and his customary industry soon won him the chairmanship of the delegation. He was a member of the Civil Service Commission under Mayor Low.

Among yachtsmen he is regarded as a prince, and was honoured by election to the coveted office of Commodore of the New York Yacht Club.

Mrs. Vanderbilt, in her own sphere, is just as active and public-spirited. She has rendered yeoman service in Red Cross and in Belgian Relief work. The Vanderbilts do a rational amount of entertaining, both at their Newport cottage and at their home in Fifth Avenue, New York. Their society activities are characterized by simplicity and commonsense.

They have two children. Cornelius IV enlisted as a private when the United States declared war against Germany.

Could Commodore Vanderbilt survey things to-day I rather think that Cornelius Vanderbilt III would be viewed by him as a not unworthy descendant

He is, indeed, an ancestor.

FRANK A. VANDERLIP

"WHAT has been the hardest step of all in your career?"

"To get out of my overalls."

That was the reply flashed back by the former farm boy and machine-shop apprentice who is to-day head of the greatest national bank in the United States, head of the American International Corporation which is extending America's foreign commercial and financial ramifications, head of the International Banking Corporation with its branches in many lands, head of the Midvale Steel & Ordnance Co., a director and constructive force in leading railroads, and upbuilder of industry.

The story of Frank A. Vanderlip's rise from poverty and obscurity to wealth and power is rich with lessons for both young America and mature America. It is a record of difficulties overcome by unconquerable perseverance, of zeal and efficiency in every station of life, of fair dealing and foresight.

"What lessons have your experiences taught you?" I recently asked Mr. Vanderlip.

"That power is nothing but a responsibility to do the right thing. Since nothing is ever settled until it is settled right, no matter how unlimited power a man may have, unless he exercises it fairly and justly, his actions will return to plague him.

"Also, in order to succeed, a young man must not only spend a full day at his work, but must devote another day learning what his work means, its relation to the scheme of things."

In the past, history was made by the spilling of blood. In future, it is to be made largely by banking and commerce.

Mr. Vanderlip to-day is the most aggressive financier in America. From his brain has come the $50,000,000 financial corporation which plans to develop new fields for American products, for American capital, and for American men. The transformation of the American dollar from a national to an international instrument is in no small measure the work of his institution. He is doing more than any other man to make New York an international financial centre comparable with London. The National City Bank, with its deposits of more than $600,000,000, ranks among the six largest banks in the world, and does more business in its head office than is done under any other non-governmental banking roof on the face of the earth.

That is the Vanderlip that the world knows.

There is a Frank Vanderlip that the world does not know, one he never mentions even to intimates. Perhaps the work of this Unknown Vanderlip may have had something to do with the success of Banker Vanderlip. It at least reveals why he *deserved* to succeed.

The Unknown Vanderlip is Vanderlip the silent philanthropist.

When a struggling reporter in Chicago, supporting six dependents, he used to rent a place near his birthplace and send group after group of city waifs to enjoy a stay there in the summer-time. At Christmas, instead of "exchanging" presents, he and his sister played Santa Claus among the poor on a scale that involved real self-sacrifice.

On entering the Treasury Department at Washington he took several of his poor boy friends with him, found them work and brought them up in his own home. Several of them have since made their mark.

He has put and is putting numbers of deserving young men through college.

He has, out of his own pocket, built a model school at a cost of $200,000 on his estate at Scarborough-on-the-Hudson where scholarships are provided for children of exceptional ability who are unable to pay the low tuition fees.

The City Bank's comprehensive plan for educating its employees and for giving a course of training to selected students from the leading universities, a vitally important movement, is a growth of this same spirit.

A friend told me how he was motoring in the White Mountains with Mr. Vanderlip when they met a poor barefoot lad whose face appealed to the banker. The car was stopped and Mr. Vanderlip chatted with the little fellow. "And Mr. Vanderlip spent the rest of the afternoon cogitating how he could take that barefoot child out of his unpromising surroundings and give him a chance to make his way in the world," he added.

Mr. Vanderlip is one of the increasing number of eminent business leaders who are more interested in making men than in making millions.

In his youth Vanderlip had to mould circumstances to his will. He had to burst the bonds of an environment that was as a straitjacket.

Of pioneer stock, he was born on a large farm not far from Aurora, Ill., fifty-two years ago. His father died when Frank, the eldest of three children, was only twelve. Duties and responsibilities early became his lot, for the farm yielded but a scanty livelihood. He had an intense thirst for knowledge and read every one of the few books he could lay his hands on. These included a complete edition of Shakespeare, the Arabian Nights, and a few old-fashioned magazines.

Since incidents illumine careers, it was significant how he spent the first money he earned.

For faithfully acting as nursemaid to thirty-seven calves during a whole summer he was allowed to choose one of them, and he sold it for twelve dollars. In a near-by hamlet hung a poster announcing that ten dollars would bring the New York *Weekly Tribune* for five years and, as a premium, a "Webster's Unabridged Dictionary." The ten-dollar bill was promptly dispatched, and for five years the country lad devoured every line appearing in the *Tribune*.

At school he was dux in mathematics, but a duffer at spelling. When he was sixteen the farm, heavily mortgaged, was sold and the family moved to Aurora. On Frank the duty of supporting the household mainly devolved, for the life insurance of his father was not touched by his prudent mother, not even to send him to college.

He took a job in a machine shop, and for running a lathe ten hours he received seventy-five cents a day. "I took this job, not because it was the kind of work I wanted, but because it was the only job I could get," he has since said.

He at once began to study his new task and the things related to it. The two things that interested him most were the new force that was beginning to create a furore in the world—electricity, and drawing. He watched the draughtsmen using mathematics, and he determined to study advanced mathematics and drawing. But there were no evening schools and no teachers. However, by paying a man fifty cents an hour—two-thirds of what he earned all day—he got lessons in descriptive geometry and draughting. The family purse sorely needed the fifty cents, so Vanderlip turned tutor, teaching algebra to other fellows in the shop.

His ambition spurring him on, the apprentice resolved that, no matter what the cost in pinching, scraping, and saving, he would go to college for a year. He went to the University of Illinois. Mrs. Scroggin, a typical Dickens character, boarded him for $2.25 a week —not, of course, in Delmonico style. His carefully kept cash book shows that Vanderlip's total expenditures for the student year reached $265! By working as a machinist on Saturdays, he earned $1.50 each week; this paid more than half his board and lodging bill.

Somewhat disappointed because the university could not give him a course in electricity (Cornell then having the only class of this kind in the country), Vanderlip, having successfully completed a course in mechanical engineering, returned home. He wrote to Edison for a job but received a stereotyped "nothing doing" reply—a disappointment for which Mr. Vanderlip has since chided the inventor.

Back to the machine shop he had to go, at $1.35 a day. It was not long before the superintendent informed him that promotion to a foremanship was in store. Instead of feeling elated, Vanderlip there and then made up his mind that he would not rest until he became something more than a foreman in a machine shop.

Shorthand lessons by mail, he concluded, might open a door from mechanical to mental occupation. The "teacher" sent him from Chicago a book and did nothing more except to correct in red ink the mistakes the machinist made. While attending to his lathe the gritty youth practised writing shorthand characters with chalk on flat pieces of iron, a picture that would have delighted the heart of old Samuel Smiles, of "Self Help" fame. His mother patiently read to him by the hour to enable him to take dictation, and he succeeded in mastering "the winged art."

Depression came, and the machine shop shut down temporarily. But Vanderlip did not let the grass grow under his feet; he immediately applied for a job with the local daily paper—"Perhaps the poorest daily paper in America," Mr. Vanderlip has since called it. The office was at the back of an undertaker's; the owner was the editor, and Vanderlip was made city editor, reporter, bill collector, and office-boy. His pay was $6 a week—when he could collect it from subscribers or advertisers. He learned to write and also to set type. His salary was raised to $8, but collections did not always reach this figure and on those sad occasions he had to go without pay.

Joseph French Johnson—now Dean of the School of Commerce, Accounts and Finance, New York University—an Aurora boy who had been educated at home and foreign universities, while on a visit to his native town, met Vanderlip, and, liking him, began to direct the young reporter's reading along economic lines. Later Mr. Johnson gave him a job as stenographer with Scudder's Investigation Agency in Chicago, of which Mr. Johnson had charge. This organization supplied brokers, bankers, and others with analytical reports on corporations and other useful financial information. Here Mr. Vanderlip spent three or four very useful years, learning to analyze corporate accounts, mortgages, annual reports, and so on. Mr. Johnson having accepted the financial editorship of the Chicago *Tribune*, Mr. Vanderlip became his successor as active head of the agency.

Johnson next got Vanderlip a job on the *Tribune* as a reporter. In two weeks his salary was raised, within a month he was assisting the city editor, and before long was assistant financial editor and, later, financial editor. Here. at twenty-five, Vanderlip made his mark.

His training as an investigator enabled him to go to the roots of things financial. Charles T. Yerkes, the traction overlord, was plundering the city and Vanderlip ruthlessly exposed one nefarious deal after another until the whole city became aroused. Yerkes did Vanderlip the honour of calling him the worst enemy he had ever encountered.

Corporate publicity, then virtually unknown, owes its growth in no small measure to the pioneer work of Vanderlip. No reporters were allowed to attend annual meetings. The enterprising financial editor, however, conceived an original and most effective idea.

"If they won't let me in as a reporter they are bound to let me in as a stockholder," he said to himself, and forthwith he purchased one share of stock in every local corporation. The *Tribune* regularly came out with exclusive reports of these meetings and its "scoops" became the talk of Chicago. It took the other newspapers a whole year to ferret out how it was done.

At eleven o'clock one night Vanderlip, who had by this time become part owner of the *Economist*, was called out of bed and told to hasten to the home of Phil. Armour. Arriving there on the run, he found the whole of financial Chicago, the governors of the Stock Exchange, the presidents of all the banks and other institutions, the Moore Brothers, Yerkes, and other notables waiting to receive him.

The astonished financial writer was told that Moore Brothers had failed, that the Diamond Match Company had gone under, that the Stock Exchange would be closed next morning, and that a financial cataclysm threatened Chicago. They wanted Vanderlip to handle the story.

"All right," he replied, "I'll do it on one condition: that every man here pledges himself not to answer one question from any newspaper man to-night." They agreed.

Rushing to the *Tribune* office, Vanderlip told the city editor to call up the editors of all the morning papers telling them that Vanderlip had an exclusive story of transcendent importance but would give it only on the strictest understanding that it be printed exactly as Vanderlip wrote it and that he be allowed to edit the headlines.

Never had such a proposition been made to the newspapers. However, all but one paper sent responsible men to get the news. Vanderlip lined them up and pledged them to the conditions he laid down. Later he drove from office to office and censored the headlines.

"It was the poorest newspaper story I ever wrote," Mr. Vanderlip admitted afterward. "The facts were told, but not in a way the newspapers would have liked to tell them. The fact that the Stock Exchange would not open next morning was mentioned in an obscure paragraph near the end of the story. But it saved Chicago much unnecessary demoralization and disaster."

When the National Bank of Illinois failed, Vanderlip was again called upon to break the news.

Hard work, incessant study, and little or no recreation characterized Vanderlip's life at this stage. Before starting his day's newspaper work, at 10:30, he attended morning classes in economics, financial history, etc., at the University of Chicago. At thirty he was still going to school! Besides, he had to do much outside work to eke out his salary, as the burden of supporting the household was on his shoulders—his grandmother, his mother, two aunts, and little brother and sister were largely dependent upon his efforts.

When Lyman J. Gage was appointed Secretary of the Treasury it was not surprising that he wanted the brilliant and resourceful young financial authority to accompany him. He went as Mr. Gage's private secretary, but so valuable did he make himself that in a few months he was elevated to the position of Assistant Secretary of the Treasury. Mr. Gage was so disgusted with the torrent of applications that poured in upon him by mail and by a constant stream of political wirepullers that he turned the handling of the whole appointment division over to a committee headed by Mr. Vanderlip. Before he had time to find his feet in Washington the ex-reporter found himself in charge of the 5,000 employees forming the Treasury force. Instead of the responsibilities staggering him, he enjoyed the experience. A writer described the Vanderlip of that day as "generous, thoughtful of others, open-minded, strong-willed, unpretentious, just, and big-hearted." He was, moreover, good-natured, enthusiastic, and optimistic.

It was the generalship he displayed in handling the $200,000,000 Spanish War loan in 1898 that gave Vanderlip a chance to win his spurs. He had to organize a special clerical staff and so efficiently did he select and train the men and systematize the statistical work that, although the subscriptions aggregated $1,400,000,000 and numbered 320,000, he was able to announce in five and one-half hours after the subscription closed within $400 of where the line would be drawn between those who would get all the bonds they subscribed for and those who would get nothing. Over 25,000 envelopes were addressed in the one day and every unsuccessful bidder received by next morning's mail the check with which he had accompanied his bid.

Vanderlip's feat did not pass unnoticed by the nation's financiers. James Stillman, the alert head of the National City Bank, told Mr. Gage that he would like to get Vanderlip as soon as he was finished at Washington. Mr. Gage and his aide assumed that a private secretaryship was in Mr. Stillman's mind. But a year later Mr. Stillman informed Vanderlip a vice-presidency of the bank awaited him—a vice-presidency of the greatest bank in the country for a newspaper writer who had never been behind a bank window a day in his life!

The stiffest test in Vanderlip's whole career came when he was installed at the City Bank. Mr. Stillman set him down at an empty desk on the overcrowded officers' platform in the old bank building. He was given nothing to do the first day. The second day also brought no duties. The third was equally barren. The fourth likewise found him absolutely idle.

Here he was, drawing a large salary and not earning a penny of it. He must do something.

In his depression and desolation his thoughts turned to Washington. An idea flashed into his mind.

He would make the National City Bank the representative of other banks throughout the country in Government bond transactions.

Vanderlip knew more about Government bonds than any other man living. He knew other banks would like to be relieved of all the red tape incidental to buying and putting up bonds to cover circulation, depositing reserves to cover note issues, etc., etc. He began to dictate a circular letter to be sent broadcast to the country's 4,000 national banks.

His plan becoming known, he was solemnly informed that it was one of the proudest traditions of the National City Bank that it had never solicited new business.

"If you never went after new business before, it is time you started now," he replied. He resumed the dictating of his circular—and the City Bank became the bank for other banks and built up the greatest bond business in the whole country.

Vanderlip's reward came in the form of elevation to the presidency eight years later.

When Mr. Vanderlip came to the City Bank, in 1901, its capital was only $10,000,000 and its deposits not far above $150,000,000; but in the following year the capital was increased to $25,000,000, while deposits had risen to over $240,000,000 when Mr. Vanderlip became president, in January, 1909. More recently deposits exceeded $600,000,000, a figure not approached by any other American institution. These deposits equal one-seventh of all the money in circulation in the United States!

The moment the Federal Reserve Act was passed, permitting branch banking, the City Bank seized the wider opportunities thus opened up. Soon the bank had branches in Petrograd, Genoa, Buenos Aires, Rio de Janeiro, São Paulo, Santos, Bahia, Valparaiso, Montevideo, Havana and Santiago, Cuba. Several other branches are contemplated, while surveys are being made in almost every civilized country with a view to dotting the world with American banks.

To buttress this plan, control of the International Banking Corporation was acquired with its branches in the Far East and elsewhere.

Every robust American would like to see the United States become the greatest financial and commercial nation on earth. Mr. Vanderlip succeeded, in 1915, in bringing together the most influential capitalistic interests in the land for the formation of the American International Corporation as an instrument to aid in achieving this end. Behind this $50,000,000 corporation stand the resources and the brains not only of the City Bank, but also of the Rockefellers, Kuhn, Loeb & Co., and other influential houses and individuals.

Ships are a nation's shoes. Hence the first step of the American International was to acquire an interest in International Mercantile Marine, the United Fruit Company, with its fleet of ninety steamers, the Pacific Mail, shipyards, etc. Plans for extending America's financial and commercial ramifications abroad and for strengthening home facilities are being perfected by the new enterprise on a scale transcending anything America has ever known.

One of Mr. Vanderlip's ambitions is to make the City Bank the Alma Mater of the coming generation of bankers. A beginning has been made by bringing the most promising students from the leading universities for a year's course in the City Bank. On finishing, the students are given positions in the foreign branches or the head office of the bank. Classes are also held for all the boys and youths in the bank. Indeed, the City Bank is almost as much university as bank.

Money-making has not monopolized this banker's attention. He did not wait until he had millions before he began to do things for others.

His belief that every citizen should give the best that is in him to the state led him to accept the presidency of Letchworth Village at the time it was proposed by the legislature to isolate the feeble-minded and epileptic. He immediately engaged a secretary experienced in philanthropy—Miss Bruere, sister of ex-Chamberlain Bruere of New York City—to give her time and best judgment to the establishment of a model state home of this type.

Recognition of Mr. Vanderlip's unselfish services has come from the educational, the commercial, and the financial world. He is a trustee of the Carnegie Foundation and of the New York University, a life trustee of the Massachusetts Institute of Technology, and possesses several honorary degrees from universities. The commercial community bestowed on him the chairmanship of the Finance Committee of the Chamber of Commerce. The bankers elected him president of the New York Clearing House. He has been frequently selected by New York mayors to serve on important committees. His pioneer and persistent work to secure for the United States currency reform, and his masterly activities in grappling with the financial crises of 1907 and 1914, won him the thanks of the whole financial community.

Even more valuable to the country were Mr. Vanderlip's day-and-night labours to insure the successful flotation of the $2,000,000,000 Liberty Loan. It is no secret that at one stage the offering threatened to fall flat. After the initial hurrah, when Washington was carried away by the first inrush of subscriptions and gave out the impression that the loan was certain to be over-subscribed forthwith, a relapse occurred. The whole country became apathetic. Then New York's leading financiers entered the field and performed miracles. They not only aroused the financial community to the enormity of the task on hand, but by their example, by the campaign they instituted, by the plans they devised, by the literature they prepared, by the posters they introduced, by the vim and force and momentum they worked up they set a pace and a precedent for other cities and districts. But for this work the result of the loan might have been less gratifying.

Leadership in the campaign was really taken by Mr. Vanderlip. He travelled hither and thither delivering inspiring, patriotic speeches to country bankers and others; he directed the whole publicity "drive"; he supplied the newspaper representatives with facts and ideas from day to day—and often late at night; and, in short, he slaved even harder than he did when he handled the flotation of the Spanish War loan in his Treasury days. Not many nights during the whole campaign did he find opportunity to see his family. Signal recognition of his services came later. When the second loan was announced Mr. Vanderlip was called to Washington to direct the popular distribution and he at once took up abode there.

As an author Mr. Vanderlip ranks high. His book "Business and Education," which includes the much-translated series of articles on "The Commercial Invasion of Europe," is still in demand. No financier's speeches arouse more interest throughout the land—this is not solely because of his position, but because of his reputation for foresight in discerning great financial and commercial movements and trends.

Perhaps the greatest single factor in Mr. Vanderlip's phenomenal success in later years has been his extraordinary ability to inspire and develop the men serving with him and under him.

His love of the country still clings so strongly to Mr. Vanderlip that he has no city house. His home life is spent at Scarborough amid ideal domestic as well as ideal scenic surroundings. Mrs. Vanderlip shares his interest in educational and philanthropic activities. They have six children.

PAUL M. WARBURG

PICTURE a party of the nation's greatest bankers stealing out of New York on a private railroad car, hieing hundreds of miles south to an island deserted by all but a few servants, and living there a full week under such rigid secrecy that the name of not one of them was once mentioned lest the servitors learn their identity and disclose to the world this historic episode in American finance.

I am here giving to the world the real story of how the famous Aldrich currency report, the foundation of our new currency system, was written.

Paul M. Warburg is popularly supposed to have been the author and writer of the Aldrich measure. He wasn't.

The Aldrich Commission, headed by Senator Nelson W. Aldrich and composed of a galaxy of American notables, visited Europe in the spring of 1908. The members and their advisers assiduously gathered banking information wherever they went and employed the ablest experts to compile for them the fullest data. The material prepared, when printed and bound, formed a unique financial library. The commissioners returned to America with the reputation of having done their gigantic work most thoroughly, and the whole country looked forward to the issuance of the Aldrich Commission report as a financial and political event of momentous importance.

Senator Aldrich did not attempt, singlehanded, to evolve a *magnum opus* out of the chaotic mountains of material turned in by an army of expert writers and investigators in Europe and at home.

Instead, he issued a confidential invitation to Henry P. Davison of J. P. Morgan & Co.; Frank A. Vanderlip, president of the National City Bank and an ex-Assistant Secretary of the Treasury; Paul M. Warburg, then of Kuhn, Loeb & Company, and A. Piatt Andrew, Assistant Secretary of the Treasury, to accompany him on an extremely important—and secret—trip. Mr. Davison had gone with the Commission to Europe as an adviser; Mr. Vanderlip was a recognized authority on banking and currency fundamentals; Mr. Warburg had written most learnedly on the subject, and Mr. Andrew had done a great deal of work for the Commission.

After a journey hedged with the utmost secrecy, the party were landed in a small boat at the deserted Jekyl Island, off Georgia.

"The servants must under no circumstances learn who we are," cautioned Senator Aldrich.

"What can we do to fool them?" asked another member of the group. The problem was discussed.

"I have it," cried one. "Let's all call each other by our first names. Don't ever let us mention our last names."

It was so agreed.

The dignified, veteran Senator Aldrich, king of Rhode Island and a power second to none in the United States Senate, became just "Nelson"; Henry P. Davison, everywhere recognized as among the ablest international bankers America has ever produced, forthwith became "Harry"; the president of the nation's largest bank became "Frank," and the quiet, scholarly member of the powerful international banking firm of Kuhn, Loeb & Co. became "Paul."

Nelson had told Harry, Frank, Paul, and Piatt that he was to keep them on Jekyl Island, cut off from the rest of the world, until they had evolved and compiled a scientific currency system for the United States, a system that would embody all that was best in Europe, yet so modelled that it could serve a country measuring thousands against European countries measuring only hundreds of miles.

After a general discussion it was decided to draw up certain broad principles on which all could agree. Every member of the group voted for a central bank as being the ideal cornerstone for any national banking system. One by one other features were brought forward and carefully pondered. Day after day for more than a week these giant intellects wrestled with their colossal problem. They worked not five or eight hours a day, but all day and far into the night. Each contributed the best in him. The actual dictating of the measure was done largely by Frank and occasionally by Paul.

As quietly as they had left, the authors of the epochal Aldrich report disappeared from Jekyl Island and slipped into New York undetected.

When Congress assembled, the aged Senator Aldrich was ill, and he summoned his trusted friends, Harry, Frank, and Paul, to Washington and they joined him in writing the message that accompanied the report to the Senate.

To this day these financiers are Frank and Harry and Paul to one another and the late Senator remained "Nelson" to them until his death. Later Benjamin Strong, Jr., was called into frequent consultation and he joined the "First-Name Club" as "Ben."

I want to add explicitly that this information did not come from Mr. Warburg; indeed, he and other members of the group will be very much astonished when they read this. While the details may not be exactly accurate in every case, the main facts are authentic beyond question.

Paul M. Warburg more than any other man had made banking reform possible in this country. Trained scientifically in European national and international banking, our anachronistic currency system shocked him.

"The United States is at about the same point that had been reached by Europe at the time of the Medicis. We have been shown bricks of the time of Hammurabi, the Babylonian monarch, evidencing the sale of a crop and similar transactions, and I am inclined to believe that it was as easy to transfer the ownership of these bricks from one person to another as it is to-day for an American bank to realize upon its discounted paper, if indeed t was not easier."

Thus witheringly he wrote in 1907. But he did more than criticize; he applied his whole talents to bringing about a cure.

It cost Mr. Warburg an effort to enter the fray. Naturally shy, averse to appearing in public or in the public prints, unable then to speak idiomatic English with perfect confidence, then a foreigner not naturalized, he shrank from coming forward. He had to be pushed to the front by friends who realized the value, the practicability, and the timeliness of his proposed reforms. Only the consciousness that the country was sitting precariously on a monetary volcano impelled him to cast aside all personal considerations and do what he considered an uncongenial but imperative public duty.

He opened fire in January, 1907, with an elaborate article on "Defects and Needs of Our Banking System," followed with a blast, "A Plan for a Modified Central Bank,' several months later, and he never ceased to raise his voice and ply his pen until currency legislation was engraved on our statute books. He was a Central Bank advocate; yet as early as 1910, realizing the political difficulties, he evolved a plan for "A United Reserve Bank of the United States," the underlying principles of which are embodied in the law now in force. The centralization of reserves under properly balanced authority and the rediscounting of an improved type of commercial paper so as to transform immobile promissory notes into bills of *exchange*, were the two cardinal reforms he constantly emphasized— reforms which were written into the Owen-Glass law.

It is no disparagement to other American bankers to say that Mr. Warburg is acknowledged to be the first authority in the land on national and international banking principles.

The depth of his sincerity and of his zeal for currency reform can be partly gauged by the fact that he gave up an income of at least $500,000 a year to accept a salary of $12,000 a year as a member of the Federal Reserve Board.

PAUL M. WARBURG

What sort of a man is this Paul M. Warburg who cheerfully made such a financial sacrifice? How did he gain his unparalleled reputation as a banking authority? What is his history?

The story differs from that of the typical self-made American of lowly birth, early hardships, and final triumph.

Paul Moritz Warburg did not have the spur of necessity to prod him forward; he was born rich, but he determined to overcome that handicap. For centuries Warburgs have figured prominently in German commerce, particularly in Hamburg. Their entrance into the banking field dates from the time George Washington was President of the United States. Mr. Warburg's great-grandfather then founded the banking house of Warburg & Warburg in Hamburg, and Warburgs have conducted it ever since, no outsiders being eligible for membership. None was ever needed, for the Warburg fathers saw to it that the Warburg sons were trained to maintain and expand the business.

Paul's drilling was thorough. On graduating from the gymnasium at 18—he was born in 1868—he was put to work with an exporting firm. His taste ran to study rather than barter. His duties included sticking price-labels on bundles of stockings, clothing, and other merchandise, keeping tab of goods handled on the docks, and other activities more menial than mental. But Hamburg's docks formed an ideal foundry for forging embryonic international bankers. Ships and men of all nations plied to and from the port; merchandise of all classes was constantly passing over the piers; all tongues were spoken, all national characteristics revealed. The high-born, sensitive, scholarly youth did not flinch. It was a tradition of the Warburg family that it did not breed idlers. He would not break that tradition.

Two years of this sternly practical commercial experience qualified him to enter the family banking house to learn the A B C of the financing of the merchandise he had handled and seen handled on the polyglottic docks. Next he was sent to England to learn how things were done in the world's financial hub. For two years he worked in one of those banking and discount firms which abound in London as nowhere else, firms whose activities have for more than a century made Britain the world's international banker. His London experience was rounded out by a few months in a stockbroker's office, a position which did not appeal strongly to the banker-in-the-making, for he had no taste for stock speculation.

France was his next training ground. Here he widened his knowledge of practical banking. Back to Hamburg he next went to finish his banking education. To round it off he was dispatched, in 1893, on a trip round the world, when, after visiting India, China, and Japan, he "took in" the United States. Here he met a young lady who captured his affections, an occurrence that was destined to change the whole course of his career.

On returning to Hamburg he was considered fit to become a member of the firm. This was not astonishing, seeing that he had gone through the mill of commerce, had gathered first-hand experience in the two leading financial centres of the world, had travelled extensively and observantly, had studied his profession from every angle, and was deeply impressed with the value of the services rendered to the world by bankers engaged in financing domestic and international trade.

Two years later he returned and married Nina J. Loeb, daughter of the late Solomon Loeb, of Kuhn, Loeb & Co. Yearly visits to the United States were followed, in 1902, by his admission to his father-in-law's international banking firm, a step induced by the illness of his wife's parents and their desire to have their daughter near them.

The idea of becoming an American citizen did not at first enter his mind. He had taken his place in the life of his native country; he was a member of the local legislative body, and also the Haendelsgewicht, a court of arbitration for the settlement of mercantile disputes and was rapidly coming to be recognized as a power in Hamburg financing.

He had not been in New York a month when Wall Street indulged in one of its frequent displays of monetary fireworks. Call money—that is, loans made from one day to another—skyrocketed above 20 per cent. He was dumfounded. Such things did not occur under the banking systems of England, France, or Germany. Why should they occur here, upsetting everything?

He at once sat down and wrote an article explaining the basic causes of the trouble. Then he promptly locked the article away!

"I did not want to be one of those who try to educate the country after they have been here a few weeks," was the reason he gave for tucking away the article, an explanation characteristic of the man.

The article lay unused for four years. During this time Mr. Warburg was carving for himself a place in American finance. His firm was then backing Harriman in railroad developments that caused the country to gasp, so bold, daring, and original were the strokes that followed one another. The Pennsylvania Railroad, also one of Kuhn-Loeb's clients, was spending many millions in defying nature and nullifying geography by burrowing into Manhattan Island. Other powerful railroad systems had to be supplied with funds. And industrial enterprises likewise demanded attention—and millions.

PAUL M. WARBURG

Mr. Warburg learned the game and played it with skill. But he was still the student, the scholar, the investigator of banking principles rather than a "Wall Street Banker" with one eye on his desk and the other on the stock-ticker tape. Bluntly, he hated speculation. His conception of a banker was a man of unquestioned integrity and reputation whose chief mission was to enable the wheels of commerce to revolve by supplying a sufficiency of funds and credit.

When the clouds which culminated in the 1907 panic began to gather, clear-sighted authorities turned their attention anew to banking reform. Mr. Warburg was one of a party of bankers and economists who gathered at the home of Professor Edwin R. A. Seligman of Columbia University and discussed the ominous outlook. Mr. Warburg enunciated his theories. They captured the intellectuals.

Professor Seligman urged Mr. Warburg to publish his views.

Mr. Warburg demurred.

Professor Seligman persisted and won.

It was natural that Senator Aldrich should have enlisted the aid of this erudite banker whose ideas were based on first-hand knowledge and practical experience, who knew every European banking system, and who had had time and opportunity to learn the special requirements of this vast democratic country. It was natural, too, that the Democrats, when their turn came to prepare currency legislation, should have turned to Warburg for guidance. They found him big enough and not too bigoted to modify his proposals in accordance with actualities instead of fatuously insisting upon the attainment of the ideal at one leap.

"The best appointment of his whole administration," President Wilson's selection of Mr. Warburg as a member of the Federal Reserve Board has been called.

In the eyes of certain Washington politicians all "Wall Street Bankers" look alike. They are a monstrous, ravenous, soulless lot, ever seeking whom they may devour, perpetually scheming how to keep their fists tightly clinched on the throats of the people. Mr. Warburg's name was received by these gentlemen with scorn and rage. They would put him through his paces before they refused to confirm his nomination! They would show up the whole "Money Trust" gang!

Mr. Warburg was incensed. He had consented to give up his profitable partnership in one of the greatest international houses in America; he had reconciled himself to sacrificing all his New York friendships; he had resolved to resign from every railroad, industrial, financial, even philanthropic office he held solely because of the hope that his example might stimulate others to accept public service and his profound conviction that the occasion demanded patriotism of a high order.

For his voluntary immolation he was being bombarded with volleys of suspicion and condemnation.

At one stage Mr. Warburg would have given a million dollars could he have unwritten his letter of acceptance to President Wilson.

Finally, he consented to appear before his inquisitors on the condition that "the affairs of my partners, who are not here as nominees," would not be taken "as a basis for discussion."

For two days he submitted to being pelted with questions, many of them insulting. Here is an example:

"You intend to go on this board, if you are confirmed, to represent what?" asked a Senator.

"To represent the country and the future of the country," Mr. Warburg replied with calm dignity.

Even his former bitterest opponents have now come to realize that Mr. Warburg is in truth striving to represent the country and its future, not any evil-motived Wall Street clique.

He has laboured incessantly to improve the working and the organization of the country's currency system; he has left no stone unturned to enlighten the public on banking principles; he has rendered invaluable service in coöperating with Governmental authorities during these crucial days to keep things on an even keel. It is, indeed, well for the nation that a man of Paul M. Warburg's calibre has been available in Washington during the last year or more.

Analyzing world prospects, Mr. Warburg—in an address before the Commercial Club of Chicago in April, 1917, on "Government and Business"—after a plea for helpful coöperation between business men and those chosen by the Government to discharge regulatory duties, said:

"In the state of the future, particularly in Europe after the war, the most efficient Government promotion of industries in many lines will be held to exist in actual Government ownership and operation. More than ever before will States become solid industrial and financial unions effectively organized for world competition driven by the necessity of perfecting a system of the greatest efficiency, economy, and thrift in order to be able to meet the incredible burdens created by the war.

"Such is the future of the world in which we shall have to maintain our own position, and it requires, on our part, thorough organization and steady leadership. Under our democratic system this cannot be furnished by changing party Governments, but can only be provided by fairly permanent, non-partisan, and expert bodies. These bodies must combine the judicial point of view with that of active and constructive business minds. They must be able to act as advisers alike to Congress and the industries concerned. They must break down suspicion and prejudice of Government against business and of business against Government. They must stand for the interest of all against the exaction or aggression of any single individual or group, be it called capital or labour, carrier or shipper, lender or borrower, Republican or Democrat.

"Our ability to handle effectually the great economic problems of the future will depend largely upon developing boards and commissions of sufficient expert knowledge and independence of character. This will be possible only if both Government and the people fully appreciate the importance of such bodies, so that the country may find its ablest sons willing to render public service worthy of the personal sacrifices it entails.

"Aristotle, in defining the essential characteristics of liberty, said: 'It is to govern and in turn to be governed,' and this thought has lost nothing of its force even though 2,000 years have passed since it was expressed. Liberty without government is anarchy. Government without coöperation of the governed is autocracy. To govern and in turn to be governed is the only form of true liberty. In this conception there is nobody governing and nobody governed. We all govern and serve alike and together. We all serve one master; the only master that no liberty-loving man need be ashamed to serve—we serve our country."

Personally, Mr. Warburg would rather solve a knotty banking problem for the benefit of the country than make a million dollars. He has given up money-making entirely, having resigned from all directorships and partnerships both here and abroad.

His home is one of the most artistically furnished in Washington. He still maintains his old home at White Plains, where he spends many week-ends and most of the summer with his wife and children.

Like his brother, Felix M. Warburg, also a partner in Kuhn, Loeb & Co., he has done a great deal of charitable and philanthropic work, especially among those of his own race. In this he has the energetic coöperation of Mrs. Warburg.

In June, 1917, Mr. Warburg received the honorary degree of Doctor of Commercial Science from New York University.

If other brainy Americans could be induced to give up money-making and dedicate themselves to public service, the United States would be a cleaner, better-governed, less-agitated Republic.

JOHN N. WILLYS

DOES American financial annals contain any story to match this?

John N. Willys, then grubbing along as an automobile selling agent in Elmira, N. Y., became uneasy, in the dark days of December, 1907, over the non-delivery of Overland cars, for which he had booked 500 orders. He hopped upon a train for Indianapolis, the Overland Company's headquarters, arrived on Saturday evening, and on Sunday morning was coolly told by the manager: "We are going into the hands of a receiver to-morrow morning."

"You are *not!*" Willys countered emphatically.

"We *are*," reiterated the manager. "Why, we paid some of our workmen by checks last night and we haven't enough money in the bank to meet them to-morrow morning."

"How much are you short?" asked Willys.

"About $350."

Indianapolis banks were paying out no real money in those memorable days. The town—like most of the United States—was on a scrip basis. But Willys meant to raise $350 by hook or by crook before the bank would open the next morning.

The interview occurred in the old Grand Hotel, where Mr. Willys had occasionally stopped. He walked boldly up to the hotel clerk.

"I want $350 cash before to-morrow morning," he informed the young man behind the desk.

"I wish you luck," came the laughing reply.

"What?" asked Willys.

"I said: 'I wish you luck,'" repeated the clerk.

"But you have to get it for me," Willys told him.

"Swell chance!" came back the clerk, still thinking that Willys was joking.

Willys wrote out a check on a little bank in Wellsboro, Pa., for $350 and sternly told the clerk: "I must have cash for that before the bank here opens to-morrow morning." The clerk again laughed.

"Isn't the check good?" Willys demanded.

"I suppose it is, but where are you going to get $350 cash? I can't get a cent out of the bank."

There and then Willys planned a money-raising campaign. He told the clerk to freeze on to every dollar that came into the office, to gather up every cent collected in the restaurant, and to empty the bar-room till. "And don't cash another check to anybody until we get this money," Willys cautioned. The proprietor, having been informed of the purpose for which the money was so urgently needed, entered into the spirit of the thing, and by midnight Willys was handed a mountain of silver dollars, half dollars, quarters, dimes, and nickels, topped off with a thick layer of one-dollar bills and a sprinkling of twos, fives, and tens.

Early next morning he planked the pile on the bank counter, to the credit of the Overland Company. The pay checks were duly met.

Within eight years John N. Willys, the saver of Overland, was offered $80,000,000 for his share of the company!

Of course, the mere raising of $350 hard cash that eventful Sunday did not bring the Overland concern back to life. It merely averted the threatened Monday morning crisis.

Instructing the company to stand off all creditors during the week, Willys hastened to Chicago and secured enough money there to meet the following Saturday's payroll. For five weeks he hurried and scurried from Indianapolis to Chicago and New York and back again, frantically trying to finance the company. The Overland plant then consisted merely of a sheet-iron shed 300 feet long by 80 feet wide, with a shopworn outfit of machinery and not enough material on hand to put out a single complete car. By frenzied scraping and cajoling, Willys procured sufficient materials to enable the company to finish enough cars to keep the working force together.

No banker would touch the concern—the bankers would not even let the company have any scrip money on tick. Creditors were clamouring for payment—the company owed $80,000 and hadn't $80 to its name.

Willys, however, was determined to stave off disaster. He was confident that he could put the enterprise on its feet with even a small amount of money. He had promised to supply 500 cars and had paid a substantial deposit to the company.

Finally he induced an acquaintance, an old lumber man, to agree to lend $15,000 real cash. This wasn't much to meet $80,000 debts, buy raw materials, and pay wages and salaries. But it emboldened Willys to proceed to have the company's lawyer draw up a proposed form of settlement with creditors. Willys undertook to pay ten cents on the dollar at once and other instalments later to those who insisted upon part cash, while his trump card was an offer of preferred stock. The draft of the agreement embodied this offer.

Alas, his lumber friend changed his mind and announced that he did not want to risk his funds. Willys, however, again demonstrated his resourcefulness by prevailing upon the old gentleman to put up $7,500.

But the agreement read that Willys stood prepared to pay insistent creditors $15,000. He was in a quandary. But not for long. He simply amended the sentence to read that he would, if called upon, pay creditors "*not to exceed $15,000.*"

When the principal creditors came together they were at first refractory. Some of them felt insulted at the terms offered. But John North Willys proved equal to the occasion. He had had years of training as a salesman of anything and everything from books to bicycles and automobiles. His eloquence, his sincerity, and his faith in the future of the automobile industry won over all the important creditors and so convinced them of the company's prospects that a majority elected to accept preferred stock for their entire claims.

It actually took only $3,500 cash to handle the Overland's $80,000 debts and to start off the reorganized company without any financial burdens around its neck.

Willys showed his financiering ability, also, in his handling of the manufacturers and others who supplied the Overland with parts. He summoned the four largest, explained to them that they might as well let the Overland have the material they had manufactured for it, painted a glowing picture of the company's prospects and convinced them it would pay them to coöperate by accepting three months' notes for additional supplies.

Immediately they consented to do this, he sprang another little wrinkle on them.

"I want you," he informed them, "to assist in reëstablishing the company's credit. I will let other people know how you have shown faith in the company, and I will refer any doubters to you. Anybody who hesitates to give us credit will be told to communicate with you. It will be up to you to convince them that we are all right."

This novel financial stroke worked beautifully.

It was in January, 1908, that the reorganization was accomplished. Mr. Willys became president, treasurer, general manager, sales manager, etc., etc. By September of the same year 465 cars had been made, sold (at $1,200 each), and delivered. And the company showed a net worth of $58,000.

In the next twelve months, on this $58,000 capital, Willys manufactured and sold over 4,000 automobiles at a total price of $5,000,000 *and cleaned up a net profit of over $1,000,000.*

Before telling of his later triumphs, it will be in order to narrate how John N. Willys first became interested in the automobile industry. It is a quaint story.

Let me give it in Mr. Willys's own words:

"I was standing looking out of a window in a skyscraper at Cleveland, Ohio, one day in 1899 when I noticed a thing on four wheels creeping along the street. No horse was attached to it. From where I was it looked exactly like a carriage. I immediately said to myself, 'That machine has all the bicycles in the country beaten hollow'—I was then in the bicycle business. I made up my mind that I would get into this new field at the first moment possible. I investigated and found that what I had seen was a Winton car; but I did not then get a chance to examine it. The total output of cars in that year was less than 4,000 for the whole country. Next year a doctor in Elmira, where I was living, bought one of them.

"I looked it over very carefully, and then bought a Pierce Motorette, built by the company which now builds Pierce-Arrow cars. It was built like a carriage but had a French motor about the size of a water bottle on the rear axle. This motor developed only $2\frac{3}{4}$ horsepower—a good motor bicycle now has 4 horsepower. The car was so low-geared that it could take hills at two or three miles an hour. It had a narrow wheel base and was smaller than the Ford car is now.

"I set off for Buffalo to see Mr. Pierce—I was then agent for Pierce-Arrow bicycles. He told me they were experimenting with automobiles, and I sat with him two or three hours discussing the future of motor vehicles. I made him promise to let me have one of the very first they turned out.

"Shortly after that I got a car, for $900, to use as a sample and to give demonstrations. That year, although everybody was anxious for a demonstration, I sold only two cars. Next year I doubled my sales—I sold four. Then I took on the Rambler agency as well as the Pierce and my sales in the following year (1903) jumped to twenty. Motor cars, you should remember, were then about at the same stage as aeroplanes are now. It was uphill, pioneer work.

"I knew there was money in it, and I was anxious to get into the manufacturing end. By 1905 it was easy enough to get orders but very difficult to get cars. The demand was far above the supply. Manufacturers became quite dictatorial; they were cocks of the walk.

"I made up my mind that the big money was to be made in making cars rather than in the selling end. But I had neither enough money nor manufacturing experience. Nor was I a mechanic. The best thing I could do, I concluded, was to form a large selling company, as I had done in bicycles, take the entire output of one or two companies, sell the cars at wholesale, and then graduate into the manufacturing end.

"So, in 1906, I formed the American Motor Car Sales Company, with headquarters in Elmira, and undertook the sale of the whole output of the American and Overland companies, both in Indianapolis. I had to put up a big deposit, but I had lived economically and had saved some money. The Overland, at that time, had been in business for six years. Its biggest year was 1906, when its total output was forty-seven cars.

"Before the panic started in October, 1907, our Sales Company had contracted to supply to dealers 500 Overland cars. I was doing well. I was anxious to branch out.

"Off I went to Indianapolis and signed a contract to distribute the Marion car. I was feeling quite happy on my way back to New York that evening when, phew! I picked up an evening paper and read that the Knickerbocker Trust Company had closed its doors and that pandemonium had broken out in New York.

"I decided to sit tight until the storm blew over. But the Overland quickly began to act suspiciously, and by the beginning of December things became so ominous that I decided to go to Indianapolis and investigate. You know what I discovered."

The Overland's troubles proved, for Mr. Willys, a blessing—a blessing much disguised at the time. The company's misfortune proved the birth of his fortune.

Up till then Mr. Willys had had a varied career. He was born, in 1873, in a place more noted for its natural beauty than as a gateway to millionairedom, Canandaigua, N. Y. From his earliest boyhood he was fond of doing little business deals with his companions; he always had something in his pockets for sale. The first real initiative he showed was when, noticing how the reins were always falling down among horses' feet, he procured and sold a dozen little clamps for holding the reins. With the proceeds he bought two dozen and quickly disposed of them all. When he grew a little older, say, eleven or twelve, he made a contract with his father to work in the latter's brick and tile factory for 25 cents each Saturday with extra pay for working a couple of hours after school, daily. But even these long hours did not stop his trading propensities.

He made a success of everything he tackled, with one exception. He became a book agent to utilize his hours after school, his specialty being a "Life of Garfield." But the returns did not satisfy his ideas of his earning power and he gave it up.

All these experiences he passed through before he had reached the age when the average boy dons long trousers.

One of his chums was a lad who worked in a laundry, and little Johnnie Willys became interested in this method of money-making. Before he was sixteen he had talked his parents into allowing him to buy, along with his young friend, a laundry at Seneca Falls, about thirty miles away. His parents hoped that a taste of roughing it in a laundry and in a boarding-house away from home would quickly cure him of his mania for business and drive him back home to his school books. They fully expected him home in a week.

The budding knights of the wash-tub and the ironing-board discovered they had been "stuck." However, they buckled down to business with grim determination.

Their knowledge of finance was so limited—the senior partner was only eighteen—that when they received a check one day for six dollars they hadn't the slightest idea how to go about turning it into cash! Willys finally summoned up courage to take it to a bank. He was not known there, and they did not care to cash it for him. Even then, however, Willys had a persuasive tongue and an ingratiating personality, and when he walked out of the bank he had the six dollars in his pocket.

At the end of a year, having succeeded in putting the laundry on a paying basis, they sold out with a net profit of $100 each. By this time Willys regretted he had not had more education. He returned home with the intention of working his way through college and becoming a lawyer. He was getting along quite well with his studies and working in a law office (one of the partners of which, Royal R. Scott, is now secretary of the Willys-Overland Company). Then his father died and young Willys had to give up his college aspirations.

Bicycles were beginning to make their appearance, and he thought he saw in them a profitable outlet for his ingenuity as a salesman. With the hundred dollars he had cleaned up on the laundry, he bought a sample bicycle, the New Mail, and was duly authorized as a local agent for the manufacturers. He induced several friends to invest in the new "safeties," and by the time he was eighteen he had organized a Sales Company, opened a store, established a repair shop in the rear, and prospered so much that by and by he opened a larger establishment in Canandaigua's main street. He advertised freely— the fancy paperweight alongside the guests' register at the local hotel still bears a Willys "ad" which cost him three dollars, not a big sum, to be sure, when compared with the $2,500,000 Willys now spends in advertising his Overland and Willys-Knight cars.

"I surely was going on the high gear," Mr. Willys remarked in discussing his youthful experiences. "I could sell any number of bicycles; but I made the mistake of taking everybody to be honest, just as I was. I found it was one thing to sell bicycles and another thing to collect the money. It needed only the upheaval caused by the free silver rumpus of 1896 to bowl me over. That was one of the best things that ever happened to me. It taught me a lesson. It put business sense into my head."

Taking a job as a travelling salesman with the Boston Woven Hose & Rubber Company, he worked hard and saved money in preparation for reëntering business on his own account. Among his customers was the Elmira Arms Company, a sporting goods store which had bankrupted four proprietors in succession. When the Klondyke gold fever broke out the owner of the store itched to get away, and was glad to sell out his $2,800 worth of stock to Willys for $500 cash. Willys installed a manager and injected some ginger into the running of the store, but retained his own job until one day, while visiting Canandaigua, he met Mr. Scott, who asked him what sort of a concern this was he travelled for. Willys opened a line of talk in eulogy of his company but was cut short by having an afternoon paper flaunted in his face with an announcement of its failure.

Astounded but not daunted, Willys decided to take personal charge of his Elmira venture. He at once made a specialty of bicycles and began to make some headway The total sales in eight months reached $2,800, of which $1,000 was profit. Gradually he worked into the wholesale distribution of bicycles and eventually took the whole output of a factory, established agencies over a wide territory, and did a business of $500,000 a year—not a mean record for a young man of twenty-seven.

Then came the automobile—and financial history.

John North Willys now employs in his factories and his sales agencies 75,000 men, a number exceeded by only one other motor company in the world. He had the distinction of being the only person to own individually a large automobile enterprise.

In the first half of 1916 the Willys-Overland Company turned out and sold over 94,000 automobiles, while his 1917 production was scheduled at nearer 1,000 cars every working day!

From ownership of the Overland, Mr. Willys branched out and secured control of other important concerns. In 1909 he took over the Pope-Toledo Company and later transferred the Overland plant to Toledo, where he employs over 18,000 men in his automobile factory and over 2,000 in the Electric Autolite Company—which had exactly forty-two employees two years earlier when he purchased it. He is also president of the Morrow Manufacturing Company of Elmira, while he controls an important rubber company and is the power behind the throne of other enterprises.

Between 800 and 1,000 railroad cars are filled daily at plants that Mr. Willys controls.

The market value of the Willys-Overland securities is about $65,000,000, and dividends are at the rate of $6,100,000 a year. And now Willys has jumped in and become the foremost figure in the aircraft industry through his acquisition of control of the Curtis Aeroplane Co. and the booking of huge orders for flying machines for war use. What the aircraft industry will develop into no man can foretell. But Willys means to be at its forefront. Yet ten years ago he had to sweat blood to raise $350 to meet the Overland payroll!

But he is the same democratic, unaffected, boyishly exuberant and enthusiastic John N. Willys as he was when he struggled with the cashing of that first six-dollar check. Wealth has not turned his head. In earning it he worked from seven in the morning to midnight daily for several years—until the doctors told him he must either drop everything and go pleasure-seeking in Europe or be prepared to become an inmate of a sanatorium. He was automobiling in France along with Mrs. Willys and their daughter when the war broke out and his limousine was promptly commandeered. But he made up for it by booking orders for a few thousand motor trucks from the Allies before he left Europe!

He still toils like a Trojan while at work, but, having organized and systematized his various enterprises, he can steal off for short trips on his magnificent 245-foot steam yacht, the *Isabel*, named after Mrs. Willys, for occasional rounds of golf; and on picture-hunting expeditions. His collection of paintings is among the most notable in the West. He enjoys life—both its work hours and its play hours. I know no man of great wealth who takes his position less pompously.

When inspecting the hundred-acre Willys-Overland plant at Toledo I visited the company's $1,000,000 modern office building overlooking the beautiful Willys Park, so named by the city in honour of its most prominent citizen, and while there I took occasion to chat with an office-boy.

"Mr. Willys is not like a boss," he told me. "He always speaks nicely to us. One morning I was coming up the stairs with my arms so full of mail packages that I couldn't open the door. Mr. Willys saw me and said: 'Wait a minute, sonny,' and he opened that door for me and went ahead and held another one open for me, too. That's the kind of things he does all the time."

They don't have strikes at the Willys plant.

THOMAS E. WILSON

ONE day Nelson Morris & Co., the Chicago packers, asked the chief clerk of the Burlington Railway to send them a young fellow to keep tab on their refrigerator and other cars. He selected his chief assistant as the man best qualified for the job. Within an hour or two the assistant returned from the stockyards. "If they offered me the whole stockyards I would not go out there to work," he declared emphatically, as he reached out for his pen to resume his clerical duties.

"Will you let me go out and look it over?" asked a nineteen-year-old youth, who had only one year's experience. His superior assented.

Off he went to the stockyards.

"I found," he said, describing his visit, "that conditions at the stockyards were not exactly salubrious. When you got there you found the plank roads floating in mud which had a knack of squirting up the legs of your pants when you stepped from one plank to another. Everything was rough and crude and uninviting—quite different from the clean and sanitary conditions of to-day.

"Inside Morris & Company's office the employees were so crowded and huddled together that they appeared to be working one on top of another—a great contrast with our handsome C. B. & Q. quarters.

"But there was no lack of business. It looked as if a fellow could find a lot to do. I thought I could see an opportunity for any one willing to work and to stay by the proposition. The prospects appealed to me, so I accepted the job at $100 a month. I was getting only $40 a month from the railroad."

That was one day in 1881.

One morning in the summer of 1916—the 21st of July—Americans awoke to find the name "Wilson & Co., Successors to Sulzberger & Sons Company," blazoned in bold type in every newspaper, in subway, surface, and elevated cars, on thousands of bill boards and on hundreds of meat establishments throughout the country.

"Who is Wilson?" every one asked.

The public was curious to know who this could be, this man whose name overnight had displaced that of a great concern which had been a household word and whose products had been familiar to every American home for sixty years. Surely he must be a man of no ordinary reputation and attainment. What had he done to achieve such distinction?

The man was the penniless clerk who was not afraid of the stockyards and its hard work.

He was Thomas E. Wilson.

Thus summarized the story savours of a fairy tale.

But when we fill in the intervening years, when we follow the unfolding of each development, when we trace the journey step by step, we find that there was nothing dramatic, nothing romantic, nothing extraordinary in it. The *dénouement* was a logical, inevitable sequence of what went before. I have not found in American business annals any story more simple, more natural, or more inspiring.

I feel it a privilege to be able to tell the story in the words of the man who lived it.

"My first work at the stockyards here was making records of our car mileage," said Mr. Wilson in reply to my inquiries. "We owned special stock cars, refrigerator cars, and others. The railroads paid us for the use of them. I didn't stay all the time in the office, but went into the yards and took an interest in the actual handling of the cars, became familiar with the car repairs, and by and by I was made superintendent of all repairing work. I also had to purchase the material used in the repair shops. Gradually we developed into building cars for ourselves and I supervised this new development.

"I broke another fellow in to take my place, as I always had a desire to trade, and I next took over the purchasing department for the whole plant—buying supplies of all kinds, machinery, and construction material.

"We were branching out, and I took charge of construction work, not only at the yards, but was given the task of locating new branch wholesale establishments elsewhere. I spent one whole winter with headquarters in Boston and covered the New England territory with branches.

"My methods of going at it?

"I would go to a town, look it over, see what Armour or Swift or Hammond was doing there, and if I thought the place would stand another plant I would buy or rent property. I would outline to our draughting department the kind of layout wanted; they would prepare a rough plan and send it to me for revision. After making such changes as circumstances made advisable, the plan would be completed and forwarded to me along with specifications. I had three or four construction men with me, who carried out the special work needed for our icing apparatus and other special equipment called for by the nature of our business.

"Before the building was finished I would look around for the best man I could find, if possible a local man, to run the business. When we had the thing safely launched, I would repeat the performance in another city. I opened many of these establishments.

"After I returned to Chicago and had taken on the management of important general construction work that we were then carrying on—we were growing, of course—Frank Vogel, who was the '& Company' of Nelson Morris & Co., pulled out, and Edward Morris, the eldest son of Nelson, who had been rapidly growing into the management of the business, took me into the office with him. I was then about thirty-two and Edward Morris was a little older.

"During the time I was working in the car department, the purchasing department, and the construction department, I had tried to learn as much as I could about the actual operating of the plant. I also took an interest in the selling end. Yes, I was always very busy—and always wanted to be busy. The days were never long enough, although I ate breakfast at 5.30 every morning, caught the stockyards 'dummy' which left Chicago at six o'clock, and seldom left before nine o'clock at night. In all the years I was with Morris & Company I was off only five days through illness.

"For fifteen years I never took a vacation, nor were there many Sundays that I did not spend at least part of the day at the yards. No, it was not laborious at all. It was fascinating. The packing business was developing and there was always something new to be tackled—just as there is to-day.

"Finally, all the superintendents were put under me. I had to look after the manufacturing and operating end of the business, in addition to supervising the construction work. I was never too tired to tackle anything. I tried to study the whole business and always was ready to take on responsibilities.

"When Edward Morris died, over four years ago, I was made president. It was his desire that his two sons—Nelson, who is now twenty-seven, and Edward, now about twenty-five—should be trained to run the business. I was very fond of him and was willing to do all I could to carry out his wishes. It was only right that the sons should succeed their father and grandfather as heads of Morris & Company. Then, too, my ambition was not to remain merely an employee all my life. As president I was, of course, on a very good salary, and had acquired an interest in a number of outside things.

"One day in the fall of 1915 I received a telephone message from the Blackstone Hotel from two New York bankers, who said they wanted to see me. I had a long talk with them. They wanted to engage me—at any salary I wanted to name—to take charge of Sulzberger & Sons Company. Ferdinand Sulzberger had died two years before, after having been incapacitated for several years, and the business was being run by his sons, Max and Germon Sulzberger. They had made a deal for the refinancing of the concern by New York banking interests, including the Chase National Bank, the Guaranty Trust Company, William Salomon & Company, and Hallgarten & Company. These interests, the two bankers told me, had now secured control of Sulzberger & Sons Company and wanted to have it built up and developed in the best way possible. After proper consideration, I felt compelled to turn down their proposition.

"One day shortly after I had rejected the offer of the presidency of Sulzberger & Sons Company, I met a friend in Chicago who hailed me with: 'So you are going with Sulzberger's.'

"'No, that's all off,' I told him.

"'Oh, yes, you are,' he came back. 'I was talking with some New York bankers and they told me you were to make the change *but that you didn't know it yourself yet.* They told me they would get you yet.'

"They did. They worked out a proposition, giving me a very substantial interest in the business and everything else I wanted. They were very liberal. And so here I am."

And now you know exactly the story behind the change in control of one of the half-dozen greatest packing houses in the country from "Sulzberger & Sons Company" to "Wilson & Company." What has not been told is the estimation in which Thomas E. Wilson is held by his fellow packers and his other friends.

He is the most natural, unaffected man imaginable. He is a giant physically and mentally. There are no hard lines in his face and his large blue eyes reveal a kindly heart rather than suggest a cold, shrewd, business mentality.

"To what do you chiefly attribute your wonderful success?" I asked Mr. Wilson.

"I am no wonder," he rebuked me. "I am no brainier or wiser than any number of other people. My whole success is traceable to the fact that I have enjoyed my work and have given to it the best in me. No job ever was too big for me to tackle. That is the foundation of success nine times out of ten—having confidence in yourself and applying yourself with all your might to your work.

"Too many men try to travel on a reputation. They stand upon their past achievements rather than daily press on toward further achievements. You cannot stake your future on the past, but on the present. A fellow must throw his whole energy into everything he undertakes and feel keenly that on this one thing, whatever it be he is doing, depends his whole future."

Mr. Wilson always had an eye to business—even when on his honeymoon. He saw in Brooklyn on that occasion a piece of property that impressed him and he immediately went and opened negotiations for its purchase. It proved one of the most profitable trades in his whole life.

He was fortunate in marrying Miss Elizabeth L. Foss of Chicago, who proved not merely in name but in deed a helpmate. She enthusiastically entered into his ambitions and gladly sacrificed her own comfort and convenience for the sake of his success. Social plans were never allowed to stand in the way of business activities. He was thirty-one when he married and already enjoying a high salary, but both agreed to undergo whatever self-sacrifice might be necessary to meet business demands, no matter how unexpected or how far they might suddenly take him from home. In other words, Mrs. Wilson, like her husband, was willing to pay the price of success.

And now their success—Mr. Wilson regards it as a joint accomplishment—is permitting them to fulfil an ambition. They have secured a 300-acre farm at Lake Forest, where both can indulge their fondness for horses and cattle. Mr. Wilson is carrying out certain theories of his own concerning the best methods of raising food cattle. The only luxury he allowed himself in his early days was a horse. To-day he keeps a string of just the kind of saddle horses his fancy favours. His 17-year-old daughter, Helen, and his 12-year-old son, Edward, have inherited this same taste, and the Wilson family often may be seen galloping along the Lake Forest country roads of an early morning.

When he plays, he plays as hard as he works. After having worked all summer at reorganizing the company and getting its various plants running in the way he desired, Mr. Wilson took his first vacation in a long while, spending three weeks in the wilds of New Mexico on a hunting trip. During that time he was completely out of touch with his office—which shows how well he knows and trusts his really remarkable organization.

Thomas E. Wilson has risen without outside aid. He was born in London, Ontario, on July 22, 1868, but the family, of Scots-Irish extraction, moved to Chicago when he was nine years old. His father made a moderate fortune in drilling oil wells and running a refinery, but met with a reverse which prevented him from sending Thomas to college. After passing through the primary and high schools in Chicago, the boy had to look for and find a job for himself. He hunted quite a while before finding an opening in the office of the Chicago, Burlington & Quincy Railroad's headquarters.

When, on his own initiative, as already told, he secured a clerical position with Morris & Company, he did not know a single soul identified with the packing trade. To-day Thomas E. Wilson is universally considered to be without a superior as an all-round, practical packer, capable of showing any one of thousands of employees how to do a task.

Not one person in Chicago, not one fellow-worker or one packer, grudges Mr. Wilson his phenomenal success. As president of Morris & Company he fought competitors fairly and squarely and treated his workmen the way he himself was treated by Morris & Company. His advent as the head of the old-established Sulzberger organization, reorganized as Wilson & Company, was hailed with genuine satisfaction by every workman and every employer in the meat business. In this case success begot no envy. Every one familiar with the stockyards felt that what happened could not well *not* have happened—or that if it hadn't happened the way it did, it would have happened some other way.

It was inevitable that Thomas E. Wilson should rise to the very top.

Mr. Wilson's latest achievement is the establishment of a sporting-goods business doing a nation-wide trade. Its products are of such quality that he is not afraid to stamp them with the Wilson trademark and Wilson guarantee.

My prediction is that, high up as he already is, Thomas E. Wilson will go farther still.

FRANK W. WOOLWORTH

A BAREFOOTED American farm lad made up his mind that he would rather work behind a counter than behind the plow. He was so green and gawky and awkward, so palpably a "hayseed," that, try as he might, no merchant would engage him at any wage. But the boy had such determination and doggedness that he agreed to serve for nothing, living meanwhile on his painfully earned capital of $50. So complete a failure did he prove at selling goods that in his next job his small pay was reduced instead of increased. But, though he agreed with his boss that he was a misfit as a salesman, he did not give in. He stuck.

To-day he is the largest retail merchant in the world.

Here are some of his 1916 sales: 50,000,000 pairs of hosiery, 89,000,000 pounds of candy, 20,000,000 sheets of music, 12,000,000 pounds of salted peanuts, 6,250,000 neckties, 42,000,000 boxes of safety matches; 9,000,000 domestic toys; 21,000,000 sticks of chewing gum; 1,700,000 nursing bottles; 15,000,000 cakes of soap; 5,000,000 phonograph records; 5,000,000 papers of hairpins; 5,500,000 rolls of wax paper—enough to wrap sufficient sandwiches to feed 170,000,000 people; 5,000,000 papers of common pins; 2,250,000 boxes of crochet and embroidery cottons.

Also:

His customers exceeded 700,000,000, a daily average of over 2,250,000.

Sales—all over the counter; no orders are filled by mail—exceeded $87,000,000 and in 1917 are running at the rate of $100,000,000, representing about 1,500,000,000 distinct and separate transactions.

He owns a store in every town in the United States of 8,000 population or more.

His stores in the United States and Canada aggregated 920 on January 1, 1917.

He controls seventy-five stores in Great Britain and plans to establish hundreds throughout Europe.

He employs between 30,000 and 50,000 men and women in his stores.

His organization is capitalized at $65,000,000—and has a market value of millions more.

He is the sole owner of the highest building in the world, 792 feet high, for which he paid $14,000,000 cash out of his own pocket.

FRANK W. WOOLWORTH

Now you know who this is.

"What is your ambition?" I asked Frank W. Woolworth, creator of the 5- and 10-cent store.

"To open a store in every civilized town throughout the world," came the reply.

And when Frank Woolworth sets his heart upon doing a thing he usually does it, no matter how numerous or how enormous the difficulties, how severe the discouragements, or how complete initial failures.

"What is your guiding business policy?" I queried.

"I look always ten to fifty years ahead and plan accordingly."

"And your basic principles?"

"Give the people such value that they will save money by trading with you; and treat your employees so well that they will give your customers satisfactory service. Volume makes for economy."

"What was your first important discovery that contributed to your success?"

"When I lost my conceit that nobody could do anything as well as I could myself, and learned to entrust duties to other people. So long as I was obsessed with the idea that I must attend personally to everything, large-scale success was impossible. A man must select able lieutenants or associates and give them power and responsibility—and we have the best business men in the world. They are all alive and know the business thoroughly."

"How do you keep in touch with 900 stores and how do you analyze where new stores should be opened?" I next asked.

"We maintain our own census all over the United States and Canada. It is kept up to date so that we know continually just which towns are growing, which ones are standing still, and which ones are dwindling. Every movement of people is reported to us and we try to diagnose coming developments. For example, when the United States Steel Corporation decided to build at Gary, Ind., we went in before fifty houses had been erected there, secured the most desirable location, and waited for the population to come. Now we have two very large and very successful stores there. It was easy to foresee what was coming. Then, by bringing together every month representatives from each of the nine districts into which the United States and Canada are divided, we keep posted on what is doing throughout the whole territory. We maintain a sort of day-to-day history of the two countries. Organization and coöperation largely explain our success."

"Isn't your purchase of a large site directly opposite the Public Library on Fifth Avenue, New York, in the very heart of the fashionable district, a distinct innovation, an entirely new departure in the development of your business?" I remarked to Mr. Woolworth, touching a subject upon which the newspapers had been commenting, not to say criticizing, very freely.

"We do things as big as that any day," Mr. Woolworth replied somewhat impatiently. "The trouble is that the people in New York don't take a sufficiently broad view. A few years from now Fifth Avenue will be like State Street, Chicago. There are more department stores on State Street and a greater volume of business done there than on Fifth Avenue. Our Fifth Avenue store will be less costly than some of our others. We established a store seven years ago in Chestnut Street, Philadelphia, the most exclusive high-price street in this country; our store is right next to Caldwell & Company, the Tiffany's of Philadelphia, and it has been very profitable. The same thing applies to Washington Street, Boston; Market Street, San Francisco; and Washington Avenue, St. Louis. Many people imagine that only the poorer classes patronize the 5- and 10-cent stores. That was true up to about fifteen years ago, but since then all classes have come to our stores in increasing numbers.

"The other evening the wife of one of the best-known lawyers in New York told me that she visited our Sixth Avenue store every week and bought things for herself, her children, and grandchildren, her purchases in a year having totalled over $600. This is by no means an exceptional case. We can sell cheaper than the department stores because of the tremendous quantities we buy. More and more every year we are taking the complete output of manufacturers of different kinds of goods; by keeping their plants running on full time from beginning to end of the year on one thing, the cost of production is reduced to the minimum, so that there are many articles we can sell at 10 cents which cost 25 cents or more in other stores. Then our overhead charge, when distributed over 900 stores, becomes only a very small percentage."

When I asked one of Mr. Woolworth's closest business associates what the former's most conspicuous qualities were, his prompt reply was: "Foresight—this is what continually astonishes every one around him. Next I would name his courage. Then he has always been a bulldog for work, and has the faculty of inspiring others with the hard-work spirit. The loyalty of his employees, the reward of generous, considerate treatment, has contributed greatly to the growth of the business."

Like Ford, Woolworth has a strong aversion to borrowing money. He gave a note for $300 for goods to stock his first store, but since he paid that off he has scarcely borrowed a dollar. There is not a cent of mortgage on the sixty-story Woolworth Building, nor is any bank in a position to embarrass him by calling upon him to pay off loans.

He could have expanded faster had he accepted borrowed capital in his earlier days, but he preferred to forge ahead slowly but surely on his own capital rather than rapidly or recklessly on borrowed funds.

Both Woolworth and Ford foresaw the infinite possibilities of supplying the multitude with meritorious but low-priced articles. Each realized that the road to millionairedom lay through system and volume. Each encountered heart-breaking obstacles at the start; each was handicapped inordinately through lack of funds; each exercised extraordinary determination, patience, and perseverance, and each had an abhorrence of placing himself or his business at the mercy of bankers or financiers. Each triumphed in his own line on a scale not equalled by any other human being. Each, also, still has unattained ambitions, so unlimited is their imagination. Each has not only become the most notable figure in his own line in the United States, but each has invaded foreign countries as part of a common plan to cover the whole earth. Each has graduated from impecunious farm boy to multi-millionaire.

One difference is that Ford is a manufacturer, Woolworth is not—"We don't manufacture a single article and don't intend to," Mr. Woolworth declares.

How did Frank W. Woolworth "get there"?

This is the first time Mr. Woolworth has been persuaded to tell in detail his early struggles. He dislikes talking about himself, but was finally induced to relate his early hardships solely because of the inspiration and encouragement the story might afford thousands of other young men now fighting an uphill battle against heart-breaking odds. Once started, Mr. Woolworth talked with the utmost frankness, describing his awkwardness and his initial failures without mincing words, glossing over nothing. He portrayed neither hero nor martyr. He simply narrated just what he went through. Biography contains no more typically American experience.

Here is an unadorned transcript of Mr. Woolworth's own conversational account of his struggles, ambitions, failures, and ultimate triumph:

"I did not have to overcome any handicap of inherited wealth which usually takes all ambition for achievement out of a young man. I inherited great physical advantages because my ancestors on both sides had been yeomanry for generations—since 1450, the genealogists tell me. I was born on a farm at Rodman, upstate (New York), but we moved to Great Bend, N. Y., when I was seven years old. We were poor—so poor that I never knew what it was to have an overcoat in that terribly cold climate. I never knew how to skate because I hadn't the money to buy skates. One pair of cowhide boots lasted a year, or rather six months, for the other six months I went barefooted. My parents and my forbears, for I don't know how far back, were Methodists, and I was brought up under the strictest discipline—dancing would have been a sin.

"I attended school in the winter and worked all summer. There isn't a thing on the farm that I haven't done. Often while I was sweating in the hayfield, I could hear the boys near by playing baseball, but the only chance I ever had of playing ball was during the recess at school in winter. It is a great advantage for a boy to start on a farm, not only for the sake of his constitution, but on the farm you learn very little of what is going on in the world; not like the young man born in the city who sees too much and knows more than is good for him.

"After leaving the public school, at sixteen, I took two winter sessions in a commercial college at Watertown, as it had always been my ambition either to become an engineer on the railroad or to get into business—behind the counter. My younger brother and I often took the old dining-room table, set it against the wall, ransacked the house for things to put on it, and then played at keeping store. How I envied the young fellow behind the counter in the village store! The farm never appealed to me—the only people farming appeals to, as a rule, are city folk—and they make poor farmers.

"After my commercial course, I tried my best to get into a store. I hitched the old mare to a cutter, went to Carthage, about seven miles away, and called at store after store looking for a job. Nobody would have me; some of them would not even talk to me. But this only made me more determined to get into a store.

"The station master at Great Bend kept a two-by-four grocery store in a corner of the freight shed, and I decided to work for him just to get the experience in selling goods and also selling tickets, making out reports, and the other simple office work that had to be done there. I became assistant station master—without pay. That was the nearest I ever got to fulfilling my boyhood ambition of becoming a railroad engineer.

"You will notice, however, that I was willing to work without pay because of the chance to get experience and learn how to do things. Not many young men to-day care to do this—they want to pick out a job that will pay them most at the start, a short-sighted policy.

"Although our sales of groceries in the freight shed averaged only about $2 a day, the job had this advantage: I got to know not only everybody who came to the station, but a good many of the people who travelled up and down the line—it was less than fifty miles long and is now a part of the New York Central system. To get on in the world it is very important to make as wide a circle of acquaintances and friends as possible and let them know what you are capable of doing.

"All this time I was persistently trying to get into a regular store. My younger brother was now able to do the work on the farm, so that I simply had to make a move and shift for myself. An uncle agreed to pay me $18 a month with board and lodging to come and work on his farm, but, although that seemed a lot of money and there was nothing else of any kind in sight, I resolved to make one supreme effort to land behind the counter, no matter how small the pay, so long as I could keep body and soul together. By this time I was nearing twenty-one, so that I had no early start in business.

"Daniel McNeil, who ran the country store at Great Bend, knowing how eager I was to get into a store, said he would let me work for him and give me the same food to eat that they put on his own table, but that he couldn't afford to pay me any wages. He said, however, that he would try his best to find a job for me in Watertown or Carthage, where the prospects would be better. I never forgot his kindness. Some people after they succeed forget those who helped them to get a start in life. I never have; I remember every person who ever said a kind word to me or helped me in any way during those days of struggle.

"Every day Mr. McNeil went to town I would go and see him in the evening to find out the news. One day he told me a man who kept a clothing store in Watertown would like to see me and asked me how I would like that kind of a job. I said, 'This is fine,' but down in my heart I didn't want to get into the clothing business at all. But situated as I was, I was ready to clutch at anything. It was a good store, but the best one in Watertown was the store of Augsbury & Moore, dry-goods merchants, and Mr. McNeil asked me to wait a few days until he could see if he could not place me there. I told him that would be the height of my ambition—to get into such a dry-goods store.

"I could hardly wait for Mr. McNeil's return from Watertown. I was overjoyed when he told me that Mr. Augsbury had agreed to look me over. Next day, you may be sure, I was in Watertown. This was in the middle of March, 1873.

"When I went into the store they told me Mr. Augsbury was at home, sick, but I asked where he lived and made straight for his house. He greeted me with 'Hello, Bub. What do you want—a job?' I was a thin, emaciated blond in those days, and I was wearing farmer's clothes. He immediately fired such questions at me as: 'Do you drink?' 'Do you smoke?' 'What do you do that's bad?' I told him I went to church every Sunday and didn't live in a locality where they did very bad things. My heart fell when he declared: 'You are too green; you have had no experience.' He added, however, that he would be in the store in the afternoon and that I might go and see Mr. Moore. Mr. Moore proved very discouraging. Finally, they both cross-examined me together. I imagine I was about the greenest fellow who ever came off a farm. They did not try to hide their opinion that I had probably no ability at all. To discourage me entirely, Mr. Moore said to me: 'If there is any mean work to be done in the store you will have to do it. You will have to deliver packages, wash windows, get down early in the morning and sweep the floor, do all the other cleaning, and any other dirty work that needs to be done. And it will be a long time before we trust you to wait on a customer. It will be the hardest work you have ever had in your life.'

"'I guess I can do it,' I replied. 'What are you going to pay me?'

"'You don't expect any pay, do you?' Mr. Moore flashed at me.

"'I don't see how I am going to live without pay,' I explained.

"'That doesn't interest us,' he snapped back. 'You should work a whole year for nothing, as a schooling. You have to pay tuition when you go to school. We will not ask you any tuition fee.'

"Imagine my predicament. When everything seemed within my reach, suddenly it was knocked on the head. Here I was, willing to do anything and everything, but I could not live on nothing. He was just about to turn me down when I said: 'Wait a minute; how long have I to work for nothing?'

"'At least six months,' he said.

"I asked him to wait until I could find out how little I could get board for, and back I came in an hour and told him that I could get a place for $3.50 a week and that in ten years I had saved $50—all the capital I had of any kind, shape, or form. I said I was anxious to meet them half-way and that I would gladly work for nothing for the first three months providing they would pay me $3.50 for the second three months. They declared these terms were unreasonable, that I should have to pay for my education. I held out, however, and finally they gave in, saying, 'We will give you a trial to see if you are any good.' They told me to come the next Monday morning, but I explained that I couldn't get to the store very early as I would ride down with my father who was to bring in a load of potatoes and thus save 33 cents railroad fare.

"Leaving my father and mother and home to strike out into the world, to tackle an uncertainty all alone, was the saddest experience of my whole life. It was the 24th day of March, 1873, bitterly cold, with three feet of snow on the ground, but as the sleigh drove away

I could see my mother standing at the door and she stood there as long as I was in sight.

"After struggling to get a heavy load of potatoes through snowbanks, we arrived at Watertown about half-past ten. I left my little bag of clothes at my boarding place—there were no such things as dress suit cases in those days—and reported for duty. Mr. Augsbury was the first one I encountered.

"Bub, don't they wear any collars in your neighbourhood?' was how he greeted me. I replied, 'No.' 'No neckties either?' I again replied, 'No.' 'Is this old flannel shirt the best you have to wear?' he next asked. 'Yes, sir,' I replied. 'Well, you'd better go out and get a white shirt and a collar and a tie before you begin work.

"I went and got properly rigged up, and shortly after I got back to the store Mr. Augsbury went to lunch. Nobody told me what to do. I hung around, feeling foolish, waiting for something to do. The clerks stared at me and sneered at me—I was a boob from the country accustomed to wearing nothing but old flannel shirts without collar or tie. At least, I imagined that was what they were thinking—and they afterward told me that that was exactly their sizing up of me. When most of the clerks had gone to dinner—lunch, as we call it nowadays—in came an old farmer and said to me: 'Young man, I want a spool of thread.' I didn't know where they kept the thread, so I went over to Mr. Moore, who was busy at his desk, and asked him. 'Right in front of your nose, young man,' he snapped without looking up from his writing. I pulled out a drawer directly in front of me and sure enough found it full of spools of thread. 'I want number 40,' said the farmer. I never knew till that moment that thread had a number. I fumbled all around the drawer looking for number 40, but could not find it. I appealed to Mr. Moore to know if we kept number 40. 'Certainly; right in the drawer in front of you,' he said quite sharply. I had to tell him, 'I can't find any.' 'Just as I expected,' he said testily as he got down from his desk and showed me the right kind of thread. He immediately returned to his desk.

"'How much is it, young man?' asked the farmer. I had to turn once more to Mr. Moore. It was eight cents. The farmer pulled out a ten-cent shinplaster. 'Mr. Moore, where do I get change?' I had to ask. 'Come right up to the desk and make out a ticket,' he ordered me. I picked up one of the blanks and studied it all over to see what I could do with it. But I was stumped. 'Mr. Moore, I don't believe I know how to make this out,' I had to confess. 'Hand it to me; I will show you,' he replied. Next I had to ask: 'Where do I get my change?' 'There's the cashier right there, can't you see him?' he said impatiently.

"No sooner had the farmer gone out than another came in with the request: 'I want a pair of mittens.' 'Mr. Moore, have we got any mittens?' I had to ask. 'Hanging right up in front of your nose, young man,' was his reply. And there they were, although I hadn't noticed them. The farmer, after a lot of fingering and trying on, selected an old-fashioned homemade woollen pair. 'How much?' he asked. I told him I didn't know, but I called over to Mr. Moore, 'How much are these mittens?' Mr. Moore by this time had had about enough of my interruptions. He replied impatiently, 'Look at the ticket; can't you see the ticket on there?' The ticket said 25 cents and in payment the farmer pulled out a $1 bill.

"This time I knew how to make out a check and where to get change, so that I finished the transaction without bothering Mr. Moore any more. I also learned where to find the price ticket on merchandise. I was keeping my eyes open as best I could.

"But as time passed, never once did I receive one word of sympathy or encouragement from a single soul. I didn't know whether I was pleasing or not, and, in order to find out, I went to the proprietors one day and told them that selling goods didn't seem to be in my line, and that I didn't seem to be able to learn the business properly. I had no idea of leaving but simply was hungry for a little encouragement. Instead, I received the reply: 'If you don't think you are going to succeed, you had better quit.' But I didn't quit. I held on, even though the other clerks made my life miserable by constantly poking fun at my ignorance and by always keeping me in the back of the store so that I had little opportunity to wait on customers except at dinner time. Only one treated me with any consideration, a young fellow named Barrett, who later became a very wealthy merchant. We remained great friends right up until his death a little while ago.

"I was determined to stick. I tried to analyze my abilities, and my conclusions were that I was a very poor salesman but that I could trim up the store, display the goods, and dress windows quite well. I realized that Mr. Moore had spoken the truth when he told me I would not be worth anything the first year. I couldn't meet customers and sell goods to them the way a good salesman could do it. But by and by when anything had to be fitted up in good shape, I noticed that they came to me to do it.

"At the end of two and a half years—the name of the firm meanwhile had been changed to Moore & Smith—I was getting only $6 a week, and when I heard of a vacancy in another store I went to apply. But when I saw how higgledy-piggledy everything was in the store, I decided to name a high salary, thinking to be turned down. I asked $10 a week, and was astonished when the proprietor, Mr. Bushnell, said, 'All right, when will you commence?' I took the job, and on this big salary I felt justified in getting married.

"However, I found conditions at this store very different and very distasteful. I tried to trim up the store to make it look attractive and also dressed the windows. Once, when I had spent a lot of time to make a really good show with the windows, Mr. Bushnell, instead of being pleased, reprimanded me, saying, 'Take it all out. We don't want any windows trimmed here.' I was told to confine myself to selling goods. This, of course, was my weakest spot.

"After I had been there a couple of months he met me in the basement one day—I had to sleep in the basement, with another young fellow, armed with revolvers, to protect the store from burglars. He unceremoniously told me there were boys getting $6 a week who sold more goods than I did, and that he could not continue paying me $10 a week. I asked if it would not be a good idea to keep the store in attractive shape and display the goods to the best advantage so as to attract customers. I told him I could do that kind of work. But he replied, 'I don't want you to do anything but sell goods, nothing else.'

"He cut my pay to $8.

"This was a terrible blow. I found I was up against a cold, cold world. I thought Moore & Smith had been hard on me, but they were angels compared to this man Bushnell. I was almost tempted to give up. I became terribly depressed. I wrote a pitiful letter to my mother. She sent me in reply the most lovely letter any one ever penned. She finished up many encouraging assurances with this sentence: *'Some day, my son, you will be a rich man.'* Although I felt sure she didn't believe that any more than I did, somehow the expression of her faith in me buoyed me up. I kept up the depressing struggle until I was near death's door from sickness. When fever came on top of nervous prostration I was almost given up for dead. For a whole year I was at home unable to do a stroke of work. During this period of poor health I became convinced that I was not fitted for mercantile life.

"About the time I recovered my strength a man who owned a little four-acre farm was so anxious to sell out that he let me have it for $900. I had no money but raised a $600 mortgage and gave him my note for the other $300. My wife and I began raising chickens, potatoes, and everything we could see a dollar in to make ends meet. After we had struggled along for about four months, I received a call from Moore & Smith to come and see them. Right off the reel they offered me $10 a week. They said they wanted to have me back to tone up the store.

"This was positively the first recognition I had ever received for the hard work I had put in. It revived my confidence remarkably. I felt that my work had begun to bear fruit. The return of my strength also had something to do with the return of my former determination to succeed, I suppose. My wife remained on the farm for a time, with visits from me about every two weeks until we rented the place and took a three-room home in Watertown. At the end of the first year we had saved $50 in addition to having lent my father, who was very hard-up, $20, and also after having paid the doctor's bills and everything else incidental to the birth of our first baby. Yes, it called for frugal management—no luxuries, no entertainments, no shows, no vacations. I worked in the store from seven in the morning till ten every night. I kept on working in this store from then (1877) until I opened my first 5-cent store at Utica, New York, on February 22, 1879.

"The rest of my story is well known."

Mr. Woolworth's trials were not to take wing the moment he hung out his shingle. How he came to take this step is worth recording. A visitor from the West told Moore & Smith, in 1878, that "5-cent sales" were proving extremely successful in a store out there and advised the Watertown firm to get together as many low-priced articles as possible from old stock, mix them with some new goods bought specially for the purpose, make a display of them, and advertise that any article in the whole collection could be bought for 5 cents. Mr. Moore went to New York, bought less than $100 worth of 5-cent articles, waited until the Fair Week and then announced the unique sale—Mr. Woolworth still possesses a copy of the handbill advertising the sale. Sewing-machine tables, other tables, and counters were heaped with such a collection of goods as Watertown had never before seen. In a few hours there wasn't a single article left. The experiment was repeated on the following Saturday and soon the "5-cent sale" craze was raging not only in Watertown, but was spreading to other towns. Dozens of men saw in this a quick road to fortune.

Mr. Moore, who by this time had come to have a high regard for Woolworth, advised the clerk to look around for a suitable location and start a 5-cent store. When Mr. Woolworth explained that he did not have the necessary capital, Mr. Moore agreed to accept his note for $300 worth of goods, and the first Woolworth store contained exactly $321 worth of 5-cent articles—the 10-cent end of the business was added later.

The store proved a failure. The craze, much overdone, was beginning to peter out. On returning from Utica with little but bitter experience for his adventure, Mr. Woolworth felt that there was nothing for him to do but resume work with Moore & Smith. Mr. Moore again backed him up, however, and this time Lancaster, Pa., was chosen by Woolworth. From the moment the doors were opened the store proved a success.

Before long one after another of the 5-cent stores which had sprung into existence all over that part of the country failed. In time Frank W. Woolworth was the only man remaining in the field. He alone had grit enough, ability enough, and foresight enough to hold on. The spirit which animated him to work gratis in the grocery store in the freight shed; to work three months, also, without pay in Watertown; and to reënter the mercantile business notwithstanding his early experiences, inspired him not to admit defeat now even though every one else had gone under.

He opened a store in Harrisburg, Pa., in June, 1879, very shortly after the opening of the Lancaster store, installing his brother, C. S. Woolworth, as manager. This venture was unprofitable and soon was dropped. But Woolworth now was more confident than ever that he had discovered his life's work and that his mother's prediction might yet be fulfilled.

"By the middle of 1880 I was so rich that I decided to take the first vacation I ever enjoyed," Mr. Woolworth told me reminiscently. "I was worth $2,000, which looked bigger to me then than $20,000,000 would now. In fact, I felt quite as rich then as I do now because I had the consciousness and the satisfaction of having made a success in business. I visited old Watertown and was received as something of a hero."

On returning to Lancaster he felt he must find another position for his brother, so he installed him in a 5- and 10-cent store in Scranton, Pa.—and the brother, now a millionaire, is there yet. After a while Mr. Woolworth's ambition led him to invade Philadelphia, but at the end of three months there was a loss of $380 and he withdrew.

Thus three out of the first five stores opened by Woolworth proved failures. This would have cowed the spirit of enterprise in most men. But Woolworth was not made of the average stuff. When his cousin, Seymour H. Knox, came to him in the following year (1882) and wanted to go into business, Woolworth arranged to become a fifty-fifty partner with him at Reading, Pa. The store then opened is running to-day at the same old location. Knox died two years ago, a multi-millionaire. Once again Woolworth invaded Harrisburg and the store there, also opened on a partnership basis with another man, is still booming. Trenton, N. J., was tapped on the same basis. By having a partner in each store Mr. Woolworth found that he could depend upon the business being properly attended, and this principle he carried out in store after store.

Becoming anxious to tackle big cities despite his experience in

Philadelphia, he opened a large store in Newark, but it also had to be closed after an unsuccessful run of six months. Elmira, N. Y., also refused to warm up to the 5- and 10-cent idea.

Failure also befell an attempt Mr. Woolworth made to establish a chain of 25-cent stores. First Reading and then Lancaster rejected this innovation so emphatically that he decided to stick to nickel and dime transactions. By this time he had been inured to reverses. Like Europe's army generals, he tried to find an opening here and there all along the line and when opposition at one point was found too strong he simply sought another line of less resistance.

It was in 1886 that Mr. Woolworth opened, not a store, but a tiny office in New York, at 104 Chambers Street, at $25 a month rent. Here he worked night and day, doing all his own bookkeeping, buying goods for all his stores, travelling all over the country to inspect promising locations, and personally answering all his correspondence. Since his first breakdown his health had never recovered fully, and at the time he was running his New York office single-handed his weight fell off to 135 pounds, although he was a large-framed man of more than average height. While in the thick of his fight for success he was stricken with typhoid fever and for eight weeks was unable to attend to business.

"This experience taught me a lesson," said Mr. Woolworth. "Up till then I thought I must attend to everything myself. But I indulged in the luxury of a bookkeeper and I also, at great effort, broke myself of the conceit that I could buy goods, display goods, run stores, and do everything else more efficiently than any man associated with me. That really marked the beginning of my success and enabled me to expand in a large way. From then on I confined my attention to important matters, to looking ahead, thinking up new plans, giving instructions to other people, placing responsibilities on them, and contenting myself with general supervision of the conduct of the business. So many thousands of merchants never get over the conceit that they must do everything themselves, with the result that they straggle along in one little store.

"A business is like a snowball: one man can easily push it along for a while but the snowball becomes so large if pushed ahead that help must be obtained to roll it—and if you don't keep rolling it, it will soon melt. No business can stand stationary for any considerable period; it either rises or falls, and, if left to itself; the tendency is for it to fall.

"In the first ten years, from 1879 to 1889, I opened only twelve stores, but I found that the greater the volume the cheaper I could buy and the better value I could give customers. I would not go into debt, however, and this alone prevented my activities equalling my ambitions. In 1895 we opened up our first huge store, in Brooklyn, and it became profitable from the start. Then we went to Washington and Philadelphia and Boston and entered New York within a week of opening in Boston, in October, 1896. Some of my associates thought I was crazy to take on such tremendous responsibilities, but I did not feel that way about it. In 1904 we invaded the West, with headquarters in Chicago. In 1905 we incorporated as a private corporation with $10,000,000 capital and in 1912, when we had some 300 stores, we combined with S. H. Knox & Company, F. M. Kirby & Company, E. P. Charlton & Company, C. S. Woolworth, and W. H. Moore, giving us a total of 600 stores."

It was characteristic of Mr. Woolworth's keen sense of gratitude toward those who had befriended him in his days of hardship that he made his aged first employer, W. H. Moore, an honorary vice-president of the $65,000,000 F. W. Woolworth Company. Both Mr. Moore and Mr. Smith were a great help to him in his start and they always remained his best friends.

European possibilities were surveyed by Mr. Woolworth in 1909 and he spent the whole summer there organizing stores in the principal cities of Britain. Inasmuch as Mr. Woolworth regards the whole world as his field, the future will probably bring great developments of the Woolworth business overseas.

These few figures show the growth of the F. W. Woolworth Company:

	NUMBER OF STORES	SALES FOR YEAR
Dec. 31, 1912	611	$60,557,767
" " 1913	684	66,228,072
" " 1914	737	69,619,669
" " 1915	805	75,995,774
" " 1916	920	87,089,270

Was there ever such a romance of nickels and dimes?

"Why did you spend so much money in putting up the highest building in the world?" I asked Mr. Woolworth.

"For several reasons. Did you know that the children's school books tell them about the world's highest building?" Mr. Woolworth replied with a significant smile. "My secretary recently received a postcard from the Pacific Coast addressed simply: 'The Highest Building In The World,' and a letter was received from Germany once with nothing but the party's name and 'Woolworth Building'—no city or country was mentioned. I noticed once in a trade paper in Europe that America was typified by a picture of the Woolworth

Building, without even the name of the building being given. Perhaps my idea was not quite so foolish as most people imagine."

Woolworth's desire to overtop every other building in the world, his ambition to cover the whole earth with his stores, his triumph after countless obstacles have been partly inspired by his boundless admiration for "The Little Corsican"—Mr. Woolworth's private office, indeed, is an elaborate copy of Napoleon's "Empire Room" and contains the famous clock and many other original articles which adorned that historic room, the whole forming an office which in grandeur eclipses anything else in the land. In his palatial home on Fifth Avenue, New York, Mr. Woolworth has installed the most wonderful musical contrivances ever created and spends many evenings entertaining his friends in his unique music room.

Amply fulfilled has been his mother's prophecy: "Some day, my son, you will be a rich man." In memory of her and his father, Mr. Woolworth has built and endowed the Woolworth Memorial Methodist Episcopal Church at Great Bend, N. Y.

Mr. Woolworth in 1876 married Miss Jennie Creighton of Watertown, N. Y., and had three daughters, Mrs. Charles E. F. McCann, the late Mrs. Franklyn L. Hutton, and Mrs. James P. Donahue.

Frank W. Woolworth's record is worthy of America, is it not?

JOHN D. ARCHBOLD

[*John D. Archbold died on December 5, 1916, just after this sketch was written*]

SCENE I

A LITTLE Ohio lad, only twelve, hungry for knowledge but poor in pocket, volunteers to light the fires in the local school and do chores around the schoolhouse if the head master will teach him Latin in the evenings. His father is dead, his widowed mother needs support, and after only one year of chores by morning and special study by night, he is sent to work in a village store.

SCENE II

At sixteen the lad, fired with ambition and totally unafraid, emigrates to Pennsylvania to join in the *mêlée* which the discovery of oil had started there. He arrives at Titusville, the centre of the excitement, without a friend to give him counsel or aid, and with few dollars in his pocket. He starts a search for work. He is a little fellow for his years, a mere slip of a schoolboy, but he finds a job as office-boy, or clerk, with an oil firm.

SCENE III

From eleven to one o'clock every day there gathers around a huge table in the best-known business building in New York a group of directors whose activities and interests transcend those of any other directorate in the world. The business built up and handled by these men and their predecessors covers every civilized and nearly every uncivilized country on the face of the earth. Their organization has been and is the greatest wonder of the industrial and commercial world. In the days of small units it became a large unit. It had learned and had practised efficiency before Bismarck had finished his work of welding Germany into one great, efficient nation. When others were content with local and domestic business, it created a national and an international business. When others were satisfied with picayune processes and appliances it evolved costly scientific methods and colossal plants. It developed its own transportation facilities by land and by sea—to-day one of its companies alone has one of the greatest fleets of steamers in operation or under construction in America, over fifty of them, plying to every important port of the seven seas, while its allied companies also have large fleets. Its sales to foreign nations have brought to this country several billions of dollars and are still bringing in a stream of gold for the sustenance of American workmen, American homes, and American enterprises. It has disbursed in dividends hundreds of millions to many thousands of stockholders—40 per cent. was the usual rate before "dissolution"—and the market valuation of the parent enterprise and its offshots exceeds $2,000,000,000.

At the head of the table where the destinies of this vast organization are daily shaped sits and has sat for years the Ohio lad who volunteered to kindle school fires and do chores to earn lessons in Latin and who, at sixteen, went out to fight the world unafraid and alone.

He is John D. Archbold, president of the Standard Oil Company of New Jersey.

"Had you any idea when you first struck the oil fields that one day you might attain something like your present position? Had you big ambitions?" I asked Mr. Archbold.

"I always was full of ambition," he replied. "In my case it was quickened by necessity. My father was a Methodist preacher and died when I was eleven, leaving us as poor as preachers usually leave their families. My eldest brother was also a preacher and teacher, with a family of his own, so he couldn't help as much as he would have liked. My second brother had joined the army on the outbreak of the War between the States. So I was anxious to do something for my mother."

The little fire-lighting-Latin incident reveals that thus early he had acumen enough to realize how best to fit himself to be of use.

He was born in Leesburg, O., on July 26, 1848, to which state his maternal grandfather, Colonel William Dana, had gone from Massachusetts in a prairie-schooner. Ohio was not then threaded with railroads, studded with manufactories, or dotted with towns. Only daring pioneers had ventured so far west in those days—toward the end of the eighteenth century. Israel Archbold, father of John Dustin, was a native of Virginia, and it is remarkable how strongly the son has inherited and preserved the polite, soft-speaking, attractive characteristics and manners of old Southern families.

His first job was as boy-of-all-work in a store in the village of Salem, O., not far from Leesburg. But though his working hours, as was the universal custom then, ran more than a full round of the clock every day, he contrived to keep up his studies. His vision even then extended beyond the cramped horizon of a country store. He assiduously cultivated self-improvement. His teacher had often during the private sessions in the evening impressed upon him that education was one of the essential weapons for the battle of life and took special pains to help the bright, persevering lad.

A diligent reader of the few newspapers he could lay his hands on, the alluring stories of fortunes being made overnight in the newly developed oil fields of Pennsylvania stirred his imagination and appealed to his ambition. The output of crude petroleum had jumped from less than 2,000 barrels for the whole country in 1859 to over 2,200,000 barrels in 1864 and had sold at more than $12 a barrel, with refined selling at 65 cents a gallon in New York. (The price now, for a vastly superior article, in bulk, is about five cents a gallon.)

Although his weekly wages as a grocery boy had gone up from only $1.50 when he started to $5 in the next two or three years, he had lived so frugally that, in addition to what he had contributed to the family support, he had saved something like $100 before he was sixteen.

He would boldly set out for the new El Dorado in William Penn's country!

It was a venturesome stroke for a boy of sixteen, especially one under rather than over average physical proportions. But young Archbold had certain pronounced qualities. He had unquestioning self-confidence. His courage was so great that it left no room for fear or doubt. He was effervescent with enthusiasm. The spirit of adventure which had spurred his grandparent to penetrate into the far-off wilds of Ohio had descended to the grandchild. Also, there was in him the embryo of what was to develop into his most conspicuous quality: ability to grasp with lightning rapidity the possibilities of a new situation and to shape his course accordingly.

Titusville had sprung up as the metropolis of the Pennsylvania oil boom. To Titusville Archbold went in June, 1864, prepared to tackle anything connected with the oil industry.

He succeeded in getting a modest position in the office of William H. Abbott, one of the largest and most reputable oil-dealing houses in the whole territory.

In three years, *before he was nineteen years of age*, he was admitted into partnership.

Why? Not because of "pull"; for Archbold had not even an acquaintance when he entered the region. Not because of his money; for his savings, all but $1,000, had gone to buy his mother a home of her own in Salem, and to send his young sister to college. Not because of his age, for he looked even younger than his nineteen years.

John Dustin Archbold had done in the oil industry what Charles M.

Schwab did in steel, what James J. Hill did in railroading, what Charles F. Brooker did in brass, what Frank A. Vanderlip did in banking, what Theodore N. Vail did in telephony, what Thomas A. Edison did in electricity, what, in short, every conspicuously successful man has done, namely, ripped off his coat, jumped into the arena, and applied both head and hands day and night in studying his business from base to copestone until master of both theory and practice, familiar with its every angle and quick to devise improved methods and to create wider opportunities.

Archbold, the office assistant, did not sit contentedly on a high stool scratching figures and keeping his collar and his fingers clean. He tramped through oozing oil fields and mud holes up to his thighs. He learned on the spot how oil wells were drilled, how the crude fluid was caught, how it was refined. He studied very specially the transportation problems. There were no pipe lines in those days; the oil had to be transported in barrels, teams dragging loads to the railroad where it was shipped to New York and other points. Furthermore, young Archbold applied himself to analyzing "indications" and became something of an expert in this important line. He quickly learned, also, how to sell.

William H. Abbott therefore knew what he was doing when he took the nineteen-year-old hustler into partnership.

A year later H. B. Porter, who had been admitted into the firm, became largely interested in a refinery at Titusville and the firm's business expanded so greatly that it was decided to open a selling agency in New York.

Although only twenty, Mr. Archbold was selected for this important post. He opened offices in the metropolis and handled not only the oil of his own concern but the product of a number of others, and built up a very extensive business.

Marketing oil was not child's play in those exciting days. Oil exchanges were opened in a dozen cities and the gambling done in oil certificates in New York and elsewhere eclipsed the speculation in securities. Fluctuations were sensational—"war stocks" have not gyrated more sensationally on the Stock Exchange during the European cataclysm. For example, the monthly average price ranged from $4 to more than $12 in 1864, from $1.95 to above $5 in 1868, and from about $3 to $4.50 in 1870, the year Mr. Archbold began business in New York. His all-round grasp of the trade, his exhaustive knowledge of transportation facilities, his faculty for making friends—Mr. Archbold is noted for his ready wit and unfailing humour —enabled him to more than hold his own with men twice and three times his age.

Mr. Archbold believed that oil should command $4 a barrel, and that he could not always get that price was no fault of his. The year 1872, as a matter of fact, was the last one in which crude oil was to touch Archbold's favourite figure—it sold temporarily as low as 20 cents a barrel when enormous new discoveries glutted the market.

It was about this time that another and more famous John D. met John D. Archbold. Mr. Rockefeller, already a notable factor in the petroleum industry, had come from the Middle West to Pennsylvania, and the wideawake Archbold was on the ground to meet him; in fact, Mr. Archbold arranged a little dinner in honour of the oil magnate's visit. Mr. Rockefeller himself has given a description of this famous meeting.

"It is not always possible," he says, "to remember just how one met an old friend or what one's impressions were, but I shall never forget my first meeting with Mr. John D. Archbold.

"At that time I was travelling about the country, visiting the points where something was happening, talking with the producers, the refiners, the agents, and actually getting acquainted.

"One day there was a gathering of the men somewhere near the oil regions, and when I came to the hotel, which was full of oil men, I saw this name writ large on the register:

"'John D. Archbold, $4 a bbl.'

"He was a young and enthusiastic fellow, so full of his subject that he added his slogan '$4 a bbl.' after his signature on the register, that no one might misunderstand his convictions. The battle cry of '$4 a barrel' was all the more striking because crude oil was selling then for much less, and this campaign for a higher price certainly did attract attention—it was much too good to be true. But if Mr. Archbold had to admit in the end that crude oil is not worth '$4 a bbl.,' his enthusiasm, his energy, and his splendid power over men have lasted.

"He has always had a well-developed sense of humour, and on one occasion, when he was on the witness stand, he was asked by the opposing lawyer:

"'Mr. Archbold, are you a director of this company?'

"'I am.'

"'What is your occupation in this company?'

"He promptly answered: 'To clamour for dividends,' which led the learned counsel to start afresh on another line.

"I can never cease to wonder at his capacity for hard work."

It was natural for Mr. Rockefeller, with his almost superhuman judgment in selecting colleagues, to have "spotted" Archbold. Indeed, the Standard Oil people had found in him a combatant of exceptional vigour. Negotiations were opened and Mr. Archbold joined the Rockefeller interests in 1875. He was by then president of the Acme Oil Company and one of its principal stockholders. In the fall of that year he was elected a director of the Standard Oil Company. Shortly after he was chosen as its vice-president and remained in that capacity until 1911, when he was selected as president.

An instance of Mr. Archbold's foresightedness was supplied in 1899 when, in giving testimony before the Industrial Commission, he urged federal charters for corporations. "Lack of uniformity in the laws of various states as affecting business corporations, is one of the vexatious features attending the business life of any great corporation to-day," he said, "and I suggest for your most careful consideration the thought of a federal corporation law."

"I am more convinced than ever that this is the only and the inevitable solution," Mr. Archbold reiterated to me.

That this is coming few clear-headed citizens can doubt. The impossibility of serving forty-eight masters is becoming more evident every year. Had such legislation been passed there would have been few "dissolution suits" by the Government, and the Standard Oil Company probably would not have been subjected to a prosecution which has accomplished worse than nothing.

Mr. Archbold's place in the oil industry is second only to that of John D. Rockefeller. That is the verdict of those best able to judge. His name is not so popularly known because of his extraordinary antipathy to appearing in public. Less has been written about the career of John D. Archbold than about that of any other American industrial leader of equal achievement. There are more facts in this sketch than have ever before been published about him. I have known and interviewed many men in many countries; I have never met one more diffident or more anxious to avoid talking for publication.

"My life has been too prosaic for your purpose," he parried. "I have simply been interested in the development of the resources of the country and the expansion of its trade at home and abroad. I have not found much time to be interested in other things."

As a matter of fact Mr. Archbold *has* interested himself in other things. He is president of the board of trustees of Syracuse University, an institution which has prospered so remarkably since his connection with it that its student roll has increased from hundreds to over 4,000, including 1,500 young women, placing it in the ranks of the foremost institutions of learning in the United States. He erected the present building of the New York Kindergarten in memory of his daughter, Mrs. Frances Dana Archbold Walcott, and endowed it. He is a director of St. Christopher's Home and Orphanage in New York and is known to have contributed generously to its support.

He has interested himself, also, in the Metropolitan Museum of Art and the American Museum of Natural History.

His friends describe him as one of the best story-tellers to be met in a day's march, as a wit who can see the funny side of most situations, and as a philanthropist who conceals from his left hand what his right hand does.

Talking of hands recalls an incident described thus in the newspapers:

While coming down the Hudson in his yacht *Vixen* in May, 1911, Mr. Archbold lost the best hand he ever held at bridge and saved two oarsmen who were struggling in the water. The *Vixen* was making her fastest speed down the river when the men were discovered, and Mr. Archbold came to the side, holding his cards in his hands. He shouted and gesticulated, and, in his excitement, released the cards, which fluttered overboard. Under his direction the yacht was manœuvred alongside the men, who were hanging on to their shell, and a few moments later they were dragged on board and their shell lifted in.

"And now," Mr. Archbold said to them, "I am at your service. Do you wish to come with me, or shall I go back with you? And in the meantime what will you have?"

The oarsmen were taken to the pier of the Juanita Boat Club, near Spuyten Duyvil, where they were landed. Before going ashore they tried to thank Mr. Archbold, but he would have none of it.

"On the contrary," he said, "I am indebted to you for a most satisfactory afternoon—but that hand of cards that went overboard was the best I ever held."

The "tainted money" talk drew from Mr. Archbold this impassioned statement in an address he delivered in 1907 to the New York Alumni of Syracuse University, a reference having been made to the subject by a previous speaker:

"If I had thought for one moment that there was any questionable taste in the university accepting one dollar of my money, I would never have given it one single cent. Every cent I have was earned through good, hard, honest toil. I say again, if my conscience were not clear that I had honestly earned every penny I possess I would never have offered the Syracuse University a single penny."

Perhaps it is Mr. Archbold's ability to extract humour from the daily round of life that has enabled him to remain in harness longer than any other of the original Standard Oil notables. He is the only man in at the birth of the Standard Oil Company in 1882 who is actively engaged in directing Standard Oil affairs to-day. Mr. Archbold was born on July 26, 1848. He married Miss Annie Mills, daughter of S. M. Mills of Titusville, in 1870 and is fond of describing this as one of the wisest things he ever did. He has two surviving daughters and one son, John F. Archbold.

He still works hard but not quite such long hours as formerly. His yacht brings him down every morning from his home at Cedar Cliffs and is daily pointed out to sightseeing parties.

I asked an elevator runner at 26 Broadway: "What sort of a man is Mr. Archbold?"

He looked astonished, as much as to say: "You surely know that." Then he spoke four words: "The nicest man ever."

I would rather have the employees' estimate of a big man than the estimate of any or all of his own cronies or clubmates.

In his will Mr. Archbold left $500,000 to Syracuse University, to which during his lifetime, it develops, he had given $6,000,000. That he had given about $500,000 to the New York Kindergarten Association in addition to having erected and endowed its building has also been disclosed by the beneficiaries, who on his death passed a resolution in which he was described as "a most kind friend to thousands of little boys and girls who, but for his kindness and interest, would have had less fair beginnings in their lives."

THE END